Irish Theatre in England
Irish Theatrical Diaspora Series: 2

Irish Theatre in England

Irish Theatrical Diaspora Series: 2

Edited by

Richard Cave and Ben Levitas

Carysfort Press

A Carysfort Press Book in association with Peter Lang

Irish Theatre in London
edited by Richard Cave and Ben Levitas

Irish Theatrical Diaspora Series: 2

First published in Ireland in 2007 as a paperback original by
Carysfort Press, 58 Woodfield, Scholarstown Road
Dublin 16, Ireland
ISBN 978-1-78874-928-2
© 2007 Copyright remains with the authors

Typeset by Carysfort Press
Cover design by Alan Bennis

This book is published with the financial assistance of
The Arts Council (An Chomhairle Ealaíon), Dublin, Ireland

Caution: All rights reserved. No part of this book may be printed or reproduced or utilized in any form or by any electronic, mechanical, or other means, now known or hereafter invented including photocopying and recording, or in any information storage or retrieval system without permission in writing from the publishers.

Contents

Acknowledgements	ix
List of Illustrations	x

Introduction
Richard Cave and Ben Levitas 1

PART ONE: RECEPTION AND CONTEXTS

1 These Islands' Others: *John Bull*, the Abbey and the Royal Court
   Ben Levitas 15

2 'Stranger in the House': Alienation and History in *The Land of Heart's Desire* and *Cathleen ni Houlihan*
   Michael McAteer 35

3 The Irish Players and the Conquest of London
   Peter Kuch 53

4 Folds in Dispersion: Yeatsian Remnants in London
   Jonathan D. H. Statham 67

5 Reclaiming Sam for Ireland: *The Beckett on Film* Project
   Graham Saunders 79

| 6 | Understanding Loyalty: The English Response to the Work of Gary Mitchell
Tim Miles | 97 |
| 7 | Traditional Routes: Challenges and Re-affirmations in the Representation of the Ulster Protestant
Wallace McDowell | 113 |

PART TWO: PERFORMANCE AND PERFORMATIVITY

8	The English/Irish Ring and Its Victorian Popularity **Jerry Nolan**	129
9	An Irish Jig? Edris Stannus, Ninette de Valois and the English Royal Ballet **Elizabeth Schafer**	143
10	Not-So-Gay-Young-Things: Mary Manning's *Youth's the Season—?* as staged in 1930s London **Cathy Leeney**	157
11	Doublings: Problematic Identities in Thomas Kilroy's *Double Cross* and *The Madame MacAdam Travelling Theatre* **Carmen Szabó**	169
12	The Transience of the Visual Image in Touring Theatre: Brian Friel's *Dancing at Lughnasa* **Enrica Cerquoni**	183

PART THREE: A STAGING HISTORY

| 13 | Chronological Table Of Irish Plays Produced In London 1920-2006
Peter James Harris | 195 |

Contributors 287
Index 289

Acknowledgements

The editors would wish to acknowledge the generosity and help of a number of institutions and individuals who made possible the conference on which this book is based: the staff of the National Portrait Gallery; Derek Hannon, Cultural Attaché, Irish Embassy in London; Warwick Gould and the Institute of English Studies, School of Advanced Studies, University of London; Colin Smythe; Gerald Lidstone and David Wiles, respectively Heads of the Department of Drama at Goldsmiths and of Drama and Theatre at Royal Holloway; Rachel Levitas; Maire Davies, Dean of the Faculty of Arts, Royal Holloway.

Thanks are due to the Board of the National Library of Ireland for permission to cite in Michael McAteer's essay letters from Frank Fay, Willie Fay, and Annie Horniman held in its manuscript collections; to A.P. Watt Ltd. on behalf of Michael Yeats for permission to include citations from Yeats's plays; to Nick Hern Books for their permission to publish the image of the cover of Gary Mitchell's *Trust*; to Field Day Theatre Company for their permission to publish the images from their production of Thomas Kilroy's *Double Cross*; to Joe Vaněk and the Gate Theatre, Dublin, for their permission to publish the images accompanying Enrica Cerquoni's essay. We extend grateful thanks to the contributors to this volume but also to all the delegates at the conference: their contributions and questions greatly assisted the authors in redrafting their papers for publication and the editors in achieving order and coherence in presenting their endeavours.

R.C. and B.L.

List of Illustrations

1 G.B. Shaw's *John Bull's Other Island* as staged at 10 Downing Street, 30 June 1911.

2 Aubrey Beardsley's poster for the 1894 production of W.B. Yeats's *The Land of Heart's Desire*.

3 The cover of the English publication of Gary Mitchell's *Trust*, staged at the Royal Court Theatre Upstairs, from 11 March 1999. (Courtesy of Nick Hern Books.)

4 Thomas Kilroy's *Double Cross* as staged by Field Day Theatre Company with Stephen Rea, Kate O'Toole, and Richard Howard, from 3 February 1986. (Courtesy of Field Day Theatre Company.)

5 Brian Friel's *Dancing at Lughnasa* as staged by the Abbey Theatre Dublin showing the set design by Joe Vaněk from 24 April 1990. (Courtesy of Joe Vaněk .)

6 Subsequent restaging of the Abbey production of *Dancing at Lughnasa* at the Lyttelton Theatre, Royal National Theatre, London, from 15 October 1990. (Courtesy of Joe Vaněk.)

7 Revival of *Dancing at Lughnasa* at the Gate Theatre Dublin from 24 February 2004. (Courtesy of Gate Theatre. Image by Paul McCarthy.)

Introduction: Irish Theatre in England

Richard Cave and Ben Levitas

It is now almost a cliché to state that English theatre would be vastly impoverished by the elimination of the Irish presence from its stages: Irish playwrights, directors, actors, managers, dancers, musicians, and singers have continually been assimilated within the theatrical and cultural hegemony centred on London. To Irish nationalist sensibilities such theatre practitioners form a long roll-call of renegade talent. To those Irish practitioners themselves, however, success on the London boards in theatres, opera houses, and concert halls has generally been viewed as a major goal, a sign of having *arrived* in terms of one's career. The situation has a long history that is as true of James Shirley and George Farquhar in the seventeenth century as it is of Peg Woffington in the eighteenth or Tyrone Power in the nineteenth; Yeats and Lady Gregory were not content with the establishing of their proto-national theatre until the troupe had found acclaim in London and Oxbridge; and even today there are dramatists who prefer to premiere their works on English stages and actors who choose to harness their talents to London performers' agencies till Hollywood calls and cinematic success brings an income allowing a triumphant return to the homeland. The gap between national and professional sensibilities, however, opens an enticing area for discussion. This collection of essays dwells on the peculiarly complex set of cultural dynamics brought into play when what declares itself to be specifically Irish is performed to an English audience. The richly diverse array of theatre offered within the category, Irish Theatre in England, is well evidenced by the material covered here; but above all it emerges as a reflexive category, continually scrutinized as it is made manifest. While the essays here tend to return time and again to shared considerations, they are most resonant in their common questioning of identity, identity in and of performance that tests repeatedly each category our title assumes: 'Irish', 'Theatre', and 'England'.

Given the long history of this cultural relationship, it may be objected that this collection of essays studying Irish theatre in England pursues the story no further back than to the mid-nineteenth century. The length and sheer complexity of this branch of performance history necessitates some form of selection. This volume has grown out of a series of lectures contributed to a conference that was mounted by the Irish Theatrical Diaspora Project in conjunction with an exhibiton held at the National Portrait Gallery in London, *'Conquering England': Ireland in Victorian England*, which explored the extent to which Irish personnel have dominated English cultural and political life. The exhibition was jointly curated by Fintan Cullen and Roy Foster.[1] Again their starting point was the mid-nineteenth century. Few if any significant cultural transitions can be dated from an exact point in time, but there was a crucial turning point that considerably affected the condition certainly of Irish people in England, and that was the Catholic Emancipation Bill, once it became law in 1829. That law effected the first of a series of subtle changes in the cultural relations between the two countries; and the theatre (whether in relation to the status of the Irish performer on the English stage or to the presenting of Irish plays for the reception of English audiences) rapidly reflected or on occasion directly engaged with the political and social factors that brought about those shifts in feeling and awareness. For the historian, Ireland performing in England affords since the 1830s a barometer that is remarkably sensitive at any given time to the intellectual, social, cultural, and political climate of the two nations.

That sensitivity may be dated from what at the time was a surprising turn of events at Covent Garden Theatre. The advertised pantomime to be performed over the Christmas season in 1830 was to be *Harlequin Pat; or, The Giant's Causeway*, penned by Charles Farley, and starring in the titular role a young Irish actor by the name of Tyrone Power, who since 1826 had been the theatre's resident player of Irish parts (the names of the roles that made up his repertoire speak volumes about English theatrical stereotyping in the period and the assumptions that lay behind such an agenda: Teg, O'Blunder, O'Brallaghan, O'Trigger, Brulgruddery). Power was billed as playing the hero, Brian Boru; the part required him to execute a jig and wield a cudgel, smashing windows to left and right; warned to beware 'a higher power', Brian demands to know: 'Is there a more powerful *POWER* than I am?' That superior force is none other than Saint Patrick, whose arrival is preceded by a rout of dancing toads and snakes crossing the stage; he transforms Brian and the other principals into the characters from the Harlequinade, then leaves in a 'car decorated with shamrock' while uttering a final couplet: 'Adieu my children – good natured be and frisky, /I go to superintend the brewing of some whisky'.[2] In light of the recent Catholic Emancipation Act, the whole conception of the pantomime is crass and offensive to Irish sensibilities. Power chose to resign from the role after some four performances. His precise reasons for so doing are not recorded, but the timing is surely significant: had he withdrawn from the role on receiving the script or during rehearsals, his action would have had no impact on theatregoers whatever (and audience-sizes at Covent Garden at this date were considerable). Four days into the run when the management would be hard-pressed to train another performer into the role at very short notice would have produced the maximum amount of chaos to pointed effect. Over the next decade Power proved to be one of the major figures on the London stage (he died in 1841), though none of his later successes was played at Covent Garden; he transformed the kinds of roles available to Irish actors both through plays written for him by the likes of Samuel Lover and Eugene Macarthy and in parts conceived and scripted by himself; all that new repertoire challenged the vicious, essentializing assumptions about the Irish temperament, which underpinned Charles Farley's pantomime and which that dramatist clearly expected to trigger English theatregoers' merriment.[3] One strategy that recurs throughout many roles in Power's new repertoire is that at some point in the drama he is required by circumstances within the plot to play-act being a stage Oirishman; he *performs* the stereotype; and in consequence an audience forcefully perceives the reduction of the character's hitherto complex personality, which is demanded by his assumption of the stereotype. These plays externalize and critique the covert ideology that shapes the creating of a stereotype. What surprises perhaps is the genial tenor with which the didactic purpose is promoted; any anger is controlled (much as later was to be the case with Boucicault's plays and performances); the appeal is to a spectator's intelligence and wider sympathies; that a sophisticated negotiation is taking place within the terms of the performance, however, is clearly signed.[4] The exploring of such negotiations between Irish artists and English spectators at different points in historical time is the enterprise behind the essays that make up the first two sections of this volume.

It was a deliberate choice of the editors, largely to illustrate the complexity of the Irish diasporic narrative when applied to England, not to organize the essays that make up this volume in a chronological sequence of subjects, but instead to group them into three distinct sections with the intention of highlighting recurring themes: issues of reception, identity, popularity, modes of representation, and the staging of history and its imperatives. The first section is organized around the historical, contextual dynamics of the theatrical event. Reception is caught within the specifics of time and place so any reading of it must attend to the exact defining of contexts and affixing of dates. Ben Levitas takes the contextualizing approach when examining the particular English success of Shaw's *John Bull's Other Island* and the precise selection of scenes that were chosen to be given as a command performance before royalty. How exactly did that royal, ministerial, and diplomatic audience interpret the Irish characters played before them? Such questions are shown to be crucially conditioned by not only Shaw's clever strategies of anti-stage-Oirishness, but by the specific social and political circumstances (the imperial and constitutional crises) that attended those strategies. Despite all the knowing inversion and exploration of Irish-English alterity in Shaw's play, Levitas suggests that there is as much resonance in the theatrical experimentation of the Abbey and the Royal Court as there is opposition. Dramatic strategies are the subject of Michael McAteer's essay, which explores how the particular staging of *The Land of Heart's Desire* at the Avenue Theatre in London in 1894 influenced the writing and staging of *Cathleen ni Houlihan* in Dublin in ways that allow a reading of the two works as complementary, and of *The Land of Heart's Desire* as more a political than a fairy play or essay in symbolist escapism. Peter Kuch starts by interpreting the word 'conquest' as a lead into a discussion of the grounds for applying the term to the Irish Players' production of Robinson's *The Whiteheaded Boy* at the Ambassadors' Theatre, London, in 1920. They next embarked on a tour of Australia with Robinson's comedy, playing before a range of urban audiences. To categorize these exploits as a further 'conquest' brings into play a whole new range of resonances in the context of an Irish company performing representations of Irish experience in various outposts of the Empire at a date when Ireland, far from being independent, was suffering under the tyrannies of the Black and Tans. The ironies are legion: Lady Gregory, for example, had astutely asked the Players to make charitable collections at the close of their performances in London to help relieve the Abbey's financial predicament in having to remain dark because of the continuing curfews. Such analysis places its emphasis on constructing the cultural gap between Irish performance and English audiences in terms that are caught in complex temporal matrices: from the state of Anglo-Irish relations to the contingencies of company management and interpretation of textual nuance.

Terms and definitions are the inspiration behind Jonathan Statham's study of the posthumous performance of Yeats's *The Unicorn From the Stars* in London in 1939. There are scant archival remains of the staging of Yeats's plays in England in the 1930s, a situation similar to that obtaining in Germany regarding the staging of his plays: what exactly is dispersed and lost, and what exactly survives to form a record from which conclusions might be drawn about reception and interpretation? As Yeats's international reputation grew, particularly after the award of the Nobel Prize, and given his involvement in his later years with such Establishment institutions as the BBC and Oxford University Press and his long sojourns abroad for reasons of health, to what extent was he still viewed in England as an Irish poet and dramatist? Was it not preferable to appropriate his name within the canons of English literature? For all its technical brilliance and insight into a fellow poet's craft, the one major English elegy on Yeats's death (Auden's) resists all Irish reference and stresses only Yeats's international value for the art of poetry. Yeats's plays themselves present a paradox, since they at once celebrate Irishness and yet resist its popular expression. Statham's use of Yeats's recurring image of the 'fold' appositely holds together the apparent oppositions of national identity and theatrical performance, showing them as cut from the same cloth. Such a theatre, he suggests, is 'always already diasporic and always already returning', always in some sense needing to acknowledge origins in the effort of escape.

Yet more intricate questions of national affiliation and categorizing surround Beckett, that most equivocal of shape-changers. Irish, French, or English: which cultural canon should he grace? The dilemma underlies the agenda structuring the *Beckett on Film* project with, as Graham Saunders demonstrates, both laughable and destructive consequences, once that agenda was put into practice; the situation was further complicated by the funding sources backing the concept. Ongoing promotion of the endeavour through festivals in Dublin, London, and elsewhere has tended to prove counter-productive. The cultural co-ordinates of Beckett's work are all the more difficult to fix when tested not so much by English theatrical performance as by new media, which allows for less of an engagement with location, than with non-location and dislocation. The disembodiment of film resonates with Beckett's existential detachment, while risking the loss of allusion to cultural memory. In an age of *Riverdance*, when Irishness is itself a reified commodity on global markets, Beckett's evasive national allegiance is also what makes him a less than all-conquering mass product. His retreat from narrow cultural labels into the meta-geography of his stagings remains resistant to easy politics and easy commodification.

The careers of few contemporary dramatists have been as cruelly subject to the shifting tides of political attitudes and policies than Gary Mitchell's, whose reception in England as the chronicler of loyalist malaise in Northern Ireland is surveyed by Tim Miles. Once fêted as an assured measure of authenticity, Mitchell is now a figure most English and Northern Irish artistic directors choose to ignore; Miles shows how the rise and fall of Mitchell's career in England is to be seen as a measure of an English vulnerability to media-manufactured 'troubles' archetypes. Representations of 'the Ulster Protestant' in contemporary plays is also Wallace McDowell's theme; but he ranges over a number of dramatists, sets them in the context of Northern Irish political and theatrical history, and shows how differently their work has been received by audiences in London, Belfast, and Dublin and how that difference is conditioned by fluctuating political circumstance. Such theatre may find affinity in English theatres because it tackles Britishness rather than Irishness in the first place. Disturbing differences are to be discerned, however, between on the one hand the diversity of theatrical representations of Ulster Protestants in recent years, and on the other the reductive uniformity of general media representation, particularly in England over the same period.

The second section moves away from issues of reception in relation to identity to engage with the ways in which identity is often within the context of theatre defined by exploring the borderline between performance and performativity. By performativity is meant a knowingly overt acting out of a decided personal choice, the conscious projection of an imagined or imaginary self for a variety of ends, political and psychological. W.B. Yeats once made the observation that, having moved to England, Oscar Wilde 'perpetually performed a play'.[5] It is perhaps not surprising that a binding theme in this volume is a sense of strategic performance, whether of the subversive outsider gaining privileged access, or of a more overtly resistant display of cultural otherness. When performativity becomes the thematic focus, Tyrone Power again offers a valid, historical touchstone. Many of his most famous roles required him to interrogate forms of role-play, which were steadily revealed to be the character's means of preserving a political integrity. Rory O'More in Samuel Lover's play of that title (Adelphi, 1837) and Gerald Pepper in Lover's *The White Horse of the Peppers* (Haymarket, 1838) deliberately assume a travesty of themselves (they role-play the stage Oirishman) before English or Dutch enemies to trick them into relaxing into their conventionalized notions about stereotypical Irishmen, where those enemies become vulnerable to Rory or Gerald's political manipulations. A self-reflexive performativity becomes the characters' moral and political armour against colonial oppression. Performativity may take, however, many forms and be motivated by a variety of ends, as the range of essays in this section reveals.

The trio of operas that became known as the Irish 'Ring' cycle exploited a prevailing English taste for sentiment and love-lorn maidens in picturesque landscapes that had been popularized by Moore's *Irish Melodies* and Daniel Maclise's illustrations to the poems in the 1840s.[6] This was the Ireland that English tourists wished to explore, but to what degree was it an Ireland of the romantic imagination, a *performed* Ireland at a considerable remove from the harsher social and political realities?[7] As Shaw was to warn in *John Bull's Other Island*, there was a dangerous potential for exploitation and commodification in overstressing the romantic delights of the landscape and an overly genial and welcoming peasantry. However, the international popularity of the operas showed that in some instances Irish theatre in England need be neither an act of obsequy nor a counter punch. Rather the operas displayed a border-crossing proclivity and an internationally viable range of signification. While that is a common enough pattern nowadays when extensive touring to international venues and festivals prevails, Irish theatre in England, as Jerry Nolan demonstrates, has a long, if selective history as an already-cosmopolitan product. The nineteenth-century phenomenon of the Irish 'Ring' showed an 'Irishness' already thoroughly blended with European mores. After the export of Moore's melodies into operetta's exotic locales by Balfe and Wallace, there came a return call, completed by the adaptation of Boucicault for *The Lily of Killarney* by Julius Benedict, a German Jew.

The concerns of the remaining essays in this section sift the performance problematics that evolve from the tension between Irish/English identities and 'theatrical' identities – and further, the reflexive recognition of that tension as it takes form, not just on the stage, but in the lives of those who take performance as their medium. This is a frame in which the 'stage name' signals a strategic performance of self that responds to pressures to conform to cultural expectations, but is not a simple masking. As Elizabeth Schafer reveals in her study of Edris Stannus/ Ninette de Valois, a sense of Irishness can be nostalgically reclaimed to the extent where it proves physically manifest in the practice such memory impels, with the Irish jig shaping the bodies of the Royal Ballet. Schafer shows how a strategic Irishness was often Ninette de Valois' trump card in establishing so wayward and 'other' an art-form as ballet within the metropolis. But was her much-prized jig any more authentically Irish than her chosen name as artist indicated an authentic French descent?

Where Power engaged with performativity as a necessary strategy for self-protection against the abuses of colonialism, Mary Manning in *Youth's the Season—?* investigates the plight of women and of sexual minorities within Dublin society post-Independence to see the extent to which such a strategy was adequate protection against the pressured, homogenizing social tendencies of the new state. But as Cathy Leeney shows in her essay, much depended for an adequate representation of Manning's argument on the actor playing in the central role. Evidence suggests that performances succeeded best when audiences experienced in the role of Desmond that unambiguously camp master of disguise and shape-changing: Micheál MacLiammóir, (English actor masquerading as Gaelic-speaking Irishman). When in such a context does performativity cease to be subterfuge and become a chosen and personally vindicated form of self-expression? Hybrid existences like MacLiammóir's and de Valois' certainly acknowledge the cultural prejudices and their power relations in the camouflage of their labels: but they also go beyond Irish and English oppositions. Leeney's essay reveals the resonances between Mary Manning's exploration of 'gender dissidence' and the cultural mobility of Alfred Willmore/Micheál MacLiammóir. Travelling in the opposite direction to de Valois, MacLiammóir found that in discarding his Englishness in a theatrical persona, he could unmask his sexuality without entirely sacrificing social acceptability. No less to the point, Leeney shows that in seeking to dramatize such subversions, Manning found the reflexive pressures of these multiple performances pushing her theatre into wholly new and challenging formal territories.

Similarly Carmen Szabó shows in her discussion of *Double Cross* how Tom Kilroy undermines our instincts to slip into simple oppositions not only by challenging their politics, but also by his performance strategies: he refuses stable character and place to employ internal dialogues, disembodied broadcast, and reportage. Szabo, in her examination of Kilroy's two plays for Field Day (the other being *The Madam MacAdam Travelling Theatre*), argues that, while acknowledging a potent politics, he draws attention to theatre's power, not by referring to its imbrication with the national struggle, but by metatheatrically insisting on its capacity to evoke heterotopia: a cultural space that is pristine. However much the intent to establish a specific Irish identity in theatrical work is heightened by its performance in an English environment, there is always a dialectical resonance that challenges that opposition. A theatre in Ireland and a theatre in England are still not merely expressions of national culture, but sites of specific and shared cultural practice: the place of theatrical performance itself. This then, becomes a case of 'Irish Metatheatre in England', in which location amplifies that aspect of Irish theatre which reflects upon the constantly conditional performance of Irish identity itself.

The common aesthetic choices and rituals of the theatre experience also create a point of unity, not only between Ireland and England, but also in a broader act of translation, internationally. If, as Enrica Cerquoni argues in discussing the scenography of diverse stagings of Friel's *Dancing at Lughnasa*, theatre belongs 'not to nations but to audiences',[8] then the theatrical space also offers a particularly useful space in the examination of national identities, since it demotes national differences as a lesser opposition than the more immediate separation of the theatrical and non-theatrical. In the troubled problematic of theatre's autonomy as an art form, refuge from the tyranny of cultural dichotomy may be sought. Performativity has distinct cultural advantages to offer in terms of both artistic creativity and audience response: it shapes a distinctive learning curve.

The final section does not derive from an initial conference presentation but from research being undertaken by Peter Harris that was largely concomitant with the *Conquering England* exhibition. The essays that comprise the earlier sections of this volume directly or indirectly chart the mobility of the theatrical idiom; and that is also, of course, to note its success as a commodity. English theatres have continually offered a lucrative market as well as critical validation for Irish dramaturgy and the practitioners engaged in staging it. What Harris's remarkable and exhaustive research demonstrates is the sheer extent of the intake of Irish theatre in its various manifestations onto London stages (and his focus is exclusively on metropolitan venues). His 'Chronological Table of Irish Plays Produced in London Since 1920' provides with wonderful precision a welcome resource: it charts the range of material available for future scholars intent on researching the multiple directions, the complex cultural resonances, the constant shape-changing but persistent presence of Irish Theatre in England.

---

[1] The conference was held on 16-17 June 2005. The exhibition was accompanied by a book, comprising annotated reproductions of most of the exhibits together with two essays by the editors. See Fintan Cullen and R.F.Foster, eds, *"Conquering England": Ireland in Victorian London* (London: National Portrait Gallery Publications, 2005).

[2] The manuscript of Charles Farley's pantomime is to be found in the Lord Chamberlain's Collection in the British Library, Cat. No. L.C.P. Add. Mss. 42905, ff.294-304b: 300, 303.

[3] A magnificent portrait of Tyrone Power at the height of his success was included in the exhibition at the National Portrait Gallery. Nicholas Crowley depicts him in the role of Connor O'Gorman in Anna Maria Hall's *The Groves of Blarney* in 1838 (Tyrone Guthrie Centre at Annaghmakerrig). See Cullen and Foster, 28.

[4] For a fuller discussion of Power's repertoire, see Richard Allen Cave, "Staging the Irishman" in *Acts of Supremacy: The British Empire and the Stage (1790-1930)*, ed. J.S.Bratton (Manchester: Manchester University Press, 1991): 83-96.

[5] W.B. Yeats, *Autobiographies* (London and Basingstoke: Macmillan, 1955): 138.

[6] Maclise's illustrations to Moore's poems and other paintings of Irish allegorical subjects featured in the National Portrait Gallery exhibition. Perhaps the most significant for the argument here is his painting of 1842, *The Origin of the Harp* (Manchester City Galleries), which was reproduced in an engraved version with Moore's *Irish Melodies*. It depicts a naked and jilted Irish maiden posing against waves and rocks in a sea-cave while awaiting her death by drowning; her long tresses of hair, some seaweed that entangles her and a shard of rock together create the shape of an Irish harp. Here in one image are both a sentimental landscape and a forlorn nude as frames for the trope of the grieving woman as emblem of Ireland, while the whole is offered as celebratory

of the birth of Irish music.
7 A similarly sanitized Ireland was still being promoted in the Irish Exhibition at Olympia, London, in the summer of 1888, which displayed girls at work industriously in various cottage settings creating luxury items for upper class English markets. See Cullen and Foster, 75.
8 Cerquoni, quoting Pamela Howard, *What is Scenography?* (London: Routledge, 2002): 33.

Part One: Reception And Contexts

1 | These Islands' Others: *John Bull*, the Abbey and the Royal Court

Ben Levitas

As scholars rework the history of the Irish revival, they may be counted upon to recount new centenaries while marking in swift succession the landmarks of change that led to independence. One hundred years since the founding of the Abbey in December 1904; one hundred since the *Playboy* Riots; since the death of Synge; since the third Home Rule Bill; since *Dubliners* and/or *Responsibilities*; since the lockout; since the Rising. One of the crucial tasks, as this flurry of reapprehendings are numbered, must be to disturb the insularity that such teleology risks – to question the long gestation by conceiving of other events that troubled Ireland from without as well as within. The Irish Theatrical Diaspora Project looks beyond Ireland's native theatre revivals to their engagement with the wider world; to the theatre traffic that reflects a social and cultural connectedness with emigrant populations, with its 'others' and with imperial politics. It is apposite, then, it should provide a counterpoint to the Abbey obsession by offering in contrast (or rather in conjunction) the influential Royal Court seasons of 1904-1907.[1]

At the crux of this comparison stands George Bernard Shaw's potent re-posing of the Irish Question, *John Bull's Other Island*, first performed on 1 November 1904. In development this play linked the Abbey and the Royal Court together; and in performance it discussed what kept them apart. As such, the substance of the play dwells with some precision on the implications of its construction: the Irish exile's backward glance, the possibility of return, the tension that exists between a topical commentary on contemporary politics and the memory of what was. Beyond that, to internationalism and the national, and the moral dimension of identity as it struggles with the responsibility of the native in an era of cultural resistance. In the success of *John Bull* and its significance within the history of the relationship between English and Irish drama can be read the complexity of a social and political landscape stretched, and perhaps distended, between locations; and an acknowledgement of the parallax of shifting viewpoints that, in shifting, change the object under inspection. At the centre, Shaw binds together the fortunes of theatrical projects that offer not lone but twin revivals, circling in a kind of wary dance.

In one sense that dance can be seen as merely the latest interaction of theatre business from each side of the Irish sea. A glance at the work of Joep Leerssen or Christopher Morash reveals centuries rather than decades of influence and counter influence between English and Irish traditions.[2] Nicolas Grene has ably sandwiched Shaw's *John Bull* between Boucicault's *Shaughraun* and Friel's *Translations*, preceding and succeeding interpretations of stage Irishness that reflexively acknowledge representations steeped in the political realities of their day.[3] But it also seems worth noting that in its coincidence with the revival, Shaw's play marks its territory as particularly attuned to the implications of a more radical separation of nations, politically and culturally. When Shaw had started out, the centripetal pull of London's literary world had been overwhelming, even while he had, with Oscar Wilde, set about what Yeats in 1891 described as their 'extravagant crusade against Anglo-Saxon stupidity'.[4] A great city of extremes, part of what London embodied was conflict, and it drew in critics keen to expose its contradictions, using whatever radical vocabularies lay to hand. In 1893, the champion of new drama, William Archer, had remarked on two examples of 'very remarkable dramatic experiment' facilitated by Jacob Grien's Independent Theatre: Shaw's *Widowers' Houses* and George Moore's *The Strike at Arlingford*.[5] Both authors had found their subjects through familiarity with socialist circles in the 1880s, whose adventures in Ibsenism had helped lay the ground for the establishment of the Independent Theatre in 1891.

If Shaw drew upon the slum landlordism he knew well from his days as a rent-collecting clerk for the Dublin land agency, his inspiration confirmed Irish experience as bound in with modern economies rather than evolving cultural resistance. Just as Shaw had in 1891 subsumed his support for the stricken Parnell within the wider campaign for moral pioneers expressed in *The Quintessence of Ibsenism*, immersion in class politics drew him toward socialist internationalist rather than Irish nationalist concerns. The punishing flamboyance of *Arms and the Man* drew on Boucicault for the purposes of turning melodrama inside out; but it was set in Bulgaria, not Ireland. Its partnering with Yeats's *The Land of Heart's Desire* at the Avenue theatre in 1894 marked a further point of departure, as trenchant as Shaw's from Dublin in 1876, at the age of 20. Hitherto, Irishmen of talent had gravitated toward London; and in one sense this auspicious double bill seemed to underline that tendency. Nevertheless, Yeats had, with his play's overtly Irish subject matter, signalled the shift back towards a drama unmediated by an Imperial host. The London-based Irish Literary Society had given rise to the National Literary Society, founded in Dublin in 1892; that in turn had given rise to the Gaelic League. Wilde's imprisonment seemed another event accelerating divergence. It was not long before the Irish Literary Theatre confirmed the momentum in 1898. As George Moore resonantly put it, the 'sceptre of intelligence' passed from London to Dublin. Shaw, it seemed, had been exiled from Ireland twice: once when he left it, and again when it left him.

By the time Shaw came to write *John Bull's Other Island*, however, the balance had shifted again. The play opens with the affable English entrepreneur Thomas Broadbent instructing his valet to pack his revolver in preparation for a trip to Ireland; his partner Doyle has been using it as a paperweight. The firearm, it seems, is a redundant melodramatic signature, rightly demoted to desk furniture from crucial plot device. An image of colonial misapprehension, the pistol is not needed, and is never unpacked. Stock characters are likewise discarded: Broadbent welcomes in Tim Haffigan, who appears, as Shaw describes him, 'with a show of reckless geniality and high spirits, helped out by a rollicking stage brogue.'[6] He wishes his host a 'top o' the mornin' and briefly continues in this expansive stage-Irish idiom until exposed as a charlatan by the altogether more stringent Irish character of Larry Doyle. Doyle reports to his friend that Haffigan is 'not an Irishman at all':

> Man alive, don't you know that all this top-o-the-morning and broth-of-a-boy and more-power-to-your-elbow business is got up in England to fool you, like the Albert Hall concerts of Irish music? No Irishman ever talks like that in Ireland, or ever did, or ever will...he flatters your sense of moral superiority by playing the fool and degrading himself and his country, he soon learns the antics that take you in. He picks them up at the theatre or the music hall (78).

As has been often noted, Shaw's opening toys with his audience's anticipation of a stereotype, and his device works whether it is a stereotype you condemn or condone. In either case the spectator is warned away from presuming the play to be predictable in its depictions of national characteristics. It also gives a clear demarcation of what counts as Irish. Haffigan, born in Glasgow, howsoever of Irish extraction, and however Irish he might appear, is not Irish. Doyle, who knows that Haffigan's father hails, as he does, from Rosscullen, is dismissive of such claims as may derive from theories of race. Landscape not blood, Shaw held, determined the Irish mind: 'There is no Irish race any more than there is an English race or a Yankee race,' he confirms in the 1906 preface. 'There is an Irish climate, which will stamp an immigrant more deeply and durably in two years, apparently, than the English climate will in two hundred' (11). Larry Doyle had elaborated this principle in an odd mix of evocative nostalgia and dread:

> You've no such colors in the sky, no such lure in the distances, no such sadness in the evenings. Oh, the dreaming! the dreaming! the torturing, heartscalding, never satisfying dreaming, dreaming, dreaming, dreaming! (81)

Condemning the imaginative torpor of his homeland, Doyle engages its potency even while his distance on this cultural characteristic places him in a separate category. He is thus situated on one hand as an antidote to the illusions of the fake Irishman, and on the other as an antidote to the delusions of the real Irishman. The latter, he observes, are most striking in the symbolic force of nationalism. 'If you want to interest him in Ireland you've got to call the unfortunate island Kathleen ni Houlihan and pretend she's a little old woman.' Doyle continues: 'It saves thinking, it saves working. It saves everything except imagination, imagination, imagination' (81). Very swiftly, then, Shaw asserts that the migrant's access to comparative cultural reference puts him in a superior position to judge. The privilege of the travelled is that observation replaces imagination. In a sense, Doyle is made a kind of *über*Irishman capable of seeing past the hindrances of false projections, whether imposed from outside by a colonizer or from inside by romantic nationalism. This contrast is thrown into further relief by the character of Broadbent, a stage Englishman whose overgrown naivety and all conquering ego Doyle consistently patronizes and which seems to neatly reverse the colonizers' tendency to infantilize their subjects. At the same time, however, this process acknowledges the potency of a new, but equally 'staged' nationality, which, as the play progresses, becomes increasingly open to reassessment. Having just been exposed by the foolery of Haffingan, the audience is on the alert for presumptions of authenticity. Shaw here uses the intrigue of finding the true Ireland as the element of suspense. After Larry Doyle's excoriations, we are avid for a glimpse into the Ireland he remembers, and eager to see for ourselves if he can be as right about that as he was about Tom Broadbent's sponging visitor.

Our curiosity is only deepened, therefore, when Act II opens with a scene that apparently belies the blast of Doyle's sardonic memory. Keegan's conversation with the grasshopper, shows a gentler and more playful imaginative impulse than heartscalding derision. He may ask the insect 'why does the sight of Heaven wring your heart an mine?' (90) but the mood is of melancholic whimsicality. Our introduction to the ex-priest gives the first reassessment of the exile's memory, altering Doyle's severe diagnoses. In the process of conjuring an Ireland to return to, Shaw negotiates the gap between an Ireland remembered and an Ireland revisited. As observation recalled in tranquillity, the imagination is brought back into play; a doubly detached witness of the new revival, Shaw airs his misgivings to give some benefit of doubt.

The reflexive disjuncture is, in part, Shaw's response to a shift in the balance between theatrical protagonists. If Irish theatre left London in the 1890s, it soon reappeared on tour, anxious to impress hard-bitten metropolitan critics. The newly formed Irish National Theatre Society had appeared first at the behest of the Irish Literary Society in May 1903, when they performed at the Queen's Gate Hall in South Kensington to a carefully assembled audience of influential arbiters of literary taste. A return trip was organized for the following spring, performing at the Royalty Theatre (off Shaftesbury Avenue) a bill of fare that included Synge's *In the Shadow of the Glen* and *Riders to the Sea*, Yeats's *The King's Threshold* and *A Pot of Broth*; and Padraic Colum's *Broken Soil*. This time Shaw absorbed the impressive innovations of their work and, even more observantly, the fact that Yeats had managed to persuade Annie Horniman, who had been a mutual patron ten years earlier, to pay for a new Dublin theatre. The Abbey was set to open at the end of the year, and for it Shaw was persuaded to produce 'a patriotic contribution to the repertory'. It was this that provided the impulse to write *John Bull*.

As is well known, Yeats praised the play, with a certain feline condescension, remarking that 'You have said things in this play which are entirely true about Ireland, things which nobody has ever said before. It astonishes me that you should have been so long in London and yet have remembered so much.'[7] It was, however, finally declined as too sizable and unsympathetic. Whatever rapprochement had seemed open in the spring of 1904 was swiftly shut. Shaw at least thought this the case: 'It was uncongenial to the whole spirit of the neo-Gaelic movement,' he wrote in the 1906 preface, 'which is bent on creating a new Ireland after its own ideal, whereas my play is a very uncompromising presentment of the real old Ireland'(7). Yet in that assessment comes an inviting confession as well as an assertion, in curious agreement with Yeats. Although loyal to his trenchant portrayal, Shaw's rejection of Celtic revivalism came with a caveat. Just as Yeats insinuated the existence of an unknown Ireland in remarking on Shaw's capacity to have 'remembered so much', Shaw acknowledges that a treatment of real 'old Ireland' might not be a full depiction of the present one.

This tendency to elicit dialectical opportunity from apparently watertight polemic is characteristic of *John Bull*, and its shape. Along with the detritus of a melodramatic past with its stock stereotype, the tight construction of the well made play is discarded in favour of a discursive elaboration of cultural labels. Shaw had already begun, with *Man and Superman*, such experimentation. But *John Bull* was the first to be performed, and its formal resistance to box-office convention offered for the theatre that could stage it a built-in art house manifesto. Yeats judged form one of the play's significant flaws – it was, he thought, 'fundamentally ugly and shapeless'.[8] Ironically, however, it is precisely its fluidity which gives shape to Shaw's attempt to resist commercial imperatives, one of the campaigns he and Yeats could count as common ground. Yeats had long before recognized Shaw's capacity to 'hit my enemies, and the enemies of all I loved, as I could never hit'.[9] More than this, the expansive form allowed the sting of Shaw's critiques of romantic nationalism to be soothed by a deeper ambivalence. As the play develops, Larry Doyle's mesmerically vituperative rejections of old Ireland are increasingly overwritten by Peter Keegan's paradoxical belief in the utility of utopian detachment, evolving the implication that a new Ireland might combine uncommercial socialist instincts with a distinctively Irish sensibility. *John Bull* concludes, therefore, closer to the common ground

Shaw and Yeats shared;[10] and this is also true of the alternative circumstance in which the play came to be first performed.

The Royal Court season of 1904-1905 was a culmination of the theatre societies upon which Shaw had largely depended for the production of his work. Principally,the Independent Theatre, already mentioned; The New Century Theatre; and the Stage Society, which gave sporadic and isolated performances of new and foreign plays that were financed by subscription. Such efforts built pressure for a more sustained attempt at establishing a ground-breaking theatre project. It came when the Court came into the possession of J.H. Leigh, who was keen to test the possibilities of a more daring programme; and when the team of the theatrical organizer J. E. Vedrenne and actor-manager Granville Barker responded to the opportunity with an innovative scheme. By giving matinees on days when the major west end venues were closed, the Court could have its pick of the acting talent available; and by offering a programme of testing material, they could convince them to perform for a nominal fee. The first production the team put on was Gilbert Murray's version of Euripides' *Hippolytus*, which Barker had been producing at the Lyric. The second, and therefore in some sense the original Vedrenne-Barker production, was *John Bull*.

The reception of the play was in fact, mixed. But it was mixed in such a way as to emphasize both the impact of the Court's influence and to guarantee Shaw's reputation – critics were divided along the lines reflecting their habitual openness to experimentation: the same critics that had admired the visiting National Theatre Society. Reviews from the *Daily Telegraph* ('great hunks of bombastic frivolity')[11] and the *Times* ('we wish he had got tired a little sooner')[12] drew attention to the unforgiving length of the play; but Beerbohm admired it,[13] William Archer declared Shaw had done 'nothing more original'[14] and for some no hyperbole could suffice. Desmond MacCarthy solemnly warned in his 1907 retrospective on the impact of the Vedrenne-Barker years that: 'Every critic of this play must stop on the threshold of his comments to remark with whatever emphasis he can command, that the performance itself was one of the best ever given in London.'[15]

MacCarthy's awe was in part a recognition of the cultural and political significance of the play. Shaw's Fabian connections with Beatrice and Sidney Webb put him in touch with influential political operators. Beatrice Webb brought the Prime Minister, Arthur Balfour, to the play on 10

November: he came back to see the play four more times, bringing the leaders of the liberal opposition Campbell-Bannerman and Asquith with him. And then, famously, came King Edward VII who laughed so hard his chair broke, throwing him to the ground. Shaw had, if not in the manner he had intended, brought down the British monarch. After that, his reputation, unlike the Royal Backside, never came back down; by the time the Vedrenne-Barker duo had split in June 1907, Shaw commanded an unassailable position at the centre of the Court roster. In that time, 32 plays by 17 authors had been produced, including groundbreaking productions of Ibsen, Hauptmann, Maeterlinck and W.B. Yeats, along with Galsworthy, Barker, and Masefield. But Shaw towered above them, with eleven different plays produced during the period. Of 988 performances in total, 701 were of his work.[16]

Given Shaw's taste for paradox and polemic, this success is not so surprising. The Royal Court Theatre occupied a peculiarly Shavian place between an establishment and a radical London. Shaw's plays provided the engine for a theatre project that could provide intellectually and artistically challenging material to a London public hungry for it. The Royal Court became a cult venue, a hub both for the political elites, and for a left intelligentsia satisfied at finding a voice that seemed to speak to them. It fed an emerging suffragist and socialist politics, evidenced by the women who dominated its day-to-day audience.[17] It became a springboard for the popularization of material previously considered taboo; and a conduit for the 'new drama' of social self-criticism. This was the theatre of Edwardian anxiety; attended by a Liberal England fascinated by premonitions of its own strange death, admired by those who chose to hasten it. On one hand steep admission prices limited the Royal Court as a venue for social upheaval[18] – it certainly fell short of a *bone fide* avant-garde[19] – on the other, as Raphael Samuel noted, Shaw's work proliferated beyond fashionable London not only into provincial theatres but to working class amateur groups in search of resonant material.[20] That a play about Ireland should have kick-started the engine of the Royal Court is not evidence merely of displaced Irish genius, but of an emerging English appetite for the contested. Within the paradox of its performance context, it could appeal to an elite alert to expert advice on the progress of land reform; and to anti-Imperialism as one element of emerging left politics.

Nevertheless, Shaw's success brings us back to some of the ambiguities at the heart of the play that sparked it off. The fact that *John Bull* proved such a hit with the British establishment inevitably draws our attention back to the circumstances of its reception. To the less radical English audience, the character of Broadbent, while clearly poking fun at a Liberal capacity for hypocrisy, seemed reassuringly warm and successful. 'It is a Saxon philistine who carries off such prizes as the sister isle has to afford.' Commented the reviewer of the *Globe*:

> An Englishman, moreover, is the genuine hero of the piece, Keegan who contests with Broadbent the supremacy of interests representing only the nebulous and mystical aspects of the Celt.[21]

What might, for an Irish audience, have operated to temper the tendency to demonize the English presence, worked within the security of its London confines to magnify his success. Ironically, Shaw's intimations of Irish intellectual superiority in Doyle and Keegan were accepted as a fair trade if mere affable cunning could bring romantic, economic and political success to Broadbent by the end of the play. For this audience, it seemed, Shaw had sugared the pill of his polemic a little too liberally.

In contrast, when the play came to Ireland on tour in November 1907, nationalists picked carefully over the play. The audience had been sensitized by the *Playboy* controversies: the opening 'riots' in January-February, and by the decision to take Synge's play on tour to England in June. The wary dance continued: ironically, the Abbey produced their London shows at the Royal Court, just as the Vedrenne-Barker company left the Royal Court for the grander Savoy Theatre. Vedrenne-Barker's move to the Savoy would prove overambitious, but their Dublin production at the Theatre Royal was no less a success than the English one. W.P. Ryan, in the (left-revivalist) *Peasant*, noted that the theatre's management had been nervous about the play's reception, but he declared, unnecessarily: 'Shaw is appreciated in the land of his birth and if he was not we believe he would be the last to employ Dublin policemen to help to ram the play down the throats of his countrymen.'[22] There was however, one jarring note. Nationalist and unionist reviewers alike (*Irish Times*, *Daily Express*, as well as the *Peasant*, and *Irish Independent*) took exception to Patsy Farrell, insisting he was a 'Handy Andy' and should be dropped.[23] Not surprisingly: Shaw describes the labourer as having a '*silliness, indicating, not his real character, but a cunning developed by his constant dread of hostile dominance, which he habitually tries to disarm and tempt into unmasking*'. This certainly places great demands upon the actor; Patsy's 'real character' never allows his own mask to slip.

Rather, silliness amplified by its own pretence, Farrell remains trapped in buffoonery, a too-subtle subaltern echo of Tim Haffingan's stage Irishman.

Despite Patsy, critics were understanding. Shaw's intentions were well advertised, not least because the 'Preface for Politicians' predated it.[24] 'Jacques', writing in the *Independent*, declared the play 'a work that appeals with intense force to anyone sensitive to the currents of thought that are disturbing the mental atmosphere of the age.' Further than that, however, he noted the social striations of a politicized audience, clearly various in its responses: if the gallery was roused by Doyle's radical speeches, the dress circle 'rocked with laughter' at Broadbent's irate liberal nationalism – while the middle-brow stalls, muttering 'who's this Shaw fellow?' were all at sea. 'Go to the gallery' he urged his readers – the most incisive reception was to be found from the cheapest seats.[25]

Just as in England, reception in Ireland revealed political difference rather than cultural sameness. Radical nationalists fastened onto the darker logic of the play. Arthur Griffith (never a man for light comedy) identified Larry Doyle as the villain: 'Of all the characters in the play, Larry Doyle is the most despicable. He is the Irishman who having deserted his country, because she is poor and weak, derides her because by his cowardice she becomes poorer and weaker.' Far from taking umbrage at Shaw's depiction of provincialized Roscullen, Griffith saw in his portrait the need to make Ireland a nation once again. Shaw's 'master stroke of satire' he decided, immune to Shaw's stab at Celtic kitsch, was 'an Irish lady humming an out of date English music hall song at the foot of the silent witness of Ireland's genius and devotion – the Round Tower'.[26] That he, like so many others, wanted to skew the play to his particular standpoint suggests Shaw's knack for charming and challenging in equal measure. But Griffith was attuned to the Doyle-Keegan opposition in a way English audiences were not. As Shaw complained: 'I have shown them the Irish saint shuddering at the humour of the Irish blackguard – only to find, I regret to say, that the average critic thought the blackguard very funny and the saint impractical.'[27]

That performances at the Royal Court and Theatre Royal should be characterized by likeable fun rather than satirical force registers an ambivalence that goes to the heart of Shaw's association with Fabian politics. The principle of permeation of social and political norms had at the time of *Widowers' Houses*, been imbued with the energy of radical, and marginal organization. By the time of *JBOI* however it had become associated less with the cutting edge of politics than with the corridors of power. In an attempt to disturb what he saw as the complacency at the heart of the Fabian Society, H.G. Wells in 1906 challenged the principle of permeation, offering a little parable to illustrate his point:

> The mouse [he said] decided to adopt indirect and inconspicuous methods, not to complicate its proceedings by too many associates, to win over and attract the cat by friendly advances rather than frighten her by a sudden attack. It is believed that in the end the mouse did succeed in permeating the cat, but the cat is still living – and the mouse can't be found.[28]

In *JBOI*, the question remains whether the mouse of Shaw's challenge to Imperial power permeated the cat all too effectively, becoming digested by an elite happy to distain its more radical suggestions and to pick clean what lessons might be construed for efficient government. The Webbs's political connections were often forged at the dining tables of the establishment, and while this obviously benefited Shaw it exposed him also. While campaigning for a socialist future, and for a more equal federation with Ireland within a socialist commonwealth, his companionable marriage to the wealthy Fabian, Charlotte Payne-Townshend, gave him a guaranteed income derived from Ireland, and spent in England.[29] His own success as a feted author was made possible by his capacity to help underwrite the Royal Court project financially. Shaw's revelation of Nora Reilly's income casts light on the relative poverty of Ireland while ironically acknowledging the difference in wealth between his wife and the Rosscullen heiress:

> **Doyle:** Nora has a fortune.
> **Broadbent:** Eh? How much?
> **Doyle:** Forty per annum.
> **Broadbent:** Forty thousand?
> **Doyle:** No. forty. forty pounds. (86)

The embarrassment of riches implicit in this exchange echoes ambivalence about simply gesturing the ruling class toward an egalitarian society. Largesse was ostentatiously evident at such events as the 1907 dinner at the Criterion, in which the exiting Royal Court management played host to the great and the good. Nevertheless Shaw kept such luxury under wry attack. The allusion to Nora's small fortune recognizes an economic difference of scale between Imperial and local elites, and contemplates the gap between the Court's resources and the Abbey's – just as the capacity to stage a play as big as *John Bull* had done, Horniman notwithstanding. Scrutiny of this process of both class-and-colonial co-option is to be detected in the trajectory of Larry Doyle's character. In the first act, as we have seen, his commentary is offered as a tentative gauge of the actual Ireland. But his declaration toward the end of the first act, that 'I wish I could find a country to live in where the facts are not brutal and the dreams are not unreal' (88) marks an early disengagement from the action of the play. Henceforth, his operation is that of someone shedding attachments, not because he does not value them, but because the value he sets by them brings a misery that affects his capacity for work. His fetishized work ethic draws him toward the 'brutal' rather than the 'unreal', just as his fatalistic acquiescence in the system becomes exposed by the discovery that subject nationality adds a layer of alienation. The internationalist independence of the worldly wise worker is recast as the colonial dependence of the economic migrant.

The process is carefully managed by Shaw. Once the action shifts to Ireland, Doyle's capacity fluctuates unevenly. His absence from Act II gives over the stage to Keegan, while allowing Broadbent the opportunity to operate unrestrained by the mordant commentary of the first act. In act three, he returns as the eloquent orator, not to deride Irish romanticism, but as a maverick thinker full of radical schemes. In his suggestion that Patsy Farrell be given a minimum wage and that the land purchase provisions of the 1903 Wyndham Land Act are a disastrous *embourgeoisment*, Doyle echoes a typically Shavian politics.[30] His paradoxical insistence on the establishment of the Catholic church offers common ground between Keegan's spiritual utopianism and his own. Nevertheless, Doyle's ready resignation to unpopularity ('I told you it would be no use' (122)) displays a reluctance to work for his own aims with the application he reserves for Broadbent's interests. From here, the logic of acquiescence is swift:

> Is Ireland never to have a chance? First she was given to the rich; and now that they have gorged on her flesh, her bones are to be flung to the poor, that can do nothing but suck the marrow out of her. If we cant have men of honour own the land, lets have men of ability. If we cant have men with ability, let us as least have men with capital (120).

Doyle derides nationalist complicity in vicious class relations, but dismisses alternatives as a circular series of non-starting failures. The same circularity, however, returns his allegiance, and his rhetoric, to the service of the wealthy. By the time we come across the play's closing argument, Keegan has replaced him as the exponent of an alternative vision, while Doyle has been subsumed within his partner's operation, no longer a foil for his foolery, but an instrument of his plans to commodify and possess. In seeking to act as a partner to Broadbent, he has been consumed by the implacable operation of the capital he represents.

What the play insists upon is that impersonal capital is still always inflected through specific socio-cultural – in this case imperialist – relations. The set piece in Act III portraying the various social groups left in the wake of the expropriation of the landlord class is a study in class difference rather than national collective identity. Shaw was at great pains to denote this diversity in terms of an accurate social signification of dress and demeanour, taking care to establish a range beyond typical Abbey peasant cabin-drama. He instructed that:

> Corny Doyle lives in a slated house...no person in rags could possibly be admitted to his parlour to listen to Doran's story...Patsy, in corduroys, is the only laborer [*sic*], and would not be treated as an equal by any of the rest; that Doran, though mill-dusty and slovenly, is a master miller, not a tramp; that Matt Haffigan dresses like a deacon or a schoolmaster when he goes to meet his priest at a land agents house.[31]

In the act of such social forensics, it becomes apparent that class is a crucial, but not all-encompassing category of difference, a fact underscored at the close by the row between the British urban working class as represented by Broadbent's valet, Hodson, and the Irish rural tenant farmer as manifest in the person of Matt Haffigan. Their argument shows national antipathy as a kind of one-downmanship of comparative suffering that blinds the combatants to common interest. At the same time, the dimension of national grievance is not discarded: Haffingan argues that Irish grievance is attested to by Irish truculence, and that is attested to by English repression. As he points out, Hodson's sheepish duty needs no muzzle. Socialist or liberal discourse notwithstanding, the colonial dimension retains its stubborn presence. Just as Haffingan invokes the Coercion Acts, so the seamless hypocrisy of Liberal rhetoric is lampooned with Broadbent's demand for a 'flag as green as the island over which it waves: a flag on which we shall ask for England only a modest quartering' (124).

The Irish reception to the play was probably all the more alert to this aspect, since the 1906 'Preface for Politicians' focused attention upon it. The preface began, after the style of the first act, to draw comparison between English and Irish values; and between Catholic and Protestant (quickly concluding that to be an Irish Protestant Socialist disposed to Irish independence within a free federation of nations was the obvious and only logical position). The emphasis on the 'natural right' to national self-determination increases as the preface continues, however, and he finishes with a long warning for British Imperialism. A recent atrocity is used as his starting point: the hanging of four men of the Dinshawai, Eygpt, following disturbances triggered by British Army maltreatment of livestock, and the accidental wounding of a local woman. Faced with angry protest, the Major had sent for help: the emissary died of sunstroke and those captured were convicted and executed for his murder. (Shaw, probably in consideration of the brutal outcome, did not allow himself a joke – aside from alluding to 'Denshavians' – which may have been difficult, considering the names of the officers involved: Lieutenant Porter, Major Pine-Coffin, and the 'victim', Captain Bull.)[32] Shaw's more serious intent was to use his analysis of the 'object lesson' of colonial injustice to set *John Bull* in that broader context:

> The whole Imperial military system of coercion and terrorism is unnatural, and that the truth formulated by William Morris that 'no man is good enough to be another man's master' is true of nations, and very specially true of those plutocrat-ridden Powers which have of late stumbled into an enormous increase of material wealth (50).

The point about this passage is the theoretical emphasis on anti-Imperialism: combining cultural difference with a framework of comparable class tensions within as well as between dominant and subject nations. Shaw's Dinshawai example was cited as principle among radical and republican readers: Frederick Ryan, James Connolly, and Terence MacSwiney among them.[33] In this context, it did the Abbey no harm for nationalist opinion to be teamed up with Shaw in defiance of the Lord Chamberlain over *The Shewing Up of Blanco Posnet* in 1909. But anti-Imperialism was far from an Irish preserve: Shaw had been briefed by the English champion of Egyptian rights, Wilfred Scawen Blunt, and the Dinshawai atrocity was no less noted by an English radical press eager to politicize the episode. The reception of the preface, like the play itself, resisted the impulse to designate simple nationalism or colonial dualities.

The connection between Irish nationalism and English anti-Imperialism could perhaps, in the years before the First World War, be considered to offer a politics of possibility consonant with Shaw's dramatic intentions. The sanguine introduction to the 'Home Rule Edition' of *JBOI* would suggest as much. Yet, that Shaw later designated this 1912 preface as a massive error, testament to 'the blindfold march' into the future, once again prepares us to be wary of teleology.[34] Did Shaw's drama sharpen English attitudes to Irish independence, helping the Liberals to pass the never-enacted 1912 Home Rule Bill? It is perhaps worth considering one special command performance. In the midst of the 1911 constitutional crisis, the Prime Minister Asquith was bullying the Lords into accepting their loss of veto.[35] On 30 June, he hosted a Coronation Party for the new King George V at 10 Downing Street, keen to pep him up for the possibility of flooding the upper house with new peerages. On his mind was also the royal visit to Ireland, just a few days away.[36] Forty-four of the social and political elite attended the banquet,[37] and after that some entertainment: the third act of *John Bull*, and a short one-act 'new woman' comedy by J. M. Barrie, *The Twelve Pound Look*.[38] The Whip's Room had been converted, down to 'every last detail' as the *Daily Telegraph* reported it, into a 'pretty little theatre...done in miniature; footlights, wings, proscenium arch, and "limes"'.[39]

The Downing Street production, was, in a sense, the Royal Court, 'done in miniature'. Granville Barker led a cast that was as close to the original as possible. Fittingly, there was also an Abbey echo: although a request to Lady Gregory for an authentic Patsy seems to have fallen on deaf ears,[40] kudos was added by W.G. Fay, who played Matt Haffigan.[41] Surely, no surer indication could there be that the *status quo* had absorbed whatever subversive power the play, or the Court, once possessed. On the verge of Home Rule, the Fabian claim could be to have inched nearer a just settlement.

But Asquith's little lesson was reductive. Shaw's play was too big to squeeze into the pocket of the establishment. The Irish issue could not be 'done in miniature' and digested after dinner like a chocolate mint. The third act alone, without the final fourth act to temper its lessons, missed something crucial. Perhaps Asquith had learned something from Shaw's attempt to train the Irish and English out of demonizing and idealizing each other, or themselves – something he wanted to pass on to the cohorts of government. Yet he had missed, under the Liberal sentiment, a darker message: that good men worked like the devil when harnessed to demonic, rapacious systems.

For it is literally in the last analysis, delivered by Peter Keegan, that Shaw steers *John Bull* successfully clear of acquiescence. Although the ex-priest is frequently interpreted as embodying the inactivity of which Doyle complains, Keegan's sudden capacity for brutal and brilliant description of the Broadbent plan at the close of the play redeems him from mere utopianism:

> When at last this poor desolate countryside becomes a busy mint in which we shall all slave to make money for you, with our Polytechnic to teach us how to do it efficiently, and our library to fuddle the imaginations your distilleries will spare, and our repaired round tower with admission sixpence, then no doubt your English and American shareholders will spend all the money we make for them very efficiently...For four wicked centuries the world has dreamed this foolish dream of efficiency; and the end is not yet. But the end will come (160).

This inspired denunciation cancels Keegan's earlier rather resigned offer to vote for Broadbent. Although he falls again into ruminations of an earthly heaven, his ability to delineate the economic dimensions of the Broadbentian future re-characterize him as a speaker with a capacity to persuade, if not his interlocutors, then the audience watching. It returns the play to cultural economy, where logics of international capital lead to Imperial ends. Its prescience has been noted, although the transition to complicity in efficient ruin was less smooth than Keegan thought. Instead of hand-holding Home Rule, there was World War, the Easter Rising, and affable Broadbent as an Edwardian memory. But its educational effects may be doubted. On tour in Ireland, in May 1916, Asquith looked blankly into the mystery of his own misgovernment and declared: 'You never get to the bottom of this most perplexing and damnable country.'[42]

'It is a pity,' commented Shaw, looking back on the Irish revolution, 'they did not begin their political education, as I began mine, by reading Karl Marx.'[43] Or, by implication, with closer scrutiny of the closing elements of *John Bull*. In providing Keegan with a last prophetic platform, Shaw had recaptured a space for a Fabian site of ideological dispute, asserting the survival of subversion. And ironically it is a stage close enough to the Abbey.[44] Allowing his spiritual utopian an economistic outburst, Shaw offered a voice capable of testifying to Ireland's various resources of insight, and the possibility that a new Ireland might combine revival and radical reform. It is this which requires the Royal Court not only to claim its place as an early herald of an English National Theatre capable of subversive drama, but as a crucial arm of the Irish theatre revival as well.

---

[1] A comparison suggested in passing by Joseph Donohue, 'What is Edwardian Theatre?', *The Edwardian Theatre: Essays on Performance and the Stage*, eds

Michael Richard Booth and Joel H. Kaplan (Cambridge: CUP, 1996): 19.
2 Joep Leerssen, *Mere Irish and Fíor-Ghael: Studies in the Idea of Irish Nationality, its Development and Literary Expression prior to the Nineteenth Century*, 2nd edn (Cork: Cork University Press, 1996) and Remembrance and Imagination: Patterns in the Historical and Literary Representation of Ireland in the Nineteenth Century (Cork: Cork University Press, 1996); Christopher Morash, A History of the Irish Theatre 1601-2000 (Cambridge: CUP, 2001).
3 *The Politics of Irish Drama: Plays in Context from Boucicault to Friel* (Cambridge: CUP, 1999): 5-50.
4 'Oscar Wilde's Last Book', *Uncollected Prose by W.B. Yeats, First Reviews and Articles, 1886*-1896, eds John P. Frayne and Colton Johnston, vol. 1 (London: Macmillan, 1970): 204.
5 William Archer, *The Theatrical 'World' for 1893* (London: Walter Scott, 1894).
6 Bernard Shaw, *John Bull's Other Island*, ed. Dan H. Laurence (New York: Penguin, 1984): 71. Subsequent quotations will be cited in the text.
7 *The Collected Letters of W.B. Yeats, 1901-1904*, eds John Kelly and Ronald Schuchard, vol. 3 (Oxford: Clarendon Press, 1994): 661.
8 *Letters*, 442.
9 Yeats, *Autobiographies* (London and Basingstoke: Macmillan, 1955): 283.
10 M.J. Sidnell, *Hic and Ille: Shaw and Yeats, Theatre and Nationalism in Twentieth-Century Ireland*, ed. Robert O'Driscoll (London: OUP, 1971): 167-68.
11 *Daily Telegraph* 2 November 1904.
12 *Times* 2 November 1904.
13 *Saturday Review* 12 November 1904.
14 Michael Holroyd, *Bernard Shaw: The Pursuit of Power, 1898-1918*, vol. 2 (London: Chatto and Windus, 1989): 99.
15 Desmond MacCarthy, *The Court Theatre 1904-7: A Commentary and Criticism* (London: A.H. Bullen, 1907): 73-74.
16 For a break-down of the plays and the number of performances, see MacCarthy, *The Court Theatre 1904-7*: 123-24.
17 Dennis Kennedy, 'The New Drama and Its Audience', *The Edwardian Theatre: Essays on performance and the stage* (Cambridge: CUP, 1996): 137.
18 Loren Kruger, *The National Stage: Theatre and Cultural Legitimation in England, France and America* (Chicago: University of Chicago Press: 1992).
19 Tracy C. Davis, *George Bernard Shaw and the Socialist Theatre* (Westport: Praeger, 1994): 60.
20 'Theatre and Socialism in Britain 1880-1935', *Theatres of the Left, 1880-1935: Worker's Theatre Movements in Britain and America*, eds Raphael, Ewan MacColl, and Stuart Cosgrove (London: Routledge and Keegan Paul, 1985). See Norman Veitch, *The People's: Being a History of the People's Theatre, Newcastle Upon Tyne 1911-1939*: 5, for a typical impulse in these years: 'Having now discovered the gold mine, Bernard Shaw, we delved enthusiastically into its precious ore.'
21 *Globe* 12 Sept. 1905.
22 *Peasant and Irish Ireland* 30 November 1907.
23 *Irish Times, Daily Express, Irish Independent* 21 November 1907; *Peasant* 30 November 1907. The allusion is to the eponymous hero of Samuel Lover's 1842

novel, Handy Andy - a hapless stage-Irish servant.
24 Frederick Ryan, the socialist writer and critic, had also approvingly reprinted extensive extracts from the recently published preface in the monthly *National Democrat* (August 1907).
25 *Irish Independent* 21 November 1907.
26 *Sinn Féin* 30 November 1907.
27 'George Bernard Shaw: A Conversation', *Tatler* CLXXVII, 16 November 1904: 242. See also Frederick P.W. McDowell, 'Politics, Comedy, Character, and Dialectic: The Shavian World of John Bull's Other Island', *PMLA* 82 (1967): 545.
28 Holroyd, *The Pursuit of Power*, 137.
29 Self-scrutiny was further enhanced by Charlotte Shaw drawing GBS into return visits to Ireland, begun summer 1905. Nicholas Grene, 'Shaw in Ireland: Visitor or Returning Exile?' *Shaw: The Annual of Bernard Shaw Studies*, vol. 5 (Harrisburg: The Pennsylvania State University Press, 1985): 45-62.
30 'What Irish Protestants Think: Speeches on Home Rule', *The Matter With Ireland*, 73, eds Dan H. Laurence and David H. Grene (London: Rupert Hart-Davis, 1962.
31 'Instructions to the Producer', Shaw Papers, BL Ms. 50615.
32 Roger Owen, *Lord Cromer: Victorian Imperialist, Edwardian Proconsul* (Oxford: OUP, 2004): 335-39.
33 See James Connolly, 'The Friends of Small Nationalities', *Irish Worker* 12 Sept. 1912. Also *Collected Works*, vol. 1 (Dublin: New Books, 1987): 431. Terence MacSwiney, *Principles of Freedom* (Cork: Talbot Press, 1921): 206-7. MacSwiney's reference to Shaw's preface, it should be noted, also drew attention to the playwright's inconsistent attitude to subject nations.
34 A judgement given in the prefatory note to the 1930 *Collected Works* reprint of the 1912 and 1906 prefaces; a further explanatory postscript, 'Twentyfour Years Later', also accompanied this edition. See *John Bull's Other Island*, ed. Dan Laurence: 53.
35 Klaus Werner Epstein, *The British Constitutional Crisis 1909-1911* (New York: Garland Publishing, 1987).
36 George V's opinion of the play is not recorded in his diary, merely a record of the fact of the performance. (Many thanks to Miss Pamela Clark, Registrar, The Royal Archives, Windsor Castle, for her assistance.) However, the Royal secretary Arthur Bigge revealed in letters to Asquith the combination of concerns: 'The King leaves for Ireland early on Friday morning next, and he desires me to say that he would be very glad if you would kindly let him have the words which you propose to make use of to Balfour...where you meet him respecting the amendments to the Parliament Bill, in regard to the creation of peers.' Letter, July 3 1911, Asquith Papers, Bodelian, Ms. A2.
37 As well as the King and Queen, the guests, according to the *Daily Telegraph* were: 'Mrs Asquith...the Duke of Norfolk, Viscount Morley, the Marquis and Marchioness of Crewe, the Marchioness of Landsdowne, the Marquis and Marchioness of Ripon, the Earl and Countess of Derby, the Earl of Aberdeen, the Countess of Minto, the Earl and Countess of Lytton, Earl and Countess Carrington, Viscount Haldane, Lady Sheffield, Lord and Lady Manners, Lord Annaly, Lord Curson of Kedleston, Lady Ashby St. Ledgers, Lord and Lady

Glenconner, the Right Hon. A. J. Balfour and Miss Balfour, the Right. Hon. Winston Churchill, Sir Edward Grey, the Right. Hon. Lewis and Mrs Harcourt, the Right Hon. D. and Mrs Lloyd George, the Right Hon. Augustine and Mrs Birrell, Commander Sir Charles Cust, R. N., Sir Edgar and Lady Helen Vincent, Professor Sir Walter Raleigh, Lady Homer, Mrs Waldorf Astor, Mrs Graham Smith, Miss Frances Tennant, Miss Violet Asquith and Mr Vaughan Nash.' 30 June 1911.
38 Barrie's play was a kind of whimsical one act sequel to *A Doll's House*: soon-to-be-ennobled Harry Sims discovers the typist he has employed for his thank-you letters to be his emancipated ex-wife. *The Twelve Pound Look* (Studio City: Players Press, n.d.).
39 *Daily Telegraph* 1 July 1911.
40 'I wonder whether you could lend us one?' Granville Barker to Lady Gregory, London, 1911. *Granville Barker and his Correspondents: A Selection of Letters by Him and to Him*, ed. Eric Salmon (Detroit: Wayne State University Press, 1986).
41 *Times* 1 July 1911.
42 Letter to Margot Asquith, 16 May 1916. Stephen Koss, *Asquith* (London: Allen Lane, 1976), 200.
43 'Twentyfour Years Later', *John Bull's Other Island*: 66.
44 Shaw's subsequent popularity at the Abbey, from the 1916 season onward, suggests that the recognition was mutual. Nicholas Grene, 'Shaw in the Irish Theater: An Unacknowledged Presence', *Shaw: The Annual of Bernard Shaw Studies*, vol. 14 (Harrisburg: Pennsylvania State University Press, 1994): 153-165.

2 | 'Stranger in the House': Alienation and History in The Land of Heart's Desire and Cathleen ni Houlihan

Michael McAteer

The Land of Heart's Desire was first performed at the Avenue Theatre in London in April 1894, opening with John Todhunter's *A Comedy of Sighs*. It was Yeats's first play to receive public performance. Although largely forgotten today, that 1894 performance was an important moment for the development of the Irish Dramatic Movement subsequently, primarily because of the extent to which *The Land of Heart's Desire* anticipates the form of Yeats's most influential contribution to cultural nationalism in the early 1900s, *Cathleen ni Houlihan*, written in collaboration with Lady Gregory. The performance effectively brought to an end the brief theatrical career of Yeats's friend John Todhunter and anticipated in a significant way Oscar Wilde's dramatic fall from grace the following year. It was also the moment in which George Bernard Shaw arrived on the London theatre scene with the instant dramatic success of *Arms and the Man*, which replaced Todhunter's drama on the double bill, launching one of the most successful careers in British drama for some decades to come. The parallels between *The Land of Heart's Desire* and *Cathleen ni Houlihan* are striking in view of the shift from a London to a Dublin audience, and this essay examines the complexities they reveal in Yeats's theatrical response to historical process through the motif of the 'Stranger in the House'.

Both *The Land of Heart's Desire* and *Cathleen ni Houlihan* address the anthropological paradox that the renewal of the family structure in the younger generation requires the intrusion of an outsider into the family circle, creating a time of uncertainty preceding and following the marriage ceremony. In *The Land of Heart's Desire* Shawn, the son of Maurteen and Bridget, has recently married. In *Cathleen ni Houlihan* Michael, the son of Peter and Bridget, is about to get married. In both plays, the discreet uncertainty generated by the presence of figures outside the family circle who are expected to renew its structure through marriage - Mary in *The Land of Heart's Desire* and Delia in *Cathleen ni Houlihan* - is projected on to figures from the Otherworld, the Fairy Child in *The Land of Heart's Desire*, and Cathleen in *Cathleen ni Houlihan*. These figures act as embodiments of the 'Stranger in the house' in both plays and there is a credible basis for regarding them as symbolic manifestations of a fundamental material change in relations between characters. As with the psychic energy generated by the intrusion of outsider figures in *The Countess Cathleen*, this familial uncertainty is connected to general historical upheaval. While responses to *Cathleen ni Houlihan* focus on the context of the 1798 Rebellion in consolidating its credentials as Yeats's most nationalist play, little attention has been drawn to the fact that *The Land of Heart's Desire* is also set in the west of Ireland at the end of the eighteenth century, in County Sligo, as indicated in published versions of the play between 1895 and 1908, not far from the Killala Bay of *Cathleen ni Houlihan*.

In reading both plays comparatively in the light of this, the critical opinion they have received needs to be reconsidered, a point that is of particular importance in relation to *Cathleen ni Houlihan*. It would be an error, however, to read this solely as a matter of empirical historical context. History is written into the fabric of both plays because Oedipal disruption within family circles is set in the context of a period of immense political upheaval in Ireland preceding the Act of Union in 1801. However, Yeats's approach of mediating historical upheaval through Oedipal tension within a private family circle calls into question the adequacy of a strictly empirical historiography in illuminating the kind of historical transformation implicit in both plays. This is particularly so for *The Land of Heart's Desire* in that the Fairy Child has no specific political resonance, unlike Cathleen in *Cathleen ni Houlihan*. The conventional critical response to the former is that it may be, in the words of Terence Brown, a 'poignantly fantastical play', but only the most tenuous of connections could be made to the historical context of late eighteenth-century Ireland, let alone the broader political upheavals taking place in

Europe and America at that time.¹ How could such a delicate, even dandyist piece of drama carry any register of fundamental historical upheaval?² In showing an intimate structural relationship between *The Land of Heart's Desire* and such an obviously political and historical play as *Cathleen ni Houlihan*, I intend to illustrate the importance of history to the earlier play. Both plays depict private family situations and economic circumstances that are historically driven by the rise of the bourgeoisie, but located in rural rather than urban surroundings. In Barbara Suess's phrase, both plays stage 'the bourgeois peasant'.³ Marx proclaims in *The Communist Manifesto* that the 'bourgeoisie has torn away from the family its sentimental veil, and has reduced the family relation to a mere money relation'.⁴ Both plays depict this reduction, but because their location is rural rather than urban, the libidinal rupture it engenders tests the limits of naturalistic representation.

Even ignoring the structural parallels of both plays, there is strong evidence to indicate that *The Land of Heart's Desire* gave rise to Yeats's part in the writing of *Cathleen ni Houlihan* with Augusta Gregory. Adrian Frazier records how Frank Fay, then a theatre correspondent with the *United Irishman*, wrote a short essay in response to favourable reviews that *The Land of Heart's Desire* received in its American performances in 1901. Frazier argues that Frank Fay's essay, published in the *United Irishman* in May 1901, in which Fay praised *The Land of Heart's Desire* as 'a beautiful little play' and in which he implored Yeats to write plays that Irish actors could perform, made an enormous impact on Yeats, inspiring him to set aside other projects in order to begin working with Lady Gregory on the play that would become *Cathleen ni Houlihan*.⁵ The essay undoubtedly sets in train a process that not only led to the production of *Cathleen ni Houlihan* but also gave impetus to the subsequent founding of the Abbey group of actors under the auspices of the Irish National Theatre Society that initially would be dominated by the Fays. However, the precise nature of Fay's comments, what they tell us about *The Land of Heart's Desire* and about its relationship to *Cathleen ni Houlihan* need to be given further consideration. Not all agree with the view Frazier presents of the piece; James Flannery sees in it an attack on Yeats's cultural prestige and the aestheticism of his plays.⁶

There is indeed much implicit criticism of Yeats's 1890s plays in Fay's essay, predictably the complaint that they were inaccessible and lacked earthiness. Fay demands that Yeats write plays that appeal to 'as large a section of his countrymen as possible', going on to state that '[t]he Theatre is a practical thing; Mr Yeats is too much of a theorist'.[7] Nonetheless, these criticisms have to be balanced with Fay's sense of the charm and allure of the earlier plays, the fact that they *could* reach the humblest of audiences, and even the phrase that Flannery draws attention to, 'beautiful corpses', is not entirely a phrase of admonition:

> I know, of course, that a poet can only give what is in him, but Mr. Yeats has shown in the beautiful *Countess Cathleen* and in *The Land of Heart's Desire* that he can speak so that the humblest can understand him, in Ireland at any rate. The plays which Mr. Yeats wishes to see on the stage of his 'Theatre of Art' remind me of exquisitely beautiful corpses. *The Countess Cathleen* and *The Land of Heart's Desire* are undoubtedly charming, aye, and moving too; but they do not inspire; they do not send men away filled for the desire for deeds.[8]

The phrase 'exquisitely beautiful corpses' expresses a late Victorian neo-gothic aesthetic within the drama of the *fin-de-siècle*, where death is subliminally invested with discreetly erotic undertones, as evident in Comte Villiers de l'Isle-Adam's *Axël* (1885), which with its heady mix of medievalism, tragedy, occultism, and love was a great influence on Yeats.[9] Certainly, Fay calls for a move beyond this form of drama, but his sentiments are much closer to it than to those of the commercial music-hall stage dominant in turn-of-the-century Britain and Ireland. It is also significant that the new appeal here is to *men* and to men to *act*. It may justifiably be regarded as a call for a theatre which is not just National but also Nationalist, given the proximity of its sentiment to that of a strong Nationalist like D.P. Moran, who complained in his essay 'The Battle of Two Civilisations' that what Ireland lacked most was manliness:

> If I were an autocrat of Ireland to-morrow and someone were to come to me and ask what I want most, I should have no hesitation in answering – Men.[10]

Such sentiment is undoubtedly present in the wish that 'a herd of Saxon and other swine' need to be 'swept into the sea along with the pestilent breed of West-Britons with which we are troubled'.[11] How far this was simply pandering to *The United Irishman* readership of the day is open to question. Fay was no lover of Sinn Féin and described the Irish to W.J. Lawrence in 1914 as 'rank conservatives', who, if they were to get Home Rule, would 'settle into the most conservative people in Europe'.[12] When Maud Gonne complained about Padraic Colum's *The Saxon Shillin'* on nationalist grounds in 1903, his brother Willie wrote a letter to Yeats attacking *Cumann na nGaedhal* interference in the theatre: 'the theatre can no more be a political organ than a temperance'.[13] If we are to take Fay's essay as a crucial motive in the creation of *Cathleen ni Houlihan*, these sentiments become invested with powerful significance, given the controversy over the impact of that play. Aside from this, the masculine force appealed to indicates the one crucial difference between *The Land of Heart's Desire* and *Cathleen ni Houlihan*: in the first play, the character transformed by a force from the Otherworld is a woman, Mary; in the second, it is a man, Michael. This needs to be given further consideration when evaluating the reasons why the first play is largely forgotten, whereas the latter continues to attract scholarly interest.

Another element that needs to be taken into account when evaluating Fay's response is how rooted his thinking is in a European context. Whereas Yeats, in his *Samhain* and *Beltaine* essays on the Irish National Theatre, looked chiefly to the precedent of Wagner, Fay, in a piece on *The Land of Heart's Desire* published in the *United Irishman* in July 1901, looked to Ole Bull, founder of the Norwegian National Theatre.[14] The precedent of Bull is a highly political one in Fay's hands, suggesting a pretext for an Irish theatre movement that would be dignified rather than mere burlesque, precisely the sentiment outlined in the inaugural statement of the new Irish Theatre Movement, written by Yeats and Gregory in 1897, in which it was proposed to present Ireland as 'the home of an ancient idealism' rather than a place of 'buffoonery and easy sentiment'.[15] Fay's allusion to Bull is clever by implying that it would be possible to create in Ireland a drama of artistic excellence that was historically grounded and relevant politically. In Ibsen, Norway had produced the most important playwright of late nineteenth-century Europe, thus making the theatrical credentials of its theatre movement indisputable. In presenting as cultural nationalism Ole Bull's motive for creating the Norwegian Theatre Movement, the precedent offered to Yeats was deeply inviting, even as it indicated a marriage of quotidian political questions that Yeats, with purely occult and artistic concerns, might have great difficulty in subjecting to his will and direction. Ben Levitas observes that even in the pages of Pearse's *An Claidheamh Soluis*, Ibsen was admired as 'a role model who had succeeded in making obscure Norwegian a linguistic force in Europe'.[16] Pearse had an Irish language theatre movement in mind that would leave the likes of Yeats out in the cold, but it illustrates the importance of European models to the contest over the form a new theatre movement in Ireland might take.

A final point to be borne in mind about Fay's *United Irishman* pieces of 1901 is precisely that they arose out of the success of *The Land of Heart's Desire* in its American performances of that year. As Frazier records, Fay was invited to write the May 1901 piece because of the positive reviews *The Land of Heart's Desire* received in its American productions.[17] This suggests that there was something about this play that worked, maybe even to the surprise of its author; and that Fay was, contrary to Flannery, not attacking plays like *The Land of Heart's Desire*, but rather acknowledging that Yeats had written the kind of play that could be produced in Ireland with powerful effect, if he lent his writing a greater degree of 'masculine' force. Indeed, it served Fay's political purpose to draw a contrast between the hostile reception the play received in its 1894 London performances and the warm reception it received in America in 1901. Given the possibility that Fay may have presumed a significant Irish American presence within East Coast and Chicago audiences, drawing a contrast between English and American receptions would serve the purpose of reinforcing his claim that Yeats's plays would have a special appeal for an Irish audience and that Yeats should direct his future compositions towards such an audience.[18]

In fact, the contrast between receptions of the play in England in 1894 and America in 1901 was not so striking as Fay presumed. It is true that the opening night at the Avenue Road Theatre in 1894 was a disaster, with the audience laughing at the play and the critics generally hostile.[19] However, this response was due to the unfortunate choice of presenting the play before John Todhunter's *Comedy of Sighs*, which was practically booed off the stage. In fact, *Comedy of Sighs* was soon to be withdrawn, while Yeats's play was retained, running for several weeks with George Bernard Shaw's *Arms and the Man*, a play that, in its diametric opposition to the decadent effeminacy of Todhunter's play, was an instant popular success with London audiences.[20] 'My little play goes on again with Shaw but goes off with Todhunter for the present on Monday,' Yeats wrote to Ernest Rhys on the 12 April 1894.[21] It is curious how the move from Todhunter to Shaw during this run, from an effeminate to a masculine theatre, prefigured the kind of shift that Fay desired for Yeats's drama in his 1901 essays. Of greater significance is the fact that, in spite of its designation as a light and somewhat frivolous play, *The Land of Heart's*

Desire survived this change in London sensibility, one that would become more emphatic subsequent to the trial of Oscar Wilde in 1895. Indeed, several reviews of Yeats's play applauded elements within it: *The Daily Chronicle*, for example, praising the 'simplicity and freshness of Mr. Yeats's diction' that separated the play from 'the dismal category of pseudo-Elizabethan blank-verse dramas'.[22] The main complaint against the play was that it was too simple in style and diction, too alien to a thespian tradition of theatricality. But even here, *The Bookman Review* hinted at the avant-garde nature of *The Land of Heart's Desire* in its review of June 1894, stating that '[w]hether it could ever be put on stage is doubtful, but certainly only under conditions which do not exist on our stage today'.[23] While one might take this as a statement of the play's theatrical shortcomings, it might also be seen as evidence of the degree to which Yeats, even in the midst of the *fin-de-siècle*, was anticipating the kind of spartan theatre of ritual that he would develop over two decades later with his Noh-inspired dance dramas, the form of theatre that most assuredly anticipates the minimalist modernism of Beckett. These responses, combined with the play's survival after the disaster of Todhunter's, undermine Fay's case that the play's first run in London in 1894 was a consummate failure.

In 'The Tragic Generation', Yeats claimed that the idea of the play, *The Land of Heart's Desire,* first came to him upon the prompting of Florence Farr that he write something for the stage in which her nine-year-old niece, Dorothy Paget, might play her first theatrical role.[24] The Fairy Child's dance and song which leads Mary's mind away from the material world, as performed by Paget on the London stage in 1894, lent the play a magical quality that endured over time. Along with *Cathleen ni Houlihan*, this was to be the only early play by Yeats to be revived at the Abbey Theatre in later years, and Joseph Hone has noted that a separate edition of *The Land of Heart's Desire* in 1925 sold ten thousand copies.[25] Its subject, the interplay of innocence and revelation, centered upon the figure of the Fairy Child, marks a historically determined change in the cultural representation of history. The recently married Mary Bruin becomes the medium for the Fairy Child, a mediation between material and non-material worlds that is conditioned by a process of exchange. In her marriage to Shawn Bruin, Mary has exchanged virginal innocence for carnal knowledge. The proper completion of this exchange, however, is predicated upon Mary's submission to her new role as household labourer.

The tension in the household at the beginning of this play arises from the fact that Mary has not yet submitted to this new role, leading to the complaints of her mother-in-law, Bridget.[26] The argumentative opening of *The Land of Heart's Desire* contrasts with the opening of *Cathleen ni Houlihan*, where the atmosphere is more one of hopeful anticipation, changing only after the Old Woman's arrival on stage. Nonetheless, as with Mary in *The Land of Heart's Desire*, Michael has not yet submitted to his new marital role. The possibility that, under the influence of the Old Woman, he will refuse it - as Mary, under the influence of the Old Book, refuses it - is the source from which the tension arises in *Cathleen ni Houlihan*. The difference between the alternatives to the conventional marriage, to which both Mary and Michael are drawn, is that the alternative presented to Michael takes the form of political nationalism.

Critical commentary on *Cathleen ni Houlihan* continues to be preoccupied by its status as a political play, one critic going so far as to claim that its proper context was that of amateur political theatre popular in nationalist circles in the early 1900s rather than European symbolist drama.[27] Lionel Pilkington stresses the fact that the 1902 production took place under the banner of *Inghinidhe na hÉireann*, claiming that the audience would not have been able to separate the action of the play from the work of that organization.[28] Ben Levitas contends that the strength of the play's impact lay in its alliance of spiritual and prosaic political dimensions of nationalism.[29] Thus, while there is some disagreement regarding the political intention behind *Cathleen ni Houlihan*, there is a growing consensus in recent criticism that its primary, even exclusive, purpose was to intervene in the movement of Irish political nationalism in the early 1900s. However, the striking similarities between Mary in *The Land of Heart's Desire* and Michael in the later play challenges this consensus. In any case, Yeats's own opinion was that a conventionally political reading of the play was not just erroneous but displayed the type of mindset the play set out to disturb. In a letter to Frank Fay dated 28 August 1904, Yeats claimed that George Moore wanted the figure of Cathleen to walk up and down continually in front of the footlights, detecting in this that middle-class pragmatism, that 'externality' incapable of attending to the subtlety of emotion Yeats sought to evoke. Paraphrasing Moore ironically, he wrote:

> [...] such emotions were impossible in drama; she must be Ireland calling up her friends, marshalling them to battle. The commonplace will, that is,

the will of the successful business man, the business will, is the root of the whole thing.[30]

Joseph Holloway's description of the audience's response to the words of Cathleen in the play, on this account at least, may have been a deeply ambivalent source of satisfaction for Yeats:

> Most of the sayings of the mysterious 'Cathleen' [...] found ready and apt interpretation from the audience who understood that Erin spoke in "Cathleen," and they applauded each red hot patriotic sentiment right heartily, and enthusiastically called for the author at the end, and had their wish gratified.[31]

The view that *The Land of Heart's Desire* is a politically nationalist play is equally as open to objection as the view that *Cathleen ni Houlihan* is an occult drama for which nationalism is only a side issue. Unlike Cathleen, the Fairy Child is not a direct political symbol of Ireland. In addition, the forces of Catholicism and Celticism clash in *The Land of Heart's Desire*; direct representation of this clash, which would have been uncomfortable for Irish Catholic nationalists (as the response to the 1899 Dublin performance of *The Countess Cathleen* attests) is avoided in *Cathleen ni Houlihan*. Donald Torchiana records how Constance Markievicz lent *The Land of Heart's Desire* political nationalist credentials when she presented a Theatre Royal performance of the play 'as played at Kilmainham Jail by women prisoners'.[32] While Markievicz would certainly have been taken with a play set in Sligo, it also suggests that she saw in the play an element of feminist nationalism in the link between Mary reading Gaelic legends and refusing to perform the role of working housewife.[33] However, Markievicz's was very much a retrospective interpretation that imposed a political nationalist perspective out of keeping with the play's original context. If the visionary force of *The Land of Heart's Desire* is to be read in relation to *Cathleen ni Houlihan*, an understanding of the political dynamic of both plays that extends beyond the local consideration of Irish political separatism is required. The earlier play signals that a political dynamic more complex than a simple assertion of a separatist aspiration is at work in *Cathleen ni Houlihan*, while this play, in turn, facilitates the illumination of the historical forces encoded within *The Land of Heart's Desire* and their attendant political form.

Early in *The Land of Heart's Desire*, Father Hart encourages Mary to leave down the book that has her distracted, asserting that pursuing her new role as worker would dissipate her restlessness:

> I have seen some other girls
> Restless and ill at ease, but years went by
> And they grew like their neighbours and were glad
> In minding children, working at the churn,
> And gossiping of weddings and of wakes.[34]

This envisages a subordinate role for women within a highly patriarchal culture, and Mary's final refusal of this carries an echo of Ibsen's *A Doll's House*, as R.F. Foster notes.[35] However, Bridget's complaints and Father Hart's attempt at persuading Mary away from the book she is avidly reading also indicate that the conflict in the play has its source in economic processes bringing designated gender roles into crisis in later eighteenth-century European society. The play initially appears as a simple conflict between values of idealism and practicality, the dreamy magical world of Celtic lore versus the mundane world of practical affairs. However, behind this lie signs of the division of labour that, Marx argues, had its origins in the family unit, but made a critical impact upon human relations within capitalist society as it developed from the sixteenth century onwards. He asserts that the work required to produce basic necessities of food and clothing in rural society were natural social relations because they were 'functions of the family' regulated 'by differences of sex and age as well as by seasonal variations in natural conditions of labour'. With the advent of commodity production in modern society, this 'natural' division of labour gradually becomes obsolescent; the traditional family unit ceases to be the form of social relation natural to material production.[36]

The economic aspects of these plays are most striking in their treatment of work and time. In his critical investigation of the operation of capitalist economics, Marx asserts that 'in the final analysis, all forms of economics can be reduced to an economics of time'.[37] The intimate relationship between time, labour, and value in both *The Land of Heart's Desire* and *Cathleen ni Houlihan* appears to bear out Marx's view of labour-time as the determinant of exchange value. The plays are set in a time of historical transition for Ireland and Europe, and, in the case of *The Land of Heart's Desire*, in a time of seasonal change: May, the month of the Virgin Mary in the Catholic tradition and the festival season of Brigid, the fertility goddess, in pre-Christian Celtic tradition. Both Catholic and

Celtic traditions are alive in *The Land of Heart's Desire*, evident in Yeats's decision to use the names Mary and Bridget for the women characters, and Bridget is as unassuming in her belief in the fairy people as she is in figures of Catholic piety. For Bridget, the eve of May is also the time of visitation, when figures from the Otherworld walk the land:

> The Good People beg for milk and fire
> Upon May Eve – woe to the house that gives,
> For they have power upon it for a year.[38]

Bridget utters these words just after Mary has given milk to an old woman who has come to the door. This figure of the milk woman recurs in drama and literature of the modernist period, carrying occult associations. This is particularly the case in Strindberg's Expressionist play of 1901, *The Ghost Sonata*, in which the aged wheelchair-bound Hummel regards the visitation of the milk maid to the student Arkenholz as a warning of imminent death.[39] Yeats's play prefigures Strindberg's through Bridget's fatalistic belief that Mary, in giving milk to the old woman, had brought evil upon the house.[40] Joyce also employs the figure in the opening episode of *Ulysses* at Martello Tower, a figure Henry Merritt reads simply as a parody of Cathleen ni Houlihan, missing the broader occult significance and the extent to which Joyce engages her - like the Martello Tower itself - as an occult presence in the 'Telemachus' episode:

> Old and secret she had entered from a morning world, maybe a messenger. She praised the goodness of the milk, pouring it out.[41]

It is possible that Yeats intended the old woman in *The Land of Heart's Desire* to be a witch; in *The Golden Bough*, Frazer describes a belief among Scottish highland clans, persisting up to the eighteenth century, that witches were abroad on May eve attempting to steal cows' milk.[42]

More importantly, there is an inverse image of the exchange of milk in *Cathleen ni Houlihan* that shows the influence of the earlier play on the later, hinting at the extent to which Lady Gregory's contribution to the writing of the later play was shaped by her engagement with the earlier. Whereas Bridget, the mother figure in both plays, laments the fact that Mary has given milk to the old woman in *The Land of Heart's Desire*, she offers the old woman milk in *Cathleen ni Houlihan*, but Cathleen refuses:

> **Bridget:** [*to the Old Woman*] Will you have a drink of milk, ma'am?
> **Old Woman**: It is not food or drink that I want.[43]

This reversal of attitudes may be attributed in part to Lady Gregory's role in the writing of *Cathleen ni Houlihan* as outlined by James Pethica, modifying earlier arguments made by Daniel J. Murphy and Elizabeth Coxhead for her share in the collaborative creation of this play.[44] Pethica argues his case on the basis of the Berg Collection manuscript draft of the play, in Lady Gregory's hand throughout and divided into three sections, prompting his opinion that the first ten pages of the manuscript, ending at the point of Cathleen's entry, were entirely hers. He also shows that a distinctive generic aspect, in which the supernatural is subordinated to a realist depiction of peasant life, reinforces the manuscript evidence of Augusta Gregory's predominant role in the creation of the play. Pethica acknowledges the precedent of *The Land of Heart's Desire* for *Cathleen ni Houlihan*, but downplays its importance.[45] The case he makes for the magnitude of Lady Gregory's input into the writing of *Cathleen ni Houlihan* is entirely convincing, yet it underplays the importance of Yeats's earlier play to the construction of the later and the possibility that Gregory was not just working from her own folklore material but also from *The Land of Heart's Desire* as she drafted sections of *Cathleen ni Houlihan*. While there is certainly a move from poetic to realistic dialogue that is distinctive of Gregory - and acknowledged by Yeats - the inversion of the exchange of milk from the earlier to the later play is one instance of the precedent set by *The Land of Heart's Desire*. This is no simple movement from symbolism to realism, but evidence of a complex engagement with the 'libidinal economy' of marriage in a particular historical and social situation.[46] Mary's response to the old woman's request for milk in *The Land of Heart's Desire* enables a liberation from the confinement to her economically secure but emotionally unfulfilling marriage to Shawn; in *Cathleen ni Houlihan*, the old woman's refusal of milk pre-empts her request for Delia's husband-to-be, Michael, thus denying Delia the economic security of marriage. Both situations involve the failure of marriage as a private economic contract governing sexual relations, and both address the pressure of material and symbolic forces weighing upon human relations in a historical situation of political upheaval. From this perspective, both plays would appear to fulfil one of the criteria for the revolutionary movement as defined in *The Communist Manifesto*: the abolition of marriage, made on the basis of Marx's claim that the bourgeois husband 'sees in his wife a mere instrument of production'.[47] Thus, there is a need to revise the nature of the collaborative enterprise that produced *Cathleen ni Houlihan*, and, more importantly, to recognize how these plays interrogate the institution of marriage within a context of historical transition and with reference to their nationalist orientation.

The Land of Heart's Desire concludes with the death of Mary Bruin while *Cathleen ni Houlihan* ends with Michael following Cathleen off stage to his certain defeat and probable death in the United Irishmen's rebellion. Both characters have rejected the economic and emotional security of marriage, though this rejection is more intentional with Mary than with Michael, who appears to be hypnotized by Cathleen. The price of this is death but the reward is the immortality of art. *Cathleen ni Houlihan* immortalizes Michael even as it depicts the force that draws him towards his probable death. This was what so disturbed Stephen Gwynn about the play, realizing that its seductive potency for young male nationalists lay precisely in this exchange. Though losing her life in the process, Mary enters the 'land of the Living Heart'[48] that remained elusive in her domestic existence. In abandoning herself to the seductive dance of the Fairy Child, she enters into the permanence of the work of art through the transitory sensuality of artistic rhythm, even as she loses the familiar certainties of social convention. A complex eroticism structures both exchanges between material existence and artistic immortality. A post-menopausal Cathleen seduces Michael away from sexual relations with Delia; a pre-pubescent Fairy Child draws Mary from her husband. (Evidently, Dorothy Paget's debut performance as the Fairy Child succeeded in harnessing the appropriately uncanny effect.) Both figures of the Otherworld are asexual, but they display the power of sexual allure over a man about to marry and a woman just married; the taboos governing cross-generational sexual attraction within bourgeois society are discreetly ruffled under the guise of Celtic romanticism. Furthermore, both Michael and Mary only achieve the condition of the work of art through death, actual or (in the case of Michael) anticipated. Thus, the exchange between the worlds of fact and imagination that takes place in both plays brings death, art, and eroticism into intimate communion with one another.

Aubrey Beardsley caught exactly this complex exchange in the haunting image he devised for both the poster and programme of the original London performances of *The Land of Heart's Desire* at the Avenue Theatre; Fisher Unwin also reproduced it, to Yeats's satisfaction, on the cover of his initial publication of the play in 1894. The image, highly innovatory in terms of current styles of publicity for London theatrical events, was retained throughout the full run of the season, even after Shaw's *Arms and the Man* replaced Todhunter's *A Comedy of Sighs*. A full-lipped, heavy–eyed woman with luxurious hair gazes intently through a slight gap in some diaphanous curtaining; it is the ambiguity of the stare that haunts the imagination, as it invites yet challenges interpretation: directed at an angle away from the viewer, the gaze might be read as critical, predatory or visionary, the thin veil suggesting that the woman is at a remove from immediate social engagement; the emotional connotations are intensely private yet indicative of a restless, potentially threatening inscrutability. If this represents Mary, does it depict her before or after her seduction into the child's fairy world? Or does it subtly suggest both states as resident within her psyche? Whichever interpretation one adopts, the radical nature of Yeats's invention is endorsed by Beardsley's image. As that radicalism relates to a specific linking of Irish history with sexual politics, it is of particular note that an English company in a commercial London theatre sustained a run of six weeks for the play and that *The Land of Heart's Desire* was robust enough to stand against Shaw's forcefully anti-romantic satire, which nightly followed its performance. (This suggests that Yeats's play was staged in a manner that encouraged London audiences to receive it as decidedly different from the conventional genre of escapist extravaganzas that were the popular fairy plays of the late Victorian theatre.) His success in London creatively foreshadowed the more rigorous but equally radical interpretation of history in *Cathleen ni Houlihan* that Yeats with Lady Gregory's help subsequently designed expressly for an Irish company (Willie Fay's National Dramatic Society) to play before Irish audiences.

---

[1] Terence Brown, *The Life of W.B. Yeats: A Critical Biography* (Dublin, Gill and Macmillan, 1998): 20.
[2] The dandy adjective for the play is not excessive, given that in an essay on Irish fairies published in *The Leisure Hour* four years previous to the first performance of *The Land of Heart's Desire*, Yeats described the Leprecaun as 'something of a dandy'. See 'Irish Fairies', *W.B. Yeats: Writings on Irish Folklore, Legend and Myth*, ed. Robert Welch (London: Penguin Press, 1993): 62.
[3] Barbara A. Suess, *Progress and Identity in the Plays of W.B. Yeats, 1892-1907* (London: Routledge, 2003): 57-63.
[4] Karl Marx and Friedrich Engels, *The Communist Manifesto* (London: George Allen and Unwin, 1948): 123.

5 Adrian Frazier, *Behind the Scenes: Yeats, Horniman, and the Struggle for the Abbey Theatre* (Berkeley CA: University of California Press, 1990): 58. Maria Tymoczko also points up the influence of Fay to the composition of *Cathleen ní Houlihan*. See 'Amateur Political Theatricals, *Tableaux Vivants*, and *Cathleen ni Houlihan*', *Yeats Annual*, 10, ed. Warwick Gould (London: Macmillan Press, 1993): 38-39.

6 James Flannery, *W.B. Yeats and the Idea of a Theatre: the Early Abbey Theatre in Theory and Practice* (New Haven: Yale University Press, 1976): 181-82.

7 Frank J. Fay, *Towards A National Theatre: The Dramatic Criticism of Frank J. Fay*, ed. Robert Hogan (Dublin: the Dolmen Press, 1970): 50-51.

8 Fay, 51.

9 Philippe-Auguste Villiers de l'Isle-Adam, *Axël* (Paris: La Columbe, 1960).

10 D.P. Moran, 'The Philosophy of Irish Ireland', *Ideals in Ireland*, ed. Lady Augusta Gregory (London: At the Unicorn Press, 1901): 39.

11 Fay, 53.

12 Fay to W.J. Lawrence, 6 November 1910, National Library of Ireland (NLI) ms. 10952(2).

13 Willie Fay to W.B. Yeats, 30 March 1903, NLI ms. 13068.

14 Fay, 103.

15 Augusta, Lady Gregory, *Our Irish Theatre: A Chapter of Autobiography*, 3rd edn (Gerrards Cross: Colin Smythe, 1972): 20.

16 Ben Levitas, *The Theatre of Nation: Irish Drama and Cultural Nationalism, 1890-1916*: 50-51.

17 Frazier, 57-58.

18 Fay, 69-71.

19 Flannery, 126.

20 Roy Foster argues that Yeats was jealous of Shaw, with rivalry over the actress, Florence Farr's affections the hidden motivation. See *W. B. Yeats: A Life*, vol. 1 (Oxford: Oxford University Press, 1997): 141. Michael Holroyd reveals that *The Comedy of Sighs* only went ahead with *The Land of Heart's Desire* because Shaw's play was not ready for the opening of Farr's season. The contrast between the message of Yeats's play and *Arms and the Man* is emphasized: "With a confusing paradox for someone presenting a fairy tale to follow Yeats's fairy tale, Shaw defined romanticism as extended immaturity." See *Bernard Shaw: the Search for Love, 1865-1898*, vol. 1 (London: Chatto & Windus Press): 304.

21 John Kelly, ed., *The Collected Letters of W.B. Yeats*, vol. 1: 1865-1895 (Oxford: Clarendon Press, 1986): 384.

22 *The Daily Chronicle*, 24 April 1894, NLI ms. 12145.

23 *The Bookman Review*, June 1894, NLI ms. 12145.

24 W.B. Yeats, 'The Trembling of the Veil', *Autobiographies* (London: Macmillan, 1955): 280.

25 Joseph Hone, *W.B. Yeats, 1865-1939*, 2nd edn (London: Pelican Press, 1971): 391.

26 Russell K. Alspach, *The Variorum Edition of the Plays of W.B. Yeats* (London: Macmillan, 1966): 181-82.

27 Tymoczko, 33-64.

28 Lionel Pilkington, *Theatre and State in Twentieth Century Ireland: Cultivating*

the People (London: Routledge, 2001): 34.
29 Levitas, 68.
30 John Kelly and Ronald Schuchard, eds, *The Collected Letters of W.B. Yeats*, vol. 3: 1901-1904 (Oxford: Clarendon Press, 1994): 644.
31 Robert Hogan and Michael J. O'Neill, eds, *Joseph Holloway's Abbey Theatre: A Selection from his Unpublished Journal, 'Impressions of a Dublin Theatregoer'* (Dixon CA: Proscenium Press, 1967): 17.
32 Donald T. Torchiana, *W.B. Yeats and Georgian Ireland*, 2nd edn (Washington: Catholic University of America Press, 1992): 185.
33 Margaret Ward notes that the militancy of Markievicz's nationalism conveyed a feminist determination to treat male conceptions, including nationalist ones, with indifference, noting her assertion that Inghinidhe na hEireann were 'always in favour of the most extreme action possible', whereas Griffith and his cohorts dreaded rioting. See *Unmanageable Revolutionaries: Women and Irish Nationalism* (London: Pluto Press, 1995): 77.
34 Alspach, 185.
35 Foster, 140.
36 Karl Marx, *Das Kapital*, vol. 1 (1887), trans. Ben Fowkes, (London: Penguin, 1990): 171.
37 Karl Marx, 'Grundrisse', *Selected Writings of Karl Marx*, ed. David McLellan (Oxford: Oxford University Press, 1977): 362.
38 Alspach, 189.
39 At first the elderly Hummel cannot see the milkmaid. Later, when she returns, only the old man and the student can see her. Hummel cringes in horror at her appearance, while Arkenholz is baffled by his reaction. See August Strindberg, 'The Ghost Sonata', *Plays: One*, 2nd edn. (London: Methuen, 1976): 161.
40 Alspach, 189.
41 James Joyce, *Ulysses* (London: Penguin Press, 1992): 15. Henry Merritt, 'Dead Many Times: *Cathleen ni Houlihan*, Yeats, Two Old Women and a Vampire', *Modern Language Review*, 96. 3 (2001): 653.
42 Sir James Frazer, *The Golden Bough*, (Herts.: Wordsworth Editions, 1992): 620.
43 Alspach, 226.
44 James Pethica, ' "Our Kathleen": Yeats's Collaboration with Lady Gregory in the Writing of *Cathleen ní Houlilan*', *Yeats Annual* 6, ed. Warwick Gould (London: Macmillan Press, 1988): 3-17. Daniel J. Murphy, 'Lady Gregory, Co-Author and Sometimes Author of the Plays of W.B. Yeats', *Modern Irish Literature: Essays in Honor of William York Tyndall*, eds Raymond J. Porter and James D. Brophy (New York: Iona College Press, 1972): 47. Elizabeth Coxhead, *Lady Gregory: A Literary Portrait* (London: Macmillan Press, 1961): 68.
45 Pethica, 7-12.
46 Notwithstanding Baudrillard's attack on Freud's libidinal economics, his formulation of labour as "slow death" standing in symbolic contrast to violent death carries a sharp resonance for *The Land of Heart's Desire*. Mary's refusal of her role as worker approximates to the type of situation Baudrillard articulates in the refusal to accept the 'gift' of wages: 'The refusal of labour, in its radical form, is the refusal of symbolic domination and the humiliation of being bestowed upon.' Jean Baudrillard, *Symbolic Exchange and Death*, trans. Iain Hamilton Grant (London: Sage Publications, 1993): 38-41.

47 Marx and Engels, 134.
48 During one of the rituals of Initiation drawn up for the proposed Celtic Order of Heroes, the Rite of the Cauldron, the initiate is instructed on the wandering nature of the human soul, travelling restlessly between the worlds of heroes, creative spirits and men, because it is 'far from the Land of the Living Heart'. NLI ms. 13568.

3 | The Irish Players and the Conquest of London

Peter Kuch

To speak of the word 'conquest' as it occurs in the title is in fact to speak of two distinct words that entered the English Language early in the fourteenth century from Latin via Old French. The first is 'conquest' from the Old French *conqueste* (now *conquête*) from the Medieval Latin *conquesta, -quista*. The second is 'conquest' from the Old French *conquêt* which itself is derived from the Latin *conquæstum*. As the *OED* advises, *conquête* and *conquêt* are still distinct in French, but in English, through the loss of the final -e and the loss of grammatical gender, the two forms ran together at an early date.

> [However], the original sense in Medieval Latin and French was 'acquisition, especially as the result of effort'; including getting by force of arms as well as by other means. Hence two lines of development: first, with the feudal jurists 'personal acquisition of estate, as opposed to inheritance', without specific reference to the mode, whether by force of arms, by grant, or (in later times) by money, called PURCHASE ... ; secondly, 'acquisition by force of arms, military conquest'. The latter of these is by far the earlier in English, and has always been ... the only popular sense.[1]

In speaking of the Irish Players' 'conquest' of London in 1920, I would like to use both senses of the word – that is conquest as 'personal acquisition of real property otherwise than by inheritance', and conquest as 'the action of overcoming or vanquishing; gaining of victory'.

To take the second meaning first. Like many 'overcomings', 'vanquishings', and 'victories', the Irish Players' conquest of London in 1920 owed its origins to a rebellion. In the immediate aftermath of the Easter Uprising, the Abbey Theatre suffered its own rebellion when several of its most accomplished actors broke with Yeats and Lady Gregory to form their own company. In part their action was fuelled by Yeats's high-handed, but ultimately justifiable, dismissal of the manager A.P. Wilson, who had been double-dealing with American and Australian impresarios interested in touring the Abbey. In part it was fuelled by the dictatorial methods of his replacement St John Ervine; and in part it was fuelled by the persistent uncertainty about the Abbey's finances.[2]

Gathering themselves around Arthur Sinclair, and hiring Wilson as their business manager, the seceding actors formed a company in May 1916 called the Irish Players. In July they played two weeks in Belfast and then toured England and the Irish provinces, before appearing in Dublin in December.[3] Though the first tour was a success, it nevertheless disclosed both the strengths and weaknesses of the new company. The Irish Players' great strength was their ensemble acting for which, over time, they were to establish an international reputation. Their great weakness was that they were essentially an actors' company, with the result that they themselves never initiated any new scripts of merit.[4] For the ten years or more the Company was active they had to rely on securing permission from playwrights whose work was not already under contract. At first this was made all the more difficult by Yeats and Lady Gregory taking out an injunction against The Irish Players to prevent them from using any of the plays from the Abbey's repertoire.

Consequently, when Lennox Robinson, a former Abbey Director, who in 1916 was working for the Carnegie Trust, wrote *The White-Headed Boy*, a shrewdly-crafted whimsical three-act play that unmasked the intrigues of provincial Irish society, and which was first staged at the Abbey with moderate success on 13 December 1916, the Irish Players could only eye the script from a distance while, for his part, Lennox Robinson could only wish that such talented performers were interpreting his work.[5]

Time, however, was to bring the two together. After 1916 the Irish Players continued to grow as a company. Touring, particularly in England, saved them from risking their fortunes in an Ireland that was becoming increasingly unpredictable and violent as a war of attrition between the IRB and the Black and Tans intensified. At the same time opposition from Yeats subsided. Though the Abbey pressed on doggedly, opening for short seasons when it could, the aging poet, who married in 1917 and who subsequently spent more and more time at Ballylee and abroad, intervened much less frequently in the affairs of the theatre. During the same period, Lennox Robinson returned to the Abbey, enhancing his reputation as a playwright with the success of *The Lost Leader* and achieving a level of rapprochement with and a degree of independence from Yeats and the Dublin theatrical establishment by combining work with the Abbey with fostering a new venture, The Dublin Drama League.[6]

Lennox Robinson's success with *The Lost Leader* also restored his relationship with the London based actor-manager and playwright, James Bernard Fagan,[7] who approached him late in 1919 or early in 1920 for permission to produce *The White-Headed Boy* in England and cast it with The Irish Players. The first public notice of these plans appeared in 'Forthcoming Revivals' in the London *Times* for 13 May 1920 under the heading 'Mr Fagan's plans' with the announcement that: 'Probably his first production in the autumn season will be Mr Lennox Robinson's *The White-Headed Boy*, which has been produced in Dublin but has not yet been seen either in England or in the United States.' Permission was granted, so J.B. Fagan went into partnership with H.M. Harwood and hired The Gaiety Theatre in Manchester whose 'Sole Proprietor and Licensee'[8] the capricious Miss A.E.F. Horniman had at one time or another quarrelled with almost everyone associated with the Abbey theatre and The Irish Players, but who had no objection to *The White-Headed Boy* being produced in her theatre. The idea of opening in Manchester was to test the play with an English audience and enable the cast to settle before venturing on a London season.

On Monday, 13 September 1920, *The White-Headed Boy* opened for a run of twelve nights, with evening performances at 7 o'clock, and matinees on Thursdays and Saturdays at 2 o'clock. Both actors and play scored an immediate success. There were fulsome reviews in *The Era* and *The Stage* and warm notices in *The Manchester City News* and *The Manchester Weekly Times*. The reviewer in *The Era* remarked that:

> it is not often that a comedy is better acted in point of fidelity and natural vivacity than this was on Monday. It is not easy to differentiate on so many points of excellence in the players. Miss Sara Allgood was fine as the fond mother, and Miss Maire O'Neill gave a most amusing delineation as Aunt Ellen; Mr Sydney Morgan's impersonation of George was realism itself—perhaps the best performance of the evening; Mr Arthur Sinclair played the opportunist John Duffy, with an admirable sense of character; Miss Nan Fitzgerald made a charming Delia, and all the other parts were ably filled. A great reception was accorded to the play, which scored an unquestionable success.[9]

The reviewer for *The Stage* concurred, observing that 'J.B. Fagan and H.M. Harwood have drawn together an excellent company of Irish artists whose interpretation and characterization carry the comedy to entire success.'[10] The 'News and Notes' column of *The Manchester City News* lauded both play and performers:

> Irish humour will never fail to please if it can be illustrated with that essential regard for Irish characteristics so excellently exemplified in 'The White-Headed Boy.' Mr Lennox Robinson has written a delightful comedy ... A strong caste [sic] help[ed] to build up that success which 'The White-Headed Boy' so well deserves.[11]

The theatre critic for *The Stage* predicted that 'judging by its reception' in Manchester there could be 'no question' of its success in London. '*The White-Headed Boy*...is full of fun and wit and Irish humour, and many times on Monday night the house was rocking with delighted laughter.'[12]

In short, the trial season was a 'conquest' in both senses of the word. Not only was it a conquest in the sense of 'the action of overcoming or vanquishing; of gaining victory' but it was also a 'conquest' in the far less well-known sense of the word—that is the 'personal acquisition of real property otherwise than by inheritance'. After Manchester, The Irish Players, by dint of the brilliance of their ensemble acting, would acquire a form of artistic 'ownership' of *The White-Headed Boy* that would not only see them with a London triumph, but would also entitle them to take the play around the world. They had given the 'definitive' performance.

The White-Headed Boy at the Ambassadors' Theatre, London

Some of the reviews of the opening night of the London season, Monday, 27 September 1920, were as laudatory as, if not more laudatory than their Manchester counterparts. As laudatory was 'C.H.J.' in *The Evening Standard* who concluded: 'There is no flaw in the company as a whole. Both play and players have won our admiration – and our gratitude.'[13] Somewhat more laudatory, the anonymous reviewer for *The Stage* exclaimed:

> *The White-Headed Boy*, in fact, almost deserves the description of brilliant, and as such is certainly among the very best comedies, Irish or otherwise, produced in town during the last decade. It kept the audience at The Ambassadors rocking with laughter.[14]

'E.A.B.' in *The Daily News* felt neither the same hesitation nor the need to consult the *Thesaurus*. For him, without doubt, the opening night of *The*

White-Headed Boy was 'a brilliant success'; the play itself 'a brilliant comedy'; the dialogue throughout was 'brilliant and yet unforced'; and the scene depicting the love and money negotiations between Aunt Ellen and John Duffy 'one of the most brilliant achievements in modern comedy'.[15] Not to be outdone, 'S.R.L' in *The Pall Mall Gazette* reached not for the *Thesaurus* but the vernacular:

> [The] main fact is that *The White-Headed Boy* is one of the most delightful of all the Irish comedies that we have had from the Abbey Theatre school. There is no wistfulness about it, but robust humour and sympathetic irony, and it goes to the tune of laughter always. It has a good deal of the cleverness of the *Playboy* and all and more than the breadth of *The Eloquent Dempsey*, and the machinery of it is so covered up with true native character that one is conscious of no trace of artificiality. It is – speaking Irishly – not merely 'brilliant'. It is actually bright.[16]

The remaining London reviewers were more discriminating. William Archer, while according Robinson the status of 'a master of comedy', and praising the play as 'a model of pure comedy, full of rich humour and racy human nature' nevertheless noted that *The White-Headed Boy* had 'one serious flaw' – 'a certain lack of crispness in the last five minutes'.[17] Finally, T.B., the London theatre critic for *The Manchester Guardian* offered the most even-handed review of the opening night:

> Mr Lennox Robinson's comedy, which has already been seen in Manchester, came to the Ambassadors' Theatre this evening, and thus gave London an opportunity of reunion with the Irish Players. They came not in that name, but their real selves were there, and that sufficed. For it meant that one could hear the English language spoken—not drawled or clipped or gabbled, but spoken with the melody that is due to it and with the vigour that is due to the drama. And one saw acting of a finish that pales the London stars to insignificance.[18]

There can be little doubt that the Irish Players in *The White-Headed Boy* had made a conquest of London; and even less doubt when they went on to have a run of 300 performances at the Ambassadors. By the end of the third month Royalty was in attendance, the 'Court and Social' section of the 'Court Circular' in *The Times* of 11 November 1920 notifying its readers that: 'Princess Mary, accompanied by the Viscount and Viscountess Sandhurst, witnessed a performance of *The White-Headed Boy* last night at the Ambassadors Theatre, while the Duke of York was present in the stalls accompanied by a large party'.[19] At the end of January 1921 and again mid-way through February of the same year, *The Times* felt obliged to reassure its readers who were theatre patrons that occasional one-off performances of other plays either during special matinees or on Sunday evenings would 'in no way interfere with the regular run of *The White-Headed Boy*'.[20]

But even conquests can themselves be conquered. The late winter and early spring of 1921 proved particularly difficult for the London Theatres. On 23 May 1921 *The Times* quoted one 'leading manager' to the effect that everybody 'connected with the theatrical business had joined the "Clan Micawber" and were waiting patiently for something to turn up'. 'At present there are few signs of a break in the "slump" and there is little prospect of a general revival of business before the opening of the autumn season', the writer went on to note. In the same column it was announced that *The White-Headed Boy* had been withdrawn from the Ambassadors that weekend,[21] advance notice having been given in *The Times* almost a month previously, on 21 April 1921, that the play, which was nearing its 300th performance, was in its last weeks.[22]

Not that the withdrawal of the play from the Ambassadors marked the end of the relationship between the Irish Players and *The White-Headed Boy*. In the summer of 1921 most of the members of the original company left for a tour of America and Canada, while those who remained formed themselves into a second group. Produced by Charles Dillingham, the original Irish Players' *White-Headed Boy* opened at Henry Miller's Theatre, New York, on 17 October 1921. From there they went to Chicago, Pittsburg, Toledo, South Bend, Indianapolis, Louisville, St. Louis, Detroit, Toronto, Buffalo, Philadelphia, Washington, and Baltimore, with a final season in Boston.[23] By May 1922 the original group was opening in Sydney, in advance of a tour that took in Melbourne and Adelaide with a return to Sydney. The final months of 1922 were spent touring Queensland. Back in London the second group, also known as the Irish Players, opened with a revival of *The White-Headed Boy* at The Aldwych on Saturday, 8 April 1922.[24]

Pre-Conquest and Post-Conquest skirmishes

Not every conquest is a seamless sequence of victories. While there is little doubt that Lennox Robinson, the Irish Players, and *The White-Headed Boy* conquered the London Stage with their 300 plus performances, playwright, players, and play lost several preliminary skirmishes and at least one subsequent one. The preliminary skirmishes were about censorship, with the result that losing these significantly reduced the power of *The White-Headed Boy* in particular and Irish drama in general to provoke debate and initiate change. The subsequent skirmish involved stereotyping, the defeat here arguably reducing the capability of both *The White-Headed Boy* and Irish comedy to affect that restoration of society which is a defining characteristic of the genre.

Most of the skirmishes over censorship took place before the play even reached the stage. In his *Preface* to the published text, which appeared in 1922, Robinson revealed that 'in its conception' *The White-Headed Boy* was 'to have been full of political meaning':

> I conceived the idea of displaying the British Empire in the form of a large, overgrown family kept together, more or less against its will, by an illogical, absurd, generous, scheming lovable mother. I made Ireland her youngest child, half black sheep, half mother's darling (or, as we say here, 'whiteheaded boy'). He was to be spoiled and petted, bullied and slapped, given too many sweets one day and shut up in the attic on a diet of bread and water the next, praised and blamed and left finally so bewildered and bemused that the only definite idea left to him is that of cutting himself free from his impossible family and making his own life in his own way.[25]

Yet, when he began to write, Robinson found that his main characters—the Geoghegans and the Duffys, the two rival families from Ballycolman, County Cork, whose attempts to outwit one another generate the comedy—took control, with the result that most of the political symbolism disappeared from the play. All that remained was one character and one speech. The character who remained was George, the elder brother, who as someone who was 'over-burdened with responsibilities' was originally intended to symbolize:

> poor harassed England, full of futile rages and firm decisions followed immediately by weak compromises, an England which would prefer above all things to be free of responsibilities with leisure and money to enjoy itself.[26]

The symbolic speech that remained comes in the third act, when John Duffy, who has only just discovered that he is now father-in-law to the feckless Denis, the whiteheaded boy, and is therefore anxious to settle him as quickly as possible, bursts out in exasperation: 'Bedad, isn't he like old Ireland asking for freedom, and we're like the fools of Englishmen offering him every bloody thing except the one thing [that he wants]?'[27]

In most circumstances such a speech would seem innocuous, but the Manchester opening of *The White-Headed Boy* took place in the year that the Black and Tans were unleashed on Ireland, while the third week of the play's London season saw the 'executions' of members of the British secret service carried out by Michael Collins's 'twelve apostles', then Bloody Sunday, and then the burning of large parts of Cork, Robinson's home city.[28] So it is not surprising that English critics and audiences were wary that whether or not what they were about to see might be politically confronting. What remains uncertain, however, is whether or not Duffy's outburst was censored when the play opened in London. The reviewer for *The Daily News* reporting on the first night claimed that the 'censor has deleted the one political allusion',[29] though the reviewer for *The Stage* reassured its readers that 'except for a couple of allusions in the third act, *The White-Headed Boy* is free from all political matter'.[30] Similarly, the reviewer for *The Pall Mall Gazette*, asserted that:

> It would be a thousand pities if the attentions of the Censor—apparently to the one (as it stands) absolutely harmless and good humoured 'political' line in the play about Ireland 'wanting to be free' and England giving her 'everything but what she wants'—should turn attention from the main fact in regard to *The Whiteheaded Boy*, Mr Lennox Robinson's new Irish comedy at the Ambassadors.[31]

Finally, the reviewer for *The Times* somewhat archly remarked that he would:

> hesitate to ascribe to the humour the quality of 'local colour', as that might seem another 'injustice to Ireland'. But the point would be relevant, were one to take seriously a hint of political feeling which the author dropped in his speech before the curtain. Fortunately the audience saw nothing political in the play and enjoyed it heartily on its artistic merits.[32]

Yet fear that *The White-Headed Boy* was overtly political continued to cause concern even when the play was approaching the end of its world tour. For example, the reviewer for *The Sydney Morning Herald* reassured its readers prior to *The White-Headed Boy* opening in Sydney a year after the London season:

> [It] has in it none of the mystic, ethereal beauty of Yeats's plays, nor is it concerned with the grim realities of life in the peat cabin so dear to Synge. It is a comedy of rural Ireland, a charming study of life in a modern Irish home, with clever satire upon the idiosyncrasies and traits of a very lovable race. It has, too, another merit, and one of inestimable advantage in view of present-day events. With neither politics nor religion is it concerned. Republicans and Diehard, Protestant and Catholic, can meet here upon common ground in the enjoyment of much wit and drollery.[33]

Whether or not the reviewer was aware, his commendation nevertheless both patronizes the play and restricts it to the level of popular entertainment.

'Drollery' and The White-Headed Boy

The epithet 'drollery' is one that was first attached to *The White-Headed Boy* at the beginning of its London season by the theatre critic for *The Times*. That it was still being used by the Theatre critic for *The Sydney Morning Herald* a year later and after the play had been toured extensively in America and Canada, not only says something about the tenacity of the attribution but also says something about the extent to which the play had become stereotyped.34 The *Times* critic had written:

> No doubt the charm of the Irish idiom and brogue for English ears helps these Irish plays in London, but we think *The White-Headed Boy* would prove comic in any language. For though much of the drollery is in the dialogue, still more of it is inherent in the characters and in the intrigue. We use the old-fashioned word, for they are really intriguers, these Geoghegans and Duffys of Ballycolman, and artful intriguers, as they might themselves say, 'at that'.35

In fact, the *OED* does not list 'intrigue' as one of the meanings for 'drollery', which is a word that first enters English in the sixteenth century. In Shakespeare's 2 *Henry IV*, II, i, 156 (1597) 'drollery' has the meaning of 'a comic picture or drawing, a caricature', although with a contiguous though slightly later use in *The Tempest,* III, iii, 21 (1610) the word simply means 'something humorous or funny; a comic play or entertainment, a puppet show, or a puppet'. By the nineteenth century, however, the word had taken on the negative connotations suggested by its earliest use—of being associated with something or someone who is 'quaint, odd, or strange'. Thus Carlyle writes of 'caricature' as 'drollery rather than humour' (1828), while Macaulay characterizes the humour of *She Stoops to Conquer* as 'quaint' by talking about the 'rich drollery' of the play. By the time the theatre critic of *The Times* came to use the word in 1920, and he seemed to use it strategically if not knowledgably, 'drollery', having entered English during the expansiveness of the Elizabethan period, had been subsumed into the discourse of imperialism as a way of both stigmatizing and stereotyping the colonized 'other'. To label *The White-Headed Boy* 'droll' is to marginalize it, to reduce its power to critique contemporary society, to deflect the laughter of recognition and self-criticism that it provokes away from the audiences who watch it in performance and towards some politically constructed stereotypical 'other'. Yet, ironically, the same critics who stigmatized the play as a piece of 'drollery' also praised it for its 'universality', though I believe it was as much its topicality as its universality that made it so popular with the audiences of the day.

Denis Geoghegan – a 20s male; *The White-Headed Boy*, a 20s play

The numerous reviews of *The White-Headed Boy* provide several clues to understanding the popular success of the play, whether the audiences were in Manchester, London, New York, Boston, or Sydney. Most critics remarked on the laughter that arose from the twists and turns of the plot as the Geoghegans and the Duffys tried to outwit one another. Most critics remarked the incisive satire on provincialism, the way Lennox Robinson had skilfully depicted a group of people who, in attempting to fulfil their individual dreams and desires, were obliged to negotiate and parley with one another. And most critics remarked the comic strength of the pre-eminent schemer, Aunt Ellen, particularly her 'love and money' scene with the widower and one-time disappointed suitor, John Duffy. In fact, Robinson himself subsequently acknowledged the significance of Aunt Ellen to the spectacular success of the play by dedicating the published version of *The White-Headed Boy* to his star character.

But the text of the play itself also contains several clues to its popular success. A number of these concern its topicality. Despite the fact that it was written hurriedly in 1916 (though there is an argument that the 1920s actually begins with the Armistice), and despite the frequently remarked 'universality' of its themes, *The White-Headed Boy* contains 'props' and 'business' that mark it as a distinctly 1920s play. When, for example, Baby asks Jane in the early part of Act III if the magazine she is looking at is *Weldon's,* and Jane replies 'No. A better paper – *VOGUE*',[36] Jane, and the young women who cluster round to comment and admire, are looking at a magazine which, even though it began publication in 1892 did not dominate until the 1920s when, in competition with *The Queen* and *Harper's Bazaar,* it established itself as the sole authority for the 'It' girl. Similarly, when Denis, the whiteheaded boy, offers his long-suffering older brother George a cigar when he first arrives home from Dublin in the middle of Act I, his gesture is significantly culturally coded. As Matthew

Hilton has pointed out in *Smoking in British Popular Culture 1800-2000*, an appreciation of tobacco and fine wine, and a taste for tailored clothing and mechanical gadgets were what distinguished the discriminating Victorian and Edwardian bourgeois male from his humdrum contemporaries.[37] And while, as Hilton and others have further argued, an extensive knowledge of these 'masculine' products also served to defeminize their consumption, the use of tobacco was particularly coded— sexually, culturally, and socially. Late Victorian and Edwardian magazines from time to time stigmatized the cigarette as 'a miserable apology for manly pleasure' that was suited only to 'the effeminate races of the Continent and the East'. Cigarette smokers were passive consumers; pipe and particularly cigar smokers were self-fashioned men of taste and refinement.[38]

Throughout the play, the central character, Denis, the whiteheaded boy, enacts a set of negotiated masculinities that had become popularly identified with a certain type of 20s male even as the play went into its London season. As the rather arch stage direction which accompanies his return home makes clear: '(... Ah! Here's DENIS at the other door. Isn't he lovely? You'd know he was from Dublin by his clothes and his smartness. He's just turned twenty-two.)'[39] As a twenty-two year old in 1916, when the play was written, or 1920 when the play was performed in London, Denis has affinities with the world of Robinson's *A Young Man from the South* (1917)[40] while also acting as a harbinger for Nick Carraway from Scott Fitzgerald's *The Great Gatsby* (1925) and Laurence Naylor from Elizabeth Bowen's *The Last September* (1929) – a type of 20s man who arguably reaches his apogee in the figure of Charles Ryder from Evelyn Waugh's *Brideshead Revisited* (1945).

Denis Geoghegan, I suggest, is the first of these to use insouciance to subvert patriarchal authority, a patriarchal authority that had sent tens of thousands of young men of his age to their death in World War One. He is also the first to mask that insouciance with a performed ennui. While the other characters in *The White-Headed Boy* bustle about giving and receiving directions, Denis waits for the strategic advantage he has come to know is so often created by the relentless pressure of other people's preoccupation with action. They are so busy asserting a specific self through action that they miss opportunities to actualize a self that would enable them to realize their desires. Style assists here. It opens a space and creates a persona that both facilitates self-actualization and enables that self-actualization to be flexible. Denis is also the first to regard his closest women friends as equals. Aware of the complexities of his own masculinity, he sees androgyny as neutral territory, a space where stereotypical gender roles can be beneficially deconstructed. In *The White-Headed Boy* Denis secretly enlists Delia as a co-conspirator to thwart the machinations of his family, his prospective in-laws, and his relatives. In short, the character of Denis Geoghegan not only embodies but more importantly prefigures many of the attributes of a certain type of 20s male. Astute audiences would have recognized the type, and would have greeted his performance with a laughter that was comprised of as much self-congratulatory knowingness as delight. Such audiences, it seems, could be found in places as varied as Dublin and Detroit, Baltimore and Brisbane, Manchester and Mount Morgan, Toronto and Townsville.

In all Lennox Robinson's *The White-Headed Boy* was performed approximately 650 times in the space of two years in some 30 cities around the world, a global triumph that was made possible by its conquest of London.

---

[1] *Oxford English Dictionary Online*, 2nd ed. (1989) accessed on 21 March 2005 through online link from <http://lrd.library.unsw.edu.au>

[2] See Peter Kuch, 'The "Abbey Irish Players" in Australia—1922' in *Irish Theatre on Tour*, eds Nicholas Grene and Christopher Morash (Dublin: Carysfort Press, 2005): 63-83.

[3] Robert Hogan and Richard Burnham, eds, *The Modern Irish Drama: A Documentary History, V: The Art of the Amateur, 1916-1920* (Dublin: Dolmen, 1984): 45. The season, which ran from 13 December 1916 into the new year, was advertised in *The Daily Express, The Freeman's Journal, The Irish Times, The Irish Independent*, and *New Ireland*, with reviews appearing in *The Freeman's Journal*, 14 December 1916: 4; *The Daily Express (Dublin)*, 14 December 1916: 7; *The Irish Independent*, 14 December 1916: 4; and *The Irish Times*, 15 December 1916: 7.

[4] Ibid., 47.

[5] Note Christopher Murray, 'Lennox Robinson: The Abbey's Anti-Hero' in *Irish Writers and the Theatre*, ed. Masaru Sekine (Gerrards Cross: Colin Smythe, 1986): 125. 'Robinson's comedies ... represent his best work. [A] feature necessary to emphasize is their strong theatricality. The characterization is so varied and the scenes in the comedies so tellingly arranged that they offered from the start excellent playing roles to the Abbey company, a matter of considerable importance where a repertory theatre is concerned'.

[6] R.F. Foster, *W.B. Yeats: A Life, II: The Arch Poet 1915-1939* (Oxford: Oxford University Press, 2003): 153-4. Murray, 'Lennox Robinson', 133, notes a letter from Robinson to James Stephens, dated 27 September 1918 cited in Michael J O'Neill, *Lennox Robinson* (New York: Twayne Publishers, 1964): 113, to support the contention that The Dublin Drama League was Robinson's brain-

child; whereas Hogan and Burnham, *The Art of the Amateur*, 152-3 claim that Yeats was the prime-mover. Finally, Ann Saddlemyer, *Becoming George: The Life of Mrs W.B. Yeats* (Oxford: Oxford University Press, 2002): 194, points out that Yeats chaired the inaugural meeting.

[7] Anon, 'London Theatres: The Ambassadors: "The White-Headed Boy"', *The Stage*, 30 September 1920: 16, reports that J.B. Fagan was 'responsible for the scene design and the production'.

[8] Advertisement for opening night in *The Manchester Programme*, 13 September 1920: 2.

[9] Anon., 'The White-Headed Boy', *The Era*, 15 September 1920: 6.

[10] Anon, 'Provincial Productions: The White-Headed Boy', *The Stage*, 16 September 1920: 18.

[11] Anon, 'News and Notes: Gaiety Theatre', *The Manchester City News*, 18 September 1920: 6.

[12] Anon, 'The Stage: Gaiety Theatre', *The Manchester Weekly Times*, 18 September 1920: 6.

[13] C.H.J., '*The White-Headed Boy*: Mr Lennox Robinson's New Play at the Ambassadors', *The Evening Standard*, 28 September, 1920: 12.

[14] Anon, 'London Theatres: The Ambassadors: "The White-Headed Boy"', *The Stage*, 30 September 1920: 16.

[15] E.A.B., '*The White-Headed Boy*: A Brilliant Success at the Ambassadors' Theatre', *The Daily News*, 28 September 1920: 5.

[16] S.R.L., '*The White-Headed Boy*: New Irish Comedy at the Ambassadors', *The Pall Mall Gazette*, 28 September 1920: 4.

[17] William Archer, 'Ambassadors Theatre: *The White-Headed Boy*', *The Star*, 28 September 1920: 6.

[18] T.B., '*The White-Headed Boy* in London', *The Manchester Guardian*, 28 September 1920: 11.

[19] Anon., 'Court Circular', 'Court and Social', *The Times*, 11 November 1920: 17.

[20] Anon, 'The Theatres: Many Changes in Prospect', *The Times*, 31 January 1921: 8; Anon, 'Reviews', 'The Ambassadors Theatre', *The Times*, 11 February 1921: 8.

[21] Anon., 'The Theatres: Waiting for Something to Turn Up', *The Times*, 23 May 1921: 8.

[22] Anon., 'The Theatres', *The Times*, 21 April 1921: 8.

[23] Interview with Arthur Shields in *The Evening Telegraph*, 15 January 1923.

[24] The advertisements in *The Times*, 8 April 1922: 10, col. 5 and *The Times*, 29 April 1922: 10, col. 5 indicate that the play opened on the 8th and closed on the 29th April 1922.

[25] Lennox Robinson, 'Preface', *The White-Headed Boy: A Comedy in Three Acts*: With an Introduction by Ernest Boyd (Dublin: The Talbot Press, 1922): xix-xx.

[26] *Ibid.*, xx.

[27] *Ibid.*, 158. The published texts ends with '…except the one thing?' though most of the newspaper reports of the speech from the opening night report it as '…except the one thing that he wants?'

[28] For a concise account of the 'executions' see Sean McConville, *Irish Political Prisoners, 1848-1922: Theatres of War* (London: Routledge, 2003): 669-70.

[29] *The Daily News*, Tuesday 28 September 1920: 5.

[30] *The Stage*, 30 September 1920: 16.

31 *The Pall Mall Gazette*, 28 September 1920: 4.
32 Reviews, *The Times* (London), 28 September 1920: 8.
33 '"White-Headed Boy": The Abbey Theatre Players', *Sydney Morning Herald*, 8 May 1922: 5.
34 It could be that the theatre critic of *The Sydney Morning Herald* merely took his cue from Ernest Boyd's introduction to the published text. Ernest Boyd, *Introduction to Lennox Robinson*, 'Preface', *The White-Headed Boy: A Comedy in Three Acts* (Dublin: The Talbot Press, 1922): xiv: 'the strength of this play undoubtedly lies in the perfect combination of form and content, and the natural unrestrained drollery of speech combined with a subject which develops realistically and logically, yet whose humour is that of cumulative effect'.
35 Reviews, *The Times*, 28 September 1920: 8.
36 Lennox Robinson, 'Preface', *The White-Headed Boy:* 130-6.
37 Matthew Hilton, *Smoking in British Popular Culture 1800-2000* (Manchester: Manchester University Press, 2000): 4, 21, 27-8.
38 Sean O'Connell, review of Hilton, *Smoking in British Popular Culture* accessed 16 May 2005 at
<http://www.history.ac.uk/reviews/paper/oconnellS.html#one>
39 Lennox Robinson, 'Preface', *The White-Headed Boy*: 40.
40 Lennox Robinson, *A Young Man from the South* (London & Dublin: Maunsel, 1917).

4 | Folds in Dispersion: Yeatsian Remnants in London

Jonathan D.H. Statham

In the 1980s there emerged an interpretive community that radically re-read the body of work we refer to metonymically as Yeats. In particular, the artists and intellectuals tied to the Field Day Theatre Company: Seamus Heaney, Brian Friel, Seamus Deane, Richard Kearney, Mark Patrick Hederman.[1] They strategically re-engaged with Yeats and other Irish writers as part of an attempt to respond to their own post-1969 situation in Ireland, Northern Ireland, and especially the newly energized relationship between those two states. For these thinkers, the emergence (in 1969) and subsequent activity of the Provisional IRA radically altered the political tension of apparently literary themes and images. Notions such as nationhood and its attendant mythologies, including those present in Yeats's writings, were seen from the perspective of new, fresher experiences of violence and the culture of violence. Indeed, Denis Donoghue felt that:

> [i]f the Troubles had not flared up again in 1968, these writers would not now, I think, be rereading Yeats, Joyce, O'Casey, Shaw and the other Irish writers in a spirit of anger and resentment. They would have been willing, as I was, to take our poetic masters pretty much on their own terms and as they came.[2]

Seamus Deane was just as clear: referring to the rise of the PIRA, he declared that '[t]he cultural machinery of Romantic Ireland has [...] wholly taken over the North'.[3] Such events clearly signalled 'the necessity of a reappraisal of Ireland's political cultural situation'.[4]

Although Field Day is a loose community of writers, most also associated with *The Crane Bag*, and mostly from the political left, the group cannot be said to have any fixed agenda or dogma. What united them was the need to respond described above. Nevertheless, there are identifiable characteristics in both the realms of politics and aesthetics. I want to name the 'point of view' that thus emerges from the Field Day Interpretation (henceforth, FDI). This unity is therefore, to some extent, a creation of my own, accrued through my readings of the Field Day writers (in particular, the philosophers and theorists) and one that could only be created retrospectively. Readers will find that some of the Field Day writers do not in fact hold the opinions I am about to ascribe to their collective; the FDI is only the trend of that body of writings.

One thing, however, is clear: the FDI is antipathetic to Yeats; an antipathy felt keenly by those critics of a slightly older generation such as Denis Donoghue, quoted above.[5] Where Joyce was seen as the demythologizer, the maker of mischief, the exile, the iconoclast, Yeats was perceived as the mythologizer, the nationalist ideologue, the Free State Senator, the idolater.[6] Richard Kearney perceives/conceives this distinction directly in relation to the politics of the Troubles; for example, in one of his Field Day papers, Kearney identifies in the Ireland of his day 'a basic polarization between a *mythologizing* form of politics [7] [...] and a *demythologising* form of politics': Yeats, he claims, 'sponsored mythology'.[8] Such an interpretation gives a clear political foothold for the use of literature, literary history and criticism as well as aesthetics in challenging Irish Republican ideologies. Donoghue even suggested that for Field Day 'the man to beat is Yeats's'[9] and indeed it does seem as if their project is founded on a 'vendetta with the Yeatsian tradition in particular'.[10] Thus it was Field Day that brought us Friel's realism and Heaney's Greek tragedies, notable in terms of the FDI not only because they follow in the wake of *Ulysses* by turning to Greek rather than Celtic mythology[11] but also because they resonate with a politics explicitly *European* in outlook.[12] This constitutes what I take to be the core of the FDI: a European postnationalism in which Joyce and Beckett can appear as heroic exiles ('Trieste – Zürich – Paris'[13]) but Yeats is thought of as explicitly *in Ireland* (Inisfree – Coole – Thoor Ballylee). By reading Yeats as ineluctably *in* an Ireland of Houlihan's four green fields the FDI can proclaim that he has left no space for 'the fifth province', an idea they take from Celtic legend: a space of the imagination that is never occupied but always open to being re-imagined, the space of the exile, always in the middle, always only here and now. A volume on 'Irish Theatre in England' therefore seemed an appropriate place to begin to question this interpretation since it licences us to think of *Yeats elsewhere*.

Nevertheless, the FDI is a highly productive point of view and I do not intend an attack: Field Day's antipathy to Yeats created, in the atmosphere of the 1980s, a political and aesthetic space of immense value. What I would suggest is that Yeats does not go whole into this interpretation, that there is a remainder, there is something left over. Without dismissing or contradicting the FDI, I want to expand beyond its own hermeneutic remit, reconfiguring its binaries as an expansion of its own project in the changed circumstances of the twenty-first century. Indeed, in this century, given the current state of the Peace Process[14] and of Europe, it is imperative that we seek this remainder, this remnant; that we ask ourselves: *what remains of Yeats*?

There is another moment in time when this question was equally imperative. 1939. In particular, December 1939. Yeats is dead: a Second World War has begun. Auden has commemorated both events in verse. For Ireland, the period known as 'the Emergency' has just begun, characterized by Irish neutrality. And in London an amateur theatre company in Kensington, the Chanticleer Theatre Company, are commemorating 'the recent death of the greatest lyric poet of the age'.[15] Under the direction of John Chandos, their choice of play is most peculiar: *The Unicorn from the Stars* – not only a play in prose but one that even Yeats himself admitted had been written in collaboration with Lady Gregory (indeed, when it premiered at the Abbey in 1907 Yeats and Gregory had been billed as co-authors). Given the contemporaneous circumstances it was also a very complexly resonant choice.

For example, at the bottom of the front page of the programme we find a note addressed to the audience:

> In the event of an air-raid warning sounding, the performance will be interrupted to advise the audience, and to allow any persons who desire to leave the theatre, after which the performance will be continued.[16]

In the play's most remarked upon (and remarkable) scene the protagonist, Martin Hearne, puts out a series of candles one by one. As he extinguishes the second candle, he says: 'We must put out the whole world as I put out this candle.'[17] The whole play centres on Martin's vision of the *monoceros de astris* trampling the world and his realization that 'where there is nothing – there is god'.[18] On one level this might seem an act of defiance: a play about visions of destruction performed in a city under threat of destruction. And the play has even more explicit moments: 'Can't you see it is the League of Unicorns' says one of the characters, referring to the uprising that Martin is leading, 'that will fight and destroy the power of England?'.[19] Also, given that most commentators of the play have noted the powerful Nietzschean logic of the play we can see that *The Unicorn from the Stars* seems a strikingly unusual choice – the BBC would surely have cancelled it.[20] What with the Nazi propaganda machine having been well aired throughout Europe during the 1930s, the association with Nietzsche, who is sometimes seen as the godfather of Nazism, must have rendered the play, at the very least, somewhat out of tune with the wartime upsurge in British patriotism, thus further complicating the resonance of Yeats's play. Indeed, in March 1940 (so presumably at least being discussed in December) there was a production of *Das Einhorn von den Sternen* in Munich.[21] The play was chosen specifically because it was thought unlikely to offend Nazi authorities and at the first performance the audience included many Brownshirts. The first and only performance was quickly cancelled because Martin's character – in conjunction with overuse of the word 'führer' – was considered insulting to Hitler.[22]

Clearly, Yeats's theme was in the thick of things. 1939 was also the year of the IRA's S-Plan[23]: under the direction of Sean Russell as Chief of Staff, the IRA had declared war on the 16 January 1939 and then initiated a bombing campaign throughout Britain. This was a high profile though badly planned and ultimately ineffective campaign (one of the bombers was the sixteen-year-old Brendan Behan; before he got round to detonating anything he was arrested and became the borstal boy he is remembered for being). In January, there was an assassination attempt on Chamberlain's son and in August the most individually devastating of the bombs killed five people in Coventry (two men, though innocent of this particular crime, were hanged for it in February 1940). By the end of the year there had been two hundred separate explosions and eighty Irishmen were in jail (many in terrible conditions).[24] It is in this context that we might best understand why no professional theatre company in London commemorated the death of the poet.[25] In context of the Nazi threat and the IRA threat (as well as the threat of collaboration)[26] we can see that in December 1939 London is beset by destruction. Meanwhile, on a stage in

Kensington, Martin Hearne calls out: 'I will begin the work of destruction.'[27]

In spite of the dark context, the director's note suggests a clear interpretation: *'The cure he* [Martin] *offers for the world's ills* [...]'.[28] So the play actually offers a solution to world war? What is important here is that Martin, having fallen a second time into a trance, completes the vision uninterrupted and so ultimately rejects the path of physical violence and especially the path of factional violence. He abandons political movements in favour of philosophical ones: '[m]y business is not reformation but revelation',[29] he says, '[t]he battle we have to fight is fought in our own mind'.[30] What Chandos's note gets absolutely right is that the mystery of this play, which is not an especially good play although (perhaps, therefore) revealing of Yeats's dramaturgy, lies in the central character, in the fact that he does indeed offer a cure for the world's ills, offers himself *as* that cure in a problematic of the individual: the mind of one's own.

Earlier I noted that many commentators have stressed the Nietzschean strains of *The Unicorn* and they have used this to 'solve' the character of Martin Hearne. Nietzsche's influence is undeniable; however, I want to suggest an alternative source for the character that has not, as yet, I think, been seriously considered: John Eglinton's *Two Essays on the Remnant*. Yeats reviewed these essays, among others by Eglinton [William Kirkpatrick Magee], in the *United Irishman* in 1901 (just a year before *Where There is Nothing*, *The Unicorn*'s predecessor) and then collected them for publication as *Some Essays and Passages* by the Dun Emer Press in 1905 (two years before *The Unicorn*). Notably, Yeats's collocation of Eglinton's texts splits up the two Remnant essays and uses them to frame the entire collection, thus precisely emphasizing them (beginning with 'Dying Nations and Regenerate Patriotism' and concluding with 'The Chosen People at Work').[31] Eglinton's thesis is a dialectic of Nation and Individual which states that the apotheosis of the Nation, 'the purpose of nationality',[32] is 'the individual grown wiser than his institutions'[33] who becomes a Remnant because s/he rebels against the Nation and goes into exile, a condition explicitly compared with the Jewish people. The Individual as Remnant, then, is that which cuts itself off from human progress as embodied in the Nation and thereby takes that progress to completion, at least to new heights:

there comes a time when the Chosen People ['a tribe of idealists, in the heart of civilization'[34]] and the State, if either are to fulfil the conditions of their existence, must take different ways, when Moses, or in our own time Thoreau, Whitman, Tolstoi, and others, appear, to call them forth to build in the wilderness the City of God. That is the period when the external application of ideas is become impossible, when the progress of the State comes to a standstill, when all development is individual and a Remnant is formed.[35]

Yeats, being Yeats, wrote a segment of his review of this hypothesis in dialogue form where a Remnant argues back at Eglinton (the premise being that Yeats has met many more such individuals than Eglinton and so is better qualified to say what they do; in other words, Yeats uses the review to steal the concept). The setting is London; Eglinton speaks first:

'You should go into the wilderness. You will be happy in the wilderness.'
'But what is the wilderness?'
'The wilderness is a country life'
'And when I get into the country what am I to do?'
'Why! read Wordsworth.'
'But I can read all the Wordsworth I think good poetry in a couple of days, and besides I am of an active disposition, I haven't a country clergyman among my ancestors for ten generations, nothing but soldiers. There was one of them that—'
'You can fish?'
'But I don't want to fish. I want to pull down Tottenham Court Road, and to build it nearer to the heart's desire.'
Then as likely as not he would go on, for the Remnant is not prejudiced:
'If I belonged to your country I could do something. There one has a chance. Your national life is not old and decadent as it is with us [[36]]. One might help to build a better civilization over there. But you must get rid of the English first. We are the makers of all vulgarity.'[37]

No 'City of God', then; but a city of (Irish)men. The Remnant is still the exile of the outward journey, the one who destroys, disperses, disseminates civilization: 'the great movement of our time is a movement to destroy civilization',[38] Yeats acknowledges; '[w]e must put out the whole world as I put out this candle'[39] says his protagonist. But Yeats's Remnant is also the one who does *not* go out into the wilderness but rather who journeys inward and rebuilds nearer to the heart's desire, 'to make the world change its image like a cloud':[40] therefore, '[t]he battle we have to fight is fought in our own mind'.[41] Eglinton's Remnant is a Chosen People who destroy civilization by departing from it, Yeats's Remnant is a heroic aristocracy who destroy civilization by remaining within it and by making it depart from itself.[42] For Yeats, the Remnant is separate(d) from society but remains within it, s/he confronts it internally with his/her status as a remainder. It is the Remnant, then, who takes us away from reformation, bourgeois administration and political violence (the two are part of the same continuum), to revelation, the metaphysical transformation of the world (this is present in Eglinton's conception too but Yeats clarifies and radicalizes it). *The Unicorn from the Stars* is Martin's realization that he is a Remnant. Yeats took this distinction and used it, not only in his plays, but as a way of thinking about his entire theatrical project:

> I was busy with a single art, that of a small, unpopular theatre; and this art may well seem to practical men busy with some programme of industrial or political regeneration [...] of no more account than the shaping of an agate; and yet in the shaping of an agate, whether in the cutting or in the making of the design, one discovers, if one has a speculative mind, thoughts that seem important principles that may be applied to life itself.[43]

The agate is like the cloud, the changing shape of the world's image: the Remnant is the stone-cutter. (We see here an early form of the subjective/objective dialectic later expounded in *A Vision*.) The shaping of the agate, of course, refers to Yeats's discovery of the *nō* theatre, an aesthetic that he experienced precisely along the lines of the inward departure I have described:

> the arts which interest me, while seeming to separate from the world and us a group of figures, images, symbols [which we might now simply call Remnants], enable us to pass for a few moments into a deep of the mind.[44]

If the *nō* aesthetic, as Yeats conceives it, mirrors the Remnant thesis in its operation then this also confirms why Martin is the central point of interest in *The Unicorn*: he is *in the wrong play*, a realist character who desperately wants to engage with what lies beyond his own reality – in this sense he is the inverse of Pirandello's *Six Characters* (they want to get into their play, Martin wants to get out of his). Perhaps this is why he must die at the end: realism as a theatrical form simply does not offer enough scope for an art of revelation. Martin ends up 'beyond the world',[45] beyond the real(m) that the realist form can present. In a sense, then, the play's ultimate failure is its most interesting facet: it creates a character who demands another kind of drama.

Yet even as Martin disperses, even as he departs, he also journeys inward for this battle in the mind: here, the super-natural is a kind of subconscious. What disperses, flows inward, because there is always a *fold*, a fold in dispersion where every motion is *revealed* in its double aspect as bi-directional. (This, of course, prefigures the double cone symbolism of *A Vision*.) Yeats, when working on the *nō*, succeeded in inventing a symbolism for this revelation: the folding of the cloth. Wherever Yeats is performed this ritual unfolds another space, a space that both departs away from the physical space (not London 1916 but the Irish Heroic Age) but also delves into the contemporary mental structures. The folds of the cloth should remind us that the stage is not where we are: it is distant from us and deep within us; it reveals us to ourselves and thus simultaneously reveals that we are not ourselves, that we are always *elsewhere*. The folding of the cloth is a ritual entirely consequent with Richard Kearney's formulation: 'the importance of being elsewhere'.[46] Yeats's drama is made of such folds, it is always already diasporic and always already returning, always already out of Ireland and remaining within it, making Ireland depart from itself (precisely the function of the fifth province: where is the middle of Ireland? goes the riddle; here and now, comes the answer). So, what remains of Yeats after the FDI, perhaps unsurprisingly, is the other places that operate in/as his theatre. In *The Unicorn*, as a realist play, the fifth province cannot unfold/enfold itself but can only be figured as a mountain spied in the distance that has yet to be climbed (how else, realistically, do you stage a space that cannot be occupied?):

> It is a hard climb to the vineyards of Eden. Help me. I must go on. The Mountain of Abiegnos is very high – but the vineyards – the vineyards![47]

I want now to conclude (or to avoid concluding) by offering, without comment although there is much to be made, the closing stanzas of Auden's 'In Memory of W.B. Yeats'. They seem to resonate with much of what I've said and, indeed, with current world affairs – the Peace Process, Europe and the events of 7 July 2005. But they also hint at why *The Unicorn from the Stars* might have seemed an appropriate if complex way to remember what remained of William Yeats in the December of 1939.

> In the nightmare of the dark
> All the dogs of Europe bark,
> And the living nations wait,
> Each sequestered in its hate;
>
> Intellectual disgrace
> Stares from every human face,
> And the seas of pity lie
> Locked and frozen in each eye.

> Follow, poet, follow right
> To the bottom of the night,
> With your unconstraining voice
> Still persuade us to rejoice;
>
> [...]
>
> In the deserts of the heart
> Let the healing fountain start,
> In the prison of his days
> Teach the free man how to praise.[48]

---

[1] These last two also initiated *The Crane Bag Book of Irish Studies* (in 1977) which, retrospectively, acted as a kind of precursor to the Field Day publications.

[2] Denis Donoghue, 'Afterword' in Field Day Theatre Company, ed., *Ireland's Field Day* (London: Hutchinson, 1985): 119-20.

[3] Seamus Deane, 'Heroic Styles: the Tradition of an Idea' in *Ireland's Field Day*: 55.

[4] 'Preface' to *Ireland's Field Day*: vii.

[5] Field Day's critical tactics could be loosely described as new historicist; thus they also rejected the critical tools of that older generation. See Quinlan, 'Under Northern Lights' in Leonard Orr, ed., *Yeats and Postmodernism* (Syracuse: Syracuse University Press, 1991).

[6] See, as an example, the 'Editorial' to Volume 2 of *The Crane Bag*: Richard Kearney and Mark Patrick Hederman, eds., *The Crane Bag Book of Irish Studies (1977 – 1981)* (Dublin: Blackwater Press, 1982): 155-7. This editorial (unsigned but, at a guess, I would attribute it to Kearney) strangely sets out to neutralize the force of Deane's article, without naming it, on Yeats and death in the previous issue. So determined is it not to let Yeats in on anything conceived as positive that it comes across as paranoid, as if Deane's article had somehow allowed Yeats to taint the *Crane Bag* by daring, to a degree (and it is only a degree), to celebrate him.

[7] In which he explicitly includes the Easter Rising and the Long Kesh Hunger Strikes.

[8] Richard Kearney, 'Myth of Motherland', *Ireland's Field Day*, 69. Since giving my paper, some of the implications of the FDI have come somewhat into focus: on Kearney's interpretation, Yeats's writings will certainly have to be banned from the UK once Tony Blair's new incitement to terrorism laws come into force.

[9] Donoghue, 'Afterword': 120.

[10] Quinlan, 'Under Northern Lights', 75 (confusingly Quinlan says this of Seamus Deane who has always seemed to me somewhat more in favour of Yeats than, say, Kearney – compare Deane's 'Heroic Styles' to Kearney's 'Myths of Motherland' in *Ireland's Field Day* and one can see that where both men perceive a double tradition under the headings of Yeats and Joyce, it is Deane who rejects a binary choice between the two positions and tries to find a third way 'unblemished by Irishness, but securely Irish' [58]).

[11] That Yeats turned to both Greek and Christian as well as Celtic mythology is conveniently elided by the FDI.

[12] See, for example, the first section of Kearney's *Postnationalist Ireland* (London:

Routledge, 1997).
13. James Joyce, *Ulysses* (London: Penguin, 1992): 933.
14. At the time of the ITD conference the IRA had not yet made their now most recent 'historic statement' and I was thinking of what almost appeared to be a crumbling of the Peace Process following bank robberies and Ian Paisley. Nevertheless, I think a re-understanding of Yeats is still relevant and the events of 7 July (surely a possible trigger for the IRA's statement, just as 9/11 had similar though less pronounced effects on the organization) make this even more imperative.
15. Theatre Programme (Theatre Museum, Covent Garden).
16. Ibid.
17. Yeats, *The Plays* (London: Palgrave, 2001): 239.
18. Ibid. *Where There is Nothing* is the title of an earlier play (written in 1902) from which *The Unicorn from the Stars* was adapted.
19. Yeats, *The Plays*, 221.
20. I have added this reference since 7/7/05 and the BBC's subsequent cancellation of their dramatization of *Greenmantle* – I couldn't resist it.
21. All information on this production is drawn from a reminiscence printed in Liam Miller, *The Noble Drama of W. B. Yeats* (Dublin: Dolmen Press, 1977): 137-8.
22. W. J. Mc Cormack gives details of another Nazi production of Yeats, this time *The Countess Cathleen*, performed in 1934; *Blood Kindred* (London: Pimlico, 2005): 164.
23. See Richard English, *Armed Struggle* (London: Pan Macmillan, 2003): 60-3; McCormack, *Blood Kindred*, 82-3; Kevin O'Connor, *The Irish in Britain* (London: Sidgwick and Jackson, 1972): 75-80.
24. O'Connor, for example, notes the significant rise in the number of IRA prison inmates in Dartmoor who were hospitalized during this period, usually as a result of beatings from the other prisoners – 'some of whom never quite recovered from the incarceration'. O'Connor, *The Irish in Britain*: 79.
25. Edy Craig had done so earlier in the year, but in her Barn Theatre.
26. In 1940, Russell himself was buried at sea wrapped in a swastika having died in a German U-boat on his way to Germany to discuss some kind of alliance.
27. Yeats, *Plays*: 227.
28. Theatre Programme, from John Chandos's Note; emphasis added. He continues: 'is only each man's individual triumph over others', but I think this is a flawed interpretation of the play – it would be more accurate if we said 'each man's individual triumph over himself'.
29. Yeats, *Plays*: 236.
30. Ibid.
31. To Eglinton's horror: he had Yeats publish a note at the front of the volume to say that had he edited the volume he would not have included 'The Chosen People at Work' at all.
32. John Eglinton, *Some Essays and Passages* (Dundrum: Dun Emer Press, 1905): 7.
33. Ibid., 5.
34. Ibid., 40.
35. Ibid., 41.
36. On which note, it seems to me that for the FDI Ireland has become old.

Interestingly, I find that my habitual mind-image of Yeats is the youthful, bespectacled portrait by his father; I picture Joyce in middle-age and then Beckett at the end of life looking as old as the earth itself. These impressions seem to be echoed and complemented by Louis le Brocquy's 'head images'.

37 Yeats, 'John Eglinton', *Later Articles and Reviews* (London: Scribner, 2000): 56-7.
38 Ibid., 57.
39 Yeats, *Plays*, 239.
40 Yeats, 'John Eglinton', p. 58. This might be a reference to Shelley's 'The Cloud' ('I change but do not die' thus opposing Eglinton's claim that 'the nation dies when it has discharged its function' – for Yeats, it metamorphoses [Eglinton, *Some Essays*, p. 6]).
41 Yeats, *Plays*, 236. My 'therefore' at this point perhaps presupposes Yeats's 'doctrine of the image' which is well known but not here discussed.
42 Compare with Deleuze and Guattari's distinction between 'the one who escapes, and the one who knows how to make what he is escaping escape'; *Anti-Oedipus* (London: Continuum, 1984): 341.
43 Yeats, 'Preface', *The Cutting of an Agate, Essays and Introductions* (London: Macmillan, 1961): 219.
44 Yeats, 'Certain Noble Plays of Japan', *The Cutting of an Agate*, 225.
45 Yeats, *Plays*, 237 (spoken by Father John).
46 Kearney, *Postnationalist Ireland*, 124.
47 Yeats, *Plays*, 239.
48 W. H. Auden, 'In Memory of W. B. Yeats', *Selected Poems* (London: Faber and Faber, 1979): 82-3.

5 | Reclaiming Sam for Ireland: The *Beckett on Film* Project

Graham Saunders

A telling incident took place during the international academic conference organized to mark Samuel Beckett's eightieth birthday held in 1986 at the Centre Georges Pompidou in Paris. As Brian Singleton recounts, Tom Bishop, the American organizer of the celebrations, was asked by Michael Colgan, Artistic Director of The Gate Theatre Dublin, if there was going to be an Irish presence in acknowledgment of Beckett's country of birth. When the answer to this was a resounding negative, Colgan immediately made arrangements for Professor Terence Brown to deliver a lecture on the subject, and for the Irish actor Barry McGovern to perform his celebrated show, *I'll Go On*, based on Beckett's prose work.[1] The story serves to illustrate two things about Michael Colgan and the subsequent *Beckett on Film* project: the importance he placed on Beckett as an artist, together with a driven and proselytizing regard for Beckett being acknowledged as a quintessentially Irish writer.

In 1991 Dublin hosted another international Samuel Beckett festival. As producer, Michael Colgan was again behind the enterprise, whereby over a three-week period from 1 - 20 October, all nineteen of Beckett's plays written for theatre were produced.[2] This ambitious theatrical event was seen in most quarters as being a genuine and worthwhile celebration of an important twentieth-century Irish dramatist held in the city of his birth, described as 'an enterprise, which spiritually brought Beckett home after his death'.[3] The event was also supported by Ireland's state broadcaster, RTE, and by Beckett's *alma mater*, Trinity College Dublin. From 1991 the Gate productions remained a permanent, if intermittent fixture on the theatrical landscape by way of a series of tours and revivals throughout the decade. In 1996 the cycle of plays was performed to American audiences at the Lincoln Centre in New York; the following year a truncated 'mini-festival' of selected plays was presented in Melbourne, Australia; and a full-scale revival took place at the Barbican Centre in London during 1999. Alan Maloney, the co-producer of *Beckett on Film*, reveals that the idea for this next project first arose from plans simply to record the 1991 Dublin performances for posterity, in much the same way that Beckett's 1975 Schiller production of *Waiting for Godot* was filmed. This became a more pressing concern following the festival's success and the various international tours that the Gate undertook: Michael Colgan wanted some sort of permanent record rather than the situation of a never-ending 'travelling circus'.[4] Moloney recalled that discussions developed regarding the feasibility of trying 'to create a cinematic feel, rather than just filmed plays'.[5] While the project's identity was inextricably bound up with its claims to promote Samuel Beckett's Irishness, its other major aim was to be a truly international enterprise in respect of the actors and directors it might attract. This strategy had a somewhat paradoxical intention, whereby it could claim both validity as a lasting testament to a uniquely Irish voice, while also laying claim to Beckett's international / universal appeal.

In terms of its aspirations for cultural significance and the scale on which it offered a 'complete' canon, *Beckett on Film* had an influential historical antecedent. This was the BBC Shakespeare television series, which was broadcast from 3 December 1978 until 27 April 1985. Crucial to each project, and indeed the catalyst behind the making of each venture, was the desire to produce a tangible record that would firmly establish the canonical status of each respective playwright. The similarities that *Beckett on Film* showed to the BBC series even extended down to the series being marketed as a definitive 'library' of the author's works, and made implicit a further important agenda that the producers of *Beckett on Film* wished to promote: namely, their endeavour in producing a complete set of the plays on film to mark Beckett out as the only twentieth-century artist ultimately to compete with Shakespeare's literary and cultural hegemony.

Michael Colgan in one interview made a telling comment that simultaneously revealed both the ambition of the project and its chief aim of canonization:

I think Beckett is the Shakespeare of the twentieth century, and I wanted to have one complete set of his plays that was going to be as faithful as possible.[6]

While earlier commentators such as Katharine Worth would doubtless agree (writing in 1986, she voiced the opinion that 'Beckett is acquiring the status of a modern Shakespeare'[7]) Colgan's insistence on Beckett's importance as Ireland's foremost dramatist can be challenged through empirical evidence at least in one quarter. Drawing on Neil Taylor's study of the most produced dramatists on BBC television since 1936 until 1994,[8] Jonathan Bignell comments:

> When the works of dramatic writers throughout the span from the ancient classical world to the present day are considered, Shakespeare, Shaw and Ibsen have their works broadcast most, and Beckett drops down the list to the fortieth most broadcast playwright.[9]

While this statistic fails to take into account other factors such as number of stage performances and revivals, not to mention Beckett's well-known reticence in giving consent for television adaptations of his stage plays, it constitutes a rebuke to the assumption that Beckett occupies the same position as Shakespeare. The names of other Irish dramatists such as Sheridan, Shaw, Wilde, and O'Casey rank higher on Taylor's list of most broadcast dramatists on television; and if that list is taken as definitive, Colgan and Maloney should perhaps more properly have been producing a series entitled *G.B.S. on Film*.

One other unstated, yet nevertheless important consideration in the international marketing of the BBC Shakespeare series was the promotion of its quintessential Englishness. Despite American financial backing and a global marketing campaign that stressed the essentially universal quality of Shakespeare, its directors and casts were drawn almost exclusively from Britain; and while the principal reason for this came from the intervention of the British actors union Equity, as Harry Fenwick sardonically observes, the whole undertaking from conception to execution was both 'gloriously British and gloriously BBC'.[10] In turn, despite the fact that its actors and directors were drawn from a far wider international ambit, conceptually Ireland dominates *Beckett on Film* on a number of levels: most obviously, the use of Irish accents adopted in *Waiting for Godot*, *Endgame*, and *Happy Days*. This stands in direct contrast to the BBC Shakespeare, where demands for a universalizing approach imposed a far greater linguistic tyranny, whereby the producers imposed a ban on British regional accents and only allowed received pronunciation; paradoxically, but not for the first time, the accent of Southern English upper-middle class became the measure of all human speech. However, before we can assess the degree to which *Beckett on Film* succeeded in its agenda, we should assess Beckett's place as a literary representative of Ireland. Whereas in Britain images of Shakespeare abound from currency to beer mats as a signifier of national identity, Beckett's relationship with Ireland is a far more problematic one.

Much of this questioning is the result of biographical fact. In 1937 Beckett set up home in Paris, and afterwards rarely spent much time in Ireland. He wrote many of his novels and plays first in French and only later translated them into English. In fact Beckett did not return to Ireland in the last twenty-one years of his life. Vivian Mercier maintained that the banning of the short story collection *More Pricks Than Kicks* (1934) by the Irish Free State was the crucial event that led to his alienation from Ireland.[11] This was compounded when Beckett refused to allow permission to have his plays performed there after an incident in 1958 at the Dublin International Theatre Festival where the Archbishop of Dublin opposed the performance of Sean O'Casey's *The Drums of Father Ned* and an adaptation of James Joyce's *Ulysses*. Beckett's response was to withdraw permission for the festival to perform *Krapp's Last Tape* and two mime pieces; he did not allow his plays to be produced in Ireland for the next two years. The practice of writing in two languages (and not including the self-translation Beckett undertook for his work in German) has also resulted in an anomalous situation where the origins and stability of Beckett's own nationality have become blurred and contested. Judith Roof, for example, notes this schizophrenic state of affairs in the Modern Language Association's decision in 1981 to categorize Beckett in its annals as both French and Irish literature. However, before this date the situation was even more bizarre: Beckett's Irish origins were ignored completely, and from 1955 onwards he had been classed solely as a French writer.[12]

However, from the mid-1980s onwards, and especially following Beckett's death, a number of major critical works were published, all of which attempted to place his work as belonging to an essentially Irish as opposed to European tradition.[13] This new approach to Beckett's work is apparent in James Knowlson's preface to the lavishly illustrated *Beckett Country*:

Though he left it for good in the 'thirties,' Ireland is present in Beckett's work not only in the localized settings of the early works or in the 'old scenes' revisited in the most recent plays or prose texts like *That Time* and *Company*, but also in some of the apparently more abstracted landscapes described in *Molloy* and *Malone Dies*, and evoked in *Not I* and *...But the Clouds*.[14]

By the 1990s two distinctly opposing strands of criticism existed concerning Beckett's place within twentieth century Irish drama. While Anthony Roche maintained that 'the presiding genius... the ghostly founding figure, is Samuel Beckett',[15] Christopher Murray's assessment of the same period saw Beckett forever destined 'to become the ghost at the feast of Irish drama'.[16] According to Murray, Beckett's marginalized position came about because his own modernistic dramaturgy was at stylistic odds with the prevailing realism exemplified by writers such as Sean O'Casey and Brendan Behan; yet Murray also believes that from *Waiting for Godot* onwards Beckett belongs firmly to the pantheon of twentieth-century Irish dramatists, 'engaged in a dialogue with Yeats and especially Synge'.[17] Beckett himself was very familiar with this particular strand of Irish drama (having frequented the theatre while he was a student at Trinity; and he was also a close friend of Jack B. Yeats). In an often-quoted letter to Cyril Cusack about his reactions to Irish drama, Beckett made his allegiances perfectly clear:

> I wouldn't suggest that G.B.S. [George Bernard Shaw] is not a great playwright, whatever that is when it's at home. What I would do is to give the whole unstoppable apple cart for a sup of the Hawk's Well, or the Saints, or a whiff of Juno, to go no further.[18]

Judith Roof identifies this tradition as partly evident through 'the Irish cadence in Beckett's language [...] in other words the Irish detritus',[19] while David Bradby observes that for the English translation of *Waiting for Godot* Beckett included several Irish idioms to locate the two tramps as Dubliners.[20] He also notes Barry McGovern's assertion that, 'Beckett had not translated his French play into English, but had rather rewritten it in Irish English'.[21] Anthony Roche argues that, given Ireland's status as a colonized nation, Beckett's decision to write in two languages would not have seemed overly out of place;[22] and the majority of critics who reviewed the Dublin premiere of *Waiting for Godot* in 1956 had no problem identifying its Irish elements. Leventhal's view is typical: 'the whole conception [...] is Irish, a fact which the original French had been unable to conceal'.[23] Yet it is also interesting to note that it took until 1969 for the play to get a performance at the Abbey, an institution which likes to see itself as Ireland's own representative 'National Theatre.'

Moreover, blithe talk of Beckett belonging to some nebulous Irish dramatic tradition has also been questioned at a number of levels. The first of these concerns Beckett's common practice of writing the plays at first in French. Michael Colgan, in a comment that, once again, indicates how important the idea of Beckett's Irishness was in the formation of the film series, sees the practice as something far more radical than merely translation: 'When he [Beckett] translated from French into English, he didn't translate, he wrote a new play'[24] (in other words that an essentially Anglo-Gaelic work emerges from the embers of the French translation). Vivien Mercier however has pointed out: 'It should be stressed that when Beckett [wrote] directly in English, he rarely makes use of Irish dialect.'[25] Beckett's British publisher, John Calder, goes even further in arguing that he often used the 'precise and economical' French language as opposed to Irish English in his work because the latter ultimately sounds 'too flowery, too rich',[26] and might subsequently lock Beckett's work into Irish theatrical tradition. It is also worth considering that despite plays including *Waiting for Godot*, *All That Fall*, *Eh Joe*, and *That Time* being identified as 'Irish' on grounds of colloquial idioms, there are still the vast majority of Beckett's dramatic works that contain little overt Irishness. Indeed, *Play* makes explicit references to small towns in Kent. If any of these views are to be believed, then grand projects such as the 1991 Beckett Gate Festival and *Beckett on Film* could be seen as imposing a false aesthetic on the work by effectively ventriloquizing an Irish voice for Beckett, whether one was intended or not. That said, although Beckett never clearly stated the accents he wished his characters to use,[27] two of his favourite interpreters were the Irish actors Jack MacGowran and Patrick Magee.

An alternative view of the Irish influence in Beckett's drama has come from those critics who see the plays as essentially vehicles by which Beckett evokes Ireland through memory. Ronan McDonald argues that even the late plays are 'crammed full [...] with names, topography and locutions from Beckett's birth place'.[28] J.C.C Mays sees these locations operating more on a subliminal basis: 'Ireland is there and not there, recalled and invented; it has a ghostly presence, more profound than reality'.[29] Judith Roof, despite recognizing the existence of these Irish reference points in Beckett's plays, sees their function as a way of detaching audiences from experiencing them in any broad Irish dramatic tradition or 'nation as a lost site and site of loss',[30] so that the place names in *Krapp's Last Tape*, for example, become evocations for the protagonist's estrangement from his country as well as from himself.

The other determining factor in Beckett's alienation from Ireland has been his refusal to let his drama engage with the society or politics of Ireland. Beckett's wireless play, *All That Fall* (1957), the most explicitly 'Irish' of his works is dismissed by Christopher Murray as only ever operating 'on the level of parody',[31] and so failing to 'engage with the conditions of Irish experience'.[32] In an often-quoted letter in 1938 to Thomas MacGreevy concerning the Irish painter Jack Yeats, Beckett expresses his 'chronic inability to understand as member of any proposition a phrase like "the Irish people"'.[33] Yet, Ronan Macdonald feels that it is unfair to cite this one letter continually as somehow proof that Beckett had completely disassociated himself from Ireland, and comments that the enduring presence, if only subliminally, of Beckett's landscapes and settings might 'point towards the colonial *erasure* of history/identity rather than the transference of it'.[34] Even in the incriminating letter to McGreevy Beckett ends by using several broad colloquial idioms: 'God love thee, Tom and don't be minding me. I can't think of Ireland the way you do.'[35] It might also be noted that Beckett's comments on the Irish People are not in themselves unique; the same kind of apparent animus lies behind Flann O'Brien's dialogues with the 'plain people of Ireland', which was a feature of his *Irish Times* column for many years.

Writing in the 1950s Vivian Mercier saw Beckett's dispassionate relationship with Ireland springing from his upbringing as a Protestant in a well-to-do suburb of Dublin:

> The typical Anglo-Irish boy learns that he is not quite Irish almost before he can talk; he learns that he is far from being English either. The pressure on him to become either wholly English or wholly Irish can erase segments of his individuality for good and all.[36]

Commenting much later in 1977 Mercier returns to the same theme, and continues in much the same vein, arguing that Beckett's muted Irish voice came about because his formative years were spent in a 'carefully insulated suburban community [which provided] little that was usable and durable'.[37] Katharine Worth argues that it is best to see Beckett as 'an Irish European',[38] but Mercier concludes that Beckett's 'universalism' cannot be located in arcane arguments revolving around competing claims of

Irish/English/French nationality, but rather 'the paradox of a unique self that has found its bedrock in our common human predicament'.[39] Nowhere was this contested and schizophrenic position made more apparent than in James Knowlson's observation that with the announcement in 1969 that Beckett had won the Nobel Prize for Literature, Ireland claimed him as its third recipient for the honour and France its eleventh.[40] Moreover, Paris also pre-empted the Dublin Gate Festival in 1991 with both the 1970 Théâtre Récamier festival and the ambitious 1981 Festival d'Automne in Paris to mark Beckett's seventy-fifth year, which combined a large scale theatrical presentation of the plays with an international academic conference at the Centre Pompidou and film and television retrospectives.

The indeterminacy of Beckett's identity hangs a useful question mark over an enterprise such as *Beckett on Film*, which not only set out to repatriate the dramatist, but also promote Beckett as a national literary figure who could also represent Ireland on the international stage. With the groundwork effectively laid by the Beckett Festival in 1991, which Campbell and Dackombe argued 'packages Beckett into a neat bundle of Irish national culture',[41] the film series in some respects presupposed the next logical step. Brian Singleton neatly summarizes the process of *festivalization* that he sees operating in Irish theatre, where certain key writers are picked out for the service they can provide internationally as arbiters for Irish culture. Singleton argues that the process also benefits the chosen writer by bringing about a fresh assessment of the canon:

> Perhaps the simplest way of determining the canonical in Irish theatre is to isolate writers whose work has been 'festivalized,' embraced by the trend of single-author marketing which recognizes that great theatre writers are the mainstay of Irish cultural capital. These writers and their works are celebrated by international recognition, and so by festivalizing their opus their lesser-known and less popular works can be consumed on the international markets, thus reinforcing their canonical status.[42]

In retrospect, the genuinely robust Irish counter-offensive festivalizing process that ultimately culminated in *Beckett on Film* had been underway shortly after the authors' death in 1989 with the inauguration of the 1991 Dublin Beckett Festival. Anthony Roche saw the enterprise as a significant 'key step in the establishment of Beckett as an Irish (as opposed to English, French, international and non-specific) playwright', [43] while Brian Singleton saw it more as an act of defiant nationalism on the part of Colgan and the other organizers, with the real intention behind the theatrical festival being 'to reclaim Beckett as Irish, a reclamation from the hijacking of Irish culture by both Britain and France'.[44] Whatever agendas may have been operating, the Beckett Festival established a new benchmark in appreciating the plays afresh through their performances in the city of the playwright's birth. Moreover, it did much to initiate a reappraisal, which resulted in the *leitmotif* of Irishness being adopted into something of the received style in subsequent productions. Having brought Beckett home, he could return to the English stage with his Irishness refreshed: Sir Peter Hall's 1997 production of *Waiting for Godot* saw the English-born actors Ben Kingsley and Alan Howard adopting Irish accents for Vladimir and Estragon. Hall also repeated the approach more recently in his 2004 production of *Happy Days*, in which Felicity Kendall (following on from Rosaleen Linehan in the *Beckett on Film* version) played Winnie with a genteel southern Irish accent.

Another major factor in the attempts of *Beckett on Film* to repatriate Beckett came from one of the principal financial backers of the project: *Radio Telefís Éireann* (RTE), the official state broadcasting network for television and radio in Ireland, which operates in broadly the same way as the BBC in Britain. RTE is also funded by a public licence fee, but with the important difference that it is also allowed to draw approximately half its funds from advertising revenue. The organization not only has a long history of promoting traditional Irish culture, but also at times of actively intervening in order to promote what is subsequently accepted *as* traditional Irish culture. Luke Gibbons gives the example of the *céilí* band, which was promoted as traditional music in the 1950s by the station's first director, Seamus Clandillion, although he himself had devised the form.[45] Such an organization, with its ability to shape new forms into an unspoken sense of tradition, seemed ideally placed as the broadcaster of choice for *Beckett on Film*.

Another of their co-sponsors makes this intention even clearer: Blue Angel Productions, an Irish-based company and a major backer of the project, had in partnership with Tyrone Productions produced *Riverdance* in 1994. *Riverdance* had become nothing short of a phenomenon, apparently reawakening a shared sense of Irish culture, both nationally and internationally. It was originally planned as a way of providing a brief interlude between acts for the Eurovison Song Contest held in Dublin that year; but, as Lance Petitt observed, 'in seven minutes, *Riverdance* produced a memorable moment in Ireland's contemporary image-making'.⁴⁶ While perhaps coincidental, the producers of *Beckett on Film* may well have seen this association as at least a fortuitous talisman in their aim to use Beckett through a media event to galvanize mass audiences to a similar sense of shared Irish identity. In a sense, the *Beckett on Film* series could be thought of as *Riverdance* in reverse: one introduced a carefully constructed ersatz Irishness to the world; the other reclaimed a hidden (but arguably equally ersatz) Irishness in an already world-famous author. Another light was cast, however, by the involvement of the other principal financial backer for the series, namely the British commercial broadcaster, Channel 4. Despite serious claims being made for the films as restoring Beckett to Irish audiences, *Beckett on Film* ultimately manifested (and simultaneously denied) a curious Anglo-Irish alliance.

The trans-nationality of the producers partly reflected the contemporary circumstance of Irish drama. Anthony Roche observes that the plays have influenced a whole new generation of Irish playwrights in the 1980s and 1990s: figures such as Sebastian Barry, Marina Carr, and Martin McDonagh have appropriated Beckett into their own work.⁴⁷ Given Eileen Morgan's point that since the 1960s the majority of Irish dramatists have by-passed their home country in order to *première* plays in London and beyond, Beckett's influence might be construed as instrumental in an odd process whereby home-grown dramatists have repeatedly become appropriated by international audiences. This in turn also suggests another reason that underscored the importance of choosing Beckett as the representative figure for Irish drama. However tokenistic, such a figurehead could, once reclaimed, also reclaim all his artistic descendents.⁴⁸ (The danger being that the attempt to preserve and canonize Beckett's drama does so at the expense of new work by living playwrights.)

The producers of *Beckett on Film* set out to accomplish this reclamation in no uncertain terms. For instance, Dublin Castle was chosen as the location for the series' launch party, with its guest list including *The Corrs* and *U2* lead guitarist 'The Edge' representing a significant quota of international Irish celebrities. Even here, however, the appetite for celebrity facilitated a certain stubborn English presence in the form of pop divas, Marianne Faithful and Lisa Stansfield, who had been resident in Ireland some years. Despite this, the launch party echoed Michael Colgan's inaugural speech at the Beckett Festival in 1991, where he first expressed the intent 'to introduce a Dublin audience to this great writer who needs to be looked at in Ireland'.[49] To this end, it is no mistake that Beckett's best-known plays were subjected to the most overtly Irish interpretation.

Many of the original actors and directors from the Gate Festival also appeared in *Beckett on Film*. *Waiting for Godot* was an amalgamation of past Dublin Gate productions and reunited (with the exception of the Boy) the Irish actors Johnny Murphy and Barry McGovern as Vladimir and Estragon.[50] *Endgame's* director was the Irish playwright Conor McPherson; the Irish actress Rosaleen Linehan repeated her role as Winnie in *Happy Days* from the Gate/Barbican production; and *Not I* (despite its casting of the American film star Julianne Moore as Mouth) was directed by Ireland's Neil Jordan. The only well-known Beckett play that escaped this treatment was *Krapp's Last Tape*, where director (Atom Egoyan) and actor (John Hurt) had no direct Irish connection.[51]

But, despite the eager intent to appropriate Beckett to an Irish milieu, in execution the project was less clear cut. Even co-producer Alan Moloney observed: 'I don't think Beckett is an Irish writer really, but the language he used is written in the rhythm of a Dublin accent.... Outside that, his writing is universal.'[52] An illustrative case in point was the film version of *Endgame*. Its director, the playwright Conor McPherson, is best known still for his 1997 play *The Weir*, which enjoyed phenomenal Broadway and West End success; he has since gone on to write other well received plays as well as writing and directing two films. McPherson was an interesting choice of director for what is probably Beckett's best-known play after *Godot*. Despite McPherson's claim that his own involvement came about because the producers wanted directors with experience in both film and theatre,[53] it is more likely that McPherson's true cachet for Colgan and Maloney came from his status as one of Ireland's most celebrated young playwrights, who could be seen as engaged in the task of reinvigorating the work of an older Irish dramatist. In addition, McPherson's other strength was that internationally his plays are somehow read as authentically 'Irish' in their sensibility and setting. He offered another route to reclaim a playwright still widely thought of as lacking such credentials. McPherson was no less keen to promote Beckett as a quintessentially Dublin writer; in interview he explained: 'The English that Beckett wrote is full of Irishisms, full of Irish inflections.'[54]

The techniques employed in drawing attention to this facet of Beckett's writing were less convincing in practice, however, since they basically consisted of the actors, Michael Gambon and David Thewlis, speaking their lines with ersatz-Dublin accents. Brian Singleton argues that the use of Dublin accents in Walter Asmus's 1991 Gate production of *Waiting for Godot* (repeated by the same two principal actors for *Beckett on Film*) was 'an act of reclamation from the received pronunciation of the English class system'.55 However, one could argue that the presence of similar accents in *Endgame* ultimately failed to produce these political resonances, becoming more akin to a mock-Irish pub, crammed full of fake signs of Irishness. John Harrington believes that, regardless of the reasons, imposing an Irish aesthetic on the play is misplaced: '*Endgame* is set in a vaguely European context which is not Ireland and not any other recognizable place.'56 Gerry McCarthy, speaking in relation to McPherson's production, also commented that the odd Anglo-Irish mish-mash of cod accents was at best off-putting, and that 'the last thing we need in a film of Beckett's work is the distraction of hearing David Thewlis [who played Clov] mix up his Irish accents'.57 The use of Irish accents in several of the canonical plays within *Beckett on Film* raises an interesting question. Writing of Peter Hall's production of *Waiting for Godot* in 1997 and its use of Irish accents by English actors, Anthony Roche noted that such interventions, 'may be taken as confirmation enough of the extent to which Beckett's Irishness is now universally conceded'.58 However, it is difficult to argue that simply doing Beckett in other voices is sufficient radically to transform the plays into something authentically 'Irish'. In fact it could be argued that the very opposite effect is achieved, that it reduces the plays by associating them with the worst kind of stage Irishness. McPherson's justification of the mock Dublin accents in *Endgame* as functioning as a mark of authenticity borders on the farcical: 'I made sure everyone had an Irish accent. Michael Gambon was born in Dublin so that was easy. David Thewlis is from Blackpool, but he picked up a South Dublin accent very quickly'.59

Ultimately, McPherson's *Endgame* becomes at best an uneasy Anglo-Irish hybrid. Even Michael Gambon's Irishness needs to be qualified; despite being born in Dublin, his family left for England during his early childhood. It is telling that to establish its so-called Irishness, *Beckett on Film* was predicated on the dubious proposition of individual claims to birth. This might have worked for the Irish football team; but in this context, it simply will not do. The given impression is that the series wanted it both ways: not only to reclaim Beckett for Ireland, but also to make him an uncontested figure of international, even universal stature. The effect was that the 'received pronunciation' of this Shakespearian claim was being glossed with a doubtful Irish brogue.

One other rather more obvious stumbling block remains in Beckett's work which prevents it from becoming another *Riverdance*: its deliberate eschewal of mass popularity. Beckett's work, after all, does not conform, either in content or style, to any media-industry standard. What *Beckett on Film* ultimately attempted to do was use the tactics of mass marketing and media to disguise the inherent difficulty of the plays. Brian Singleton observes that much the same attempt to make Beckett palatable also happened in 1991: the Gate season was marketed as an 'event' through the simultaneous staging and celebration of the plays' essential Irishness, together with the hosting of a prestigious academic summer school:

> Beckett's work outside such a huge marketing venture remains unapproachable. Perhaps it was only the cachet of the event which was the success, rather than the work itself, as his plays like those of Yeats, still remain outside the contemporary repertoire.[60]

Singleton argues that given the bubble of excitement temporarily created from the immediacy of the festival, it would be easy to jump to the conclusion that Beckett's work had suddenly been rediscovered as an exciting new cultural force. However, outside of the rarefied festival air, the demands that the plays make upon audiences were always liable to puncture the claims made for them. *Godot* might be a commercial standby, and *Not I* might have played to 87% capacity houses at the Royal Court during its first run; however it is hard to see mass audiences regularly turning out for *Come and Go* or *Ohio Impromptu*.

Beckett on Film looked to popularize Samuel Beckett. Frost and McMullan see such attempts as the "commodification" of an icon.[61] An enterprise such as *Riverdance* is suited to the internationalism of the Eurovision Song Contest, and its two Irish-American dancers successfully managed to combine traditional Celtic dancing with contemporary American styles to reinvent a traditional cultural form for global consumption as something definably 'Irish'. In contrast, Beckett's work cannot be so easily appropriated or made so overtly popular. And while his work and striking facial features are globally recognized, the drama contains inherent difficulties that Beckett deliberately built into their structure and which will always mitigate against them being seen as any form of 'brand'.

That this aspect of his work ultimately hampers its mass dissemination (rather than any failing on the part of *Beckett on Film* itself) was ironically recognized by the very broadcasters involved in its production, as was evident when the series *premièred* on Irish television from 19 March to 2 April 2001. Despite Colgan's hope that national interest would be aroused by a season of films that re-appraised the work of a Dublin-born playwright, RTE screened the series well outside peak viewing times. The earliest showing of 9.30 in the evening was for *Krapp's Last Tape* and *Act Without Words II*. The remainder of the films, including *Waiting for Godot* and *Endgame* were broadcast after 10 o'clock at night. Audience figures during the week of the Irish *première* also proved to be disappointing. The back-to-back screening of *What Where*, *Footfalls*, and *Come and Go* attracted an audience of 121,000; *Happy Days* and *Endgame* attracted 87,000 and 92,000 viewers respectively, while *Krapp's Last Tape* was the most successful in attracting 136,000 viewers. On the night that the series began, the largest recorded audiences (460,000) tuned in earlier at 8pm to watch the imported British soap opera *EastEnders*, followed by a Dublin variation on the form called *Fair City*, which attracted even more viewers (743,000). By the time it came to *Waiting for Godot* at 10.30pm figures had dropped significantly to 87,000. As would later be the case with its broadcast on Channel 4 in Britain, decisions over scheduling became a major problem.

It should also not be overlooked that, in considering the national and transnational aspects of Beckett, one audience stood customarily askance. Unable to access southern broadcasts, Northern Ireland had to wait for Channel 4's subsequent showing. Suspicions about Beckett, based on religious and political prejudices, were clearly seen when David Trimble, then leader of the Ulster Unionist Party in Northern Ireland, was asked if he had seen any of the *Beckett on Film* series and gave the enigmatic reply: 'I am not well acquainted with Samuel Beckett. I come from Northern Ireland so it wasn't an obvious subject.'[62] Trimble subsequently admitted to seeing an amateur production of *Waiting for Godot* in his youth, but his initial comment, coming from someone who sees Ireland's destiny as ultimately bound to Britain, seems to imply that for many Northern Irish Protestants Samuel Beckett, despite also being a Protestant by birth, is both suspiciously nationalist and Fenian in sensibility.

Yet in Beckett's centenary year, alongside the host of international academic conferences in places as disparate as France, America, and Japan, performances of the dramatic work at least served to reinforce notions of Beckett belonging firmly to a tradition associated with the Irish Diaspora, rather than self-imposed exile from his homeland. At London's Barbican Centre a joint assault was launched, with screenings from the *Beckett on Film* Project alongside new and revived stagings from the Gate Theatre. One production – an adaptation of the 1965 television play *Eh Joe* – with Michael Gambon and Penelope Wilton – effortlessly made the journey from Dublin to the heart of London's West End in twice-nightly sell-out performances. Elsewhere, Peter Hall revived his 1998 production of *Waiting for Godot* in the cities of Bath and London replete with Irish accents for Vladimir, Estragon, and Lucky. Michael Gambon also donned a suitable accent for the new production of *Embers* broadcast on BBC Radio 3 (directed by the Irish actor Stephen Rea) in April 2006, as did Penelope Wilton as the haunting voice in *Eh Joe*.

In one sense there is nothing wrong in these revivals highlighting the Irish dimension to Beckett's work, but one of the problems of being associated with a Diaspora is the tendency to overly romanticize the claims and importance of the homeland. In Beckett's centenary year and since, whether one takes one's perspective from the standpoint of academic Beckett Studies or of theatrical performance, the trends for dissemination paradoxically sustain an uneasy balance, poised between 'International Beckett' and 'Diaspora Beckett'.

---

[1] Brian Singleton. 'The Revival Revised', *The Cambridge Companion to Twentieth-Century Irish Drama*, ed. Shaun Richards (Cambridge: Cambridge University Press, 2004): 267-8.
[2] With the exception of *Eleutheria*, which has remained unperformed for copyright reasons.
[3] S.E. Wilmer, 'Introduction', *Beckett in Dublin*, ed. S.E. Wilmer (Dublin: Lilliput Press, 1992): 1.
[4] Aleks Sierz, Unpublished Interview with Michael Colgan, January 2001.
[5] Aleks Sierz, Interview with Alan Moloney. See the *Beckett on Film* website, <http:www.channel 4.com/plus/beckett>.
[6] Sierz, Unpublished Interview with Michael Colgan.
[7] Katharine Worth, *The Irish Drama of Europe from Yeats to Beckett* (London: Athalone Press, 1986): 264.
[8] See Neil Taylor, 'A History of the Stage Play on BBC Television', in *Boxed Sets: Television Representations of Theatre*, ed. Jeremy Ridgman (Luton: John Libbey, 1998): 23-37.

9 Jonathan Bignell, 'Beckett at the BBC: The Production and Reception of Samuel Beckett's Plays for Television', *Drawing on Beckett: Portraits, Performances and Cultural Contexts*, ed. Linda Ben-Zvi (Assaph: Tel Aviv University, 2003): 178.
10 Harry Fenwick, 'Transatlantic row breaks over the BBC's most Ambitious Drama Series', *Sunday Telegraph*, 24 September 1978.
11 Vivian Mercier, *Beckett/Beckett* (Oxford: OUP, 1977): 38.
12 Judith Roof, 'Playing Outside with Samuel Beckett,' *A Century of Irish Drama: Widening the Stage*, eds Eileen Morgan, Shakin Mustafa and Stephen Watt (Bloomington: Indiana University Press, 2000): 159.
13 The first major work in this reinterpretation was Eoin O'Brien's *Beckett Country* (London: Faber, 1986). Others include, John Harrington's *The Irish Beckett* (Syracuse: Syracuse University Press, 1991); Mary Junker, *Beckett: The Irish Dimension* (Dublin: Wolfhound Press, 1995); and Declan Kiberd, *Inventing Ireland* (Cambridge: CUP, 1996), particularly the chapter, 'Beckett's texts of Laughter and Forgetting', (530-50).
14 James Knowlson, Foreword to Eoin O'Brien, *Beckett Country* (London: Faber, 1986): xv-xvi. The relationship between Beckett's writing and his Irish background was not a completely new critical development. Writing back in 1971, Marilyn Gaddis Rose drew attention to the fact that even prose works such as *Texts for Nothing* (1950-2) and *How It Is* (1961), which seem to ignore time and space, in fact make deliberate topographical allusions to the Irish landscape. See 'The Irish Memories of Beckett's Voice', *Journal of Modern Literature*, (1971): 311 –17. One also cannot ignore Katharine Worth's *The Irish Drama of Europe: From Yeats to Beckett*.
15 Anthony Roche, *Contemporary Irish Drama: From Beckett to McGuinness* (Basingstoke: Gill and Macmillan, 1994): 4. Like Katharine Worth's earlier book *The Irish Drama of Europe from Yeats to Beckett*, Roche maintains that much of Beckett's drama comes from an older tradition, such as the detailed comparison he draws between *Waiting for Godot* and W.B Yeats's *At the Hawk's Well* (24-8).
16 Christopher Murray, *Twentieth Century Irish Drama: Mirror up to Nation* (Manchester: University of Manchester Press, 1997): 148. Despite Murray's reservations, the inclusion of a chapter on Beckett in the recent *Cambridge Companion to Irish Drama* (Cambridge: Cambridge University Press, 2004) seems to suggest that his position is less marginalized than it was in the past.
17 Ibid.
18 James Knowlson, *Samuel Beckett: An Exhibition* (London: Turret Books, 1971): 23.
19 Roof, 147.
20 David Bradby, *Waiting for Godot* (Cambridge: Cambridge University Press, 2001): 40.
21 Bradby, 185.
22 Roche, 4.
23 A.J Leventhal, 'Dramatic commentary', *Dublin Magazine* 31 (1956): 52.
24 Alan Riding, 'Finding New Audiences for Alienation', *The New York Times*, 11 June 2000, section 2.
25 Mercier, 42.

26 John Calder, 'Remembering Sam', *Beckett in Dublin*, ed. Steve Wilmer (Dublin: Lilliput Press, 1992): 124.
27 In her biography of Beckett Deirdre Bair seems to imply that originally Beckett had required the actress Billie Whitelaw to deliver Mouth's lines in *Not I* in an Irish brogue. See *Samuel Beckett* (London: Vintage, 1990): 688.
28 Ronan McDonald, *Tragedy and Irish Literature: Synge, O'Casey, Beckett* (Basingstoke: Palgrave, 2002): 141.
29 J.C.C. Mays, 'Irish Beckett, a Borderline Instance,' *Beckett in Dublin:* 145.
30 Roof, 159.
31 Murray, 148. Vivien Mercier also concurs: 'In *Watt* and *All That Fall*, only the working class characters - the railway-station staff and the man driving the cart loaded with manure - speak in dialect.' (42).
32 Murray, 6. Yet even here there are strongly opposing views. Ronan McDonald in *Tragedy and Irish Literature* sees it as 'fallacious to assume that [Beckett] occupies some sterile, evacuated imaginative site, in quarantine from its own historical context' (142).
33 Cited in Patricia Coughlan, '"The Poetry is Another Pair of Sleeves": Beckett, Ireland and Modernist Lyric Poetry', *Modernism and Ireland: The Poetry of the 1930s*, eds Patricia Couglan and Alex Davis (Cork: Cork University Press, 1995): 180.
34 McDonald, 142.
35 Cited in Coughlan, 180. Many thanks to David Pattie for contributing to this paragraph.
36 Vivian Mercier, 'Beckett and the Search for Self', *New Republic*, 13 September 1955: 20.
37 Mercier, *Beckett/Beckett*, 38.
38 Katharine Worth, 'Beckett's Irish Theatre', *Perspectives of Irish Drama and Theatre,* eds Jacqueline Genet and Richard Allen Cave (Gerrards Cross: Colin Smythe, 1991): 39.
39 Mercier, *Beckett/Beckett*, 45. Harry Cockerham makes a similar point: 'Arguments over whether he [Beckett] is properly a French or an Irish writer are therefore necessarily sterile and it may indeed be that his example and the fact of his existence as a bilingual writer will do much to break down barriers between national cultures and encourage a trend towards a comparativism in literary studies. If any claim has validity, it is that this tidy categorization is excessively constraining, Beckett is the world.' See 'Bilingual Playwright,' *Beckett the Shape Changer: A Symposium*, ed. Katharine Worth (London: Routledge and Kegan Paul, 1975): xxiii.
40 Knowlson, Foreword, *Beckett Country*, xxi.
41 Julie Campbell and Amanda Dackombe, 'The Beckett Festival at the Barbican Theatre, September 1999', *Journal of Beckett Studies,* Spring (1999): 91.
42 Singleton, 259.
43 Anthony Roche, 'Pinter and Ireland', *The Cambridge Companion to Harold Pinter*, ed. Peter Raby (Cambridge: Cambridge University Press, 2001): 175. Roche argues that such was the success of the Beckett festival that Michael Colgan attempted to do the same in 1994 with the English dramatist, Harold Pinter.
44 Singleton, 268.

45 Luke Gibbons, *Transformations and Innovations in Irish Culture* (Cork: Cork University Press, 1996): 73.
46 Lance Pettitt, *Screening Ireland: Film and Television Representation* (Manchester: Manchester University Press, 2000): 177. Many thanks to David Pattie for contributing to this paragraph.
47 Roche, *Contemporary Irish Drama*, 244, 257.
48 Eileen Morgan, Shakin Mustafa and Stephen Watt, eds *A Century of Irish Drama: Widening the Stage* (Bloomington: Indiana University Press, 2000): xviii.
49 Eileen O'Halloran and Susan Schreibman, 'Dublin Salutes Beckett', *The Beckett Circle: Newsletter of the Samuel Beckett Society*, 13 (1990): 1.
50 Alan Stanford, who played Pozzo, was also in the Dublin production. He is English, but resides permanently in Ireland.
51 Although Hurt had played the role of Krapp when the Gate production came to the Barbican Theatre in London during 1999, the actor who originally played Krapp in the 1991 Dublin production was the Irishman, David Kelly. Familiar to British television audiences for playing a whole host of stereotypical Irishmen during the 1970s and 1980s (notably the role of Albert - the one armed dishwasher in the situation comedy *Robin's Nest*), Kelly first took on the role of Krapp at a remarkably young age in 1959, when he appeared in the Irish premiere of the play at Trinity College's Player's Theatre. Kelly was also involved in *Beckett on Film*, playing 'A' in *Rough for Theatre I*.
52 Aleks Sierz, Unpublished interview with Alan Maloney.
53 Conor McPherson, Unpublished Interview with Aleks Sierz, 20 January 2001.
54 Riding, The New York Times.
55 Singleton, 268.
56 John Harrington, 'Samuel Beckett and the Counter-Tradition', *Cambridge Companion to Twentieth-Century Irish Drama*, ed. Shaun Richards (Cambridge: Cambridge University Press, 2004): 172.
57 Gerry McCarthy, 'Screen Test', *Sunday Times*, 11 March 2001.
58 Roche, 'Pinter and Ireland,' 175.
59 Riding, The New York Times.
60 Singleton, 269. Many thanks to David Pattie for contributing to this section.
61 Everett C. Frost and Anna McMullan, 'The Blue Angel Beckett on Film Project: Questions of Adaptation, Aesthetics, and Audience in Filming Samuel Beckett's Theatrical Canon', *Drawing on Beckett*, 218.
62 'Pandora', *The Independent*, 9 July 2001.

6 | Understanding Loyalty: The English Response to the Work of Gary Mitchell
Tim Miles

> It was around the time of *The Force of Change* that I think he (Mitchell) began to write for an English audience.[1] (Paula McFetridge, Artistic Director of the Lyric Theatre, Belfast)
>
> You could read a thousand newspapers and not get such a vivid sense of why violence and hatred won't be laid to rest in the province, and why Unionist anger is turning in on itself.[2] (Brian Logan, *Time Out*, review of *As the Beast Sleeps*)

On 14 February 2004 Paula McFetridge, artistic director of the Lyric theatre in Belfast, was interviewed about the work of the playwright Gary Mitchell. She seemed clearly impressed: 'His achievements are remarkable given where Gary has come from'. She was referring to Rathcoole, an estate in north Belfast, described by *The Irish Times* as 'a microcosm of place, and time, and mindset'.[3] Rathcoole, Mitchell's home until recently, is a heartland for the loyalist paramilitary organization, the Ulster Defence Association (the UDA). Mitchell's 'achievements' include some thirty works for stage, screen and radio, chronicling the struggles of working class loyalists to redefine their identities in the context of the developing peace process. In his plays violence has not been put to rest, it has just changed from old sectarian hatreds; now Protestants attack other Protestants. McFetridge went on to criticize Mitchell for not being what she called 'forward looking'. She praised the 'originality' of his early work but claimed she had not even seen his most recent, *Loyal Women*. This lessening of her interest in Mitchell's work was, in part, she claimed because he had 'begun to write for an English audience', that Mitchell wrote characters who 'wore shell suits, chain smoked and cursed like fuck'. Mitchell, she asserted, was now providing stereotypes, little more than 'stroppy Prods'. To the English, McFetridge continued, 'we have become sexy and risqué', as they see in Mitchell's enclosed worlds of perpetual, and perpetuating, violence something supposedly raw and exciting. McFetridge is a Catholic; these were personal comments that were not expressed as representing the views of the Lyric theatre. Nevertheless, Mitchell's greatest success in England, *The Force of Change*, has never been produced in Ireland, on either side of the border. This essay will consider the possible reasons why Mitchell's work seemed to so impress English critics, and why the success of his work may be fading as quickly as it began.

Mitchell's first stage play in England was *In a Little World of Our Own*. It had premiered, not in Belfast, but in Dublin, in February 1997 in an Abbey Theatre production at the Peacock. Eamon Hughes has commented on a strange 'bouncing back' effect, whereby Ulster theatre seems only able to view Protestant writing clearly 'through the prism of London or Dublin ... as though there is some need for external validation'.[4] The play itself, like much of Mitchell's work, is a 'thriller' (in that the drama is driven by a sense of physical danger), and a 'whodunit'. In the play, a Protestant family fear reprisal when the daughter of the leader of the local Ulster Defence Association is murdered and suspicion falls upon the learning-disabled Richard, the youngest member of the family. A friend of the family, Walter, hitherto seemingly timid, argues that the family should shoot Richard as a symbolic act to prevent reprisals from the UDA:

> ... 'cause it's not about the wound, it's about the act and it's about the will to carry out the act, that's remorse and that's respect.[5]

However, the murderer turns out to be Ray, Richard's over-protective brother, an Ulster 'hard man' and UDA enforcer, motivated to commit the crime, in part, as an attack on what he sees to be the 'namby pamby ways'[6] of the UDA leadership as they make concessions to the peace process, and also to defend the honour of his brother. The play ends with an injured Ray, shot by the UDA, urging his younger brother to kill him before any further reprisals can be delivered. Richard raises the gun and is commended for doing so: 'You're the man. You're the fucking man'[7] are Ray's last words, and the final lines of the play. Loyalty, and indeed love, has led to violence; defence has led to aggression; and Ray's legacy to his brother has been to teach him how to use a gun, indeed to commit the biblical sin of killing one's own brother. To Mitchell, the effects of 'the troubles' are still being felt, and through violence. That is their legacy.

In Ireland the play had been a huge critical and commercial success, winning the *Irish Times* best new play award. Embracing the spirit of the peace process and cross-border co-operation, the play became the first Abbey production to be performed in Belfast at the Lyric Theatre, when it opened there in August 1997. Eight months later would see the signing of the Good Friday Agreement. McFetridge talked about how 'unusual it was to have a working class Protestant voice at the Lyric', how 'real' the work felt, and 'how important' it was 'for *all* people to tell their stories'. However, controversy surrounded the play from the beginning. Ophelia Byrne in *State of Play: Theatre and Cultural Identity in Twentieth Century Ulster* claimed the production was troubled with '...public denials that theatres in Northern Ireland thought it too dangerous to handle... '.[8] The Lyric, though having the play in development, did not produce the finished piece, nor did Tinderbox (the company who had produced Mitchell's first stage play in Ulster, *Independent Voice*). This was, to Mitchell, the result of anti-Protestant bias within Ulster theatre. In an article entitled 'Balancing Act' in *The Guardian* Mitchell talked about knowing Protestant actors who had changed their names 'to sound more Catholic' and claimed that the Lyric had wanted *In a Little World of Our Own* set, not in Belfast, but in Birmingham: 'Prods in Belfast – too political'.[9] The Lyric have always denied this.

Despite, or perhaps even because of, this allegation, in March 1998 the production transferred for a short run at London's Donmar Warehouse. The controversy that the play had caused in Belfast seemed to have crossed the Irish Sea, since English critics were largely polarized in their responses: either fiercely admiring or as fiercely damning. Nicholas de Jongh, for example, writing in *The Evening Standard* described the play as 'fascinating',[10] and Michael Billington in *The Guardian* called it 'passionate drama', describing Mitchell as 'a skilful dramatist'.[11] Benedict Nightingale, writing in *The Times*, mysteriously quoted an anonymous 'senior figure in the Irish theatre' who claimed that Mitchell's plays are 'urban and tough and about Irish life as it really is, not as you like to pretend it is'.[12] Michael Coveney in *The Daily Mail*, however, claimed that the only reason Mitchell had been appointed writer-in-residence at the National Theatre was because he was 'superficially competent, fashionably

Irish, and not a Republican'.¹³ He was, however, in the minority. To most English critics, here was a play dealing with people on the violent margins of Ulster loyalism, presenting them as morally complicated, with differing identities, afraid for their futures and, at times, ignorant of their past. This was something rarely seen on the English stage, they argued, and it was authentic, passionate and visceral.

In a Little World of our Own signalled the start of a series of London successes for Mitchell. In March 1999 *Trust* opened at the Royal Court, and then in the spring of 2000 *The Force of Change* became Mitchell's most successful play in England, opening upstairs at the Royal Court, and winning *The Evening Standard* 'Most Promising Playwright Award' and the Royal Court's own 'George Devine Award' for the best new play. Later in the same year it transferred to the larger Jerwood Space downstairs at the Court. *As the Beast Sleeps* was produced at the Tricycle theatre in September 2001; and *Loyal Women*, Mitchell's only full-length play with a predominantly female cast, came to the Royal Court in November 2003. In all cases the reviews were generally positive and those who found fault usually did so as a result in seeing shortcomings in Mitchell's stagecraft not in his thematic content, or in his politics. Lynn Gardner in *The Guardian*, for example, found that *The Force of Change* 'though never less than gripping, is always drama rather than theatre'¹⁴ and was unhappy with the 'televisual' nature of the play. Significantly, few of the English critics challenged Mitchell's treatment of his principal theme: loyalist identity and the problems in adapting to the demands of the peace process.

Since *Loyal Women*, no Mitchell play has been performed in England. *Splinters* was commissioned by the Tricycle in 2003, but not produced. Perhaps surprisingly, neither *Loyal Women* nor *The Force of Change*, despite the latter being lavished with awards in London, has ever been produced in Ireland, north or south. In Ireland it seems his success may have faded as quickly as it began. Eamon Hughes at the conference 'The Ulster Literary Theatre and its Legacy' talked about how Protestant writers like Mitchell would 'seem to be a sensation' before fading quickly, far more so than their Catholic counterparts.¹⁵ John Wilson Haire, for example, another Ulster Protestant had a major success in England with his play *Within Two Shadows*, produced in 1972 at the Royal Court, winning many awards, only for his subsequent work to receive far less critical attention.

One of the champions of Mitchell's work in the English press has been Michael Billington in *The Guardian*. He justifies his praise on three grounds: Mitchell's use of metaphor, his sense of moral complexity, and his apparent authenticity (that he depicts the world of Ulster loyalists exactly how it is). The last point is exemplified by this observation from his review of *Marching On* where Billington claims that the play 'fulfils one of drama's most basic functions: the anthropological recording of the country's customs'.[16]

To look firstly at Mitchell's use of metaphor: Mitchell's dramatic world is often that of disintegrating families, or of conflict within the workplace, and here the internal divisions act as metaphors for the collapse of a wider political union with Britain, and of divisions within the concept of loyalism. Mitchell's plays tend to be dialogue-driven but metaphors may often also be visual. There are, for example, a number of occasions where characters will be decorating or undertaking DIY, and seemingly very badly, papering over the cracks literally and metaphorically. Both *As the Beast Sleeps* and *Loyal Women* start like this, acting as metaphors for Mitchell's attitude towards the peace process: that it looks impressive but has no lasting foundations.

Contradiction and conflict, both internal and external, mark Mitchell's work. In commenting on *Loyal Women*, Billington states that 'it is his ability to convey the contradictions within the Protestant community that make Mitchell a major writer'.[17] Billington admires, for example, the way Mitchell leads us to sympathize with Ray from *In a Little World of our Own*, the loving brother and committed loyalist, helping us to see him, human and vulnerable, as a victim of circumstances, that, despite his violent ways, he is driven by brotherly love as well as a desire for revenge. In so doing Mitchell also comments on the degree to which loyalist paramilitary activity is inherently paradoxical: if you attempt to pledge loyalty to the State by breaking the very laws that support the State, you undermine that which you wish to maintain. Loyalty may be a noble act but it can have terrible consequences.

This notion of contradiction, of conflicting loyalties, is reflected in what is almost a *leitmotif* in Mitchell's work: the police officer with divided convictions, who faces emotional collapse once he has been forced to compromise his integrity, however good his intentions may have been. *Marching On*, for example, finishes with Christopher, the RUC officer who faces conflict between his loyalty to his family who want to march down the traditional routes on the 'glorious twelfth', and his loyalty to his role as a police officer whose job it is to stop them. This is conflated with his sense of personal injustice:

> Well, here's the thing – who's stopping them marching? –Me. And who's to bring him in? -Me. And who's to do this Scottish fucker for shagging his sister? -Me. And who's not allowed to see his own kids? Me-me-me-fucking me. Well, fuck it. Fuck it all, fuck the lot of you.[18]

To Mitchell, authority, as represented by the police officer, is collapsing. Structurally, matters are no better. In *As the Beast Sleeps*, for example, each link in the chain of command, from UDA enforcer, to UDA area leader, to the community's specific political representative, is successively undermined and threatened from within. Authority is reduced to anarchy, and order leads to chaos. These are the paradoxes in Mitchell's work that Billington admires.

In the television documentary, *Red, White and Blue: A Protestant Tale*, Mitchell talks about emotional contradictions, and his motivation to write. He comments on his 'beautiful feelings' towards the children in Rathcoole and his empathy with 'their sense of hopelessness'.[19] He writes to try and reconcile this with the 'ugly feelings' of his youth and his belief in an exclusively Protestant Ulster. In Mitchell's first produced stage play *Independent Voice*, subsequently broadcast on BBC radio, a journalist on a local newspaper, hitherto content with publishing innocuous stories and filling the paper with jokes and puzzles, decides instead to write a story about the UDA's involvement in drug dealing. Convinced that he is now a vehicle for justice, he follows this with a story about alleged child abuse in a local foster home. These actions trigger a chain of events leading to the murder of the supposed child abuser, who is almost certainly innocent; and then to the ambitious would-be leader of the local UDA effectively taking control of the paper now that he has realized the power of stories. The journalist sought truth and independence but, in so doing, ends up as little more than a mouthpiece peddling lies. His idealistic actions, in fact, make matters worse. The bleakness of this position is all too clear. In *As the Beast Sleeps* Kyle spends much of the play trying to be loyal: to his wife, who wants him to provide for their family; to Freddie, his fellow member of the UDA, who wants him to help re-start the war with the hated 'taigs'; and to the UDA leadership, who want him to try and maintain the peace by leading a punishment squad, to demonstrate his loyalty by 'punishing' his friends. Despite, or indeed because of, Kyle's attempts to be loyal to all three, he ends up alone, accused of treachery by all sides. Loyalty is complicated and comes at a price.

Billington's third reason for praising Mitchell, his 'authenticity', is one shared by a number of the English critics; they make claims for Mitchell's supposed truthfulness, a position with which Mitchell himself is often keen to agree. In an article entitled 'Truth and Nail' in *The Guardian* published just before the opening of *The Force of Change*, Mitchell is quoted as saying that 'It's the reviews that scare me ... someone leaving the theatre saying that I have not been completely truthful'.[20] The author of the article, Fiachra Gibbons, goes on to say that 'Mitchell argues that you cannot be a true loyalist unless you are loyal to the truth'.[21] In the most recent publication on Mitchell's work in *Modern Drama* in Spring 2005, Richard Ranking Russell takes for the title of his piece, 'Loyal to the Truth: Aesthetic Loyalism in *As the Beast Sleeps* and *The Force of Change*' and refers to Mitchell as an 'unblinking chronicler'. To Russell, Mitchell's excellence lies in his being 'objective'.[22]

This notion of Mitchell's authenticity is problematic. His authoritativeness comes from what Billington calls 'anthropological recording', that this is a 'real' picture of life in Rathcoole. However, by simply accepting Mitchell's supposed truthfulness, we may limit our ability to challenge the work. Those critics who have wanted to see more in Mitchell's plays have found a certain impurity there; they view his 'truth' as very much a partial one. Jennifer Cornell, writing in *The Canadian Journal of Irish Studies*, notes that there are surprising omissions from Mitchell's work:

> It is the absence of other, equal truths – ones, for example, that explore the energy, ingenuity and determination of working-class Protestants who have organised themselves into residents associations, action groups, and community councils dedicated to the constructive pursuit of their political aspirations and the creative expression of their identity.[23]

In her paper 'Namby-Pamby Ways Don't Get Results: Cultures of Machismo and Violence in the Work of Gary Mitchell', Nadine Holdsworth quotes Billy Mitchell, the former loyalist paramilitary convicted of murdering a fellow loyalist:

> When you incite people to form armies and then walk away, you create a monster and that monster does what it wants. [...] Basically, I think Mary Shelley could have written Frankenstein about us.[24]

Holdsworth is making a point about the legacy of violence and how that is reflected in Mitchell's work. She is quite right. *The Force of Change*, for example, ends with a police officer deciding that the only way to combat the paramilitaries is to threaten them with violence. The violence is self-perpetuating. However, Holdsworth does not go on to explain that Billy Mitchell has, in fact, shed any attachment to violence and now works for peace through organizations like EPIC (Ex-Prisoners In the Community) and refers to himself as a 'pacifist':

> On nearly every interface people are working together on both sides. [...] They work on the ground – I'm quite optimistic about that. Hurts are being healed right across Belfast.[25]

These 'healed hurts' seem never to appear in Mitchell's plays, something that English theatre reviewers have curiously ignored. However, another form of violence against the 'other' has, in many ways, replaced the sectarian violence of 'the troubles'. According to *The Guardian* in January 2004 in an article entitled 'Racist War of the Loyalist Street Gangs' we read that Northern Ireland holds 'the UK's highest rate of racist attacks'. The article goes on to state that 'there are 4,000 – 5,000 Muslims in Northern Ireland, most of them born locally, but there is no purpose-built Mosque for fear of attack'.[26] In the council elections of 2004 the British National Party for the first time fielded candidates in Northern Ireland. Some of the former high security prisons are now being used to house asylum seekers. None of this is reflected in Mitchell's work. No person of colour is ever referred to, or anyone who does not come from a Christian heritage. Of the English press it was left to Sean Docherty in *The Socialist Review*, commentating on Mitchell's play, *Trust*, to point out the limitations of his enclosed worlds of Protestant in-fighting:

> It is totally unconvincing to restrict the drama to their own ghettos and families. After all, Rathcoole, one of the biggest housing estates in Europe, used to be mixed – Catholics and Protestants living together. They found work in the surrounding factories. The Catholics and the factories have now disappeared. Why? Real trust would have been found in the commonality of interests Protestant workers have with their Catholic counterparts, a trust that has been manifested in numerous common struggles throughout Irish history.[27]

It could be said that Mitchell is being authentic within the limitations of his own experience. However, in *Red, White and Blue* he talks about working as a civil servant and realizing that he had more in common with one of his Catholic colleagues than many of his Protestant ones. Strangely, this realization does not seem to inform his work. Instead, he feels a need to keep returning to the heartland of loyalist paramilitary activity. He justifies this by claiming that his work transcends the specificity of his subject matter: 'I don't write about Northern Ireland. I write about people.'[28]

There are formal reasons that help explain Mitchell's success outside Ireland. Billington refers to his 'rare gift of speaking to his community while, at the same time, reaching out beyond them'.[29] It is arguably Mitchell's use of theatrical realism and a populist form, the thriller, which has allowed his work to travel. *In a Little World of Our Own* utilizes the conventions of Greek tragedy. There is an Aristotelian unity of time, place and action, with the single action being the destruction of the family. The family friend, Walter, acts as both chorus and messenger, bringing news of the off-stage violence; and the plays ends with Ray's death, as the world without finally engulfs the world within. Furthermore, Mitchell's characters face dilemmas within structures familiar to an English audience: the family and the work place. Characters also face personal dilemmas applicable to circumstances outside Ulster loyalism. Kyle in *As the Beast Sleeps*, for example, is caught between the competing demands of his wife, his friend, his boss, and his own conscience. So, this may help explain why Mitchell's work was for a period a success in England; but it does not help us understand why his work ceased being performed in Ireland, while three major productions were appearing on the London stage.

A significant comment from the English tabloid newspaper, *The Sun*, was quoted in the programme for Conal Morrison's play, *Hard to Believe*: 'Ulster is not another country. It is another planet.'[30] Alan F. Parkinson in his book *Ulster Loyalism and the British Media* explores the thesis that the British media have misrepresented the Ulster loyalists, who have in turn failed to present themselves in a positive way. He argues that loyalists have failed to understand the demands of the media age, and that from partition onwards Ulster loyalism had been marginalized from most British narratives, both political and cultural. He says that the British media were ill-prepared to cover 'the troubles' when they started, and ill-informed about Northern Ireland's history and peoples. They concentrated on portraying loyalists as what he calls the 'bigots in the bowler hats'. This, Parkinson suggests, provided a scapegoat for successive erring British Secretaries of State. He goes on to suggest that the media concentrated on 'quizzing the government', on the high profile 'miscarriages of justice', and the allegations of 'shoot to kill' against British troops, and of abuses against Republican prisoners. Feature films such as *Michael Collins* and *In the Name of the Father* helped further change British public opinion, during the 1980s and 1990s, to seeing Republicanism as increasingly occupying the high moral ground. Thatcher's broadcast ban not only failed to prevent Sinn Féin having the 'oxygen of publicity' but created further sympathy among the British public. Loyalists, conversely, were seen more and more as entrenched, inflexible and irrelevant. Ian Paisley was the man who always said 'no'. To the British, Ulster loyalists were, indeed, 'from another planet'. So, Mitchell's vision, given this reading of history, tended to confirm its view of loyalists as committed to outdated tribalism while, at the same time, challenging it, by presenting them as morally and emotionally complex. David Edgar has consistently endorsed Vaclav Havel's view that if a playwright delivers all an audience's expectations then this promotes boredom, but if none are delivered then this is caprice. For the drama to work they need their expectations both challenged *and* confirmed. Mitchell's work, in England, if one accepts Parkinson's view of history, did just that. Jennifer Cornell, however, takes the view that '*As the Beast Sleeps* will only confirm stereotypes of Ulster Protestants despite its author's commitment to challenging them'.[31]

It seems reasonable to assume that their experience of Northern Ireland for most English audiences is one they have derived not from life but through the media and through art, a mediated perspective. Few people consider Belfast as a holiday destination. Christina Reid, when she was writer-in-residence at the Lyric, recounts how a group of youngsters from the Catholic Falls Road, who had never been to a theatre before, were invited to see a production of O'Casey's *The Shadow of a Gunman*.[32] They talked loudly during the play, lit cigarettes and ate crisps but, on the whole, appeared to be engaged by the drama. However, Reid was surprised when they all laughed at the shooting of Minnie Powell. When asked about this, they replied that to them such violence was real, lived experience, and to see it represented in this way was comic. Their lived experience overruled any appeal to empathy. This context, of the lived versus the mediated experience, is something on which the English press largely fail to comment. In his review of Danny Morrison's IRA thriller *The Wrong Man* which premièred in London in March 2005, Dominic

Cavendish said in *The Daily Telegraph* that 'No theatre on either side of the Irish border would touch this, apparently. Full marks to the brave Pleasance for doing so.'³³ Though as Quentin Letts was quick to point out in *The Daily Mail*, ' deep in the badlands of Islington' hardly requires the same level of bravery, as it would do if you produced it in Belfast in the heart of the struggling peace process.³⁴

It is perhaps instructive, at this point, briefly to compare Mitchell's work with one of the most popular plays performed in Ireland in recent years, *The History of the Troubles (Accordin' to my Da)*, written by Martin Lynch together with the comedy partnership Conor Grimes and Alan McKee. The play has been a huge commercial success in Belfast, having three sell-out runs at the Grand Opera House. However, in England, when it came to the Tricycle in June 2003, it was largely savaged in the press and did little better at the box office. Sarah Hemmings, for example, in *The Sunday Times* called the play 'feeble'.³⁵ Ian Johns writing in *The Times* was rather more perceptive when he stated that 'for a non-Irish audience it sometimes feels as though you are not in on the joke'.³⁶ One scene sees the thirteen-year-old Colm explaining to his father that he does not want to grow up because:

> ...adults kill people over whether you're Irish or British, and...and blow people up in pubs...and shoot people at their front doors in front of their families and other horrible things...³⁷

His father is understandably worried. He asks Colm what he does want instead and gets the reply: 'I'd rather sit in m'room, listen to Stuff Little Fingers and masturbate all the time'.³⁸ There is a big laugh. This scene, and indeed the play, acknowledges the very real pain of the 'troubles', while demonstrating Ulster's move to 'normalization': Colm is, in fact, just like most other thirteen-year-old boys, in Belfast, Dublin, London, or any other place, obsessed by thoughts of sex and popular culture. While acknowledging the pain of 'the troubles', the play offers the prospect of normality, something which, to the people of Belfast, is hardly trivial. Put the play on in London and it is not much more than extended vulgarity. Rhoda Koenig, writing in *The Independent*, for example, referred to the Tricycle production in London as having 'tired sub-Benny Hill gags' and entitled her piece 'When tragedy is no laughing matter'.³⁹

This geographic contextualization is further conditioned by the cultural politics of Northern Ireland, which presents an almost bi-polar position: write about the 'troubles', or look to the future. In *The Guardian* on 5 June

2005 the academic and novelist, Linda Anderson, urged writers to move on from hackneyed thrillers: 'the impression is given that violence in Northern Ireland is inherited, bred in the bone, that the situation is hopeless, that anyone involved in the political process is pathologically damaged'.[40] She was not, but she could have been, talking about Mitchell: the description fits perfectly. Paula McFetridge speaking on BBC television in May 2005 talked of 'the end of the single community drama' and again about the need for theatre to be 'forward looking'.[41] Funding bodies in Ulster want work to be produced that 'brings people together' across the divide. But perhaps the reality is a little different. In the 2003 general election the largest winner was Ian Paisley's hard-line Democratic Unionist Party. David Trimble, joint winner of the Nobel Peace Prize, lost his seat. Cornell quotes Arnold Wesker when he states that any theory of art, which concentrates on how the world should be, not how it is, 'is more about wish-fulfilment than truth'.[42] Mitchell claims, as has been observed, that he is 'loyal to the truth'.

There is an intricate ethical dimension to the experience of Mitchell's dramas in performance. In order to engage in them, we need to feel some emotional empathy for his hard men of violence, to acknowledge that Ray, for example, from *In a Little World of Our Own* is in some degree tragic, in that he is incapable of redefining himself away from the violence and tribalism with which he has grown up. The key question is, however, at what point does what Mitchell calls 'opening up' to try to understand such a man, become an act of justification for his actions, with which we, as the audience, through our need for engagement, have become complicit? If we are, then such complicity in England may indeed be 'sexy and risqué', but in Ulster it is a far more serious response.

In Brian Friel's play, *The Home Place*, the English landlord in Ireland, Christopher Gore, begs his housekeeper to marry him and leave for South America to be 'anywhere where roles aren't imposed on us – where we'll be free of history and heritage and the awful burden of this'.[43] In Marie Jones' play *A Night in November* the hitherto committed Ulster loyalist, Kenneth, finishes the play believing in a vision of a united Ireland, having freed himself from his sectarian upbringing: 'I am free of it. I am free of it. I am a Protestant man. I am an Irish man.' [44] Similarly, Robert Welch's play, *Protestants*, ends with a vision of a world liberated from the ties of religious affiliation. Conversely, Mitchell's plays end with bleakness and often violence. It is this bleakness that Nicholas Kent pointed to, when questioned in interview by Richard Cave about his decision not to produce any of Mitchell's plays at the Tricycle Theatre since *As the Beast Sleeps* in 2001.⁴⁵ Maybe Mitchell will free himself 'from the role that history' has given him. If he does not, then he runs the risk of being abandoned by even his English admirers. This would be the final ironic metaphor for that abandonment by the British state, which the loyalists in his plays so deeply fear.

At the time of writing, April 2006, Gary Mitchell is in hiding. He and his family were attacked by renegade members of the UDA in December 2005. According to Henry McDonald in *The Guardian*, this was for two reasons: 'Mitchell's exploration of Ulster loyalism and its identity crisis and that the loyalist paramilitary groups have begun to fragment'.⁴⁶ However, Mitchell, speaking on the BBC, claimed his attackers were motivated because they saw him as some sort of collaborator:

> Images of myself winning awards in Dublin is enough to give these people the impression that I've sold out or done something against them.⁴⁷

In his radio play, *Stranded*, a tone poem about the isolation of certain Ulster Protestants, a character speaks of 'The BBC, Fenian scum, the lot of them, with their reports from Derry, and its Ireland this and Ireland that'.⁴⁸ It is hardly surprising that Susan McKay entitled her book: *Northern Protestants, An Unsettled People* (2000). This harsh and challenging title makes for a stark contrast with what Mitchell sees as the overwhelmingly positive English attitude towards the peace process:

> When I go over to London, people say 'Oh, how lovely now that you have peace'. BBC Northern Ireland told me that I wouldn't be working for them unless I wrote about the peace process, and it would have to be positive. How can I write a positive drama about the peace process when terrorists are blowing up my car? [...] As for England, you are a second-class citizen if you do not come from London or Metro-land. If I were a Muslim writer whose work upset members of my community so much that some were threatening to kill me, then it would be a *cause célèbre* [...] But because this is Northern Ireland what is happening to my family is not part of the peace process narrative.⁴⁹

He perceives English attitudes towards him, his work and Northern Ireland to be vastly at odds with the truth.

To conclude: the English press have been enthusiastic over Mitchell's work since *In a Little World of Our Own* opened at the Donmar. Many critics believed that through his visceral plays of loyalist in-fighting they could understand the violent margins of loyalism. However, this English response to Mitchell's work has been conditioned by cultural, political and historical factors, which are in their turn shifting as a result of the developments of the peace process, and the changing cultural dynamics between Belfast and London. These factors are also in their turn influencing what is produced and how. Gary Mitchell's plays in the view of English audiences may at one time have been 'sexy and risqué' but they are perhaps now no longer as significantly a 'part of the peace process narrative'.

---

[1] Paula McFetridge, Personal Interview with author, 13 February 2004. All subsequent comments by McFetridge are from the same interview unless otherwise stated.

[2] Brian Logan, Review of *As the Beast Sleeps*, *Time Out*, 26 September 2001: 149.

[3] Mic Moroney, 'The Mitchell Principles', *The Irish Times*, 25 February 1998. See <http://scripts.ireland.com/search/highlight.plx?TextRes=2%In%20a%20Little%.../fea2.ht>, accessed 19 January 2001.

[4] Eamon Hughes, speaking at *It's Own Way of Things: A Celebration of the Ulster Literary Theatre*, Queens University, Belfast, 23 October 2004.

[5] Gary Mitchell, *In a Little World of Our Own* (London, Nick Hern, 1998): 51.

[6] Ibid., 4.

[7] Ibid., 61.

[8] Ophelia Byrne, ed., State of Play: The Theatre and Cultural Identity in Twentieth Century Ulster (Belfast: Linen Hall Library, 2001): 126.

[9] Gary Mitchell, 'Balancing Act', *The Guardian*, 5 April 2003, <http://www.guardian.co.uk/arts/features/story/0,11710,929911,00.html>, accessed 20 January 2004.

[10] Nicholas de Jongh, *The Evening Standard*, 5 March 1998, reprinted, *Theatre Record*, 26 February–11 March 1998: 283.

[11] Michael Billington, *The Guardian*, 5 March 1998, reprinted, *Theatre Record*, 26 February–11 March 1998: 284.

[12] Benedict Nightingale, *TheTimes*, 6 March 1998, reprinted, *Theatre Record*, 26 February–11 March 1998: 284.

[13] Michael Coveney, *The Daily Mail*, 13 March 1998, reprinted, *Theatre Record*, 26 February–11 March 1998: 283.

[14] Lynn Gardner, *The Guardian*, 10 November 2000. See <http://www.guardian.co.uk/arts/reviews/story/0,,699671,00.html>, accessed 31 August 2004.

[15] Eamon Hughes, 23 October 2004.

[16] Michael Billington, 'Summertime and the Rioting is Easy', *The Guardian*, 17 June 200. See <http://www.guardian.co.uk/Archive/Article/),4273,43030189,00.html>, accessed 19 January 2001.

[17] Ibid.

[18] Gary Mitchell, *Marching On* (unpublished script): 135-136.

[19] Red, White and Blue: A Protestant Tale, Brian Waddell Productions, broadcast

on BBC1, January 1998.
[20] Mitchell, quoted by Fiachra Gibbons, 'Truth and Nail', *The Guardian*, 10 April 2000. See <http://www.guardian.co.uk/arts/story/0,,177744,00.html>, accessed 5 January 2006.
[21] Ibid.
[22] Richard Ranking Russell, 'Loyal to the Truth: Aesthetic Loyalism in the work of Gary Mitchell', *Modern Drama*, 48.1 (2005): 186-201.
[23] Jennifer Cornell, 'Walking with Beasts: Gary Mitchell and the Representation of Ulster Loyalism', *Canadian Journal of Irish Studies*, 29.2 (2003): 33.
[24] Nadine Holdsworth, 'Namby Pamby Ways Don't Get Results: Cultures of Machismo and Violence in the Work of Gary Mitchell', The Twelfth Annual Central New York Conference on Language and Literature, 28 October 2002.
[25] Billy Mitchell, BBC Radio Ulster, 15 April 1999, recorded as part of the Millennium Memory Bank (British Library Sound Archive, catalogue number C/900 10617).
[26] Angelique Chrisafis, 'Racist war of the loyalist street gangs', *The Guardian*, 19 January 2004. See <http://www.guardian.co.uk/Northern_Ireland/Story?0,,1120112,00.html>, accessed 6 January 2006.
[27] Shaun Doherty, 'The Real Betrayal', *The Socialist Review*, 229, April 1999. See <http://pubs.socialistreviewindex.org.uk/sr229/theatre.htm>, accessed 23 January 2003.
[28] Mitchell, 'Balancing Act'.
[29] Billington, 'Summertime and the Rioting is Easy'.
[30] *The Sun*, quoted in the programme of *Hard to Believe* by Conall Morrison, The Riverside Studios, London, 2–26 September 2004.
[31] Cornell, 31.
[32] Christina Reid speaking on *Irish Arts Week*, March 2003 (British Library Sound Archive, catalogue number B/1092/4).
[33] Domenic Cavendish, *The Daily Telegraph*, 22 March 2005, reprinted, *Theatre Record*, 12–25 March 2005: 345.
[34] Quentin Letts, *The Daily Telegraph*, 23 March 2005, reprinted, *Theatre Record*, 12–25 March 2005: 345.
[35] Sarah Hemmings, *The Financial Times*, 9 June 2003, reprinted, *Theatre Record*, 21 May–17 June 2003: 709.
[36] Ian Johns, *The Times*, 5 June 2003, reprinted, *Theatre Record*, 21 May–17 June 2003: 710.
[37] Connor Grimes, Martin Lynch and Alan McKee, *The History of the Troubles (Accordin' to my Da)*, (unpublished script): 67.
[38] Ibid., 67.
[39] Rhoda Koenig, 'When tragedy is no laughing matter', *The Independent,* 05 June 2003. See <http://enjoyment.independent.co.uk/theatre/reviews/article107591.ece>, accessed 19 January 2001.
[40] Linda Anderson, quoted in Maev Kennedy, 'The Trouble with Fictional Troubles', *The Guardian*, 2 June 2005: 8.
[41] Paula McFetridge, speaking on *The Culture Show*, BBC2, 12 May 2005.

42 Cornell, 33.
43 Brian Friel, *The Home Place*, (London, Faber and Faber, 2005): 67.
44 Marie Jones, *A Night in November*, (London, Nick Hern Books, 2000): 108.
45 During the conference, *Irish Theatre in England*, National Portrait Gallery, London, 16 June 2005.
46 Henry McDonald, 'Playwright hits back against intimidation', *The Guardian*, 29 January 2006. See
<http://www.guardian.co.uk/Northern_Ireland/Story/O,,1697432,00html>, accessed 15 April 2006.
47 'Playwright driven out by idiots', BBC News, 22 December 2005. See
<http://news.bbc.co.uk/2/hi/entertainment/4551870.stm>, accessed 19 January 2006.
48 *Stranded* by Gary Mitchell, dir. Pam Brighton, BBC Radio 3, 11 August 1995.
49 McDonald, 'Playwright hits back against intimidation'.

7 | Traditional Routes: Challenges and Re-affirmations in the Representation of the Ulster Protestant

Wallace McDowell

The aim of this article is to offer an overview of the way in which Ulster Protestants have been portrayed on stage for English audiences, as well as to examine just what sort of Ulster Protestantism(s) are represented. To do so I intend to offer, as a context, some of the preliminary findings of my research into the relationship between the Protestant/Unionist/Loyalist community and the theatre within Northern Ireland before examining how this community has found itself represented theatrically in England in the work of three playwrights. As someone born and bred in Protestant East Belfast, but who has also lived in England for fifteen years, my position is necessarily dual, approaching the subject as insider and outsider. However, I thought it would be useful to begin by briefly considering just what preconceptions such audiences in England are likely to bring with them at the start of the twenty-first century. What images are conjured up in minds on this side of the Irish Sea when the term 'Northern Ireland' is paired with words such as 'Protestant', 'Unionist' or 'Loyalist'?

On the night of 5 May this year, I sat up into the early hours watching the results of the general election come in along with their analysis by various panels of experts. The following day, I tuned in to the BBC's parliament channel which was broadcasting the election programme transmitted from Belfast. To the eye, everything looked as it had the night before. There was the usual mix of presenters, pundits and results, familiar-looking graphics and captions, and returning officers announcing the results. I had, however, spent a long enough time away from Northern Ireland for the whole thing to sound completely alien. The punditry included no discussions on social issues – nothing about health or welfare or taxes which had been the mainstay of the election campaign in Britain. A different vocabulary was in use – the 'sell out', the 'traitor', 'decommissioning', 'kneecapping', 'gangsterism' and, above all, that highly contested phrase, 'the people of Northern Ireland'. The contrast was a salutary reminder of the difference of perception of events inside and outside the region. Back at the election coverage, the final image one was left with was that of Ian Paisley's count in North Antrim where, having been returned with yet another thumping majority, he preceded his vote of thanks to the returning officer with a vote of thanks to God, leading the faithful in a rousing rendition of the hymn *Praise God from whom all blessings flow*. This image of Ulster Protestantism – the dour, voluble and intransigent figure of Paisley – has arguably been the one with which viewers in mainland Britain have become most familiar over more than three decades.

Recently, I have taught a module on Theatre and National Identity to a third year group at the University of Warwick. The module examined theatre in Ireland, with two seminars devoted to the North. We looked at plays by Frank McGuinness, Stewart Parker, Gary Mitchell, and Marie Jones, in an attempt to separate out those strands of ideas around national identity which apply more directly to the Protestant and Unionist cultures found in Northern Ireland. As an exercise, at the end of the module, I asked the students to draw up two lists. Both were to consist of up to five adjectives describing how each student saw the Ulster Protestant, one list based on the plays we had examined, the second on images and opinions drawn from wider media – television and radio news, documentaries, newspaper articles. The most frequently used words from this second list were largely predictable: 'angry', 'violent', 'stubborn', 'sectarian', and 'bigoted'; conjured up, one imagines, by media images of bowler hatted and sash-clad men congregating to confront the police in an attempt to march down a stretch of road where they were clearly unwanted. The list based on the students' studies of the plays, however, threw up content which was both more varied and more nuanced: terms such as 'repressed', 'disillusioned', 'lonely', 'introverted' 'regressive', 'confused', and 'divided'. This poll with its admittedly small sample does encapsulate some important points about the perceptions in England of

Ulster Protestant identity. These were, after all, students from various parts of England with only a peripheral, media-centred understanding of the Northern Ireland situation.

Most importantly, it should be noted that any broad-brush approach to grouping all Ulster Protestant, Unionist, and Loyalist opinions into virtually a single identity, which is the case with much UK media coverage, is profoundly misleading. Although, as Brewer points out, 'it is commonplace to argue that Ulster Protestantism is a monolith, striding through Irish history like a leviathan, made stronger by its centrality of purpose and identity',[1] this view from the outside masks a wide variety of both Protestant churches and political unionism. There are a plethora of churches ranging from mainstream Presbyterian and Anglican, through Baptist, Methodist, Congregationalist, and tens of other tiny groups, to the hellfire preaching and anti-papist demagoguery of Free Presbyterianism. Similarly, the once dominant version of political unionism, the Ulster Unionist Party, has fragmented on a number of occasions, finally resulting in the party's remnant being reduced to just one MP at the recent General Election. It is more useful to think of Ulster's Protestants as occupying positions on a continuum, one which is capable of including a range of different expressions of identity from the rugby supporter who travels to Dublin to watch the (all-Ireland) national team play, followed by a few pints in local pubs; to the family travelling from Belfast to Dun Laoghaire to catch the ferry to Fishguard, ensuring before the journey that the car is full of petrol, sandwiches have been packed and flasks filled, so that there will be no reason to spend money across the border and thereby fuel the economy of the hated Republic. Whereas it could be argued that Catholic Nationalism, to a sizeable degree, exists on one faith and two linked political traditions (those of nationalism and republicanism), Ulster Protestantism offers a heterogeneity of beliefs and opinions where political unionists will disapprove of working-class loyalists, loyalists will feel betrayed by political unionism, Presbyterians will regard the Church of Ireland as the embodiment of woolly liberalism and Ian Paisley claims almost papal infallibility.

The divisions within political Unionism have been well laid out by Norman Porter, who identified the differences between what he called 'cultural Unionism' (those who identify themselves in terms of Protestant-Britishness) and 'liberal Unionism' (for which life shared with the rest of the United Kingdom holds more importance than a particular religious element). Porter sets these divisions within a call for a new approach, which he calls 'civic Unionism', which would recognize both the 'Britishness' and 'Irishness' of the people of Northern Ireland. He argues that this is:

> located within a political-philosophical horizon which accommodates questions of cultural identity, liberal emphases on the entitlements of individuals and a substantive understanding of politics in which the practice of dialogue is central.[2]

At the time of writing, when majority Unionism is represented by the DUP (who became the largest party at the last election) such advocacy would appear to be little more than wishful thinking. However, much of my current research suggests that all across Northern Ireland there are many people within Protestant communities who have found that the results of the Peace Process that began with the ceasefires of 1994 have led to a new stream of self-questioning about who they actually are. This can be seen in a range of activities from the increase in membership of the Ulster-Scots Society, to the growth and development of the network of community arts organizations in Protestant working-class areas – something which has lagged far behind similar movements in nationalist areas. In looking at where the theatre fits in with this cultural self-reappraisal, it is worth noting that traditionally, the Protestants of Ulster have had something of an ambivalent relationship with theatrical representation. Christopher Morash has drawn our attention to, as he puts it:

> the existence of an Ulster Protestant theatre tradition extending from eighteenth-century productions of *The Battle of Aughrim*, through countless amateur productions in Orange Halls, to more interrogatory works by writers like Stewart Parker and Graham Reid in the late 1970s and 1980s.[3]

However, it is equally true that the majority of playwrights, actors, and directors currently working in the North are from a Catholic background,[4] that the only producing repertory theatre in Northern Ireland (The Lyric in Belfast) was founded with a nationalist ethos, and that time and again research interviewees from Protestant communities have told me that the theatre is, somehow, not for them.

The position of the Lyric Theatre is an interesting one, in that although its long history of production in Belfast has seen it take on the mantle of an artistic institution within Northern Ireland, the founders, Mary and

Pearse O'Malley, who moved from Dublin to Belfast in the 1940s, sought specifically to organize theatrical presentations which were non-indigenous in nature. Roy Connolly sets out the relevance of this background when he writes that 'For the O'Malleys the Lyric stage…provided an important counter-hegemonic space where their preferred reality could be realized and embedded in the local consciousness.'[5]

The hegemony referred to here is that of Britishness and Ulster Unionism, and the counter-hegemonic activity took the form of the theatre's celebration of cultural and historic landmarks in the Republic of Ireland (such as the fiftieth anniversary of the Easter Rising in Dublin) while ignoring similar landmarks associated with the Northern Ireland state, alongside a theatrical programme which privileged playwrights from the south over those from the north. As Connolly points out: during the Lyric's first, seventeen-year-long amateur incarnation, 'out of 180 plays produced only four were by Northern Irish writers'.[6] Connolly goes on to note that this state of affairs continued after the theatre became a professional one in 1968:

> With the exception of producing works by John Boyd (who had a formal relationship with the theatre as its Literary Advisor), the Lyric conspicuously ignored the submissions of other Ulster writers including Stewart Parker, Graham Reid, Stewart Love and Robin Glendinning. It chose instead to champion the work of a succession of dramatists from the Republic.[7]

I would argue that the behaviour of the Lyric in its early decade exemplifies the double-bind in which writers from a Protestant background whose work stages debates around Protestant issues in Ireland – they are fewer in number to begin with than their counterparts from a Catholic/Nationalist tradition, already operating in a small, Northern pool largely disregarded by the Lyric in favour of playwrights from the Republic. In addition, those playwrights who are present find it more difficult to achieve main stage professional production in Northern Ireland. Although the Lyric has seen, in the post-O'Malley period, artistic leadership largely in the hands of incomers from England and Scotland, this trend has remained. For example, the reputation of Gary Mitchell, the one playwright to have emerged from the Protestant working class in Belfast over the last fifteen years, was founded in Dublin, cemented in London with only two commissions and subsequent premieres at the Lyric Theatre, Belfast, in the form of *Tearing the Loom* (1998) and *Marching*

On (2000). Indeed, the London stage has been crucial to the formation of Mitchell's reputation as a writer, his plays having been staged at the Royal Court, the Tricycle, and the Donmar Warehouse as well as his being made Writer in Residence at the Royal National Theatre in 1998.

Turning to the relationship between the theatre and Protestant communities in Northern Ireland, the early stages of my research show that this relationship is, at best, somewhat unenthusiastic. For example, both the Artistic Director of the Lyric and the manager of the Waterside Theatre in Derry[8] remarked on how difficult it was to get Protestant schools involved in theatre outreach programmes.[9] Such programmes were enthusiastically taken up by Catholic schools when offered yet uptake on the Protestant schools was dependent on the key involvement of individual teachers who already had an interest in the theatre. In both cities, outreach schemes which were offered equally to both communities were taken up 70%-80% by Catholic schools. At the Waterside, free tickets were on offer for a performance by a children's theatre company called Life of Pie in October 2004. When an audience analysis was done in terms of where schools were coming from to see the performance, it was discovered that half of them were Catholic schools that had travelled over the border from County Donegal. Schools travelling from predominantly Catholic/Nationalist places such as Strabane, Castlederg and Omagh, 'were prepared to travel thirty, thirty-five or forty miles' as Ian Barr put it, 'but with only one local Waterside school attending'.[10] Records on the involvement of community groups show such involvement to follow that found with the schools. The marketing director at the Lyric told me that responses she received from Protestant community groups demonstrated that 'there was a kind of prejudice against this place because of what the Lyric means. People would say 'It's not our kind of venue. It's not going to do our kind of play.'[11] This discrepancy has been taken up in a report commissioned by one of the Protestant community's arts organizations, the Ballymacarratt Arts and Cultural Society, which was entitled *Prods can't act, sing or dance*. In the foreword to this report, the society's cultural development worker, George Newell wrote of its title that:

> this saying is one many people in Protestant areas interested in arts and culture may be familiar with, as it was the common view of previous generations. Any young Protestant interested in arts, culture or drama could well have been warned off from artistic pursuits by constant repetition of this phrase.[12]

Actor and playwright (and from a Protestant background) Tim Loane offered an interesting angle on this point when he described Belfast as a:

> city built upon industry, upon nuts and bolts, ropes and steelworks. The psyche of the city, the psyche of the North of Ireland, is one that is about concrete things to do with certainty and belief and faith and unshakeable things ... so that psyche does not lend itself to creative writing, or creativity in many ways, because creativity is asking questions, raising doubts, saying that there is uncertainty and saying that there are things over and above concrete and steel that are important.[13]

How, then, does this contextual backdrop inform representation of Ulster Protestantism on English stages? Do such representations tend to reaffirm the homogenous image of the dour, bowler-hatted, bigot, convinced of his or her own rectitude and brooking no opposition? Or does (as my tiny *vox pop* would suggest) the more nuanced view of the identity get a hearing, the differences and variety within coming to the fore?

To examine this I will now look at certain character aspects within three plays which have been staged in London over the past thirty years: *Rat in the Skull* by Ron Hutchinson (Royal Court, 1984); *Pentecost* by Stewart Parker (Tricycle Theatre, 1989); and *A Night in November* by Marie Jones (Tricycle Theatre, 1995). There are, of course, notable omissions from this short-list – Frank McGuinness, Gary Mitchell, Christina Reid, Bill Morrison, and Graham Reid spring immediately to mind. To highlight just one example from this excluded list, McGuinness's *Observe the Sons of Ulster Marching Towards the Somme* (1985) is a remarkable play made all the more so by the fact that the author is a Southern Catholic (actually, a Donegal northerner) speaking primarily to his own fellow-countrymen about this strange breed to their north. The play has already been extensively discussed. It is sufficient here to note that, as Nicholas Grene points out, 'McGuinness seeks an understanding of the psychological, spiritual and political ethos of Protestant Unionism, resisting the crude stereotyping of it which has been all too common among Irish nationalists.'[14] I would argue that the play fulfils a similar function for audiences in England, staging a plurality of Ulster Protestant identities. As such, the play works to challenge the situation, noted by Parkinson, in which 'the British public remain perplexed by Ulster's Protestants and this confusion has led to the formation of a number of negative responses'.[15]

Working in reverse chronological order, I will first look at *A Night in November,* a one-handed play which follows the journey of social security clerk, Kenneth McAllister, from sectarianism to salvation. He abuses his position by deeming a (Catholic) claimant to be unavailable for work because by taking his mother down to Dublin on the train he is technically out of the country. He gloats to his (again Catholic) boss over getting membership of the golf club – which operates a discreet Protestant-only policy. He then attends a World Cup qualifying match in Belfast between Northern Ireland and the Republic alongside his foul-mouthed and deeply bigoted father-in-law Ernie, who regards the visitors as representing not their country but the IRA. At the height of the match, the father-in-law leads chants of 'Trick or Treat' and 'Greysteel seven Ireland nil' going round the ground, a reference to the Greysteel massacre at Hallowe'en 1993 when seven Catholics were gunned down in a bar. This is Kenneth's 'Damascus' moment. He says: 'I felt sick, I felt such shame...ashamed of him, ashamed that I'd married someone who came from him, ashamed of standing in the same place as men like him.'[16]

The play concludes with Kenneth flying off to the United States to follow the Republic's team in the finals alongside a group of Irish supporters he describes as: 'This wild and wonderful harmless celebration of human beings just simply bringing out the best in themselves ... just a parade of the best there is in human nature' (107). The very last words he speaks summarize the journey he has made: 'I am a Protestant Man, I'm an Irish Man' (108).

The play manages to interweave a clear and simple set of binaries such as 'Protestant-Catholic', 'good-bad', and 'desirable-undesirable'. The Catholic characters are presented entirely in a positive light whereas the Protestants are projected as mean-spirited at best, violently sectarian at worst. Jones constructs the notion that if only Ulster Protestants could embrace their underlying Irishness then the scales would drop from their eyes and they would be able to take their rightful place at the heart of the everlasting celebration that is the Irish nation. That this was less than convincing can be read in reviews of the London production. Brian Logan wrote in the *Guardian* that 'Jones fails to persuade us that Ireland's fractured identity is so easily resolved'[17] and Charles Spencer in the *Daily Telegraph* called it a 'self-congratulatory wallow in liberal guilt'.[18] Critical responses such as these show that, in England, the simplicity of the scenario presented in the play was queried. In Ireland, however, performances of the play were greeted with both critical acclaim and public adulation. Margaret Llewellyn-Jones notes that when the play was performed in Dublin, 'there was a long, standing ovation for this performance of a hybrid identity'.[19] Whether such a 'hybrid identity' exists is, I would contend, at the very least open to question. I interviewed a (self-declared) Protestant and Loyalist theatre producer who attended that performance in Dublin and who, far from being moved to ovation, found himself glued to his seat at the end. He told me that he 'watched as eight hundred people stood and cheered at the end of that show'. He not only failed to recognize the cultural representation on stage, but felt specifically excluded from it; 'I felt as though my insides were being ripped out.'[20]

In 1974 an amalgamation of Unionist Politicians, Protestant workers and Loyalist Paramilitaries organized a strike which successfully brought down the power-sharing executive set up in Northern Ireland. This period forms the background to Stewart Parker's *Pentecost*, in which four friends in their twenties and thirties, two Catholic, Lennie and Marian, and two Protestant, Ruth and Peter, find themselves trapped in a house by the state of lawlessness on the streets outside. The house has been previously occupied by the recently deceased Lily Matthews, who had lived there for over seventy years, and has now been inherited by Lennie. His estranged wife, Marian, wants to buy the house from him so it can be kept, via the National Trust, as:

> A whole way of life, a whole culture, the only difference being, that this home speaks for a far greater community of experience in this country than some transplanted feeble-minded aristocrat's ever could.[21]

Of the two young Protestant characters, Ruth arrives at the house first having finally run away from her brutalizing policeman husband. Peter, the final arrival, now lives in Birmingham and has developed a 'plague on both your houses' attitude to 'The Troubles'. It is, however, on the character of Lily that I would like to concentrate here. Although she is dead, she appears to Marian three times, a personification of the house in which the play takes place. Parker describes the house in the initial stage directions as 'in spite of now being shabby, musty, threadbare, it has clearly been the object of a desperate, lifelong struggle for cleanliness, tidiness, orderliness – godliness'. (171) The condition of the house stands for the way in which Ulster Protestants have traditionally liked to see themselves and for others to see them. In her first appearance she immediately objects to Marian's Catholicism, saying 'I want no truck with any of yous, stay you with your own and let me rest easy with mine' (181). Her husband, Alfie, was one of only two young men from their street who had returned alive from World War One – a period of iconic reverence to Ulster Protestants – and together they had lived in the house, surviving at one point an attack from a Catholic mob which had destroyed most of their belongings. Lily exhibits all the traits of the bigot; she tells Marian she can 'smell her mass off her'; she makes a reference to 'over-sized' Catholic families as 'runty litters running the streets, whelped by your kind, reared with a half-brick in their fists, and the backsides hanging out of their trousers' (211); and finally she refers to Marian as the Antichrist. Marian finally finds Lily's diary which showed that she had become pregnant by an English airman when Alfie was away looking for work. When the child was born she left it on the doorstep of a Baptist church and the remainder of her life was spent in lonely, tortuous and very Protestant repentance:

> He [God] alone was witness to the torment that I've suffered every living hour in this house where the very walls and doors cry out against me, there was never anybody to tell the knife that went though me a dozen times a day (231).

Although the play ends on an optimistic note, indicating that change for the better is possible, it is also possible to read once more a representation of Protestant characters who come across as negative in comparison with their Catholic counterparts. Only Peter seems able to escape the dourness and drudgery of the Ulster Protestant character, and this has been through a literal escape, across the water to England and, for part of the time, to the United States, where he experienced a stand-off between black students and armed police which he likens to the Northern Ireland situation. His position as an exile gives him the opportunity to comment both from within and without, a perspective which allows him to refer to what is happening to the 'Protestant tribe' with the memorable phrase 'a lingering tribal suicide' (216). Although the play offers a much more nuanced representation of Ulster Protestantism than *A Night in November*, with a richer vein of both personal and political views, it is, I would contend, a play which will resonate very differently with audiences that have grown up with an intimate knowledge of the conditions in Northern Ireland than with those the play faced in London, where audience preconceptions would arguably tend to be amplified and reaffirmed rather than challenged. Indeed, in his review of the 1996

Donmar Warehouse production by Rough Magic, Alastair Macaulay initially talks of finding the play easy to resist because 'it is set in Belfast during the Troubles...a setting that is not my idea of a good night out'.[22] He describes the negative presentation of Lily as 'the embodiment of "respectable" Protestant self-righteousness and bigotry'.[23] Lyn Gardner also uses the word 'bigot' in her review of the same production and goes on to note how Ruth has left her husband 'who batters her with his RUC truncheon'.[24] This would seem to imply that the battering occurs, at least in part, because the assailant is a policeman.

Rat in the Skull, as well as offering a more complex view of the Ulster Protestant than the other plays in this brief examination, also has the benefit of dealing directly with the perceptions held in England about people from Northern Ireland. Roche, a suspected IRA bomber, has been picked up by the police in England under the Prevention of Terrorism Act. An RUC Detective Inspector, Nelson, has been dispatched from Northern Ireland to help in the interrogation. His first words on arrival at the airport indicate that he is aware of how he is regarded in England: 'Belfast-bound or Belfast-been you're set apart. Cut out from the other arrivals and departures. Corralled off. Unclean. Infected. Bearing madness, sweating sin.'[25]

On being taken to see Roche, Nelson ticks off the young English PC for referring to the prisoner as 'Paddy', not because the term, or other such as 'Mickey', 'taig' or 'Fenian bastard' are not to be used, but because 'each one of those has a shade of meaning a beardless sprig like yourself is not capable of understanding' (13). As part of the interrogation Nelson systematically works his way through all the fictions, myths and misperceptions about both Northern Catholics like Roche: 'And off he sets, in a beret two sizes two big, and a borrowed pair of sunshades, to war with a mother's blessing ringing sweetly in his ears, "Fuck those Orange bastards, son"' (15), as well as Northern Protestants like himself:

> Six footers every one, and a fine burly sight of it we make in the back kitchen of an evening, under the ten foot by ten photy of the Queen, helping each other into our uniforms, and stuffing the pork chops and the tatty bread down our gobs off real china plates showing scenes of the Royal Wedding and drinking the tay from Coronation Day Presentation Mugs (16).

Nelson is not speaking here for Roche's benefit, but for that of his English audience. His construction and subsequent undermining of Northern Ireland's stereotypes is for the ears of the English audience who hold those stereotypes – PC Naylor, the audience sharing the interrogation room and, by extension, those occupying the stalls of the Royal Court Theatre.

Nelson manages to break down Roche's stance of silence not through traditional interrogation methods, but by talking about Irish history, initially by a reference to de Valera's telegram of condolence to the German government on the death of Hitler. Roche, to whom this is news, is forced by his incredulity to enter into a conversation with his interrogator. However, the play is not centrally about staging a debate between representatives of the two sides in Northern Ireland. What it examines is how the situation and its participants are viewed from the outside, and from England in particular. The English audience are shown, as Billington notes, how 'Irish Catholics and Protestants are bound together by history and a fierce pride in a way that the English will never comprehend.'[26] Nelson sends the young PC off to get some tea and, left alone with Roche, assaults him, which results in the case falling apart. The key encounter is the subsequent one between Nelson and Superintendent Harris, who is investigating the assault. Harris states his view that there are:

> the two brands of Paddy, in your little corner in the north. It's my job to know. I can by now almost, not quite, tell you apart by looking ... acquaintance with your lot Nelson, wonderfully enlarges one's understanding of the animal that's in us all. With all his instincts still in tact, the pelt still bristling under the string vest and Burton's suit (26).

Harris sums up the official English line on Ulster's Protestants when he describes material from the Hendon police training manual for officers preparing for any engagement with the Northern Ireland conflict: 'Narrow, bigoted, thrifty, ambitious and tough, a grim stern people, powerful for good and evil' (26). This is the view that Hutchinson allows Nelson to playfully subvert. The audience sees, at first glance, a career RUC detective who mouths the expected anti-Catholic sentiments and ends up assaulting an IRA prisoner – everything appears to follow the script. But at all times, Nelson is playing his own game with his English colleagues, wrong-footing their expectations and constantly writing and re-writing a text of his own. Nelson understands Roche, a member of the tribe with whom his own tribe is at war. What he also recognizes is that the British, the larger tribe to which his own Ulster Protestants claim allegiance, do not recognize or understand them at all. *Rat in the Skull* is a deeply nuanced play, which asks a series of difficult questions about how identity is approached, worn and performed. On the occasions when one thinks one has an identifiable handle on what is making Nelson tick, the moment is subverted and slides away. Although the play predates the current round of political negotiations by more than a decade, it anticipates some of the debates around cultural identity within Protestant communities discussed in my introductory section.

It may well be that, in light of the previously noted lack of production opportunities in Northern Ireland, the option of 'Irish theatre in England' is even more important for playwrights who endeavour to stage issues around Ulster Protestantism than it is for other Irish writers. English theatres (alongside theatres in the Republic) still seem to offer the best opportunity for professional main stage production. It is clear how far the ambivalent relationship between Protestant communities and culture (in general) and the theatre (in particular) affects the writing of plays, their eventual staging and the reception they receive within the community which is being staged. It may be that in representational terms, the Protestants of Ulster need to decide whether they exist in a vicious or a virtuous cycle. If the former, cultural expression will go on much as before and the wider world will see the same characters too infrequently and in two dimensions. If the cycle is to be virtuous, not only must the heterogeneity and pluralism that exists within various aspects of Protestantism, Unionism, and Loyalism be allowed to come more to the fore, but it will be for the people themselves to adopt a more outgoing vision of cultural self-presentation and to accept in greater numbers, that theatre is indeed, somehow, for them. As Stewart Parker, Ron Hutchinson and, most recently, Gary Mitchell, have found, the paradox remains that rather than within Northern Ireland, such theatrical representations must be steered to the stages of the Royal Court, the Tricycle, the Donmar Warehouse, and others in England.

---

[1] John D. Brewer, 'Continuity and Change in Contemporary Ulster Protestantism', *The Sociological Review*, vol. 52, no. 2, May 2004: 268.
[2] Norman Porter, *Rethinking Unionism*, (Belfast: Blackstaff Press, 1998): xvii.
[3] Christopher Morash, *A History of Irish Theatre, 1601-2000* (Cambridge: Cambridge University Press 2002): 260.
[4] This statement is anecdotal in nature – it is based, however, on the author's involvement with the Lyric Drama Studio from 1979-1981, his full-time employment at the Lyric Theatre between 1990 and 1999, and his involvement with Equity with five years as chair of the Northern Ireland Committee and four years as Northern Ireland Councillor on the governing body of the national union.

5 Roy Connolly, 'Making Institutions: The Cultural Identity of the Lyric Theatre, Belfast', *Irish Studies Review*, vol. 11, no. 3, 2003: 309.
6 Ibid., 311.
7 Ibid.
8 The Waterside area of Derry is on the East Bank of the Foyle River, and is predominantly Protestant and Unionist. The Cityside area, which takes in the old walled city, is almost entirely Catholic and Nationalist.
9 Interviews with Paula McFetridge, Artistic Director Lyric Theatre Belfast, 16 February 2005, and Ian Barr, General Manager, Waterside Theatre Derry, 19 November 2004.
10 Interview with Ian Barr, General Manager, Waterside Theatre Derry, 19 November 2004.
11 Interview with Una NicEoin, Education Officer, Lyric Theatre Belfast, 16 November 2004.
12 Brid Ruddy, *Prods can't Act, Sing or Dance* A Report of the work of the Ballymacarrett Arts and Cultural Society, 2000.
13 Interview with Tim Loane, actor, writer and director, 18 February 2005.
14 Nicholas Grene, *The Politics of Irish Drama* (Cambridge: Cambridge University Press, 1999): 247.
15 Alan F. Parkinson, *Ulster Loyalism and the British Media*, (Dublin: Four Courts Press, 1998): 12.
16 Marie Jones *A Night in November* (London: Nick Hern Books, 2000): 71. Subsequent references are cited in the text.
17 Brian Logan, 'A Night in November', *The Guardian*, 13 July 2002: 25.
18 Charles Spencer, *Daily Telegraph*, 13 July 2002: 21.
19 Margaret Llewellyn-Jones, *Contemporary Irish Drama and Cultural Identity*, (Bristol: Intellect 2002): 145.
20 Interview with Jonathan Burgess, theatre producer, 19 November, 2004.
21 Stewart Parker, *Plays* 2, (London: Methuen 2000): 208. Subsequent references are cited in the text.
22 Alastair Macaulay, 'An Odd Foursome', *Financial Times*, 10 September 1996: 15.
23 Ibid.
24 Lyn Gardner, 'Mothers who care too much', *The Guardian*, 12 September, 1996: 9.
25 Ron Hutchinson, *Rat in the Skull* (London: Methuen, 1984): 10. Subsequent references are cited in the text.
26 Michael Billlington, 'First Night: Pride, Prejudice and Ritual Revenge', *The Guardian* 12 October 1995: 2.

1 G.B. Shaw's *John Bull's Other Island* as staged at 10 Downing Street, 30 June 1911

2 Aubrey Beardsley's poster for the 1894 production of W. B. Yeats's
The Land of Heart's Desire.

TRUST

GARY MITCHELL

3 The cover of the English publication of Gary Mitchell's *Trust*, staged at the Royal Court Theatre Upstairs, from 11 March 1999. (Courtesy of Nick Hern Books.)

4 Detail of flyer for performance of Thomas Kilroy's *Double Cross* at the Royal Court Theatre, London, May 1986. (Courtesy of Field Day Theatre.)

5 Brian Friel's *Dancing at Lughnasa* as staged by the Abbey Theatre Dublin showing the set design by Joe Vaněk from 24 April 1990. (Courtesy of Joe Vaněk.)

6 Subsequent restaging of the Abbey production of *Dancing at Lughnasa* at the Lyttelton Theatre, Royal National Theatre, London, from 15 October 1990. (Courtesy of Joe Vaněk.)

7 Revival of *Dancing at Lughnasa* at the Gate Theatre Dublin from 24 February 2004. (Courtesy of Gate Theatre: image by Paul McCarthy.)

Part Two: Performance And Performativity

8 | The English/Irish Ring and Its Victorian Popularity

Jerry Nolan

The English/Irish Ring entered the British musical repertoire as a result of the practice of Victorian operatic companies, who often presented three very popular operettas in sequence, during the last quarter of the nineteenth century. At first, the sequence was known as the English Ring, but gradually it became better known as the Irish Ring. The operettas brought together were Michael William Balfe's *The Bohemian Girl*, William Vincent Wallace's *Maritana*, and Julius Benedict's *The Lily of Killarney*. The composers of these works never envisaged anything like such a Ring Cycle, which nevertheless became popular with music-lovers in opera houses throughout the world, and continued to be frequently performed in Britain into the twentieth century by companies like the Carl Rosa Opera Company.

The Bohemian Girl was first produced at Drury Lane Theatre on 27 November, 1843 when Julius Benedict was the musical director there and had invited Michael William Balfe, a much travelled Dubliner, to conduct the first performance with stage direction by Alfred Bunn. Balfe's operetta, using the bare bones of a story which can be traced back to Cervantes, was given a hurried and somewhat misleading title because the heroine was an Austrian who had been raised as a gypsy, a fact which the English title obscures with its mistranslation of the French term 'bohemienne', which means 'Gypsy Girl', (although the operetta's setting was, indeed, Bohemia). In spite of some harsh reviews from the London critics, *The Bohemian Girl* ran for more than a hundred performances and that success was quickly followed by German, Italian, and French performances which ensured the European-wide and American popularity of *The Bohemian Girl*.

Maritana was by William Vincent Wallace (1812-65), an extremely widely-travelled Waterford man. First produced at Drury Lane on 15 November 1845, with Alfred Bunn again as stage director, its tale, based on a French play, was set in Spain and told the story of a Spanish street singer who became intriguingly involved with the King of Spain. While the critic of *The Athenaeum*, H.F. Chorley, feeling very unimpressed by the display of musical eclecticism, dismissed Wallace as in search of a style amid his half dozen of different manners, *Maritana* was an immediate success with the public and was soon being produced in Vienna, Hamburg, Prague, Sydney, and Cape Town.

Julius Benedict, who had been involved in the performances of both *The Bohemian Girl* and *Maritana* at their London premieres, composed music for *The Lily of Killarney* with its libretto adapted from a recent play by Dion Boucicault, the remarkable Dubliner who was bestriding the Atlantic Ocean as actor/author rather in the manner of a popular modern celebrity. Benedict's operetta, his most successful work, reflected in music the strengths of Boucicault's version of the story of the traumatic love of an Irish squire for his Irish peasant lover. *The Lily of Killarney* was first produced at Covent Garden in 1862 to great acclaim, after which it was immediately staged at the principal theatres throughout Germany.[1]

The hybrid nature of the three operettas entranced Victorian audiences. The three distinct stories featured: a singing gypsy in Bohemia, Arline, who was an Austrian; a famous street singer, Maritana, native to Spain; and a Colleen Bawn, Eily O'Connor, an Irish peasant beauty. Two of the composers of the operettas were cosmopolitan Irish – Balfe and Wallace – and the other composer, Benedict, was a German Jew who had settled in London to become the darling of the Victorian musical establishment. Obviously impresarios became aware of a few publicity advantages to a reference to Wagner's *Der Ring des Nibelungen*, as they promoted as the 'English Ring' the three operettas whose premieres had all been staged in London. Only gradually did English, Irish, European, and American lovers of the operettas become increasingly convinced, that in spite of the sheer eclecticism of the works – perhaps even because of such a rampant eclecticism? – the works were essentially Irish! One contributory factor to such a view may well have been that when the memorable songs were detached from the operettas in recitals, they sounded to the ear of the music lovers, very much in the tradition of Thomas Moore's *Melodies*. Soon Moore's most popular melodies such as 'The Last Rose of Summer', 'The Harp that Once Through Tara Halls', and 'The Minstrel Boy' began to be sung side-by-side with selections of songs from the Irish Ring such as Balfe's 'I dreamt I dwelt in marble halls' and 'Love smiles but to deceive'; Wallace's 'Tis the harp in the air' and 'Yes! let me like a soldier die'; and Benedict's 'The Moon has raised her lamp above' and 'Eily Mavoureen'. Many songs from the Irish Ring entered the repertoire of the concert hall and drawing room world, where a growingly ubiquitous band of Irish tenors, including James Joyce's father and John McCormack, sang the melodies to very appreciative audiences especially, though not exclusively, among the Irish middle-class – the world poignantly evoked in Joyce's description of Miss Morkham's party in 'The Dead' (*Dubliners*).

Moore, whose *Melodies* audiences began to link with the Ring, was the son of a Dublin merchant and grocer from Aungier Street and one of the first Catholics educated at Trinity College Dublin. He made his lasting mark as a London émigré on those levels of English society who adored Lord Byron, and the *Melodies* are often marginalized by critics who say that they appealed mostly to a sentimental idea of Ireland popular with 'every guilt-ridden voluntary exile'. Yet for very many years after their publication, the melodies of Moore greatly appealed to many who never left home. Indeed, the historical context of the popularity of the melodies, the settings of some 130 poems, composed and published in ten instalments between 1808 and 1834, was very near the very centre of the Irish cultural revival which took place during the first half of the nineteenth century. During his years at Trinity College Dublin, Moore formed close friendships with the United Irishmen, Edward Hudson and Robert Emmet, and an enthusiasm for things distinctively Irish was a strong factor in inspiring Moore's *Melodies*. Moore's later performances of his songs were heard as intensely Irish by London's aristocracy, who saw in the ever performing Moore a great Irish patriot. In 1846 there was a magnificent collected edition published which was illustrated by the outstanding Irish history painter, Daniel Maclise (1806-1870), whose very special contribution was acknowledged in Moore's Preface: 'An Irish pencil has lent its aid to an Irish pen in rendering the honour and homage to our country's ancient harp.'[2]

The image was no mere symbolic flourish; Ireland's ancient harp played a crucial part in Moore's early encounter with the beauties of Irish native music at the Belfast Harp Festival of 1792. The first flush of his enthusiasm was much stimulated by *A General Collection of the Ancient Music*, collected by Edward Bunting and published in 1796.[3] However, Bunting declined to provide the ancient airs for Moore's words and Sir John Stevenson was commissioned to do so by William Power, the Dublin music-seller. Like many future Irish musicologists, Bunting was uneasy about aspects of the Stevenson versions: 'The beauty of Mr. Moore's words in a great degree atones for the violence done by the musical arranger to many of the airs which he has adopted.'[4] The impact of Moore's *Melodies* was much more than musical because they were to become the inspiration of much iconography in Irish art throughout the nineteenth century. One of Moore's key nationalist melodies was 'The Origin of the Harp', which was superbly illustrated by Maclise. The harp became the archetypal Irish musical instrument and a symbol of Irish cultural nationalism. In the age of Moore's *Melodies*, there was the significant replacement of the 'formalized winger-maiden' harp of ascendancy Ireland topped by the imperial crown by more realistic images of the early Irish harp to represent music-making among all the Irish.[5] Eventually the Society for the Preservation and Publication of the Melodies of Ireland was founded in 1850 with George Petrie as its first President.[6]

Frederic William Burton played a significant part in the propagation of the rediscovery of Irish origins. During a tour of the West by the antiquarians in 1840, Burton sketched Paddy Conneely, the Galway Piper, for George Petrie – Conneely is depicted playing the Irish uileann (elbow) pipes - and the piper joined the harper as an exemplar for Irish musicians. Burton produced a most arresting watercolour 'The Aran Fisherman's Drowned Child' in 1841, establishing (a good half-century before Synge) an image of how Aran seemed to represent the ages of life in pre-Famine Ireland – an iconic image which has not yet been widely explored by cultural historians.[7] Burton, a friend of Thomas Davis, designed a memorable frontispiece in 1845 for the very widely read collection of verses by the Young Ireland writers for *The Nation* newspaper. One of the last significant events in that first Irish cultural revival occurred in 1857 when Sir William Wilde organized a group sailing from Galway to Inishmore, on board the Galway Hooker, which was a grand reunion of the most prominent enthnologists and antiquaries, with the Provost of

Trinity College there to preside over their formal meetings. Many local singers were invited on board the Hooker, or turf boat, and sang while George Petrie, antiquary and painter, played on his violin and noted down the music; and Eugene O'Curry, old Celtic scholar, wrote down the words in Irish which Whitely Stokes, young Celtic scholar, then wrote down in English. Back on the islands, Frederic Burton painted watercolours of the islanders and Samuel Ferguson, poet and archivist, sketched ruins and antiquarian objects.[8]

The fact that Irish peasant life was being researched and enthusiastically appreciated by the antiquarians as the link with the Celtic past on an island was largely being ignored by the English public.[9] What that public was made most aware of was the recurring image of the Irishman in *Punch* cartoons which featured Paddy as a retarded creature with low forehead, bulging eyes, heavy jaw, and slobbering mouth – clearly on a low level of the evolutionary ladder![10] One Punch cartoon by Leech, published on 8 April 1848, bore the headline: 'The British Lion and the Irish Monkey'.[11] Bridging the gulf between the English perception of the Irish as apes and Young Ireland's perception of their ancestors as akin to the gods lay at the root of Dion Boucicault's Irish plays *The Colleen Bawn* (1860), *Arrah-na-Pogue* (1864), *The Shaughraun* (1874), and *Robert Emmet* (1884). The performance of these plays enabled Boucicault in middle age to transcend the world of Victorian theatricals by writing and appearing in plays which trenchantly challenged the Irish world according to *Punch*.[12]

The Colleen Bawn was first staged in New York at Laura Keene's Theatre on 29 March 1860 and then staged at the Adelphi Theatre, London, on 10 September 1860 for a run of 278 performances, then a record. It was the last play which Queen Victoria saw three times during February and March 1860 before she went into a long mourning after the deaths in quick succession of her mother and husband.[13] According to most reports, the audiences (including the Queen) responded well to Boucicault's overall view of Ireland. Indeed, his wide-sweeping and masterly melodramatic panache called out for much more music. Boucicault had already included the songs: 'Oh, Limerick is beautiful', 'Cruiskeen Lawn', 'Pretty Girl Milking her Cow', and 'Brian O'Linn'; but the music of Thomas Baker would pale before the songs in Benedict's *The Lily of Killarney,* which were credibly transferred to the picturesque region of County Kerry, already known from popular engravings.[14] The

Lily of Killarney was destined to become the third operetta in the English/Irish Ring and would provide the clinching argument for audiences that the Ring was quintessentially Irish; its flow of Irish music and sentiment moving gracefully through the Bohemia of Balfe and the Spain of Wallace until it was at last all brought back home in terms of setting and characters to the Ireland of Boucicault and Benedict. Yet *The Lily of Killarney* also contained an inner drama capable of touching raw nerves, especially among Irish audiences, which stemmed from the fact that the operetta's ultimate source was Gerald Griffin's novel of 1829, *The Collegians*.[15]

In Griffin's story, written during his time in London, the squire Hardress Cregan secretly marries the beautiful peasant girl, Eily O'Connor. When Cregan changes his mind, he suggests to his faithful hunchbacked servant Danny that Eily should be dispatched to America to join her father in pleasant exile. Shortly afterwards, Eily's dead body is found in a pool, and her murder becomes a crime to be solved. When Cregan meekly follows his widowed mother's command to become engaged to Anne Chute, a girl of his own class, he suffers agonies of remorse over Eily's death because he knows that he simultaneously deeply loved her and wanted her to die. Cregan clashes with his mother when he confides to her his innermost thoughts and feelings, which she disdainfully brushes to one side. The hunchback Danny is arrested and, when questioned, tries to incriminate his master who is then arrested at the reception organized for his wedding to Anne Chute. Cregan is tried, exiled, and dies on board the convict ship. Griffin saw Cregan's fate mainly as a result of his immature susceptibility to the influences about him, especially his subservience to the arbitrary will of his mother. The most powerful emotions portrayed in the novel are the feelings of guilt and anguish within Cregan whose other emotions of friendship for his fellow collegian, Kyrle Daly, tortuous love of poor Eily, and utilitarian attachment to Anne are much more sketchily depicted.

Griffin's biographer, John Cronin, has concluded that *The Collegians* was Griffin's greatest work because it had a hero whose psychology paralleled the author's own.[16] Ethel Mannin has suggested that the artist in Griffin was frustrated by his Catholic moralism – apparent in his failure to explore Cregan's feelings for Eily and Anne – but also notes that Griffin told his brother (and future biographer) Daniel that he could see Edmund Kean playing Cregan at the wedding party just before his arrest for murder, so despite pious restraint Griffin himself sensed the theatrical possibilities of the work.[17] Boucicault's interest in the novel led to the construction of the drama around Cregan's predicament, with most emphasis on the intrigue between mother and servant, the impact of the threats from the agent Corrigan, and the great unease generated by the match-made marriage necessary to secure the future of Torc Cregan. Mrs. Cregan's enthusiasm for the Anne Chute solution signals to Danny Mann the need to dispose of the Colleen Bawn. But in Boucicault's adaptation, Eily's life is saved and Myles-na-Coppaleen, a minor character in Griffin, is transformed into a major character crafted to be played by Boucicault himself. Myles – masterful poacher, outlaw, and rank social outsider – shoots dead Danny Mann before he has the time to push Eily deeper into the lake. This shooting of Danny produced one of the most sensational *mise-en-scène* in all Victorian theatre – the so-called scene of the 'watery grave' with Boucicault himself as an Irish incarnation of a Prospero orchestrating the staged revels. Myles's immediate explanation of Danny's death as an accident – he thought he was shooting an otter at the time! – is believed by all for the greater good of the local community. Myles hides Eily whom he loves but who really still loves the undeserving landed squire Cregan. The magnanimous act of the vagabond's surrender of Eily to Cregan conjured up a fleeting yet memorable image of a kind of harmony in rural Ireland, offered as the only effective alternative to the destructive schemings of the Cregan matriarch.

The plotting of events in Griffin's original novel was based on sensational events which had actually happened. Early one morning towards the end of July 1819 the body of a young woman was washed ashore near Kilrush, County Clare – the dead woman was later identified as Ellen Hanley from Ballygahane, County Limerick, a sixteen year old girl who had disappeared from the home of her uncle and guardian and who was then secretly married in a mock wedding to the son of a local gentry family, Lieutenant John Scanlan. Eventually Scanlan was arrested for murder when a soldier searched the family castle, and Scanlan's boatman and devoted henchman, Stephen Sullivan, was also tracked down to Tralee Goal in County Kerry, where he was being held under another name for passing off forged banknotes. After two trials, both men were hanged for the murder – Scanlan in March and Sullivan in July 1820. The trial attracted enormous interest largely because Daniel O'Connell, the Catholic Liberator, defended Scanlan by arguing that Sullivan was the sole murderer without the complicity of his master. Griffin who may well have attended the trials as a young reporter, expressed sympathy with Cregan, his version of Scanlan, because he saw him as the victim of an overambitious mother who bullied him to marry Anne Chute within his own class: unlike Scanlan in life, Cregan escaped the hangman's noose, but he did not survive long on board the convict ship.[18] Griffin's budding interest in the case, unlike Boucicault's later interest, was to represent in *The Collegians* in his novel a personal impression of the entire structure of provincial Irish society of his day: the Chutes of Castle Chute, the Cregans of Roaring Hill, the strong farmers, the Dalys, torn between feelings for the Gaelic past and the Anglo-Irish present, the English of the Garrison, the peasants, the landless men, the horse traders, the boatmen. The novel's subtitle was 'A Tale of Garryowen' and Griffin wrote that 'the days of Garryowen are gone, like those of ancient Erin; and the feats of her once formidable heroes are nothing more than a winter's evening tale.' A debate rages throughout the novel between the present and the past which runs the gamut from abuse to satire, from invective to geniality. It was such realism in Griffin's novel that led the culturally 'monocular' Daniel Corkery to damn Griffin as 'the type of non-Ascendancy writer who under the stress of moulds of his time wrote Colonial Literature.'[19] On the contrary, Griffin's novel teemed with evidence which exposed the ailing body and tortured soul of rural Ireland between the Union and the Great Famine: the country's declining native language, the after-effects of the savage Penal Code, the Catholic middle class emerging without an Irish Parliament, memories of the failed 1798 Insurrection and Emmet's heroic gesture, a disturbed age of Rackrents and Whiteboys, the many emigrants drifting abroad. Corkery failed to see how Griffin had managed to write a tragic novel about pre-Famine Ireland, a sense of tragedy which prompted Griffin himself to give up writing in 1838 and to join the order of the Christian brothers where he tragically died of typhus fever in 1840, at the early age of forty-one.

Many rumblings about how the Irish nation stood surfaced in the whole saga of *The Colleen Bawn*: from its beginnings in the infamous murder trial in Limerick which led to the hanging of a squire and his lackey in 1819, in spite of the Kerryman Daniel O'Connell's spirited defence of the squire; through to Griffin's version of the events as a national tragedy; its transformation into the energetic romanticism of Boucicault's play and then even more so in Benedict's operetta. *The Lily of*

Killarney celebrated in memorable fashion a visionary union of the gentry and the peasantry in County Kerry, encapsulating something of that vein of idealism which was one of the striking characteristics of an ever reviving Irish spirit over many centuries, but associated in this period with the ideals of the contrasting expressions of that spirit in the works of Moore and Boucicault. Time's inevitable critical reversals of reputation have occurred in the instances of Moore and Boucicault, a reversal which has spread to an obscuring of the full significance of the pioneering enthusiasms and discoveries of the whole generation of Irish antiquarian scholars inquiring into the language, customs, and music of Connacht.

The Victorian popularity of Moore's *Melodies* has caused them to be viewed by the twentieth-century Irish critical establishment as amounting to little more than symptoms of the 'bourgeois' and the intellectually undemanding nature of Moore's cultural nationalism, a view which conveniently ignores their historic appeal across all classes and ages. Perhaps the decisive factor in this view is the unquestioning acquiescence in the canon of Irish poetry laid down by W.B. Yeats. Inspired by Yeats, the true believers' conclusions run as follows: 'Any selection of poems from Irish writers of poetry of the nineteenth century is bound to be bedevilled by the discrepancy between the quality of some of the poems and their representative status. More bluntly, it may be said that some of the best-known poems are, to present-day tastes, among the worst...propagandist, full of standard clichés and rhythmic vulgarities.' Not only is Thomas Davis named as the chief offender but Moore is found guilty of effectively exploiting 'infantile romanticism' and even Moore's poetic masterpiece, 'Lalla Rookh: An Oriental Romance', which had a most interestingly thinly veiled Irishry, is summarily dismissed as 'of abnormal, languor and longuers'.[20] Seamus Heaney, Ireland's current national poet, has likewise distanced himself from Tom Moore, Ireland's pre-Yeatsian National poet, by quoting James Joyce's *A Portrait of the Artist as a Young Man* for the opinion of Stephen Dedalus who remarks that the memorial statue of Moore on College Green, Dublin, had the indignity of a 'servile head' and little more than 'a Firborg in the borrowed cloak of a Milesian', 'an emblem of nineteenth-century Ireland's cultural and political debilitation.' Heaney then contrasts unfavourably the Tom Moore sculpture in College Green and the Henry Moore semi-abstract sculpture of Yeats in St Stephen's Green which for him at least displays the all conquering Yeats as 'a universal symbolic force, an energy released and a destiny discharged.'[21] Whatever about the relevance of Stephen's remarks to any current questioning of the value of Moore's contribution to the Irish Nation, Joyce - in spite of his declared early sympathy for the poetry of the outsider, James Clarence Mangan - included many references to Moore's *Melodies* in *Ulysses* which suggests to what extent the songs were part of the music-making in Dublin during 1904. There is also a reference in *Ulysses* to a performance on 16 June 1904, by the Elster-Grimes Grand Opera Company at 8.00 pm in The Queen's Theatre, 209 Great Brunswick Street (now Pearse Street), which they announced as 'the Irish opera', *The Lily of Killarney*.[22]

The hostility to the popularity of Tom Moore's poetry in his lifetime was mainly political in motivation. Charles Gavin Duffy mounted a defence of Moore as early as 1842. Duffy wrote before reviewing Moore's life:

> 'But,' said my friend, 'why, in the devil's name, did you put the little Whig into *The Nation*, at all?' 'Because he is an Irishman, of whose genius Ireland is proud, and for whose services she is grateful.'...When the rest of Moore's poems and the music of the Melodies are to be had, his fame will be as great as ever. Our patriots, too, are intolerant with Moore, because he is not all-out Irish...Now, fair play is a jewel. Let us remember what Moore was, and what he has done.'[23]

Perhaps the fact that Moore was an Irish constitutionalist reformer need not now be held too much against him, in a period when the heat of Irish revolutionary republican politics seems to be entering a period of adjustment during which more all-embracing historical perspectives might well appeal to more than the few. Apart from the issue of Moore's poetic nationalism, there has been another discussion among dedicated advocates of Irish traditional music about the 'damage' inflicted on traditional tunes in Moore's *Melodies*, all part of the very specialized debate about Bunting's arrangements of Irish folk tunes in 'the modern art-music system of major and minor keys'.[24] Why stop 'the traditional music' and 'the art music' flourishing side by side in the concert halls and the opera houses?

Boucicault's popularity has suffered a fate similar to Moore's decline of reputation. When W.B. Yeats, Lady Gregory, and Edward Martyn in 1899 founded the Irish Literary Theatre in Dublin to bring about a dramatic shift away from the London to Dublin theatres, they proclaimed 'We will show that Ireland is not the home of buffoonery and of easy sentiment, as it has been represented, but the home of an ancient idealism.'[25] The legacy of *The Colleen Bawn* and *The Lily of Killarney* contained some elements of buffoonery and easy sentiment, only to be expected in the popular genre of Victorian melodrama; but, for all that, Boucicault's Irish plays drew much from an ancient Irish idealism and even more significantly cultivated the seeds of a view of the Irish peasantry much researched during the first Irish cultural revival in the nineteenth century. What damned Boucicault in the eyes of later influential critics was his association with promoting 'the Stage Irishman': 'Boucicault found a formula for buffoonery and sentimentality which it became the mission of J.M. Synge, W.B. Yeats and even Bernard Shaw...to counteract and to replace with an authentic picture.'[26] What can now be seen clearly is the glaring gap in the Irish Dramatic Movement, perpetuated by the policies of the Abbey Theatre, which opened as emerging dramatists failed to learn from the comic idealism of Boucicault's view of the country and the tragic realism of Griffin's anatomy of a crumbling Irish society. In a handful of symbolist plays by Edward Martyn, now largely forgotten, and a slightly larger handful of visionary plays by Synge, often crudely misinterpreted in frequent performances, there was far too little building on the legacy of the antiquarian revival. Perhaps the later revival dramatists, rummaging for inspiration in forms of folk poetic and Ibsenite drama, were put off by Boucicault's stagecraft, given 'the little room' the severely constricted spaces on the Abbey Theatre stage allowed. Nevertheless, his vibrant theatrical language and dramaturgy could have been given a local habitation in the Irish Dramatic Movement, an objective which his immediate pale imitators, like Hubert O'Grady, J.W. Whithead and P.J. Bourke, singularly failed to achieve.[27]

The advent of the cinema was to steal some of Boucicault's clothes when Sidney Olcott, director of Kelem Films, began to film versions of *The Colleen Bawn*, *Arrah-na-Pogue* and *The Shaughraun* on location in County Kerry around 1910 and replaced the famous spectacular stagecraft with camera angles on Killarney's beauty spots while the captions of silent cinema much reduced the dramatic impact of the language. When *The Lily of Killarney* was filmed in 1934 with Stanley Holloway and shot almost entirely in England by Twickenham Studios, apart from tourist prologue views of Killarney, the utterance of Boucicault's Hiberno-English language began to sound like a send-up; and thus was launched the tradition of producing Boucicault's Irish plays as send-ups, so much so that even the very words 'Irish melodrama' became a term of abuse on the lips of many rarefied critics.²⁸ The recent exception to the twentieth century's recurring bad habit of sending up Boucicault's Irish plays in performance was Garry Hynes's 1995 production of *The Colleen Bawn* at the Royal Exchange Manchester which, apart from the spot-on casting and deft use of an arena space, brilliantly incorporated into the action Paddy Cunneen's music vigorously played by a Ceildh Band. Surely even the staunchest defenders of the ambiguous legacy of Yeats can now venture to accept that the much vaunted Irish Dramatic Movement, by failing to absorb the imaginative legacy of Boucicault, fell well short of what might have been realized with a more informed understanding of the rich theatrical tradition that preceded the foundation of the Irish Literary Theatre in 1899?

It seems to be one of the regrettable facts of Ireland's unfolding cultural history that one period's 'canonical' preference of the only authentic style, is inevitably replaced by another 'definitive' version, as the wheel of public taste, driven by new generations of scholarly publicists, continues to turn. In this saga, the role of the independent critic should be to construct a case against factional exclusiveness and in favour of an arguable inclusiveness which draws wisdom from the many very different periods in the history of the arts in Ireland in favour of a cultural plurality. Part of the reason for the falling off in performances and popularity of the English/Irish Ring has to be linked to the changing critical attitudes to Victorian operettas among music lovers world-wide, in the context of the all-conquering grand operas of Wagner, Verdi, and Puccini – unlike Vienna, neither London nor Dublin has learnt to treasure the grand tradition of operetta. Nowadays there can be little doubt that a revival of popular interest in the performance and appreciation of the Ring very much depends on an *Irish* revival of a once important but now undervalued manifestation of Ireland's early nineteenth-century cultural revival on the world stage. So may the day come soon when on the last night of the Irish Ring in cities like Dublin, London, New York, and Sydney, audiences again have the opportunity to experience live the Ring's supreme musical moment approaching its grand conclusion, when Hardress Cregan sings one of the great Irish love songs, composed by the German/Jewish/English Benedict: 'Eily Mavoureen'!

---

[1] See *The Oxford Dictionary of National Biography* [*Oxford DNB*] (Oxford: University Press, 2004-5) for Clive Brown's entries for William Vincent Wallace (1812-1865), Michael William Balfe (1808-1870) and Sir Julius

Benedict (1804-1885). <www.oxfordnb.com>
[2] *Moore's Irish Melodies* (London: Longmans, 1846): a publication with 218 floral borders and many black-and-white illustrations. This illustrated edition has been recently republished in facsimile (New York: Dover Publications, 2000).
[3] See Michael Heaney's entry for Edward Bunting (1773-1843) in *Oxford DNB*.
[4] Quoted by Seamus Deane, 'Thomas Moore (1779-1852)' in *The Field Day Anthology of Irish Writing [FDA]* vol. 1, ed. Seamus Deane (Derry: Field Day Publications, 1991): 1053.
[5] See *Eighteenth-Century Ireland 1998* for Catherine Jones, ' "Our Partial Attachments": Tom Moore and 1798', 24-43; and Barra Boydell, 'The United Irishmen, music, harp and National identity', 44-51.
[6] See *Oxford DNB* for Marie-Louise Legg's entry for George Petrie (1790-1866).
[7] See Marie Bourke's 'The Aran Fisherman's Drowned Child', *The GPA Irish Arts Review Yearbook* 1988: 190-196 which includes colour reproductions of 'Paddy Conneely, the Galway Piper'(pencil and watercolour) and 'The Aran Fisherman's Drowned Child' (water-colour on paper), both in the collection of the National Gallery of Ireland. See also Marie Bourke's 'Rural Life in pre-Famine Ireland: A Visual Document', *Ireland: Art into History*, eds B.P. Kennedy and Raymond Gillespie (Dublin: Town House, 1994): 61-74.
[8] Jeanne Sheehy, *The Rediscovery of Ireland's Past* (London: Thames & Hudson, 1980): 29-30.
[9] See *Oxford DNB* for the following entries: Paul Caffrey on Frederic William Burton (1816-1900), Fergus Kelly on Eugene O'Curry (1794-1862), Paul Denman on Samuel Ferguson (1810-1886), Nollaig O Muraile on Whitley Stokes (1830-1909), James McGeachie on William Wilde (1815-1876).
[10] R.F. Foster, *Paddy and Mr Punch* (London: Allen Lane, 1993): 178-84.
[11] *Drawing Conclusions: A Cartoon History of Anglo-Irish Relations 1798-1998*, eds Roy Douglas, Liam Harte and Jim O'Hara (Belfast: Blackstaff Press, 1998): 47.
[12] For the texts of these plays, with the exception of *Arrah-na-Pogue*, see *Selected Plays of Dion Boucicault*, chosen and introduced by Andrew Parkin (Gerrards Cross: Colin Smythe, 1987). For an extract from *Arrah-na-Pogue*, see *FDA* 2, in the section 'Fenianism 1858-1916', ed. Seamus Deane, 209-31.
[13] Richard Fawkes, *Dion Boucicault: A Biography* (London: Quartet Books, 1979): 122-3.
[14] *The Lily of Killarney*, libretto by John Oxenford & Dion Boucicault with music by Julius Benedict: overture with 22 songs and books of piano arrangements (London: Boosey & Co. 1862).
[15] Gerald Griffin, *The Collegians*, 3 vols (London: Saunders & Otley, 1829).
[16] John Cronin, *Gerald Griffin 1803-1840* (Cambridge: University Press, 1978): 69.
[17] Ethel Mannin, *Two Studies in Integrity* (London: Jarrolds, 1954): 68.
[18] See also the *Limerick Leader*, 8 May 1999, for an article about the local demands for the erection of a Colleen Bawn statue in the locality where she was murdered.
[19] Daniel Corkery, *Synge and Anglo-Irish Literature* (Cork: University Press, 1931): 8-9.
[20] For dismissal of Davis and Moore see *FDA* 2: 1 and 1: 1053-4 respectively.
[21] *FDA2:* 783. See Terence Brown, *Ireland's Literature* (Mullingar: Lilliput Press,

1988): 14-27 for a chorus-line of witnesses testifying that Moore was 'the poet of bland wish-fulfilment' with quoted testimony from various critics including Stopford A. Brooke, W.B. Yeats, Paddy Kavanagh and Tom Paulin.
22 See Don Gifford & R.J. Seidman, *Ulysses Annotated* (Berkeley:University of California Press, 1988), for details in Index of references to Moore's *Melodies*, Boucicault's plays and Benedict's Irish opera.
23 Reproduced in *FDA* 2: 1250-54.
24 Tomás O Canainn, *Traditional Irish Music* (London: Routledge & Kegan Paul, 1978): 14. See also Nuala O'Connor, *Bringing it all back home* (London: BBC Books, 1991): 167.
25 Quoted in R.F. Foster, *W.B. Yeats: A Life, vol 1: The Apprentice Mage 1865-1914* (Oxford: University Press, 1997): 184.
26 *FDA* 2: 505, part of the introduction to the section 'Drama 1690-1800', edited by Christopher Murray.
27 Ben Levitas, *The Theatre of Nation* (Oxford: Clarendon, 2002): 19-26.
28 Kevin Rockett, Luke Gibbons & John Hill, *Cinema and Ireland* (London: Croom Helm, 1987): 7, 212ff., 229.

9 | An Irish Jig? Edris Stannus, Ninette de Valois and the English Royal Ballet

Elizabeth Schafer

In 1957, Ninette de Valois was one of the most powerful people in the world in international classical ballet. Her ballet company, which, after the Second World War, had been invited to make its home at the theatre in Covent Garden, had, in 1956, acquired the 'Royal' stamp of approval, and had been renamed the Royal Ballet;[1] Margot Fonteyn, the company's star dancer, and de Valois' particular protégée, had helped the Royal Ballet conquer America, and thus earned British classical ballet the international respect it had never had before; de Valois' school for training ballet dancers of the future, at White Lodge, Richmond, was thriving. It was at this point in her career that de Valois chose to publish a memoir (partly to raise more funds for the ballet school) and in this memoir she very clearly and very self-consciously constructed herself as Irish.[2]

De Valois' claim was to a very particular kind of Irishness: romantic Celtic Irishness rather than republicanism. However, the claim is thorough and is implicit in the very title of her book: *Come Dance With Me* is taken from W.B. Yeats:

> 'I am of Ireland,
> And the Holy Land of Ireland,
> And time runs on,' cried she.
> 'Come out of charity,
> Come dance with me in Ireland.'[3]

The autobiography devotes its first chapter, entitled 'An Irish Jig', to establishing de Valois' Irish identity: she was born Edris Stannus on 6 June 1898; her family, Anglo-Irish Protestants, had been in Ireland since the early seventeenth century, and they lived at Baltiboys, a large stately home two miles from the village of Blessington, County Wicklow. De Valois' early years were generally happy and stimulating, although her education was Anglicized, and English governesses were hired, partly in an attempt to get rid of the Stannus children's Irish brogues (10). De Valois prefaces, and so contextualizes, anecdotes about her childhood with a declaration of her belief that in childhood 'each hour...is lived in full, and that is a rare event in later life' and that 'In the process of growing up a child soon ceases to be himself, (sic) for he is an atom that the world soon splits asunder' (3). This locates de Valois' Irish childhood as not only seminal but also something of a lost Eden.

Crucially, however, de Valois makes the avowed declaration that Ireland made her a dancer, and that had it not been for an early encounter with the Irish jig, she might never have danced; the implication of this claim is that she might also never have founded the Sadler's Wells Ballet, the English Royal Ballet, she might never have choreographed, she might never have nurtured the careers of dancers such as Fonteyn, Alicia Markova, Robert Helpmann. The catalyst in making de Valois a dancer is, in de Valois' rendition of events, the herdsman's wife, Kate Finnigan, who had formerly been nurse to de Valois' mother:

> In that quiet country existence we were cut off from all communal interests and school life. Memory does not clarify why Kate singled me out and taught me how to execute an authentic Irish jig on the stone floor of that kitchen. If she had not done so, as this book will show, I might never have become a dancer. I adored my jig, for it was my first experience of any self expression (10).

In her work on theatrical memoirs and autobiographies, Jacky Bratton has argued that such anecdotes

> [...] may be understood not simply as the vehicle of more or less dubious or provable facts, but as a process of identity-formation that extends beyond individuals to the group or community to which they belong.[4]

To the dance community of 1956, when de Valois was writing her memoirs, her Irishness was in tension with her French sounding name, and with her position at the centre of English Ballet, but de Valois is categorical in tracing all her achievements back to the foundational moment of this Irish jig. Of course there are questions to be asked here: for example, what, in the first few years of the twentieth century was considered to be 'an authentic Irish jig', as practised in Blessington,

County Wicklow? De Valois is implicitly contrasting the 'authenticity' of what she was taught in the unconventional, unsophisticated dance school of the stone floored kitchen, with less authentic Irish jigs in circulation elsewhere.[5] Whilst the nineteenth century had fostered a great interest in recovering and recording 'authentic' folk culture, music, and dances, and held up access to authenticity as a desideratum, de Valois' claim here for 'authenticity' in her training in the jig might be seen to sit slightly uneasily with her privileged class background. However, as Bratton argues, with anecdotes:

> [...] the testing and probing to which we should subject them should always be aimed at understanding who said what and why, within the context of their own perception of the world (131).

So the authenticity of Kate Finnigan's jig, and the circumstances of her teaching it to Edris Stannus, are less important than the fact that the claim to this authenticity was made so publicly in 1957 by Ninette de Valois.

It is important to register here that, unlike some dancers who, despite their highly trained skills in physical communication, are less interested in verbal communication, de Valois always loved writing, and she wrote tirelessly to promote and advertise her ballet. During her long career de Valois published three books which combined reminiscences and propaganda;[6] she wrote articles for the primary dance publication of the period, *Dancing Times*; in later life she also published poetry. So it seems reasonable to assume that de Valois was acting very self-consciously and deliberately when she located Irish dancing as so seminal in her career. In addition de Valois identifies her first public performance as revisiting this foundational moment: attending children's parties were occasions which the painfully shy Edris usually hated, but on one occasion a Miss Leggatt Byrne performed a dance. De Valois narrates how:

> Something within me underwent a complete change. I forgot the awful party and the crowd of people; a curious critical faculty suddenly arose within me and I found myself consumed with interest, but not overcome with admiration. [Miss Leggatt Byrne] wore a wide accordion-pleated dress edged with lace and my mother informed me that she was executing a skirt dance. (16)

Skirt dancing became extremely popular during the early 1890s. It usually featured 'the dexterous and gentle manipulation of light, long fabrics', and became particularly popular at the Gaiety, the Alhambra and the Empire in London.[7] It became notorious not only because of its potentially erotic overtones but because of the large numbers of amateur dancers displaying their skills, or lack of them, in public. Miss Leggatt Byrne's 'skirt dance' certainly invoked the professional/amateur divide as far as young Edris was concerned and in a moment that de Valois identifies as completely out of character, Edris offered to perform her Irish jig as a response, or riposte, to the 'skirt dance'. The metropolitan fashion, designed merely to foreground the flirtatious charms of the performer, was to face up to the competition of a national dance, rigorously expressive of tradition and community. De Valois claims:

> I experienced no fears; I had no thought for the people surrounding me when I stood in the middle of the room waiting to start. [...] I can remember very distinctly hoping - as a fully-fledged professional might – that [the pianist] would get things right and that she would understand what I wanted. (16)

De Valois' perception of young Edris's incipient professionalism invokes a very popular trope in performers' memoirs and autobiographies and this trope clearly functions to mark out territory:[8] the true professional is distinguishable from the aspiring amateur, whereas in real life this distinction often becomes blurred. However, de Valois also marks out territory in her denigration of the skirt dance she witnessed, when she sums up the incident in heavily value-laden terms, terms which implicitly privilege Irishness: the child Edris 'sensed the difference between an exhibition of fancy dancing and an authentic National dance' (73).

Not all of de Valois' early encounters with dance in Ireland were steeped in Irishness. Her first visit to a professional theatre, for example, was to see the pantomime of *The Sleeping Beauty* at the Gaiety Theatre, Dublin. De Valois claims that, fifty years later, in 1956, she could still remember details from this performance and the 'clear-cut joy' of it (15). Although pantomime did allow for localized jokes, *The Sleeping Beauty* was, primarily, part of the international theatrical repertoire; and staging the balletic version in 1939 and again in 1946 was to be the triumph of de Valois' career as artistic director. Lauded when performed on her company's first visit to America, the production rapidly became globalized theatre by the standards of the day.[9]

At the age of seven, de Valois left Ireland. The Stannus family were in financial difficulties partly because de Valois' father, who served in the Boer War and was later to die in the First World War, lived a life of hunting, horse racing and partying which necessitated selling off more and more of the Baltiboys estate, the family home, which had actually been inherited by de Valois' mother.[10] De Valois moved to Deal in Kent, to live with her maternal grandmother, an uprooting she characterizes starkly and dramatically:

> There and then I deliberately tore my heart out and left it, as it were, on the nursery window-sill. I remember nothing of the journey, for Ireland had faded – Ireland with its sights and sounds, its soft air and smell of burning peat (18).

And her memoir again invokes Yeats:

> I have spread my dreams under your feet;
> Tread softly because you tread on my dreams.[11]

De Valois' relocation to Deal also, however, gave her an opportunity to ponder on her colonial heritage. Her new home was decorated with the skin of a tiger shot by one of de Valois' many military forbears; relics of the battles he had fought in on behalf of the British Empire; and engravings where

> English soldiers with beards, moustaches and sun helmets were depicted in noble last stands, sometimes kneeling four-square, with fire spitting from their rifles in defiance of hundreds of natives, who leapt down the hillside with daggers between their teeth (22).

De Valois' various encounters with mementoes of colonialism, and colonization, seem to me to be important in helping us to acknowledge the colonizing impulse in her own work: in later life de Valois set up, as it were, colonies of her ballet company and school in countries as diverse as Turkey, Iran, Korea, and Egypt but her influence can be detected in almost any country where her disciples worked.[12] While de Valois had first hand experience of colonialism during her time in Ireland (1898 – 1905 was a period when the issue of Home Rule would be difficult to avoid entirely even for a seven year old), her mixed heritage also included refugee, French Huguenot ancestry, and Scottish *émigré* descent: de Valois' mother, Lilith Graydon-Smith, had a Scottish grandmother, Elizabeth Grant, who was famous for writing *Memoirs of a Highland Lady* (173). Consequently it seems ironic that de Valois, the descendant of colonizers as well as the colonized, was so successful in building her dance empire in so many countries except in any lasting way in the country she identified as home, Ireland.[13]

In fact it was only after the relocation to England that de Valois the serious dancer began to emerge.[14] De Valois' talent for dancing was identified by her grandmother, and her mother then 'remembered the episode of the Irish jig' (26). De Valois' own dance style was developed by means of classes at Mrs Wordsworth's School of Deportment, which specialized in amateur, decorative 'Fancy Dancing'; then, rather more professionally, de Valois began training at the Lila Field Academy for Children when she was around thirteen years old; she gained extensive professional experience with the yearly Lyceum pantomimes, where she was principal dancer 1914-1919; she performed soubrette roles in revues; and, at various stages in her career, she had classical teaching from Edouard Espinosa, Enrico Cecchetti, and Nicolas Legat.[15] However, most English professional dance work available in this period tended to be in pantomime, revues, musical comedy, opera ballet and music hall. Indeed de Valois' career included professional engagements as a child dancer at what seemed like 'every old pier theatre in England' (31), and the dance profession was not respectable simply because dancers exposed far more of their bodies in public than any other category of performer apart from, perhaps, circus workers. There were few sustained work opportunities for British dancers in classical or modern ballet, the area de Valois wanted to work in, where principal dancers were expected to present themselves as French or Russian. Consequently it was logical for the Anglo-Irish Colonel's daughter, Edris Stannus, to take the stage name of Ninette de Valois right at the beginning of her professional career, around 1913: 'My mother gave me the name Ninette for the theatre when I was too young to say much about it, but I had a lot of French blood in me.'[16]

After a wide variety of professional dance work, de Valois joined Diaghilev's Ballets Russes in France for the period 1923-5, years that she found stimulating, exciting and fulfilling. In *Come Dance With Me*, de Valois' reminiscences of this period are often linked in with reflections on Irishness, Englishness, and Russianness. For example, de Valois remembers:

> I was musical by Russian standards, and had, in the opinion of my fellow artists, a considerable and very accurate technique. But my projection and general attack were faint in comparison with the Russians, my personality reserved, and stamina (outside technical feats) for the hardship of the life - low. [...] Russians can be physically indefatigable; they can also be astonishingly inaccurate in their repetition of any set movement, and thus, the sustaining of Russian vitality is free from the tiring restraint of discipline and accuracy: they are consistently concerned with the uninhibited projection of themselves. It must be admitted that sometimes projection of energy is not, with Russian dancers, always distributed equally between the physical and the mental;

there is, more than often, a magnificent dynamic offering in one or the other direction: the banks may be flooded over, adding dramatic effect to the landscape. This gives much exhilaration and pleasure to witness, provided that you do not happen to be something on the bank (62).

These are broad generalizations, but, as reflections on dance technique, which the various dancers had acquired by means of undergoing the same strict regime of training, de Valois' comments have some value, especially when she considers the dance work of the exiled Russians, who had trained under the Tsarist system.[17] The dancers 'had lived cloistered lives in the Russian State Schools; now they were further bound together by the *émigré* spirit, cut off as they were from the land of their birth' (66) and a common point of contact in their exiled existence was not only the memory of their training but also the familiar rituals of daily repetition of exercises and rehearsal of dance routines.

During her period with the Russian Ballet, de Valois danced the choreography of Fokine, Massine, Nijinska, and Balanchine, and, significantly, de Valois describes all of these choreographers in terms of exile, and as deeply influenced by 'the roots from which they had had to cut themselves off' (63). De Valois also identifies Massine as expanding the horizons of dance character work 'including the basic elements of national dances' (63), which, presumably complemented her own interest in national dances, especially Irish and, later, English.

De Valois specifically states that life in Diaghilev's company 'was colourful' but 'to a native of Ireland the pattern did not strain, nor did my state of exile tug at my heart strings' (65). This statement is difficult to unpack precisely but it is important that in 1957, looking back to her twenty-five-year-old self, de Valois still constructs herself 'as a native of Ireland' and in 'exile', the trope of 'the exile', like that of the 'wild goose', being particularly potent in Irish writing in the post-Famine period. While de Valois' sense of Irishness does invoke some clichés, when she talks generally, for example, of 'an Irish sense of martyrdom' (39), it is important to remember that she was only a generation away from Parnell, and that the notion of martyrdom for her own generation was politically loaded. And de Valois takes pride in recording that the Russian dancers felt she was more like them than the 'other English members of the Company' (66).[18] Although this phrase actually classifies de Valois as English, she is also 'other' than English, and she quickly follows this up with a claim to 'Celtic blood' and explains that she 'became heavily involved in stating the case of the Irish' (66) to the other dancers, a case which she illuminated by stating 'that to call an Irishman an Englishman was as incorrect as to call a Russian a Pole!' (67)

After de Valois left Diaghilev she began running her own Academy of Choreographic Art in South Kensington.[19] Because de Valois wanted to expand her horizons and, specifically, wanted to found a serious ballet company in Britain, in 1926 she turned to Lilian Baylis, the manager of the Old Vic theatre. De Valois agreed to introduce dance training at the Vic, and to work for starvation wages: her 'carrot' was the hope that Baylis would refurbish and reopen the derelict Sadler's Wells theatre, which would give de Valois a base for the foundation of a permanent ballet company.[20] Although Baylis, famously, had been running both an opera company and a Shakespeare company on a shoestring for over ten years, she also had a great passion for dance, and had actually made a living as a dance teacher in South Africa in the period leading up to the Boer war, where she had taught 'Fancy Dancing', and techniques that de Valois had herself learnt during her time with Mrs Wordsworth's School of Deportment.

Baylis and De Valois were from very different backgrounds, and had very different world views: Baylis's family was dominated by musicians and social workers, who dedicated their lives to good causes particularly in the area of social housing, and were used to working side by side with slum dwellers. Baylis was sure she was on a mission from God in running the Old Vic and saw social outreach as just as important as production values. The fact that de Valois and Baylis worked so well together is a real tribute to both women's commitment and determination. Indeed de Valois' choreography and movement work for her pioneering cousin Terence Gray, who in his experiments with production styles at his Cambridge Festival Theatre was not unduly concerned about whether or not his theatre made a profit, and her artistic work with Yeats together represent almost the antithesis of most work that was on offer at the Old Vic when de Valois joined the company. The Old Vic was offering cut-price opera and Shakespeare and its target audience was the poor of Lambeth; Gray and Yeats had different aims from each other, but both were more interested in the intelligentsia than local slum dwellers filling their theatres. However, where de Valois and Baylis really connected was in their total, almost ferocious dedication to the job in hand, their willingness to attempt what others assured them was impossible, and their pragmatic, strategic thinking. Both women were also linked by their outsider status;

both were women succeeding in areas of management where traditionally men predominated, but both were also marked by colonial and colonizing experiences. Although she was born a Londoner, between the ages of eighteen and twenty-four Baylis had worked in South Africa as a musician and dance teacher, and her accent, which many misrecognized as cockney, was South African. By comparison with Baylis, de Valois seemed of the establishment; but I would argue that her sense of connectedness with Ireland gave her an outsider status as well, and this outsider status may well have helped both women in achieving what those who were comfortably and unequivocally 'inside' the establishment felt to be impossible. Their experiences of exile, expatriate life, and the absence of a beloved 'home', as well as their familiarity with the phenomenon of empire in action, must have marked these two women and the astonishing theatrical empires that they built.

It was at the Vic-Wells that Ninette de Valois' choreography became prolific. The company started small and could only offer token wages, but it gave dancers the chance to work in London for nine months of the year, an offer no other British classical dance company of the time could rival, and a range of roles that few other companies could compete with.[21] While the company did eventually work up to staging the large scale classical works, featuring guest principals such as Lydia Lopokova, Alicia Markova, and Anton Dolin, the company chiefly featured new ballets. These were often choreographed by de Valois, Frederick Ashton, and, later on, Robert Helpmann: all three tailored their ballets to the resources of the young Vic-Wells company. This was a great advantage as far as Baylis was concerned as such ballets tended to avoid huge, and so expensive, corps de ballet. Expenses were also kept to a minimum as de Valois often waived her royalties.[22] The emphasis on new work meant that the Ballet company acquired a cutting edge modernity, which played alongside tradition in its classical work; but if, as de Valois claims, her dancing looked back in some way to that foundational Irish jig, it has to be asked whether her choreography did as well. This is not to argue that de Valois' choreography can be excavated for traces of Irish jigs but to suggest that an emphasis on precision in footwork, a characteristic of de Valois' choreography and of her own style as a performer, might relate to her encounters with Irish dancing.[23] Long after Edris's Irish jig, de Valois continued to be fascinated by folk dancing and national dance, which she felt always influenced any country's choreography, even in the realm of classical ballet.[24] Indeed many early ballet works, in the form of the aristocratic court masques, included national or folk dance in the form of divertissements, and one of de Valois' favourite modern ballets was *La Fille Mal Gardée*, choreographed by Frederick Ashton, a ballet that contains sustained influences and direct quotations from English folk dancing.[25]

De Valois also had her eyes on the future and alongside her ballet companies she continued to run her school. The Royal Ballet School had national dancing as part of its curriculum from its early days; and from 1971 students had to master national dance for their annual performances.[26] Repetitive training such as that demanded by the discipline of classical dance reshapes the body, develops some muscles at the expense of others, expands some movements, and restricts others; the real impact of dance training can, for example, be seen clearly in the state of ballet dancers' feet after years of dancing on *pointe*. Irish dancing, with its focus often located in the legs, with back upright, would produce a different body development than, for example, ballroom dancing, belly dancing or ice skate dancing. Whilst the dominant mode of dance at the Royal Ballet School was of course classical ballet, the inclusion of national dancing in its curriculum means that generations of English ballet dancers were moulded, in a small but possibly significant way, by the legacy of Edris's Irish jig.

The actual dance work that de Valois did in Ireland, however, was comparatively short lived. During the period 1928-1934 she artistically supplemented her work at the Vic-Wells by collaborating with Yeats, visiting Dublin every three months or so, helping to establish a training school there and choreographing for, and performing in, Yeats's *Plays for Dancers* (88). De Valois felt deeply honoured by Yeats's invitation:

> I would work among those people whose efforts to establish the Irish Theatre were in progress at the time that I struggled with an Irish Jig in a farmhouse at the foot of the Wicklow Hills (88).

Although prone to essentialist generalizations in her reflections on Irish theatre – 'the Irish are natural actors' (89) - her six years of collaborating with Yeats were 'happy inspiring years', although 'the English scene eventually crowded them out' (97). Perhaps the most concrete inheritance from this period, when de Valois was interacting intensively with Yeats's work, is her poetry, mostly written in later life and often offering homage to Yeats in its style. Lord Drogheda, in his 'Foreword' to de Valois' first collection of poems, certainly claims them as

'Irish': 'it is Edris, the Irish girl, who emerges as the author of these sensitive moving poems'.[27] Similarly Graham Bowles invites readers to approach de Valois' poetry through the lens of her Irishness, declaring enthusiastically:

> The setting for this prelude of childhood was as important to [de Valois] in her future as an artist as was that of the Lake District to Wordsworth or the Dorset landscape to Hardy. Ireland, its countryside and its people were, and have remained, intrinsic to her whole being.[28]

At the end of *Come Dance With Me*, de Valois returns to Irishness, and travels to her now much changed childhood home. She experiences a moment she identifies as Chekhovian in registering the complete and utter *pastness* of her life in Ireland but goes on to close her book by offering the Irish jig as a metaphor of her life, and indeed her body:

> [...] my Jig of the Wicklow Hills is stiffening up a bit----for over the years it has travelled quite a long way....
> I would say that this Irish Jig, with its lively adventures, has recorded as much as can be of any interest to the younger generation of jigs that roam the wide world today.
> I must not forget the reader; for he [sic] has danced with me from Blessington Fair to Covent Garden Market. It has been a lengthy journey and I thank him for his charity (223).

By constructing her life and her body as an Irish Jig, de Valois comes close to embracing the romantic and spectatorial position of Yeats's oft-quoted line: 'How can we know the dancer from the dance?'[29] As a trained dancer, de Valois knew precisely how much blood, sweat, and tears, how much rehearsal, how much repetition, how much sheer slog goes into dance performance and her elision of the dancer and the dance here seems almost disingenuous. But as a dancer and choreographer de Valois always valued character, the theatrical, and acting; and in her memoirs, and in life, she certainly exhibited an ability to play with personae and personal identity: she is not only an Irish Jig, and Edris Stannus, but she is 'Madam' to many of her ballet associates, and publicly she became Dame Ninette de Valois after 1951.[30] In addition, although this character is completely absent from the book, in private she was Mrs Arthur Connell, a doctor's wife.[31]

De Valois never entirely let go of Edris Stannus. Late in her life in 1992, she commented:

> I don't know anyone any more who calls me Edris. It's rather a serious little name, I suppose. You outlive it, rather, a name like that.[32]

In fact one person who continued to call her Edris was Alicia Markova, whom de Valois had met as the young Alice Marks, when both dancers were in exile in France, working for Diaghilev. But it was de Valois herself who did most to ensure Edris's survival simply by inscribing Edris and her jig so securely into de Valois' memoirs. And what Edris crucially gave to de Valois was strategic Irishness, something that was easier to deploy perhaps in England in 1957 than at other times during de Valois' lifetime when Irish issues were more burning.[33] What strategic Irishness gave to de Valois was an ability to be always something of an outsider, even when firmly ensconced at the very heart, the Imperial centre, within an *establishment* of her own creating.[34]

---

[1] The phenomenal growth of de Valois' company also produced the touring Sadler's Wells Ballet, which still exists today as the Birmingham Royal Ballet.

[2] Ninette de Valois, *Come Dance With Me: A Memoir*, 1898-1956 (London: Hamish Hamilton, 1957). Subsequent references are cited in the text.

[3] W.B. Yeats, "I am of Ireland", *The Variorum Edition of the Poems of W.B.Yeats*, eds Peter Allt and Russell K. Alspach (New York: Macmillan, 1977): 526. Another formidable Irish woman, Mary Robinson, also saw great possibilities in the line 'Come dance with me in Ireland' and used it as a successful campaigning slogan.

[4] Jacky Bratton, *New Readings in Theatre History* (Cambridge: Cambridge University Press, 2003): 102. But see Chapter 5 'Anecdote and mimicry as history' in general.

[5] The dust jacket blurb takes this a step further by constructing Kate Finnigan as 'a peasant woman', whereas the fact that she had been de Valois' mother's nurse, and that later she was the family's cook in London suggests something more complicated than unadulterated 'peasant' pedigree.

[6] The books are : *Invitation to the Ballet* (London: John Lane at the Bodley Head, 1937, reprinted 1953); *Come Dance With Me*; and *Step by Step: The Formation of an Establishment* (London: W.H.Allen, 1977).

[7] Quotation and information on skirt dancing taken from Catherine Pedley-Hindson, 'Interruptions by inevitable petticoats: the historiographical problem of late nineteenth-century dance', paper delivered at the TAPRA conference, Manchester September 2005. Miss Leggatt Byrne's attire is not in the classic skirt dancing tradition but I am assuming that de Valois' mother knew a skirt dance when she saw one.

[8] Bratton comments that 'stories about the definition of what is professional behaviour are an important focus of anecdote' in such memoirs and autobiographies (123).

[9] It has been lovingly restored to the repertory during 2006, the year of the seventy-fifth anniversary of the company's foundation. This is perhaps another instance of de Valois investing anecdote with the status of myth.

[10] Lieutenant-Colonel Stannus (DSO) died in 1917 at Messines Ridge.

[11] W.B. Yeats, 'He Wishes For the Cloths of Heaven', *Variorum Poems*, 176.

[12] The founding of the Turkish National Ballet took place as a result of an invitation

to de Valois from the Turkish Government in 1947. For de Valois' widespread influence see Kathrine Sorley Walker, *Ninette de Valois: Idealist Without Illusions* (London: Hamish Hamilton, 1987): 287. In the recent seventy-fifth anniversary celebrations of the founding of the Royal Ballet, the Australian Ballet, the National Ballet of Canada and the two State Ballet companies of Turkey (Ankara and Istanbul) were invited to give showcase performances at Covent Garden as "celebrating the profound impact Dame Ninette de Valois had on the international ballet scene" (*About The House*, February 2006: 36-37).

[13] Her work for Yeats at the Abbey Theatre and her founding of a ballet school in Dublin survived from 1928 to 1934. Deirdre Mulrooney in writing a history of professional theatre dance in Ireland, *Irish Moves* (Dublin: The Liffey Press, 2006) mourns the loss of so much archival material from this period, though she does manage to include the reminiscences of two of de Valois' Dublin pupils, Freda Freeman and Doreen Cuthbert.

[14] Mary Clarke, *The Sadler's Wells Ballet: A History and an Appreciation* (London: A&C Black, 1955) records that de Valois spent two years at art school before focussing on dance.

[15] Details from Clarke (5); and see *Step by Step* (11-21) where de Valois classifies each of her mentors as masters of (respectively) the French, Italian and Russian schools.

[16] "'Call Me Madam'. Meredith Daneman interviews Ninette de Valois", *Sunday Telegraph* 2 February 1992. De Valois was using this stage name at least as early as July 1913, when she was reviewed in *The Stage* (Sorley Walker 8).

[17] De Valois' experiences of living amongst the exiled community of Russian dancers presumably helped make her anti Soviet, and anti communist but she constructs herself as anti-Bolshevik as early as 1918 (39).

[18] De Valois also claims a *Daily Mail* reporter was convinced that she was Slav (67).

[19] See Walker (62) and Clarke (37). At first de Valois deployed the idiosyncratic spelling 'Choregraphic' and 'Choregraphy' in advertisements for her school and this was the subject of some debate for a while in the pages of the *Dancing Times*; but, by the time she was working with Terence Gray at the Festival Theatre in Cambridge after 1926, she had begun to refer to herself in programmes by the more traditional spelling, 'choreographer'. The academy was initially funded by De Valois' stepfather. After metamorphosing into the Vic-Wells school, in 1947 it was reborn after the disruptions of the Second World War as the Sadler's Wells School, and in 1955 it became the Royal Ballet School, based at White Lodge, Richmond Park.

[20] See Walker (152).

[21] Marie Rambert's company at the Mercury Theatre was the Vic-Wells company's only significant English competitor. De Valois writes "a tribute" to the Mercury Theatre and the work undertaken there by Rambert in the 1930s in *Step by Step* (44-46).

[22] The Vic-Wells, however, had to pay royalties to the Camargo Society for de Valois' ballet *Job* because the first production of this ballet had been funded by the Society.

[23] Meredith Daneman, a biographer of Fonteyn and a ballet dancer herself, avers

that 'footwork' was 'de Valois' great strength' in *Margot Fonteyn* (London: Penguin Viking, 2004): 60. Walker (10) emphasizes the importance of de Valois' early training with Espinosa who 'specialized in good footwork'. De Valois' last dancing appearance was 27 April 1937 as the maid Webster in *A Wedding Bouquet*.

24 Richard Cave in a private communication, but see his forthcoming volume, *Collaborations: Ninette de Valois and W. B. Yeats* (Alton: Dance Books, 2008). My interest in the Irishness of de Valois' work does not deny the internationalism of her approach; but even at the age of 102 de Valois was still insisting that each country 'should be allowed to develop its own style', by rooting its ballet in its national dance traditions. In this interview with Maina Gielgud, she also draws parallels between the distinctiveness of the spoken language of a country and its dance language – see 'The Dance Insider Interview: Dame Ninette de Valois, interviewed by Maina Gielgud: <www.danceinsider.com> (visited 14 November 2005).

25 De Valois' personal passion for English Morris dancing is well attested: see Walker (22, 64, 98). The final group of illustrations in *Step by Step* is of "the boys of White Lodge" (the Royal Ballet School); two show them performing Morris dances. Walker records that de Valois learned and regularly performed circa 1926 the "one Morris dance traditionally permitted to women" (64).

26 See Walker (297).

27 Lord Drogheda, 'Foreword' to Ninette de Valois, *The Cycle and Other Poems* (London: Sadler's Wells Trust, 1985).

28 Graham Bowles, 'Introduction' to Ninette de Valois, *Selected Poems* (Manchester: Carcanet Press, 1998), published on behalf of the Friends of the Birmingham Royal Ballet.

29 W.B. Yeats, 'Among School Children', *Variorum Poems*, 446.

30 De Valois credited Gordon Hamilton with first calling her 'Madam' (see 'Call Me Madam'). She also acquired nicknames as various as 'The Games Mistress' (Walker, 86, 154) and 'The Romanov' (Walker, 41).

31 Dr Arthur Blackall Connell (d.1986) had a general practice in Barnes, London, and later in Sunningdale, Berkshire.

32 'Call Me Madam'.

33 However, it is also important to acknowledge that in 1957, when de Valois was restating her Irishness very emphatically in *Come Dance With Me*, some landlords in London put up signs stating 'No Irish'. My reading of de Valois' 'strategic Irishness' has been informed by Emma Cox and her rereading of Gayatri Chakravorty Spivack's 'strategic essentialism' in 'Shakespeare and Indigeneity: Performative Encounters in Australia and Aotearoa-New Zealand' unpublished M.Phil thesis, University of Queensland, 2005, although both Spivack and Cox are focussing upon indigenous, rather than expatriate issues.

34 Significantly the sub-title of de Valois' second volume of autobiography reads: "The Formation of an Establishment".

10 | Not-So-Gay-Young-Things: Mary Manning's *Youth's the Season—?* as staged in 1930s London

Cathy Leeney

> It is true that when realism first arrived it seemed to bring new life to a commercialized and stagnant drama, but today it spreads stagnation and death wherever it has established itself.[1]

In this characteristically forthright statement of 1932, Mary Manning at once expressed her disdain for the style then associated with the Abbey Theatre, and her vigorous enthusiasm for all that was challenging to it and that was at the core of the Dublin Gate Theatre's ambitions. She also pinpointed the crisis in Irish theatre in the 1930s: how to deal with realism as a theatrical style. If Ireland, as a nation, was in a phase of political consolidation, this process had a dubious role to play in cultural life generally, and in theatre in particular. The stalwarts of Abbey Theatre programming from the late 1920s into the 1930s (Macnamara, Robinson, George Shiels) were perceived as realist playwrights, but 'mining a lighter vein', appealing to audiences through entertainment value:

> A style had been found in which to bridge the gap between urban and rural; the core value of this style was amusement, laughter, rather than satire or applied judgement.[2]

Manning's achievement in *Youth's the Season-?* is to sharpen amusement with satire, to cut a swathe through the complacencies of the young state, its insecure self-satisfaction, its isolationism, its narrowness. She used expressionist elements to represent what realism could not, or did not allow to be accommodated: that is to say, diversity of sexual identity, and its metonymic relationship with diversity within national identity.

Manning's work challenges homogenous definitions of Irishness. Significantly, she does so through the tropes of youth, urbanity, and sexual non-conformity; in this way she interrogates the terms of nationality. She explores identity through the categories of class and gender, and makes joking reference to nationality as a source of meaning. In *Youth's the Season-?* Manning uses the urban, Protestant middle class as an image of the outsider. It is her best play of that decade. In it, realism is shattered by expressionism, that is by techniques of stage montage, which surpass their use by, for instance, Noël Coward in *The Vortex*. *Youth's the Season-?* is formidably entertaining, while having a dark core of violence.

Here I will argue that Manning's play presents a crisis that was not unique to post-colonial Dublin, but that resonated in subtly different ways with London audiences when the play travelled there in 1937 to the Westminster Theatre as part of the Longford Company tour. This was six years after its premiere at the Dublin Gate in 1931 in a production directed by Hilton Edwards, and starring Micheál MacLiammóir. Critical reactions to the play in Dublin and London reveal common elements: in both cities critics expressed a robust resistance to the challenges the play poses in its mix of genres, and in its representations of gender dissidence.

The crisis coded in the play revolves around two issues: one is the role of the homosexual character as outsider, and the codes and conventions that controlled and obscured the representation of homosexual identity. Here the differences of reception resolve on two points: firstly, the powerful London context created by the success of Noël Coward's plays, and the tropes of sophistication and youthful crisis he had created and, at the same time, skilfully masked. Following from the issue of the coding of homosexuality is the way that this impacts on the representation of femininity, and the identification that Manning proposes between the homosexual man and the unconventional woman as parallel outsiders. The second issue of interpretation concerns casting, and importantly the presence of Micheál MacLiammóir, playing Desmond, in the 1931 Dublin Gate production. Reviews of the production in Dublin, and then six years later in London, indicate how ways in which the play concerned Ireland specifically (as a drama of post-colonial failure) disappeared at the Westminster Theatre, and *Youth's the Season-?* became a play about a group of hectic, and rather unpleasant young men and women struggling with conformity, and finding that gender non-conformity leads to self-hatred, despair and death.

One unidentified reviewer described with distaste how the play dealt with 'a couple of abnormal young men' and expressed amazement that it got past the censor, unlike Lillian Hellman's *The Children's Hour*.³ S/he attributed this to Manning's use of a comic frame. Several London reviewers mentioned the influence of Coward; but, in contrast with Coward in, say, *The Vortex* (1923; produced 1924), Manning confronts the audience with the absolute sacrifice demanded at the time from characters embodying sexual transgression in homosexuality, or in non-conformist femininity. Critics of Manning in both cities, however, resisted this confrontation. What was unpalatable was read as unconvincing. In Dublin, the characters were seen as too anglicized, not convincingly Irish. Christopher FitzSimon comments on the Dublin reception of the play:

> Predictably, the Hope of the Gaels section of the press did not appreciate *Youth's the Season-?* at all, and did not care to believe that the characters in it were Irish.⁴

In London, the characters were seen as not sufficiently Irish, although patently not English. In both cities critics were disturbed and displeased by the violent ending of the play, when it had apparently been working so successfully as a satiric comedy of manners.

But Manning was consciously writing about an Ireland that was moving on from the clichés of the cultural renaissance. As she herself described the process more recently in interview:

> We were going through the difficult and hazardous process of becoming a nation once again. [...] Dr. Drumm's electric trains, the Shannon Scheme pylons, so disturbing to Paul Henry's skyline, the cinemas dominating every city, town and suburb, bone-shaking bus services, and miles and miles of red-brick villas springing up in all directions – that was the real Ireland.⁵

Manning wrote about the Protestant upper middle classes of Dublin as an image of these modern anomalies in the young state. She uses the technique of genre instability in all her extant plays of the 1930s, and throws definitions of Irishness into relief through the presence of other nationalities on stage. In this way she achieves, perhaps most effectively in *Youth's the Season-?* , the sense of a common crisis, regardless of nationality. Beyond the props of national identity (whether they be sartorial, cultural, or ideological) she asks how this aspect of identity divides the characters one from the other. She opposes the signs of national allegiance with another set of props that sustain all her outsider characters: these objects and behaviours were an eloquent expression of allegiance to a wider, more pluralistic and cosmopolitan world; they are the cigarette-holder, the dressing-gown, the cocktail, and a kind of behaviour and discourse that might be described as camp.

Manning has acknowledged the influence of the polished society comedies of Coward, whose sophisticated English style of internationalism offered a radical alternative to peasant, or even 'big house' realist drama.[6] Coward's characters are urban creations, never more so than when we meet them in the country. Manning's plays remind us that Irish life was also to be lived in Rathgar and Ballsbridge, as well as in farmhouse kitchens and in Dublin's inner city. There was resistance in both Dublin and London to the fact that characters who lounged or who posed melodramatically over lampshades, who admired their hair in mirrors, and who drank too much gin were also Irish. These may sound like petty points of reference; however, they functioned as a code, and resistance to the code meant resistance to three fundamental markers: class difference, diversity of religion, and gender transgression within the definition of what it was to be Irish. Manning succeeds in revealing and challenging narrow definitions of masculinity and femininity, and, by extension, narrow definitions of Irishness. Hers is a far from sanguine vision of Ireland in the 1930s: its self-absorption, its social complacency, its reining-in of the energies of its younger generation, all lie just beneath the comedic surface of the play, and are not always masked by it.

Manning borrows the title for her play from one of the songs in Gay's *The Beggars' Opera*, but puts it into the interrogative voice. The play opened at the Dublin Gate Theatre in 1931; it was revived in 1932, and again in 1937 by Longford Productions, which is the staging that was played on that company's London tour to the Westminster Theatre. The action in three acts is set on three consecutive days in March, that notoriously volatile time of year. It concerns the younger generation of the Millington family and their friends. Ingenues and ingenus dominate the cast. Some of the actors in the 1931 production must have enjoyed the opportunity to play rather younger than their actual ages, and while they could still do so without straining the audience's credibility. MacLiammóir was thirty-two in 1931, but played Desmond Millington as 'about twenty', a 'youthful invert in a cyclamen polo jumper.'[7]

The play revolves around the troubled and troubling Terence Killigrew, a *'shambling literary loafer'* whose dissipation is off-set by the *'neatness and respectability'* of his silent *Doppelgänger*, Horace Egosmith.[8] The undecidability of Terence's identity is most vividly theatricalized in the mirroring of him by this mute figure, dramatizing the repressive force of the ego where, as Elizabeth Wright explains, 'the ego-instincts, concerned with self-preservation and the need to relate to others, are in conflict with the sexual instincts as the dynamic core of the energies in the conscious.'[9] Manning discussed the role of this silent character with Samuel Beckett, and seen in retrospect Terence himself is very much a Beckettian figure.

Manning's *doubling* of Terence and Egosmith anticipates Friel's splitting of Gar into Public and Private in *Philadelphia, Here I Come!* but the two playwrights have very different goals. Gar's dual presence allows Private to speak in the play where Public cannot speak in his life. Terence's alter-ego, by contrast, expresses the tacit power of the status quo in conflict with the expressive individual. When Terence frees himself of Egosmith, his liberation leads him to self-destruction. It is in this double bind that the real darkness of the play lies. With the violent suicide of Terence onstage Manning bursts the seams of her social comedy. Terence seethes with the 'inexplicable emotion' that Alisa Solomon associates with a straining at the limits of realist representation.[10]

The girl-next-door is Toots (played by Betty Chancellor in both Dublin and London). She functions as an onstage audience, and she forms a triangle of alienation with Desmond and Terence; she witnesses Terence's suicide in the closing moments of the action. Her own broken romance with an alcoholic allows her to function also as a version of the 'woman with a past', a figure that Nicolas de Jongh links with coded re-presentations of homosexual identity as seen in plays by Oscar Wilde.[11]

Act I of *Youth's the Season-?* is carefully structured to establish the major characters and situations. In Act II this structure is disrupted by the free staging, the introduction of several new characters, and an expressionist carnival atmosphere in which relationships are jeopardized or destabilized. This disruption is powerful enough to change the direction of the play irrevocably, so the atmosphere in Act III is one of uncertainty, even anxiety, leading to the catastrophic ending. A feeling of apprehension is suggested in the first act, but this is skilfully undercut by a kind of camp flippancy that de Jongh has identified as the coded 'diction' of the sexual dissident (17). So Manning invites the audience to re-assess the early scenes of the play in the dark context of its closure.

As Terence descends further into self-hatred and despair, his progress is paralleled in the character of Desmond, whose hopes provide the second major theme of the action: Desmond's plan is to escape Dublin for London, where a friend can offer him a start as a designer. However, his courage will not carry him to a complete break for independence, and he requires his father to approve his scheme and to subsidize it. Mr. Millington never appears on stage, yet his presence is very much felt. His values are those of the rigid societal structure that, regardless of the recent republican revolution and ensuing independence, still remained in place. This was specifically true in the cities, where 'Anglicized cultural norms had taken firm hold, along with the cinema, the popular press, golf-clubs and race meetings.'[12] The tenacious residue of colonial influence is revealed, clung to all the more in a context of post-colonial identity crisis.

Terence's suicide shatters the form of the play as comedy of manners, and reveals the order that is reaffirmed as coercive. But what is the oppressive order that is at issue here, and who are the myth-makers behind Terence in his role as scapegoat? If it is patriarchal order that is being questioned, the issue of gender ordering relates to it directly, and explicates both its breakdown and its re-establishment. The critical unease with the shift from comedy to violence relates perhaps to ways that the play opens an interrogation of patriarchy, its class, gender and national associations.

In *Youth's the Season-?* the resonances sustained by individual characters are deepened through linkages and mirrorings between the characters. These expand into veiled disputations on masculinity and femininity. Toots, Desmond, and Terence (they all mirror one another) are the most dislocated people in the play. On witnessing Terence's suicide in the closing moments, Toots exclaims 'Somebody! Let me out!' (404) It is tempting to read this placing of Toots in the play as metaphorical of the place of young Irish women in the emerging Free State: crucial to it, yet suffocated and demoralized by its antiquated values. Written at a time when female emigration from Ireland was preponderant (in contrast with emigration from other European countries), *Youth's the Season-?* comments on the price women paid to stay at home.[13] Manning dramatizes the woman-as-outsider in her shared predicament with the homosexual-as-outsider by mirroring Toots in Desmond and Terence. The deconstruction of gender polarities opens a space for the representation of woman as subject, not defined in relation to man.

The most innovative aspect of *Youth's the Season-?*, theatrically speaking, is the staging of Act II. To celebrate his twenty-first birthday Desmond holds a party in his 'studio', which is situated at the top of the Millington house; the event comprises the entire second act. The acting area is presented as an arena, where '[*a*] *seat cut from the wall encircles the room*' (350). Freeing the stage space from the paraphernalia of furnishings, Manning moves the action out of the restrictive frame of the diachronic, and into the theatrical time-frame of the present moment of performance. So, the setting of Act II extends the dramatic impact of *Youth's the Season-?* from comedy of manners to expressionist tragedy.[14] Identity, especially gender identity and gender relationships, is represented here as performative. De Jongh has identified aspects of dramaturgy whereby, given the impossibility of representing homosexuality directly onstage, the playwright may express an encoded homosexual sensibility. Aside from what de Jongh terms 'diction', 'techniques and strategies of disguise, and an apparent empathy with outsiders from the conventional family unit were the signs of this sensibility' (123). The outsider status of Terence, Toots, and Desmond is confirmed in Act II, and is emphasized in the sense of behaviour or identity as performance. Through the structured fluidity of the stage space, the movement of performers in and out of light, in short, through this break with realism, Manning creates an area of possibility. The coding becomes less robust, and in the fractures, the audience glimpse, occasionally, direct articulation of Desmond's and Terence's sexuality, and of Toots as a fellow outsider with them.

Wilde's place as homosexual icon stands as an elusive intertext in the business of defining the gender representations in the play. The crucial connector here is Micheál MacLiammóir, who played Desmond in the Dublin production.[15] Just as Wilde may be said to have reinvented himself in London, to have created a powerful cultural and sexual persona, so Alfred Willmore reinvented himself as an Irishman. Eibhear Walshe reveals Willmore's move as a reversal of Wilde's, for Wilde was escaping Irishness to embrace 'self-consummation' in London, while MacLiammóir 'by quitting London for Dublin, [by] embracing Celticism, and remaking himself as an Irishman' was escaping identification with what Walshe perceives was 'a particular and threatening concept of "the Homosexual"'.[16] Somewhere, then, in the space between Irishness and homosexuality MacLiammóir was able to live, as Walshe argues, as an 'openly homosexual public figure.'

However, it is important to remember that MacLiammóir's persona was, in every sense, framed by theatricality. The trope of performance here becomes a mask, one that interrogates the notion of identity as anything but a mask. Such a notion of identity could not be accommodated within a search for essentialist post-colonized certainties based on difference from all that was seen as English. The irony is that Irishness was itself such a mask, requiring the inventive energy of what was called a 'renaissance' but was in many respects more a virgin birth. In MacLiammóir's case, 'Irishness' was a mask which distracted from his identity as homosexual; thus, MacLiammóir as Desmond in Dublin was unambiguously camp, but not unacceptably so.[17] MacLiammóir did not appear in the London revival in 1937; but even if he had, one may speculate that the coded resonances of his performance as Desmond would not have created the same impact for a London audience, as they would have been unaware of his Dublin profile as a leading *artistic* Irishman.

In the 1931 production (revived in 1932) it was possible for Dublin audiences to read the codes of Desmond's tragedy, given that MacLiammóir was playing the part, at two levels at least: artistic Irishness, and homosexuality. Such a reading was not available to audiences at the Westminster Theatre: certainly the note of distaste that strikes in a number of the London reviews is not evident in the Dublin responses. As de Jongh has pointed out, casting may be crucial in defining homosexual stereotypes as they appear in the theatre (144). Extra-textual as it is, the issue of casting serves as an invitation to imagine how the gender meanings in *Youth's the Season-?* might revealingly be emphasized in a contemporary production, appealing to an audience for whom gender playfulness is a routine part of popular culture. In the context of such a production, the gradually darkening setting of the ending of Act III (395) becomes a strikingly defeatist vision of young Ireland, a site of claustrophobia, gender oppression, forced conformity, and self-inflicted violence. The link between Toots and the gender codings around Desmond and Terence were, I would argue, unreadable in 1931, but would, in a present-day performance of the play, be central to its meaning.

In *Youth's the Season-?* Manning dramatizes the failure of the nascent state to exploit the energy of its most privileged youth; furthermore, between the conservatism of the old, ascendancy order, and the tendentious narrowness of nationalist values, there lies no space for lives outside confining notions of masculinity and femininity. The play works to link gender nonconformity with self-immolating violence. By refracting Toots' lack of future through the crises of Terence and Desmond, Manning suggests that young womanhood and homosexuality are parallel conditions of alienation. Theatrically, *Youth's the Season-?* exploits the semiotics of camp sophistication to interrogate Irishness as an homogenous set of characteristics closely allied with strict gender polarities. The expressionism in Act II of *Youth's the Season-?*, the dynamic use of stage space, and the resultant fallout in the uneasy disjunctions and jarring conclusion of Act III mark the play as a brilliant example of the codings de Jongh has described, here placed under extreme pressure.

Critical reactions in Dublin and London then, although separated by six years, were pointedly in tune. However, where Dublin audiences laughed comfortably at the mannered performance of Micheál MacLiammóir as Desmond, there is a definite note of distaste in the London responses to what one commentator disdainfully called 'abnormals'. In both cities there was scepticism as to whether the characters qualified as authentically Irish; in both cities there were concerns about the ending of the play in violence (the *News Chronicle* headline exclaimed with intriguing inaccuracy 'Like *Hamlet* Tacked on to a Farce'[18]); and in neither city is there critical evidence of an appreciation of how the play refuses to be diverted from the dark side of its comic surface; rather this was seen as a fault, and seen to be a more grievous fault in London than in Dublin. Only *The Times* reviewer expressed an awareness of a weight of 'symbolism' [his/her word] that 'never fully declares itself'.[19]

In a report on a symposium held at the Gate Theatre in 1932, entitled 'Should the Theatre Be International?', *Motley* quotes Hilton Edwards's view that he would 'prefer that Irish drama was incidentally national rather than consciously national'.[20] Manning's plays of the period promote this preference, while sustaining a high level of technical skill, and a healthy respect for audience appeal. Manning complimented Denis Johnston on the impact of his *The Old Lady Says 'No!'* when it was revived at the Gate Theatre in 1931, saying that the play was 'the voice of Young Ireland [...] and [...]must be heard'.[21] Her own rendering of that voice, in *Youth's the Season-?* demands to be heard, as it expresses the pain, uncertainty, comedy, self-pity, and bitterness of youth, and of the young country itself.

---

[1] *Motley* 1 (7) (Dublin, 1932): 2-3.

[2] Christopher Murray, *Twentieth-Century Irish Drama: Mirror Up to Nation* (Manchester: Manchester University Press, 1997): 114.

[3] An unidentified press cutting in Mary Manning's private archive (Cambridge, Mass.).

[4] Christopher FitzSimon, *The Boys: A Double Biography* (Dublin: Gill & Macmillan, 1994): 78.

[5] Mary Manning in interview with the author, Cambridge, Mass., 15 September, 1994.

[6] Ibid.

[7] Micheál MacLiammóir, 'Some Talented Women', *The Bell*, 8. 2 (Dublin, 1944): 117-27.

[8] Mary Manning, "Youth's the Season-?", *Plays of Changing Ireland*, ed. Curtis Canfield (New York: Macmillan, 1936): 330. Subsequent references are cited in the text.

[9] Elizabeth Wright, *Psychoanalytic Criticism*, 2nd ed. (Cambridge: Polity Press, 1998): 33.

[10] Alisa Solomon, *Re-Dressing the Canon: Essays on Theater and Gender* (London: Routledge, 1997): 46.

[11] Nicholas de Jongh, *Not in Front of the Audience: Homosexuality on Stage* (London: Routledge, 1992): 14. Subsequent references are cited in the text.

[12] R.F. Foster, *Modern Ireland 1600-1972* (London: Allen Lane, 1988): 538.

[13] J.J. Lee, *Ireland 1912-1985: Politics and Society* (Cambridge: Cambridge University Press, 1989): 376-7.

[14] Denis Johnston's expressionistic deconstruction of Irish history, *The Old Lady Says 'No!'*, played at the Gate in July 1929. Part II opens with a tea party which invites the same fluid staging suggested by Manning for Act II of *Youth's the Season-?*

[15] An important aspect of the gender meanings in the 1931 production evolved because, as well as directing the production, Hilton Edwards (MacLiammóir's partner) also played the part of Terence.

[16] Eibhear Walshe, 'Sodom and Begorrah, or Game to the Last: Inventing Micheál MacLiammóir', *Sex, Nation and Dissent in Irish Writing*, ed. Eibhear Walshe (Cork: Cork University Press, 1997): 150-52. Walshe argues that Yeats's persona offered MacLiammóir a way of re-claiming aestheticism, and what might be termed effeminacy in some people's books, as detached from their Wildean association with homosexuality.

[17] Walshe, 150.

[18] *News Chronicle*, 7 October, 1937.

[19] *Times*, 9 October, 1937.

[20] Motley, 6.

[21] FitzSimon, 63.

11 | Doublings: Problematic Identities in Thomas Kilroy's *Double Cross* and *The Madame MacAdam Travelling Theatre*

Carmen Szabó

Michel Foucault defined the term 'heterotopia' as a location used by a culture to create a space 'as perfect, as meticulous, as well arranged as ours is messy, ill constructed and jumbled'.[1] This virtual space engenders a process referred to by Foucault as 'the heterotopia of the mirror', in which the Self reconstitutes itself into reality. The analysis of the following two of Thomas Kilroy's 'identity plays' will focus on the 'heterotopia of the mirror', the way in which these plays reflect the construction of virtual identities that emanate from the 'safe' haven of mythology or from an ideal image of power induced by the structure of the colonial centre.

Society in general forces individuals to define themselves in social terms, but Thomas Kilroy's characters especially in *Double Cross*, are more problematic, haunted by ideas of belonging and treason. Their existence is defined by a liminal state, in between identities, always balancing between reality and the fiction they created for themselves, and often between Ireland and England. Their hypothetic self, the Irishness they historically and biographically embody, urges them to construct an image completely opposed to the original and based on language and power. The burden of a colonial, fragmented sense of Irishness is replaced by the burden of pretending to fit the society of the oppressor, the society of power. The role of the victim is exchanged for a role of power not by building on the basis of the identities they acquired at birth, but by completely denying those in an attempt to enter the power society and maybe disrupt it from the inside. The problematic issues of identity and of choosing between opposing identities present the characters with new questions of belonging and treason.

Margret Boveri discusses the problem in her book *Treason in the Twentieth Century*, where she observes that, by definition, traitors are 'externally two-faced and internally divided'.[2] These individuals are usually challenged by the problem of homelessness, where home involves the deeper issue of belonging. Boveri notes the existence of several traitors who 'learned to love two countries and were torn between their allegiances' and of those she calls 'border people' who were neither exactly homeless nor displaced in the ordinary sense of the word but 'are torn between the two cultures which pull at them'.[3]

Thomas Kilroy's *Double Cross* was first produced in the Guildhall in Derry/Londonderry as part of the annual Field Day enterprise on 13 February 1986, then toured Northern Ireland and the Republic and went across the Irish Sea to the Royal Court in London. In production, then, the performances were no less liminal than in theme. The play presents two historical characters 'with one foot in Ireland and the other in England',[4] fighting to belong to the powerful centre by mimicking the postures of the British colonial power, but being always reminded of the fact that they actually belonged to the colonized Other that they continuously denied. According to Anthony Roche, 'the play corresponds to the Field Day debates: relation between language and identity, crossing of established boundaries, betraying of self and others'.[5] It is also, in Roche's view, consistent with Kilroy's previous plays: 'debating the notions of personal freedom, resisting the pressures of social conformity and marking out a space of existential possibility'.[6] Kilroy wrote in an introduction to the 1994 edition of the play:

> I wanted to write a play about nationalism and in a real sense *Double Cross* derives from the whole debate about national identity which Field Day did so much to promote in the 1970s and 1980s.[7]

However, by 1997 Kilroy's opinion about the reasons behind the creation of *Double Cross* changed, as he moved away from Field Day and more towards his personal creative aesthetic for the play. He states in an interview with Paul Brennan and Thierry Dubost:

> That particular play, *Double Cross*, was written out of a kind of rage. A rage against the whole nature of fascism. A rage against the kind of power residing in role-playing, in costuming, in uniforms, a rage against

militarism, and I was writing about two characters, two figures, that really came out of anger in me.[8]

The issues of identity present in Kilroy's play are problematic not only because of their challenging of the traditional views on Irish identity but also, at a closer look, because of their undermining of the Field Day principles of identity discussed in the company's pamphlets. The Field Day identity discourse is controversial, given the changes that occurred within it along the fifteen years of the company's theatrical enterprise. At the beginning of the 1980s the Field Day ideologists were influenced by the emerging post-colonial identity discourse, advocating the ideological move from the hyphenated identities which were determined by the binary structures towards a more open hybrid identity, determined by the fragmentation and deconstruction generated by the postmodern theoretical discourse. However, by the end of the 1990s Seamus Deane, Field Day's main ideologist, considered that plurality and multiplicity do not represent a viable solution to the problem of Irish identity. They constitute only decoys of tradition and conservatism used by the structures of power to falsely challenge themselves, just to be able to prove the fallibility of heterogeneity and liberalism and reimpose their own, traditional patterns.[9] This continuous balancing between different, opposing ideas of identity induced a sense of unrest within the structures of Field Day, making it difficult for the playwrights working with the company to reflect their complex and controversial theoretical stands.

In Thomas Kilroy's *Double Cross*, the two main characters, Brendan Bracken and William Joyce, subscribe to this difficulty of grasping any kind of genuine identity. The only apparent reality of the characters is represented by the historical data that builds up their biographical identities presented by the playwright at the beginning of the play. However, the manipulative tendency of historiography is kept in mind; the historical identities of the characters are subverted as well, thus creating a vacuum of identity, a lack of substance that can be traced back to the Field Day discourse on identity and ultimately to the failure of this discourse to secure a valid vision of Irish identities. This element of unsureness was no less emphasized by the itinerant nature of the production itself, moving, as the play moves, across boundaries. Performed at the Royal Court, Kilroy's complex explorations of betrayal and projection offered proliferations of complexity – a *Double Cross* doubled and redoubled.

Talking about the creation of identity in contemporary times, Jacques Derrida considered that 'the self-affirmation of an identity always claims to be responding to the call or assignation of the universal, the inscription of the universal in the singular'.[10] This view seems to be further complicated in the case of Joyce and Bracken as they want to be introduced in the globality of the British Empire or any Empire for that matter, by completely denying the singularity of their Irish origins. In their development, the two characters seem to be increasingly torn between an identity they desire but which is ultimately forbidden to them and an identity they possess but which they completely deny. The structure of the play follows the two apparently separate lifelines. After presenting the official biographies of both characters, Kilroy divides the play into two acts or, rather, into two interacting halves – The Bracken Play: London and The Joyce Play: Berlin.

In a combination of physical performance and video technique the two characters define themselves as 'Other'. Bracken, on stage, sees Joyce as a 'vulgar little shit from Connemara, full of fight, ready to take on anyone. You know the kind of Paddy'.[11] Joyce is presented as the epitome of an Irishman, an outsider, thrown out of Oswald Mosley's British Union of Fascists since 'the Irish are always being thrown out of something or other, aren't they?' (18) The response comes from the video screen where Joyce, wearing black shirt and tie, gives his own description of Bracken's character. Until this point in the development of the play, the dialogue is given a parallel structure, with the characters addressing the audience directly. By starting to react to each other, the characters disrupt the apparent balance of their relationship, thus creating an unusual dialogue between presence and absence, between stage and screen, between Self and Other. Joyce describes Bracken as the son of a Tipperary stonemason who rose to the top of British politics by being a trickster and a clown, a court-jester entertaining Winston Churchill. The rapid staccato of the dialogue between the two expresses concerns with the problems of acting and doubling.

The audience witnesses a continuous interpenetration between different layers of reality: history penetrates fiction and fiction penetrates the realm of performance in a need to redefine the boundaries of the world. The English language as vital feature of these mixed worlds determines the Babel of realities. The power of language as means of colonization is underlined by Bracken's opinion that in the future 'the whole world will be divided between those who speak the language [English] and those who don't' (21). Winston Churchill likewise observes that England's power to colonize so many territories was determined by the use of English and by the imposition of the language and culture upon the victims rather than by the use of force: 'we have always taken more captives with our dictionaries than with our regiments' (21).

The centripetal power of the centre is so strong that the periphery feels a permanent attraction towards it and a need to imitate it so that it can fit within the structures of power. The new slogan of existence in such a reality is 'Imitate that you may be free' (22). However, the stories of the narrators also raise the question of post-colonial existence, the tendency of a now independent periphery to appropriate the language and the image of the oppressor in a conscious or subconscious intent to dominate or disrupt the centre from the inside.

The last scene of 'The Bracken Play' becomes crucial in the economy of the piece as we witness the imminent transformation of Bracken into Joyce. The Actor and the Actress enter the stage and change the cardboard figures, thus preparing the space for the transformation. They help Bracken to disrobe to Joyce: 'beneath the overcoat there is the fascist black shirt and tie. Spectacles removed. Wig removed to a close-cropped hair. A scar is exposed the full length of the face.' (47) The choice of the playwright to have this transformation on stage reinforces, for the audience, the illusory notion of identity laid bare by this metatheatrical device. The difference between the two characters lies only in costuming, in pretending and acting. To create a connection between the two parts of the play, the final scene of 'The Bracken Play' builds up a space of crossing, of borderline between the two sides of the Self.

After disrobing, the actor who plays Joyce now appears in the middle of a crowd in Manchester, advocating the teachings of Oswald Mosley's British Union of Fascists. By allocating Joyce a position already within the British power structures, Kilroy determines a close spatial relationship between the two characters. Joyce's appearance on stage at the start of his play may bear a double interpretation. The first is that of continuation – the play of the Self continued by the play of the Other, both treated as inseparable halves of the same being. The second interpretation might be that of breaking structures, of Joyce reacting against the compliance of Bracken's life within British political society. Both interpretations acknowledge the identity of the two characters, their external sameness, as far as their place of origin is concerned, and their interior, self-identification.

The image that opens 'The Joyce Play' is intended to mirror the first scene of 'The Bracken Play'. If the phone determines Bracken's appearance, Joyce's space is determined by the radio, 'a battery of different radio stations over the air' fills the atmosphere created in the first scene. The artificial, mechanical voices address the audience in an attempt to dramatize the wide spectrum of 'free' radio stations in Britain, all directed against Britain's involvement in the war. Even the BBC Home Service expresses the disapproval of the general public. All these fragmentary voices seem real, genuine reports of a nation at war. This belief is dismantled by Bracken, who appears on the video screen – changing places with the Joyce of the first part – and addresses the nation as Minister of Information in order to discourage the audience from listening to such broadcasts as they are all enacted by people in Rundfunkhaus, the broadcasting centre in Berlin, led by the Irish traitor Lord Haw Haw, William Joyce. With this emphasis on the importance of the Voice in the manipulation of reality, Kilroy touches yet again upon the problematics of the construction, through language, of 'invisible', presumed identities.

The two narrators, the Actor and the Actress, appear on stage in order to set the background for The Joyce Play. The story of William Joyce unfolds in front of the audience, having as a central moving power the 'VOICE' and the manipulation of the historical events through the use of different voices – as the Actor puts it: 'our hero sits at the centre of the most extraordinary factory of voices ever assembled in the history of radio' (52). By entering the world of William Joyce, the two narrators exist under the spell of the spoken word and they start manipulating it by miming Churchill, for example: 'Get Brendan on the phone. Something has to be done about this chap Haw Haw' (53). Voice and time – the obsession with clocks – are considered to trigger the imagination of the people in such a multiplying 'Tower of Babel'. Through the radio, Joyce can release 'the most potent subversion of all: the imagination of the people' by manipulating time – announcing different times for bombings – and voice – putting on/enacting different voices and languages. On air, time, space and language lose their boundaries and become slippery notions, the traditional ways of measuring time, for example, are easily transformed in Dalian flowing clocks, time being in the speaker's power to manipulate.

The relationship between William Joyce and England relies on invention. Joyce reinvents an England of his desires through his voice on the radio, while England, through Bracken and the Ministry of Information, reinvents Joyce into a Nazi traitor and, by considering him a traitor, actually acknowledges Joyce as part of the British Empire. The Actor presents this relationship as 'the Principle of Circularity' or 'the Double Cross Effect'. The Double Cross effect constitutes the centre of Kilroy's play, both parts being based on the idea of invention and imagination. Acting always one against the other, the two parts are at the same time identical and opposed, following the relationship pattern between Self and Other. Thus, Bracken's Ministry of Information is doubled by Joyce's Ministry of Misinformation, a doubling that is seemingly opposed. It is based, according to the Actress, on the principle of 'absolute duplication' (55).

In the final scene of the play Joyce and Bracken meet on stage, mirroring the beginning and thus finalizing the circularity of the play. The playwright uses the same video projection technique to bring Bracken on stage: 'On the video Bracken appears as if behind bars or a grille of iron' (78). The meeting is supposed to take place in Joyce's prison; however, the audience knows from the beginning of 'The Bracken Play' that they never met, according to Bracken himself. Thus, the mood of the scene is one of 'reverie', of a dream sequence that creates a surreal image in the final instances of the play. Bracken tends to identify Joyce with the brother, the hateful double that troubled him for a lifetime. The theme of the continuous search ('I have searched everywhere else. I searched the streets. I have only begun the search' (78)) reinforces the image of the lost soul, migrating from one place to another in order to find his identity. After years of pretending and fictional creations of identity, Bracken begins his search for his true Self in an attempt to find the brother he has always avoided. With Joyce's conviction and death, Bracken is refused the comfort of having a double, a shield that he could always use in protecting his own Self by projecting his negativity onto the Other.

Through the issues discussed, Thomas Kilroy's play – however deconstructive it might be – has managed to become an integral part of the Field Day enterprise. Brian Friel considered that *Double Cross* challenges questions of 'betrayal and an exploration of the necessities of treason' and thus enters the 'canon' of the company, being considered the second 'core text' after Friel's *Translations*.[12] The Field Day production, directed by

Jim Sheridan, seems to have solved, at least partially, the controversial problems of identity emerging in the play by using innovative techniques. However, the confusing identity discourse that surfaces both in the text and in the production, relates back to the ideological texts of the company, the problems of identity creation in Northern Ireland and the voicing of this process in the Field Day plays.

Notwithstanding, Kilroy continued to challenge the ideological structures of Field Day with his second play for the company, *The Madame MacAdam Travelling Theatre* (1991), directed by Jim Nolan. The play is, on the surface, a tragicomedy about the role of theatre and the power of performance in a world at war. During the Second World War, a travelling theatre company run by Madam MacAdam arrives from a war-tormented Belfast into the apparently peaceful and neutral town of Mullingar in the Irish Free State. The actors and the locals interact within a scenario having at its basis two main ideas that determined the Shakespearean vision of theatre: 'all the world's a stage' and 'the stage of fools'. All through the play there is a constant confusion between reality and illusion on and off stage, the interaction between players and audience being structured in a Chinese-box style by creating plays within plays and illusions within illusions. Everything on stage appears to be a simulacrum, where all different elements are put together in a collage that surpasses reality.

Kilroy did not venture into extreme techniques of theatrical production as one could witness in postmodern performances where the fragmented text and the elements of multimedia are combined in a continuous tale of degradation and 'death of theatre'. *The Madame MacAdam Travelling Theatre* goes towards another type of postmodern theatrical thinking, that of bringing together different traditional techniques and new ways of theatrical expression in such a way as to make the audience recognize both the new elements of creation and the historical and political ideas embedded within this new frame. Thus, in this play Kilroy uses transvestism and theatrics itself as means of interrogating issues of identity and as tools to expose the codes constructing everyday discourse. Through *The Madame MacAdam Travelling Theatre*, Kilroy deconstructs the image that Field Day created of themselves as a travelling theatre with the greater plans of transforming or, at least, of influencing the established master narrative of culture in Northern Ireland, the Republic, and in England.

I would venture to argue that this often-surfacing 'hidden' critique is one of the main causes for the play's almost complete failure in production. *Madame MacAdam* incorporates a multitude of issues and discourses that can be easily related back to the Field Day enterprise: the idea of the travelling company, the necessity the members of the company feel to regain the greatness of the past by working against the established trends, the discussions of the role of the theatre in a conflict zone. However, Kilroy sometimes changes the tone of the discourse from a dramatic account of the problems that the company faces, both theoretically and practically, in a zone of conflict, to an ironic rendering of their futile efforts, in certain instances alluding almost directly to Field Day's choice of plays. Lyle Jones, the main actor of the imaginary Madame MacAdam theatre company, advocates a position that sustains, above all, the importance of performance. For him, theatre means acting, but the actors cannot exist without the audience and thus they have to satisfy every need or wish the spectators might have. This relationship between audience and actors justifies everything the actors do, even the choice of 'rubbish' melodramas just because 'the Irish simply adore' them.[13] In Lyle's opinion there is no difference between these 'Hibernian melodramas' and Shakespeare's *Hamlet* – what is important is that the actors always offer their best performance to the audience. Theatre itself has only the role of pleasing the audience and providing aesthetic beauty. This view (expressed by Jones) refers back to the Field Day Theatre Company's decision in 1983 to refuse David Rudkin's commissioned play *The Saxon Shore* and stage instead Athol Fugard's play *Boesman and Lena*. The reason for this change was shortly explained to Rudkin in a letter, the board of directors considering the play problematic for the 'ecumenical' audience attending the premiere in Derry's Guildhall – but it contains a logic that perhaps also took account of the awaiting Royal Court patrons.

The ghostly space created at the beginning of the play is one under surveillance. The 'distant sound of a bomber approaching' frees the play 'from a fixed place and moves it into a zone of threat and uncertainty'.[14] This borderline space is characteristic for the artistic vision of postmodernism: there are spaces of indeterminacy and distress where the two forces defining them – the centrifugal and centripetal forces – are combined in creating a theatrical vision of 'reality'. It is difficult to define the actual position of the performance within the established rules of theatrical perception given the multiple layers of aesthetic production that spring to life from the very first scene. The brightly painted van of the Madam MacAdam Travelling Theatre appears on stage creating the illusion of theatre within theatre. The metatheatrical device of bringing on stage another theatre with its own audience doubles the accepted relationship between audience and production. The duality of the structures is a characteristic of Kilroy's plays; his characters always in balance between reality and fantasy, between being performers and individuals. Such identities, created through a mixture of roles and real life, subscribe to Kilroy's constant assumption that the notion of character has disintegrated. Thus, there is a constant communication between the production and the audience in an attempt to delineate the possible structures of the performance.

Like the metatheatrical device of theatre within theatre, which opens up issues of theatricality and performance, Madame MacAdam becomes the mouthpiece of two spaces which overlap in the play: the space of pretending and that of the reality surrounding it. With Madame MacAdam, Thomas Kilroy creates a viable link between the artistic experience and the viewer.

Madame MacAdam's view on theatre postulates that there is always a threat in the art of performing, in the lack of balance between illusion and reality. Rabe represents one example of this dangerous imbalance. He would like to project reality on stage and solve the problems of the world within the space of theatre, which could provide catharsis for the audience but it is far from truth and reality. Madame MacAdam observes: 'I'm afraid he may look on life as just a larger stage with a larger audience' (57). On the other hand, Lyle Jones, Bourke, and the LDF men see the illusion of theatre everywhere. They apply the same rules of theatrical performance to the real world around them. They are acting on the great stage of fools without realizing that there is a determining difference between the illusion of theatre and reality. Lyle Jones is always acting, making Madame MacAdam see theatre everywhere around her. For Jones, participating in the farce at the races is as much part of theatre as it is playing on stage.

The discussions on the theme of theatre and the different views on the art of performance develop in a space very open to pretending and acting. Madame MacAdam observes: 'This is an extremely dangerous country. How can you perform theatre before a population of performers? They constantly complete one's lines for one'(46). The representatives of this space use theatre and pretending as a way of life.

By the collision of these two worlds, that of the travelling company and that of the local people, Thomas Kilroy creates a gigantic stage where through discussing different views on theatre, he tries to give a possible solution for the position of theatre in the contemporary world. Kilroy's insistence on fragmentation illustrates his belief in the necessary acceptance of diversity and sums up his vision of the world thus contributing to but also destabilizing the general vision represented by the Field Day policy of a theatre.

The path followed by both productions subscribed to the direction taken by all the other plays performed by the Field Day Theatre Company: premiere in the Guildhall, Derry, followed by tours in Northern Ireland, the Republic and ultimately, England. *Double Cross* opened in Derry on 13 February 1986 and successfully toured smaller venues in Northern Ireland and the Republic, reaching the Abbey and then moving across the sea to The Royal Court in London. The dynamic morphology of the reviews also corresponds to the critical tendencies of the three national spaces where the play was performed: in Derry and the other venues in Northern Ireland, the reviews focused almost exclusively on the spatial importance of the Guildhall and on the political allegiance of the audience rather than on the production itself. Moving across the border to venues in the Republic, the reviews tried to create a balance between the theatrical qualities of the performance and the political and ideological importance and fame that surrounded Field Day. Reaching The Royal Court, the reviews got more and more focused on the production in all its elements: actors, staging, dramatic structure. The importance attributed by Field Day to the theatre critics in England is discussed by Stephen Rea in an interview with Kevin Jackson in September 1989:

> Sometimes local critics cannot get beyond the local context perhaps because they lack theatrical experience. This is contrasted with the mature criticism of some British critics, who put what we do into a world context.[15]

Rea's comment reflects the change in the ambitions of Field Day as it slowly crossed borders between the cultural semiotic groups of subculture and dominant culture.[16] Starting off as a mixture of anti-cultural and sub-cultural elements, the Field Day Theatre Company became part of the dominant cultures on both sides of the Irish Sea. As celebrity was starting to envelop the proceedings of the company, the main ambitions changed profoundly: Field Day did not intend to be a 'rural', 'travelling', and overtly political company anymore. Paradoxically, Field Day wanted to break free from the political ideologies that defined it from the very beginning and, accordingly, the company expected its 'local' critics to change their discourse overnight and focus more on the theatrical and performance qualities of their productions rather than on the political milieu that constantly followed and determined the company's theatrical enterprise.

Thomas Kilroy's *Double Cross* presented audiences on both shores of the Irish Sea with characters that raised challenging questions in relation with issues of identity and belonging, focusing on the differences but also on the complementary character of two cultures that force individuals to exist in a space 'in-between'. Following the success of *Double Cross*, *Madame MacAdam* was expected to reach the same heights, given its theme – the importance of theatre within the community, and the visually innovative way of rendering it on stage. However, Jim Nolan's production of the play failed, and by the time it reached Dublin, Kilroy was already thinking about withdrawing from the Field Day directors' board, which he eventually did a few months later. The importance of this failure was reflected in Kilroy's dramatic decision to say farewell to the Irish stage, thus re-enacting in a certain way the dilemma of his own characters – his return to The Abbey five years later with a version of Pirandello's *Six Characters in Search of an Author* was something of a poetic twist. The sense of failure was no less apparent in the further theatrical development of the Field Day Theatre Company, which, after Brian Friel's public resignation in 1994, produced only one more play, Frank McGuinness's version of Chekhov's *Uncle Vanya* in 1995. Kilroy's *Madame MacAdam* became the last original play that the company produced, and its lack of success proved to be a bad omen for Field Day's theatrical enterprise.

The relative decline of the company's theatrical productions in the period between Kilroy's two plays reflects not only the secession between the main personalities of the company, but also the pronounced gap that was being created between the ideological wing of Field Day, led by Seamus Deane, and the theatrical wing that remained without the public support of its leader, Brian Friel, from as early as 1990. Kilroy's *Madame MacAdam* was unlucky enough to become the first play put on stage by the company after the rupture between Friel and Rea in 1990, caused by

Friel's decision to offer *Dancing at Lughnasa* to the Abbey. However, the failure of the production reflected, more than anything, the pronounced lack of communication between theory and performance within the company, a communication that defined all the previous productions. It also showed the slow but certain realization that the company had failed to impose its theoretical discourse within the frame of Irish Studies; and even more so, within the theoretical environment of the second half of the 1990s, the ideologies developed by Field Day were challenged more and more often.

The innovative tendencies that the company wanted to intertwine in the fabric of Irish culture slowly turned into obsessions and blurred the theoretical perspectives of the company's aesthetic agenda. The continuous need to reconsider tradition, history and myth, to deconstruct the stereotypical binary oppositions that determined Northern Irish society and to attempt a new definition of Irish identity, 'free of Irishness' but securely Irish, changed utterly the internal morphology of the company. The theatrical side of Field Day, responding in part to the celebration of its craft offered by English critics, was drawn into conflict with the critical and academic voice of the company. It is this tendency that is visible within the texts of the plays put on stage by the company after 1990, reflecting the reactions of the playwrights against the shift within the company, and the transformation of Field Day from a theatre company into a critical label.

Twenty-six years had passed since the first production of the Field Day Theatre Company, Brian Friel's *Translations*, was set to change the theatrical and cultural perceptions of representation. The continuous past, the almost impossible attempt to create a past tense in the present of the performance, determined the vision of the plays the company put on stage, placing identity and history at the centre of the critical discourse; and in turn placing that critical discourse at the centre of the English, as well as the Irish, stage. The binary oppositions started to be discussed and deconstructed, if still not completely annihilated. The central issues of language, identity, and history were shaken from the calcified frameworks that defined them, and challenged by new voices representing a new critical language. However, with a combination of successes and failures, Field Day prepared the discourse of Irish studies for a new millennium that slowly starts witnessing the dissolution of traditional binary structures and the movement out of the continuous past.

1 Michel Foucault, *Discipline and Punish: the Birth of the Prison* (New York: Vintage Books, 1979): 57.
2 Margret Boveri, *Treason in the Twentieth Century* (London: Macdonald, 1956): 57.
3 Ibid., 58.
4 Stephen Rea, founding member of Field Day, defined what a Field Day play should be in an interview with Kevin Jackson: 'a play of ideas, involved with language, involved with looking at imperialism, and looking at men who have one foot in Ireland and one foot in England'. *The Independent*, 15 September 1989: 18.
5 Anthony Roche, *Contemporary Irish Drama – From Beckett to McGuinness* (New York: St. Martin's Press, 1995): 190.
6 Ibid., 210.
7 Thomas Kilroy, *Double Cross* (Oldcastle: Gallery Books, 1994).
8 Paul Brennan and Thierry Dubost, *Études Irlandaises*, vol. 26-1, Spring 2001: 9.
9 See Seamus Deane, 'Canon Fodder: Literary Mythologies in Ireland', in Jean Lundy and Aodán Mac Póilin (eds.), *Styles of Belonging: The Cultural Identities of Ulster* (Belfast: Lagan Press, 1992): 22-32
10 Jacques Derrida, *The Other Heading – Reflections on Today's Europe*, (Bloomington: Indiana University Press, 1992): 73.
11 Thomas Kilroy, *Double Cross* (London: Faber and Faber, 1986): 18. Subsequent references are cited in the text.
12 Brian Friel, programme notes to Thomas Kilroy's *Double Cross*, 13 February 1986.
13 Thomas Kilroy, *The Madame MacAdam Travelling Theatre* (London: Methuen, 1991): 17. Subsequent references are cited in the text.
14 Roche, *Contemporary Irish Drama*, 209.
15 Stephen Rea in an interview with Kevin Jackson, 'Running Wilde on the Road', *The Independent*, 15 September, 1989: 18
16 For detailed information on issues of cultural semiotics and the relationship between anti/sub culture and dominant culture, see Jørgen Dines Johansen and Svend Erik Larsen, *Signs in Use – An Introduction to Semiotics* (London: Routledge, 2002).

12 | The Transience of the Visual Image in Touring Theatre: Brian Friel's *Dancing at Lughnasa*

Enrica Cerquoni

This article evolves as an investigation of the dynamics of theatrical space and scenic art whose mutable boundaries have taken on the role of provocative agent in shaping images and states of a nation. As Czech scenographer Jaroslav Malina has claimed, 'stage design, just as other areas of national culture, seeks its own national identity'.[1]

Given the connection between theatrical representation and issues of Irish national identity, it is particularly revealing to explore those issues as embodied in scenic representations. Scenography, with the dimensions of the visual and of the physical, as a critically overlooked yet penetrative and implosive area of theatre practice, can disclose aesthetic and ideological insights in relation to those matters. To look at Irish theatre from an angle other than 'words' exposes alternative forms of expression. This undermines the saturated myth of Irish theatre as exclusively 'verbal', and insists on the adaptive capacities of touring theatrical production as it shifts its physical, along with its geographical and temporal, space.

The assumed monolithic identity of Irish theatre as a theatre of 'words' is ideologically marked. If Una Chaudhuri and Elinor Fuchs can refer to scenographic practice globally as 'the most obvious site'[2] in the new spatial turn which has debunked Aristotelian hierarchy and reshuffled dramatic structures, this view would hardly apply to scenic art in an Irish theatrical context, where scenography has been stripped of its semblance of obviousness. In the critical context of a diasporic Irish theatre, words and images have long incarnated a contesting tension between self and alterity: scenography and the whole dimension of the visual have most often been edited out of the critical discourse, the latter more focussed on perpetuating a construction of Irish theatre as definitively logocentric yet utterly falsifying and unreflective of the plurality of the Irish theatrical experience in the twenty-first century. Because of the invisibility of the visual component, the theatrical memory that is being transmitted is a maimed and elliptical one, inhabiting discontinuity and a theatrical 'negative space of absolute loss'.[3] The inclusion of the visual component in the calcified fabric of critical seeing can present a danger for the exclusionary verbal ontology of theatrical nationhood in Ireland. As Heidi Gilpin argues, paraphrasing Norman Bryson, 'the visual experience is never fully organized by a centralized ego: there is always an excess in vision over and beyond what the subject can master in sight'.[4]

In order to highlight the ambiguous and complex relation between scenography and national identity in accounting for alternative experiences, identities and histories, in this article I will focus on Brian Friel's *Dancing at Lughnasa*, a pivotal play in the Irish canon and for more than one reason. Firstly, it was written specifically for the Abbey Theatre in Dublin, the National Theatre in Ireland, in 1990, when the images of the nation and of Irish theatre were undergoing complex processes of diversification and formal changes. Secondly, from an aesthetic and thematic viewpoint, in *Dancing at Lughnasa* Friel tackles the culture-defining conflict at the core of an infected critical practice. The play performs and makes problematic the dialectics of division between the verbal and the visual, between words and images, between what is spoken and what is shown, between the shaking 'memory framework' of Michael's narratorial voice and vision, and the stage events, the visual and corporeal energies, 'the scenes of real life', with their mostly female ensemble within a 1930s country home location. Finally, the play has had a diverse and successful stage history from the 1990s onwards, first in-house, then internationally, following its reproduction on the stage of the English National Theatre. As such, *Dancing at Lughnasa* has visually marked an era of national and theatrical reshaping, providing a wide spectrum of performance images in the void of visual documentation.

For the purposes of this exploration I will therefore focus on and refer to selected aspects of scenic presentation in the original production of the play in 1990: the Abbey Theatre production which went to England before touring elsewhere and was revived at the Abbey, in 1999 and 2000. These scenic aspects from the original production will be counterbalanced by images of stage design from a more recent, non-touring, Irish production, so as to highlight images and concepts where the theatre artists' inventiveness and the spectators' visual perceptions interact to evoke transient, provisional and permeable notions of nationhood, identity, and belonging. Transience is a key-factor for this visual journey through Friel's *Dancing at Lughnasa*: it becomes scenic image and national metaphor within the play in the touring and non-touring productions under scrutiny in this article. The transience of the travelling visual image raises questions in relation to audiences in Ireland and England and their reception of the performed play.

In relation to transience and scenography, the scenographer Jaroslav Malina offers an interesting point of reflection:

> Every stage design is transient, it perishes with the end of the production for which it was intended. Its short life is very often played out in the field of popular culture. Its memory, photographs of it, designs, exhibits, can penetrate the field of elite culture: museums, galleries, posters and so forth. Its transient life is then lengthened and experiences a new interpretation which each person projects into it. Its transience becomes its strength.[5]

This statement has strong implications in reference to the unresting power of the set design created by Joe Vaněk for the Irish premiere of Friel's *Dancing at Lughnasa* in the Abbey Theatre, directed by Patrick Mason in 1990. As the production went touring to London, New York, Melbourne, and Sydney and was revived several times in Dublin (last time in 2000), the setting had to be rebuilt and recreated, sometimes with variations in accordance with the physical reality of the different hosting sites. Because of its vast popular and critical acclaim, this set design has become iconic of the theatrical imagery of the play, thus pointing to the scenographer's role as 'visual director'[6] in unlocking the visual impact of the play. Because of its 'transient' and nomadic visual history, Vaněk's scenic image has turned into an emblematic mirror of the mutating state of the nation. A further evidence of the role of Vaněk's set image is that in 2004, Vanek's setting was one of the central pieces of the Abbey scenic art exhibition held at the Irish Museum of Modern Art as part of the events celebrating the Abbey Centenary. In the catalogue accompanying the Abbey exhibition, the photographic reproduction of Mason's and Vaněk's *mise-en-scène* as cover image visualized its centrality within the artistic scenario of the exhibit.

Joe Vaněk's set for the Abbey production in 1990 presented a thrusted-out stage image which was realistic just on the surface: details present, but distilled. The overall feeling is more that of a fragmentary quotation from reality than reality itself. Vaněk's angular and edgy open box, with the single diagonal wall containing all the necessary props and objects, such as turf stack, the radio, the range, the iron, the buckets and so on, has its line of power in an unruly field of golden wheat rising potently in a dramatic wedge behind the house and extending towards a visually discordant focal point. Extending the spectator's visual field beyond the physical confines of the stage, the dotted expanse of corn, like an open-ended and fleeting image from an Impressionist painting, conjures up the irresolvable ambiguity and complexity of the play's inward landscape. Mason's and Vaněk's premiered stage image has known multiple incarnations in its touring history throughout its subsequent decade. The symbolic power of this obtrusive and commanding visual presence shifts and renews through the diverse spatial adaptations and scenic modalities: intimate and atmospheric in Dublin, framed and sharp in London (National, Lyttleton Theatre, 1990-1991), popular and cinematic in New York (Broadway, 1992), abstract and stylized in Melbourne and Sydney (1992-1993).

In all the diverse spatial transformations the challenge is to preserve the thrusted-out image, which translates on the Abbey's 'very wide and unfocussed stage and auditorium'[7] the immediacy of the characters and their intimacy with the audience. For the transfer to the National in London, which was the seminal site for the travelling visual image, crucial in establishing its iconic status, the physical reality of Lyttleton's stage and auditorium – the repertory system and the fixed position of seats – required some changes. Joe Vaněk writes how:

> by stopping the walls six feet short of the stage edge and extending the floor only between black, textured slabs that connected with similarly textured side flats [...] I endeavoured [...] to keep a sense of that thrust.[8]

However, the final effect is of a sharper frame than had been the case in Dublin. Michael Coveney caught the achievement in the *Observer*:

> [the] shimmering wheatfield, flecked with poppies' [and holding] the history of a nation in a burning glow of reminiscence, in the aftermath of Catholic imperialism before the loss of joy and identity in the urban diaspora.[9]

The multi-dimensional image transmitted by Vaněk's scenic creation captured the spirit of the Irish nation in the early 1990s, when Mary

Robinson had just been elected president and 'there was a very real sense of the take-off of the Irish internationally, culturally, and politically'.[10] It was a nation in a germinal state of flux, where boundaries were becoming permeable and provisional, and notions of identity and nationhood re-invented and renegotiated. The production at the Lyttleton therefore marked a crucial repositing of the Irish nation (and National Theatre) in an English national (and National Theatre) context, a moment of changed reception and of cultural re-perception. The London performance indicates how, transposed from culture to culture, Vaněk's scenic environment has continued to contaminate and be contaminated, each time in an attempt to disclose 'differentness' to the onlooker's world of experience. Yet, when it was revived in its original cultural context years later (1999 and 2000), that very conceptual image did not speak to its audiences with the same strength as before: the concept behind the mutable scenic constructions had stayed the same, whereas the nation and its identity values had continued to morph. As a consequence, Vaněk's epoch-making image appeared more as a nostalgic attempt to look backwards and to recapture a past state of the nation. Audiences were confronted with an image which had become the memory of a memory, thus reiterating the narrator's tragic distance from the events and experiences of the play.

In 2004 the Gate Theatre in Dublin became the hosting site for a production of *Dancing at Lughnasa* under the direction of Joe Dowling, with the set design of Robert Jones and lighting design of Rupert Murray. Jones's visual response presented the audience with a conceptual image which contracts the expansiveness of the Mason-Vaněk image and excavated the dark and subterranean forces of the play. Here spectators were faced with a darkened and austere miniature-space which engulfed the pitch-brown exterior of a tiny farmhouse, with the narrow field as its decentered backdrop. A key image in this recreated, gloomy theatrical locale was the presence of a frame which had been superimposed on the more external frame of the proscenium stage of the Gate. The rectangular greyish frame, marble-like and abstract in its style, as the visualization of the play's memory framework, created a perceptual and emotional bridge between the performance space and the audience space. Within that visual filter of the frame, the austerity of the space intensified this opening tableau of gloom, isolation, and uncertainty. As soon as the play began, the revolving platform, on which the dark exterior of the house rested, revealed as its interior a contrastingly brightly-lit kitchen; then, as the tableau animates, the action started unfolding under the warm light. Yet, the visual impact of that sombre opening image of the farmhouse, like a shadowy Nativity, banished any nostalgia from the spectator's experience and functioned as a constantly surfacing visual reminder of the disturbing recesses of the play's fictional world.

The shift of the visual focus from the animated field, as it is in Vaněk's conception, to the abstract inner frame, as in Jones's vision, went along, in the Gate production, with a reinterpretation of the narrator's role. The actor performing Michael, Peter Gowen, moved anxiously across the whole onstage and offstage, thus traversing memory, 'reality' and the 'elsewhere'. In and out of his role, as if existentially denied a full possession of it, his own painful and problematic interpretation reopens the relationship between the flux of memory and the scenes of 'real' life, between the verbal and the visual, favouring a possibility of a rebalance between the two dimensions. The visual elements become so alive as to nearly spill out of the framing power of words and take on an ontological existence of their own. Nicolas Pussin's dictum that 'nothing is visible without boundaries' is here given visual stage expression.[11] It is as if spectators are invited to access the play's complex world through a series of multiplying frames which, one within the other, undermine the effect of one, unitary perspective and paradoxically lead to what Bleeker defines as 'an absence of frames, an absence that would allow for a direct access to the plenitude of being'.[12]

This battlefield of representational boundaries creates liminal zones of indeterminacy where performers and audiences can participate in the process of making meanings. These borderline moments suspended between change as created within Jones's bleak stage imagery revisualize a disquieting image of the Irish nation today: they hint at the downturn that has followed the prosperity and success of the 1990s decade, thus pointing towards the social and cultural limbo that post-millennium Ireland seems now to inhabit. In this layered and fluctuating condition, the experience of home and identity as a 'transient' set of relationships outside nationality and territoriality can be at once challenging and unsettling. The nation has been exposed to the opening of borders and has encountered 'otherness': it may now have to face the impossibility of embracing that otherness.

Pavis's typology of *mise-en-scène* as a confrontation between directors, 'visual directors'[13] and textual practice is relevant here to help to assess briefly the ideological weight and repercussions of the two scenic images.¹⁴ From the analyst's taxonomy two dimensions of *mise-en-scène* seem to serve our critical purpose: one is what he calls the 'autotextual' *mise-en-scène*, when productions tend to approach the playtext as a world of its own, with its own internal cohesion and logic, hermetically closed upon itself; the other is the 'ideotextual' one, when the interpretive strategy seeks relevance in the outside world and the new circumstances of reception, thus creating a relation of continuity between the play's world and the audience's world. While it could be argued that both productions' conceptual images tend towards the 'ideotextual', it seems to me that the status of the Mason-Vaněk transient stage composition has journeyed from 'ideotextual' to 'autotextual'. Beyond and apart from its physical adaptations and reinventions, its unchanged, surviving core image in the revived productions in 1999 and 2000 has broken the continuity between the play's perceptual world and the audience's perceptual world and engendered an unexplored fracture between the two worlds. The premiere production's diasporic trajectory, beginning in London, charted a process of reinvention and adaptation to new stages, which, however open-ended, masked a lack of change in its sense of Irishness, rather like a emigrant space relying on memory. The scenic image, sealed in a chamber of its own, was revealed upon its return as the entrapping and falsifying visual consciousness of the nation, now become a tragic witness to the space/time-specificity of production values. By contrast, Dowling's and Jones's compressed scenographic choice engendered an edgier feel of phenomenal strangeness, which unleashed again the spirit of the play and its current, disturbing topicality from the oppressive halo of past familiarity and knowability. Recalling Roland Barthes, it could be contended that the Mason-Vaněk scenic image, had evolved into his notion of '*studium*', having initially released and then submerged the play's '*punctum*', or as Barthes would have it, the 'element which rises from the scene, shoots out of it like an arrow and pierces [us]'.¹⁵

Given the multiple visual possibilities conjured up by each production's unique theatrical vision, it seems to me that there is more to Irish theatre than just 'words'. This visual quest has also proved how the aesthetic and ideological impacts inscribed in the mutable identity of scenographic art in touring and non-touring productions can have a foundational role in making and breaking images of theatrical nationhood.

The vast diversity of each production's image and scenographic realization asks spectators to ponder on the shifting and vulnerable nature of concepts such as nationhood, identity, and belonging. With each production, the scenic transposition seeks to reinvent Irish theatrical locations which, less burdened by national traditions and inherited visual formats, are characterized by inclusiveness, open-endedness, non-linearity, and multi-dimensionality. Such a representation foregrounds a move away from a bordered, stable and coherent notion of Ireland and 'Irishness' and opens up uncomfortable and unfamiliar zones of fragmentation, complexity and contradiction.

In view of the problematic and transient revisualizations of self and place which emerge in the spatial poetry of each production under scrutiny, this visual journey has revealed the fallible and precarious cartography of received notions of Irishness and identity in the hybridity of our current world. While this ontological vacuum interrogates the truth-value of identity as a point of origin in the cultural imagery of third-millennium European Ireland, it also asserts how theatre works. 'Plays', in Howard's words, 'do not belong to nations but to audiences'.[16]

---

[1] Jaroslav Malina, 'Theatrical Space in Postmodern Times: Concepts and Models of Space Analysis', *Space and the Postmodern Stage*, eds Irene Eynat-Confino and Eva Sormova (Prague: Prague Theatre Institute, 2000): 16.

[2] Una Chaudhuri and Elinor Fuchs, eds, *Land/Scape/Theater* (Ann Arbor: The University of Michigan Press, 2002): 2.

[3] Kevin Whelan, 'The cultural effects of the Famine', in *The Cambridge Companion to Modern Irish Culture* eds Joe Cleary and Claire Connolly, (Cambridge: Cambridge University Press, 2005): 152.

[4] Heidi Gilpin, 'Tracing displacement and disappearance', *Corporealities*, ed. Susan Leigh Foster (London: Routledge, 1996): 108.

[5] Jaroslav Malina, 'What actually is stage design – now for the tenth time...', *Prague Quadrennial: 2003* (Prague: Theatre Institute, 2003): 21.

[6] Pamela Howard, *What is Scenography?* (London: Routledge, 2002): 25.

[7] Joe Vaněk, 'Inspired Lughnasa: Designing for Friel', *Sightline*, January 1991: 17.

[8] Ibid.

[9] Michael Coveney, 'Arts (Theatre): Glee follows the Big Band', *The Observer*, 21 October 1990: 8.

[10] Joe Dowling, 'Joe Dowling in conversation with Miles Dungan', *Rattlebag*, RTE Radio 1, 25 February 2004.

[11] Quoted in Marc Robinson, 'Robert Wilson, Nicolas Pussin, and Lohengrin', *Land/Scape/Theater*: 176.

[12] Maaike Bleeker, 'Look who's looking!: Perspective and the Paradox of Postdramatic Subjectivity', *Theatre Research International*, 29 (2004): 32.

[13] Howard, 25.

[14] For the notion of 'autotextual' and 'ideotextual' in relation to *mise-en-scène* see

Patrice Pavis, *Theatre at the Crossroads of Culture*, trans. by Loren Kruger (London: Routledge, 1992): 36-9.
[15] Roland Barthes, 'The Phenomenological Attitude', *Critical Theory and Performance*, eds Janelle G. Reinelt and Joseph R. Roach (Ann Arbor: University of Michigan Press, 1992): 377.
[16] Howard, 33.

Part Three: A Staging History

Chronological Table Of Irish Plays Produced In London (1920-2006): Introductory remarks

Peter James Harris[1]

The work of Irish dramatists has been a constant presence in London theatres since the end of the seventeenth century, when George Farquhar's *Love and a Bottle* was first staged at the Theatre Royal, Drury Lane. In the latter half of the eighteenth century comedies by Arthur Murphy, Oliver Goldsmith, Richard Brinsley Sheridan, and John O'Keefe were drawing enthusiastic audiences, while in the nineteenth century it was plays by Boucicault, Wilde, and Shaw that were filling West End theatres. However, it is generally accepted that, thanks to the impetus provided by the founding of the Irish Literary Theatre in 1897, the twentieth century witnessed a growth of unparalleled proportions in terms of activity by Irish playwrights. On 8 December 2005 the Irish Government's Minister for Arts recognized the central role played by the theatre in Irish culture with the announcement that the Abbey Theatre can now look forward to a second century in a prestigious new theatre to be constructed on a site in Georges Dock, adding 'further lustre to its distinguished reputation for fostering Ireland's world class playwrights, actors and producers'. Nonetheless, more than eight decades after Independence, Irish playwrights and their agents continue to procure a London staging of their work in order to have the best possible chance of obtaining the critical

---

[1] The research presented here was conducted during Dr Harris's appointment as Visiting Research Fellow at the Drama and Theatre Department, Royal Holloway University of London, under the supervision of Professor Richard Allen Cave, and was funded by the São Paulo State Research Support Foundation (FAPESP).

attention and commercial success deserved by their writing. To a certain extent, therefore, it may be argued that the London theatres provide Irish dramatists with a benchmark by which they can measure the progress of their careers. At a wider level, London provides a mirror which reflects the physiognomy of the Irish theatre as a whole.

For the purposes of analysis, of course, generalized affirmations are of no value whatsoever. If the image of Irish drama seen in London is to be discussed it must first be described as accurately as possible. It was to this end that the cartographic exercise whose results are here set out was undertaken. The Table which follows is intended to serve as a map of the Irish play on the London stage from the decade which ushered in the Free State up until the present day. It is presented as an implement which, it is hoped, will assist future research and stimulate discussion. Like any tool, however, it is subject to parameters which must be understood by those who intend to make use of it. The data are presented in six columns as follows:

Year

The information is set out chronologically and covers the period from January 1920 until December 2006. The first column highlights the year in which a given presentation took place and is intended to facilitate access to the remaining information. Following each year the figure in brackets is the total number of productions staged in London that year. This serves as a useful guide to the general level of activity in the London theatre, and makes it possible to establish a concept of proportionality between the number of Irish plays staged in London in any given period and the total number of productions seen in London in the same period. Thus, it can be established that the 1,657 Irish plays registered here represent exactly 5% of the total of approximately 32,800 productions staged in London in the period covered by this survey. Furthermore, on a decade-by-decade basis it can be seen that this proportion is subject to very little variation. In the 1920s, for example, 5.1% of the plays seen in London were of Irish origin, while, in the period from 2000 onwards, the proportion was 4.5%. Viewed from this perspective the much-vaunted 'Irish invasion' of the 1990s becomes rather less impressive, since precisely 5.0% of the plays staged in London in that period were Irish, a lower percentage than the 6.4% represented by the 1960s.

A note of caution should be sounded, however, before too much weight is placed on these figures. Theatre is an ephemeral art form and the attempts to chronicle the detailed history of the London stage have been no less subject to periodic evanescence. As a result, the information for a panoramic survey must be culled from numerous sources, whose methodologies are not homogeneous. In J.P. Wearing's *Calendars of Plays and Players*, for example, the author includes operas and ballets in his survey of London performances. Although he lists performances at studio theatres such as the Unity he does not include these in his overall total of productions for any given year. On the other hand, *Theatre Record* does not cover opera and ballet performances but attempts to give information about every fringe theatrical venue. For the period from 1976 to 1980, when there was no published collation of each year's performances, it will be seen that an approximation is given, which is simply based on the average annual number of productions for the preceding fifty-five years. Despite such limitations, the correlation between the total number of London productions and the number of Irish plays staged in any given year holds true throughout the period. Thus, at one extreme, in the depths of the Second World War, the lowest number of productions staged in London in any one year was 167, in 1941, a year in which not a single Irish play was put on. At the other, 1999 was the year which witnessed the most intense theatrical activity in London, with 804 productions. Of those plays 51 were Irish, partly as a result of the Dublin Gate's Beckett festival, which gave London the benefit of 19 different plays in as many days but which nonetheless swelled Irish participation to just 6.3% of the total for that year.

Finally, observers of the Irish theatre in the U.K. will be interested to note the exceptional level of activity in 2006, when 53 Irish plays were seen in London theatres (including, it has to be said, three play-readings in the Royal Court's celebration of its 50th anniversary), representing 7.9% of the total number of plays staged in the city that year. It remains to be seen whether these statistics mark the beginning of a more significant 'Irish invasion' than that of the 1990s.

Author

The second column lists the author(s) of each of the plays listed. The name is registered as it was found in the source. Thus, for example, J.B. Fagan is sometimes registered as James B. Fagan, and St John Ervine as St John G.

Ervine. It should be stressed that it was not considered appropriate to limit the scope of this survey to a rigorous definition of Irishness by place of birth, although the huge majority of the dramatists included are indeed Irish as so-defined. There are, for example, a number of English-born dramatists who, for personal, political, or artistic reasons, have set one or more of their plays in Ireland. In some cases these dramatists have been assumed by critics and public alike to be Irish. Thus, Thomas Shadwell and his son Charles are included, from the seventeenth and eighteenth centuries respectively. More recently, it would have been equally inconsistent to exclude dramatists like Tyrone Guthrie, Lady Longford, David Rudkin, Martin McDonagh and Declan Donnellan on account of their English birth certificates. In other cases, it was felt important to include individual plays which have focused on Ireland in a significant manner, even though their authors may not have been Irish themselves. It was therefore decided to include such plays as Elsie T. Schauffler's *Parnell*, Howard Brenton's *The Romans in Britain*, and Helen Edmundsen's *The Clearing*, since the plays may be considered to be Irish even though their authors are not. Important adaptations of Irish plays are also included, like Mustapha Matura's Trinidadian version of *The Playboy of the Western World* and Mark-Anthony Turnage's opera based on *The Silver Tassie*. It was deemed more appropriate that subsequent researchers should be able to apply selection criteria according to individual needs rather than limiting the information a priori.

Title (First Appearance)

In addition to the title of the work this column also registers the year in which a play was first made available to the public. This normally implies the year of the stage premiere, but in some cases could refer to the publication of the playscript if this occurred first. In a small number of instances it has proved impossible to determine the year of a play's first appearance, in which case the lacuna is represented by means of asterisks. Where a play was presented in a double or triple bill this fact is indicated by the use of curly brackets { }. Since all productions are necessarily either a premiere or a revival it was felt that to categorize every entry in this way would overload the table with repetitive information. However, the interval between a play's first appearance and the year of a given production is of considerable utility when analysing the production history of a play or the artistic policy of a theatre.

This column also contains information where necessary to identify the source of plays that are either translated or adapted from other plays, which has been a growing tendency in the Irish theatre over the past couple of decades.

Comment

This space has been utilized to include relevant information about the characteristics of a particular production, especially where this makes it clear that the production itself was imported from Ireland. The names of notable directors are registered, and the column also indicates the genre of a production where it is not a 'straight' play.

Date

The date registered here is that of the production's opening night in London. Productions are listed in strictly chronological order, with the exception of those where this information was unavailable. Where a precise date is not known the lacuna is represented by asterisks.

Venue (Run)

The last column in the table sets out information about where a particular production was staged and for how long. These matters are not as straightforward as they might appear to be at first sight. Restricting this survey to the theatres of the West End would have resulted in a very incomplete picture of the Irish play on the London stage, particularly in the last thirty-five years, which have witnessed the exponential growth of fringe theatre. However, for budgetary and other motives, fringe venues are often less than successful at publicizing their productions, with the result that smaller fish may occasionally slip through the net. For this reason, the information presented here cannot be regarded as absolutely definitive but rather as a work in progress. To this end, the author would welcome any information about gaps, which may be sent by e-mail to peter@ibilce.unesp.br .

With regard to the question of the length of a production's run, this information is of great utility in giving a quick, rule-of-thumb notion as to the play's commercial success. Whilst one appreciates that the number of performances a play receives is governed by a complex series of factors in addition to its box-office appeal, it is generally true that a theatre management will find the means to extend the run of a play that is selling well. Unfortunately, however, this information is not always easily available. Up until the end of the 1950s the meticulous research of J.P. Wearing enabled him to calculate the exact length of the run for virtually every play staged in the West End. From 1981 onwards *London Theatre Record* (subsequently, *Theatre Record*) published the opening and closing nights of each production's run. For this period, therefore, a calculation of the number of performances was made on the basis of the number of *days* that a production was running, with no attempt to include matinées. This calculation was not made for plays staged at the theatres operated by the Royal Shakespeare Company and Royal National Theatre, whose repertory system makes it impossible to apply this methodology. In the latter section of the table, covering the period from 1981 onwards, the approximate calculation of a production's run is not indicated by 'c.' Prior to this period, however, where the majority of the figures are precise, the use of *circa* indicates that a calculation was made.

* * *

In conclusion, it should be pointed out that the information presented here forms the backdrop for a project which focuses specifically upon the reception of the Irish play on the London stage, so this table is part of a work-in-progress. However, it is very much hoped that publication of this initial mapping of the terrain will be of benefit to other researchers in the area.

CHRONOLOGICAL TABLE OF IRISH PLAYS PRODUCED IN LONDON (1920-2006)

A chronological listing of data concerning Irish plays staged in London in the period from 1920 to 2006, including author's name, title (with the year of the play's first public appearance), date of London opening, venue and, where known, the length of the London run in performances.

Principal sources:

1920-29: WEARING, J.P. *The London Stage 1920-1929: A Calendar of Plays and Players.* (Vol. 1: 1920-1924; Vol. 2: 1925-1929; Vol.3: Indexes.) Metuchen, N.J. & London: Scarecrow Press, 1984.

1930-39: WEARING, J.P. *The London Stage 1930-1939: A Calendar of Plays and Players.* (Vol. 1: 1930-1934; Vol. 2: 1935-1939; Vol.3: Indexes.) Metuchen, N.J. & London: Scarecrow Press, 1990.

1940-49: WEARING, J.P. *The London Stage 1940-1949: A Calendar of Plays and Players.* (Vol. 1: 1940-1949; Vol. 2: Indexes.) Metuchen, N.J. & London: Scarecrow Press, 1991.

1950-59: WEARING, J.P. *The London Stage 1950-1959: A Calendar of Plays and Players.* (Vol. 1: 1950-1957; Vol. 2: 1958-1959 and indexes.) Metuchen, N.J. & London: Scarecrow Press, 1993.

1960-68: MERRYN, Anthony (ed.). *The Stage Year Book 1961.* 30th edition. London: Carson & Comerford, 1961.
—. *The Stage Year Book 1962.* 31st edition. London: Carson & Comerford, 1962.
—. *The Stage Year Book 1963.* 32nd edition. London: Carson & Comerford, 1963.
—. *The Stage Year Book 1964.* 33rd edition. London: Carson & Comerford, 1964.
—. *The Stage Year Book 1965.* 34th edition. London: Carson & Comerford, 1965.
—. *The Stage Year Book 1966.* 35th edition. London: Carson & Comerford, 1966.

———. *The Stage Year Book 1967*. 36th edition. London: Carson & Comerford, 1967.
———. *The Stage Year Book 1968*. 37th edition. London: Carson & Comerford, 1968.
———. *The Stage Year Book 1969*. 38th edition. London: Carson & Comerford, 1969.

1969-75: PARKER, John (ed.). *Who's who in the theatre. A biographical record of the contemporary stage*. London: Isaac Pitman (15th edition, 1972; 16th edition, 1977).

1976-80: British Theatre Association (BTA) scrapbooks, organised by Enid Foster and now held in the archives of the Theatre Museum, Blythe House, Kensington Olympia.

1981-90: *London Theatre Record* – fortnightly publication which collates reviews of every first-night performance of plays staged in the London area.

1991-2006: *Theatre Record* – as above, but renamed to register the publication's widened focus which now includes regional professional productions in addition to London first nights.

YEAR	AUTHOR	TITLE (FIRST APPEARANCE)	COMMENT	DATE	VENUE (RUN)
1920 (414)	G.B. Shaw	*Pygmalion* (1913)		10/2/1920	Aldwych (78)
	St. John G. Ervine	*John Ferguson* (1915)		23/2/1920	Lyric, Hammersmith (65)
	Richard Brinsley Sheridan	*The Rivals* (1775)		8/3/1920	Old Vic (13)
	Dion Boucicault/J. Benedict	*The Lily of Killarney* (1862)	Musical version of *The Colleen Bawn*	18/3/1920	Old Vic (3)
	Lord Dunsany	{*The Glittering Gate* (1909)}		21/3/1920	Lyric, Hammersmith (1)
	G.B. Shaw	{*The Dark Lady of the Sonnets* (1910)}		21/3/1920	Lyric, Hammersmith (1)
	G.B. Shaw	*Pygmalion* (1913)		10/5/1920	Duke of York's (24)
	W.B. Yeats	*The Land of Heart's Desire* (1894)		18/5/1920	Old Vic (1)
	Lennox Robinson	*The Whiteheaded Boy* (1916)		27/9/1920	Ambassadors (292)
	G.B. Shaw	*You Never Can Tell* (1899)		27/9/1920	Everyman (20)
	Richard Brinsley Sheridan	*The School for Scandal* (1777)		25/10/1920	Old Vic (15)
	G.B. Shaw	*You Never Can Tell* (1899)		22/11/1920	Garrick (9)
	G.B. Shaw	*O'Flaherty, V.C.* (1917)		19/12/1920	Lyric, Hammersmith (2)
1921 (375)	G.B. Shaw	*You Never Can Tell* (1899)		24/1/1921	Everyman (8)
	G.B. Shaw	*Candida* (1897)		7/2/1921	Everyman (14)
	G.B. Shaw	*Great Catherine* (1913)		18/2/1921	Shaftesbury (1)
	G.B. Shaw	*The Doctor's Dilemma* (1906)		21/2/1921	Everyman (28)
	Oscar Wilde	*A Florentine Tragedy* (1906)		22/2/1921	Kingsway (1)
	G.B. Shaw	{*How He Lied to Her Husband* (1904)}		14/3/1921	Everyman (19)

	Author	Play	Notes	Date	Venue
	G.B. Shaw	{The Dark Lady of the Sonnets (1910)}		14/3/1921	Everyman (19)
	G.B. Shaw	{The Shewing Up of Blanco Posnet (1909)}		14/3/1921	Everyman (19)
	Dion Boucicault/J. Benedict	The Lily of Killarney (1862)	Musical version of The Colleen Bawn	17/3/1921	Old Vic (2)
	W.B. Yeats	{Kathleen ni Houlihan (1902)}	Abbey Players	6/4/1921	Ambassadors (1)
	J.M. Synge	{In the Shadow of the Glen (1903)}	Abbey Players	6/4/1921	Ambassadors (1)
	Lady Gregory	{Spreading the News (1904)}	Abbey Players	6/4/1921	Ambassadors (1)
	G.B. Shaw	Major Barbara (1905)		18/4/1921	Everyman (28)
	G.B. Shaw	Man and Superman (1905)		23/5/1921	Everyman (23)
	Lord Dunsany	If (1921)	Première	30/5/1921	Ambassadors (180)
	Lady Gregory	{The Workhouse Ward (1908)}	Abbey Players	10/6/1921	Court (1)
	J.M. Synge	{Riders to the Sea (1904)}	Abbey Players	10/6/1921	Court (1)
	Lady Gregory	{The Rising of the Moon (1907)}	Abbey Players	10/6/1921	Court (1)
	G.B. Shaw	{The Dark Lady of the Sonnets (1910)}		20/7/1921	Queen's (29)
	G.B. Shaw	{The Shewing Up of Blanco Posnet (1909)}		20/7/1921	Queen's (29)
	J.M. Synge	The Playboy of the Western World (1907)	Directed by J.B. Fagan	25/7/1921	Court (48)
	G.B. Shaw	John Bull's Other Island (1904)	Directed by J.B. Fagan	9/9/1921	Court (43)
	G.B. Shaw	Heartbreak House (1920)	Directed by J.B. Fagan	18/10/1921	Court (63)
	W.B. Yeats	The Land of Heart's Desire (1894)		14/11/1921	Kingsway (21)
	Lord Dunsany	{Cheezo (1921)}		15/11/1921	Everyman (24)
	Lord Dunsany	{The Tents of the Arabs (1917)}		15/11/1921	Everyman (24)
	Lord Dunsany	{A Night at an Inn (1916)}		15/11/1921	Everyman (24)
	Lord Dunsany	{The Lost Silk Hat (1921)}		15/11/1921	Everyman (24)
	Oliver Goldsmith	She Stoops to Conquer (1773)		12/12/1921	Court (59)
	J.M. Synge	{In the Shadow of the Glen (1903)}	The Irish Players	26/12/1921	Everyman (22)
	William Boyle	{The Building Fund (1905)}	The Irish Players	26/12/1921	Everyman (22)
	Oliver Goldsmith	She Stoops to Conquer (1773)		26/12/1921	Old Vic (7)

1922 (361)	St. John G. Ervine	Mixed Marriage (1911)	The Irish Players	23/1/1922	Everyman (80)
	G.B. Shaw	Fanny's First Play (1911)		6/2/1922	Everyman (28)
	J.M. Synge	Riders to the Sea (1904)	The Irish Players	13/2/1922	Ambassadors (17)
	W.B. Yeats	Kathleen ni Houlihan (1902)	The Irish Players	27/2/1922	Ambassadors (25)
	G.B. Shaw	Arms and the Man (1894)		6/3/1922	Everyman (21)
	Dion Boucicault/J. Benedict	The Lily of Killarney (1862)	Musical version of The Colleen Bawn	16/3/1922	Old Vic (2)
	Lady Gregory	Hyacinth Halvey (1906)	The Irish Players	18/3/1922	Ambassadors (24)
	G.B. Shaw	Getting Married (1908)		27/3/1922	Everyman (21)
	St.John G. Ervine	Progress (1922)	Première	3/4/1922	Little (63)
	Lennox Robinson	The Whiteheaded Boy (1916)	The Irish Players	8/4/1922	Aldwych (24)
	G.B. Shaw	Misalliance (1910)		18/4/1922	Everyman (22)
	G.B. Shaw	You Never Can Tell (1899)		16/5/1922	Everyman (20)
	J.M. Synge	Riders to the Sea (1904)		4/7/1922	Aldwych (1)
	G.B. Shaw	Candida (1897)		24/7/1922	Everyman (14)
	G.B. Shaw	Widowers' Houses (1892)		4/9/1922	Everyman
	James B. Fagan	Treasure Island (1922) – from R.L. Stevenson		23/12/1922	Strand (137)
1923 (301)	G.B. Shaw	The Philanderer (1905)		29/1/1923	Everyman (21)
	Dion Boucicault/J. Benedict	The Lily of Killarney (1862)	Musical version of The Colleen Bawn	15/3/1923	Old Vic (2)
	G.B. Shaw	The Doctor's Dilemma (1906)		2/4/1923	Everyman (28)
	G.B. Shaw	Major Barbara (1905)		28/5/1923	Everyman (21)
	G.B. Shaw	Candida (1897)		18/6/1923	Everyman (21)
	Gerald MacNamara	Thompson in Tir-na-n-Og (1912)		29/6/1923	Scala (9)
	Gerald MacNamara	The Throwbacks (1917)		2/7/1923	Scala (6)

	"George Birmingham"	*Send for Dr. O'Grady* (1911)	First performed Gaiety, Dublin as *Eleanor's Enterprise*	4/7/1923	Criterion (45)
	G.B. Shaw	*Fanny's First Play* (1911)		9/7/1923	Everyman (21)
	George Moore	*The Coming of Gabrielle* (1913)	First performed as *Elizabeth Cooper*	17/7/1923	St. James's (3)
	G.B. Shaw	*The Dark Lady of the Sonnets* (1910)		17/9/1923	Kingsway (40)
	Oscar Wilde	*The Importance of Being Earnest* (1895)		21/11/1923	Haymarket (61)
	James B. Fagan	*Treasure Island* (1922) – from R.L. Stevenson		24/12/1923	Strand (55)
	Richard Brinsley Sheridan	*The School for Scandal* (1777)		26/12/1923	Old Vic (10)
1924 (422)	G.B. Shaw	*Back to Methuselah: Part I* (1922)		18/2/1924	Court (4)
	G.B. Shaw	*Back to Methuselah: Part II* (1922)		19/2/1924	Court (4)
	G.B. Shaw	*Back to Methuselah: Part III* (1922)		20/2/1924	Court (4)
	G.B. Shaw	*Back to Methuselah: Part IV* (1922)		21/2/1924	Court (1)
	G.B. Shaw	*Back to Methuselah: Part V* (1922)		22/2/1924	Court (4)
	Richard Brinsley Sheridan	*The Rivals* (1775)		10/3/1924	Old Vic (9)
	Dion Boucicault/J. Benedict	*The Lily of Killarney* (1862)	Musical version of *The Colleen Bawn*	13/3/1924	Old Vic (2)
	G.B. Shaw	*Saint Joan* (1923)		26/3/1924	New (244)
	G.B. Shaw	{*The Man of Destiny* (1897)}		11/6/1924	Everyman (13)
	G.B. Shaw	{*Augustus Does His Bit* (1917)}		11/6/1924	Everyman (13)
	G.B. Shaw	*Getting Married* (1908)		9/7/1924	Everyman (33)
	G.B. Shaw	{*The Man of Destiny* (1897)}		27/8/1924	Everyman (15)
	G.B. Shaw	{*How He Lied to Her Husband* (1904)}		27/8/1924	Everyman (15)
	G.B. Shaw	*Back to Methuselah: Part I* (1922)		10/9/1924	Court (4)
	G.B. Shaw	*Back to Methuselah: Part V* (1922)		12/9/1924	Court (4)

	G.B. Shaw	The Devil's Disciple (1897)		24/9/1924	Everyman (26)
	G.B. Shaw	Fanny's First Play (1911)		29/9/1924	Regent (2)
	G.B. Shaw	Pygmalion (1913)		30/9/1924	Regent (2)
	G.B. Shaw	Man and Superman (1905)		1/10/1924	Regent (3)
	G.B. Shaw	Candida (1897)		2/10/1924	Regent (1)
	G.B. Shaw	{The Dark Lady of the Sonnets (1910)}		3/10/1924	Regent (2)
	G.B. Shaw	{The Man of Destiny (1897)}		3/10/1924	Regent (2)
	G.B. Shaw	{How He Lied to Her Husband (1904)}		3/10/1924	Regent (2)
	G.B. Shaw	Arms and the Man (1894)		6/10/1924	Regent (1)
	G.B. Shaw	The Devil's Disciple (1897)		8/10/1924	Regent (1)
	G.B. Shaw	You Never Can Tell (1899)		9/10/1924	Regent (1)
	G.B. Shaw	The Doctor's Dilemma (1906)		9/10/1924	Regent (1)
	Lennox Robinson	Crabbed Youth and Age (1922)		15/10/1924	Dramatic Art Centre
	Richard Brinsley Sheridan	The Duenna (1775)		23/10/1924	Lyric, Hammersmith (145)
	G.B. Shaw	Misalliance (1910)		27/10/1924	Everyman (14)
	G.B. Shaw	The Philanderer (1905)		26/12/1924	Everyman (18)
	Oliver Goldsmith	She Stoops to Conquer (1773)		26/12/1924	Old Vic (8)
1925 (408)	G.B. Shaw	St. Joan (1923)		14/1/1925	Regent (132)
	Richard Brinsley Sheridan	The Rivals (1775)		5/3/1925	Lyric, Hammersmith (93)
	"Lynn Doyle"	Persevering Pat (1913)	First performed Belfast as Love and Land	13/3/1925	Little (27)
	Dion Boucicault/J. Benedict	The Lily of Killarney (1862)	Musical version of The Colleen Bawn	19/3/1925	Old Vic (2)
	G.B. Shaw	Caesar and Cleopatra (1906)		21/4/1925	Kingsway (78)
	Lennox Robinson	The Round Table (1922)		11/5/1925	Wyndham's (21)
	Lady Gregory	Mirandolina (1910) – from Goldoni		17/8/1925	Everyman (7)
	G.B. Shaw	Pygmalion (1913)		7/9/1925	Regent (18)

	Author	Play	Notes	Date	Theatre (perfs)
	G.B. Shaw	*You Never Can Tell* (1899)		11/9/1925	Regent (9)
	G.B. Shaw	*Man and Superman* (1905)		14/9/1925	Regent (7)
	G.B. Shaw	*Getting Married* (1908)		18/9/1925	Regent (9)
	G.B. Shaw	*The Doctor's Dilemma* (1906)		21/9/1925	Regent (16)
	G.B. Shaw	*Arms and the Man* (1894)		25/9/1925	Regent (21)
	G.B. Shaw	*Mrs. Warren's Profession* (1902)		28/9/1925	Regent (9)
	G.B. Shaw	*Fanny's First Play* (1911)		2/10/1925	Regent (8)
	G.B. Shaw	*Candida* (1897)		9/10/1925	Regent (5)
	J.M. Synge	*The Playboy of the Western World* (1907)	The Irish Players	12/10/1925	Royalty (40)
	G.B. Shaw	*Major Barbara* (1905)		16/10/1925	Regent (3)
	Lady Gregory	*The Rising of the Moon* (1907)	The Irish Players	17/10/1925	Royalty (26)
	G.B. Shaw	*Man and Superman* (1905)		23/10/1925	Royalty (5)
	G.B. Shaw	*The Devil's Disciple* (1897)		2/11/1925	Regent (6)
	Sean O'Casey	*Juno and the Paycock* (1924)	Transferred to Fortune 8/3/26 – Irish Players, produced by J.B. Fagan	16/11/1925	Royalty (202)
	Norman Frost / Kingsley Lark / Patrick Barrow	*Nicolette* (1925)	Musical, first performed Gaiety, Dublin, 31/8/25	18/11/1925	Duke of York's (12)
	G.B. Shaw	*Overruled* (1912)		30/11/1925	Regent (4)
	G.B. Shaw	{*The Shewing Up of Blanco Posnet* (1909)}		26/12/1925	Regent (42)
	G.B. Shaw	{*Androcles and the Lion* (1912)}		26/12/1925	Regent (42)
1926 (394)	Oliver Goldsmith	*She Stoops to Conquer* (1773)		18/1/1926	Old Vic (14)
	G.B. Shaw	*The Man of Destiny* (1897)		1/2/1926	Regent (7)
	G.B. Shaw	*John Bull's Other Island* (1904)		8/2/1926	Regent (19)
	James Joyce	*Exiles* (1918)		14/2/1926	Regent (2)
	G.B. Shaw	*Mrs. Warren's Profession* (1902)		3/3/1926	Strand (68)

Year	Author	Play	Notes	Date	Theatre
	Dion Boucicault/J. Benedict	*The Lily of Killarney* (1862)	Musical version of *The Colleen Bawn*	18/3/1926	Old Vic (2)
	G.B. Shaw	*Saint Joan* (1923)		24/3/1926	Lyceum (53)
	T.C. Murray	*Autumn Fire* (1924)	General Strike 4/5 – 17/5/1926	13/4/1926	Little (c.62)
	Sean O'Casey	*The Plough and the Stars* (1926)	Transferred to New 28/6/26	12/5/1926	Fortune (133)
	G.B. Shaw	*Back to Methuselah: Part I* (1922)		18/5/1926	Court (1)
	Kate O'Brien	*Distinguished Villa* (1926)		12/7/1926	Little (64)
	G.B. Shaw	*Widowers' Houses* (1892)		26/7/1926	Everyman (16)
	J.B. Fagan	"*And so to Bed*" (1926) – from Pepys		6/9/1926	Queen's (334)
	G.B. Shaw	*Arms and the Man* (1894)		16/9/1926	Everyman (19)
	Dion Boucicault	*The Octoroon* (1859)		15/11/1926	Fortune (1)
	G.B. Shaw	*The Doctor's Dilemma* (1906)		17/11/1926	Kingsway (37)
	Lord Dunsany	*The Lost Silk Hat* (1921)		25/11/1926	Everyman (14)
	Lennox Robinson	*The Whiteheaded Boy* (1916)	The Irish Players	13/12/1926	Criterion (53)
	G.B. Shaw	*Pygmalion* (1913)		19/1/1927	Kingsway (25)
1927 (380)	George Farquhar	*The Beaux' Stratagem* (1707)		20/1/1927	Lyric, Hammersmith (143)
	Sean O'Casey	*Juno and the Paycock* (1924)	Transferred to Vaudeville 14/2/1927 – Irish Players, produced by J.B. Fagan	24/1/1927	Criterion (63)
	G.B. Shaw	*Man and Superman* (1905)		10/2/1927	Kingsway (44)
	J.B. Fagan	*The Greater Love* (1927)		23/2/1927	Princes (53)
	Dion Boucicault/J. Benedict	*The Lily of Killarney* (1862)	Musical version of *The Colleen Bawn*	17/3/1927	Old Vic (2)
	George Shiels	*Professor Tim* (1925)	The Irish Players	22/3/1927	Vaudeville (37)

	Author	Play	Notes	Date	Venue
	Richard Brinsley Sheridan	St. Patrick's Day; or The Schemeing Lieutenant (1775)		28/3/1927	Old Vic (12)
	St. John Ervine	The Lady of Belmont (1924)		6/5/1927	Arts
	Sean O'Casey	The Shadow of a Gunman (1923)	The Irish Players	27/5/1927	Court (66)
	J.M. Synge	Riders to the Sea (1904)	The Irish Players	27/5/1927	Court (20)
	Kate O'Brien	The Bridge (1927)		31/5/1927	Arts
	Bernard Duffy	The Cainer (1915)		15/6/1927	Court (14)
	Oscar Wilde	The Florentine Tragedy (1906)		26/6/1927	Arts
	G.B. Shaw	Overruled (1912)		3/8/1927	Everyman (19)
	Richard Brinsley Sheridan	The School for Scandal (1777)		8/11/1927	London Hippodrome (1)
	G.B. Shaw	The Glimpse of Reality (1927)		20/11/1927	Arts (4)
	G.B. Shaw	Getting Married (1908)		5/12/1927	Little (24)
	G.B. Shaw	Back to Methuselah: Part I (1922)		9/12/1927	Wyndham's (1)
	G.B. Shaw	You Never Can Tell (1899)		26/12/1927	Little (26)
1928 (463)	G.B. Shaw	Man and Superman (1905)		16/1/1928	Little (27)
	G.B. Shaw	{The Fascinating Foundling (1928)}	First professional performance	28/1/1928	Arts (4)
	W.B. Yeats	{The Land of Heart's Desire (1894)}		28/1/1928	Arts (4)
	G.B. Shaw	Mrs. Warren's Profession (1905)		6/2/1928	Little (7)
	G.B. Shaw	Back to Methuselah: Part I (1922)		5/3/1928	Court (10)
	G.B. Shaw	Back to Methuselah: Part II (1922)		5/3/1928	Court (9)
	G.B. Shaw	Back to Methuselah: Part III (1922)		12/3/1928	Court (9)
	G.B. Shaw	Back to Methuselah: Part IV (1922)		12/3/1928	Court (9)
	Dion Boucicault/J. Benedict	The Lily of Killarney (1862)	Musical version of The Colleen Bawn	15/3/1928	Old Vic (2)
	G.B. Shaw	Back to Methuselah: Part V (1922)		19/3/1928	Court (11)
	Richard Brinsley Sheridan	The School for Scandal (1777)		26/3/1928	Old Vic (14)
	George Moore	The Making of an Immortal (1928)		1/4/1928	Arts (2)

	Oliver Goldsmith	*She Stoops to Conquer* (1773)		16/8/1928	Lyric, Hammersmith (78)
	J.B. Fagan, et al.	*The Beetle* (1928)		9/10/1928	Strand (30)
	Richard Brinsley Sheridan	*The Critic; or, A Tragedy Rehearsed* (1779)		24/10/1928	Lyric, Hammersmith (77)
	Lady Gregory	{*The Workhouse Ward* (1908)}	The Irish Players	25/10/1928	Arts (4)
	T.C. Murray	{*Birthright* (1910)}	The Irish Players	25/10/1928	Arts (4)
	J.M. Synge	{*In the Shadow of the Glen* (1903)}	The Irish Players	25/10/1928	Arts (4)
1929 (455)	Lennox Robinson	*Give a Dog . . . .* (1928)		20/1/1929	Strand (1)
	St. John G. Ervine	*The Ship* (1922)		28/1/1929	Everyman (24)
	G.B. Shaw	*Major Barbara* (1905)		5/3/1929	Wyndham's (63)
	Richard Brinsley Sheridan	*The Rivals* (1775)		11/3/1929	Old Vic (14)
	Lennox Robinson	*The Far-Off Hills* (1928)		30/3/1929	'Q'
	St. John Ervine	*Jane Clegg* (1913)		29/5/1929	Wyndham's (21)
	St. John Ervine	*The First Mrs Fraser* (1928)		2/7/1929	Haymarket (632)
	G.B. Shaw	*The Apple Cart* (1929)		17/9/1929	Queen's (285)
	Sean O'Casey	*The Silver Tassie* (1929)		11/10/1929	Apollo (66)
	G.B. Shaw	*Captain Brassbound's Conversion* (1900)		7/11/1929	Everyman (12)
	Richard Brinsley Sheridan	*The School for Scandal* (1777)		28/11/1929	Kingsway (121)
	Lady Gregory	*The Workhouse Ward* (1908)		4/12/1929	Lyric, Hammersmith (22)
	G.B. Shaw	*Arms and the Man* (1894)		23/12/1929	Court (23)
	G.B. Shaw	*Pygmalion* (1913)		30/12/1929	Court (8)
1930 (455)	G.B. Shaw	*Man and Superman* (1905)		6/1/1930	Court (23)
	G.B. Shaw	*The Doctor's Dilemma* (1906)		13/11/1930	Court (8)
	G.B. Shaw	*The Philanderer* (1905)		20/1/1930	Court (8)
	J.B. Fagan	*Bella Donna* (1911) – from R. Hichens		25/1/1930	Regent (12)

	Author	Play	Note	Date	Theatre
	G.B. Shaw	‡Androcles and the Lion (1913)‡		24/2/1930	Old Vic (23)
	G.B. Shaw	‡The Dark Lady of the Sonnets (1910)‡		24/2/1930	Old Vic (23)
	G.B. Shaw	Misalliance (1910)		17/3/1930	Court (47)
	W.B. Yeats / G. Antheil	Fighting the Waves (1929)	Ballet Play	28/3/1930	Lyric, Hammersmith (1)
	Oliver Goldsmith	She Stoops to Conquer (1773)		19/4/1930	Lyric, Hammersmith (25)
	Sean O'Casey	The Plough and the Stars (1926)	The Irish Players	2/6/1930	Duchess (40)
	G.B. Shaw	Sainte Jeanne (1923) - Translated by A. & H. Hamon		10/6/1930	Globe (11)
	George Farquhar	The Beaux' Stratagem (1707)		11/6/1930	Royalty (92)
	G.B. Shaw	Annajanska, the Bolshevik Empress (1917)		27/6/1930	Grafton (26)
	Oscar Wilde	Lady Windermere's Fan (1892)		3/7/1930	Everyman (25)
	Oscar Wilde	The Importance of Being Earnest (1895)		7/7/1930	Lyric, Hammersmith (104)
	G.B. Shaw	The Fascinating Foundling (1928)		7/7/1930	Players'
	Lennox Robinson	The Far-Off Hills (1928)	The Irish Players	1/9/1930	Everyman (62)
	G.B. Shaw	The Devil's Disciple (1897)		2/9/1930	Savoy (51)
	Lennox Robinson	Give a Dog . . . (1928)		15/9/1930	Embassy
	George Moore	The Passing of the Essenes (1930)		1/10/1930	Arts (13)
	Oscar Wilde	A Woman of No Importance (1893)		11/10/1930	Regent (12)
	J.M. Synge	The Playboy of the Western World (1907)	The Irish Players	28/10/1930	Criterion (30)
1931 (555)	J.B. Fagan	The Improper Duchess (1931)		22/1/1931	Globe (348)
	Lord Dunsany	If (1921)		12/2/1931	Arts (13)
	G.B. Shaw	Arms and the Man (1894)		16/2/1931	Old Vic (24)
	G.B. Shaw	Fanny's First Play (1911)		4/3/1931	Court (29)
	Dion Boucicault/J. Benedict	The Lily of Killarney (1862)	Musical version of The Colleen Bawn	14/3/1931	Old Vic (5)

Author	Play	Company	Date	Theatre
Sir Frank Popham Young	{The Accomplice (1931)}	The Irish Players	15/3/1931	Arts (1)
Lady Gregory	{The Jail Gate (1906)}	The Irish Players	15/3/1931	Arts (1)
Una O'Connor	{Love at First Sight (1931)}	The Irish Players	15/3/1931	Arts (1)
Aubrey Ensor	(The Perfect Plot (1931)}	The Irish Players	15/3/1931	Arts (1)
Rosalind Wade	{Strange Adventure of a Maiden Lady (1931)}	The Irish Players	15/3/1931	Arts (1)
G.B. Shaw	Widowers' Houses (1892)		22/3/1931	Prince of Wales's (2)
G.B. Shaw	Mrs. Warren's Profession (1902)		30/3/1931	Court (14)
G.B. Shaw	Saint Joan (1923)		6/4/1931	His Majesty's (48)
George Shiels	The New Gossoon (The Girl on the Pillion) (1930) Title changed on transfer to Duchess 27/4/1931	The Irish Players	7/4/1931	Apollo (39)
G.B. Shaw	Man and Superman (1905)		10/4/1931	Court (1)
Richard Brinsley Sheridan	The Duenna (1775)		22/4/1931	Lyric, Hammersmith (21)
St. John G. Ervine	The First Mrs. Fraser (1929)		25/4/1931	Regent (12)
G.B. Shaw	Pygmalion (1914)		4/5/1931	Kingsway (16)
G.B. Shaw	Man and Superman (1905)		18/5/1931	Kingsway (16)
Oscar Wilde	Salomé (1896)		27/5/1931	Gate
Lord Dunsany	The Lost Silk Hat (1921)		31/5/1931	Fortune (2)
St. John G. Ervine	The Ship (1922)		10/6/1931	Fortune (29)
Oscar Wilde	Lady Windermere's Fan (1892)		12/6/1931	His Majesty's (1)
Rosalind Wade	Episode (1931)		21/6/1931	Everyman (1)
Oscar Wilde	Lady Windermere's Fan (1892)		4/7/1931	Regent (12)
T.C. Murray	Autumn Fire (1924)	The Irish Players	21/9/1931	Everyman (16)
Lord Dunsany	{A Night at an Inn (1916)}		5/10/1931	Savoy (16)
Oscar Wilde	{Salomé (1896)}	Transferred to Duke of York's 21/10/31	5/10/1931	Savoy (30)

	James B. Fagan	And So to Bed (1926)		26/11/1931	Globe (72)
	James B. Fagan	Treasure Island (1922) – from R.L. Stevenson		26/12/1931	New (27)
1932 (472)	Dion Boucicault/J. Benedict	The Lily of Killarney (1862)	Musical version of The Colleen Bawn	17/3/1932	Sadler's Wells (2)
	G.B. Shaw	Heartbreak House (1920)		25/4/1932	Queen's (48)
	Oliver Goldsmith	She Stoops to Conquer (1773)		5/5/1932	Kingsway (29)
	Oscar Wilde	The Importance of Being Earnest (1895)		4/6/1932	Regent (12)
	G.B. Shaw	Too True to Be Good (1932)		13/9/1932	New (47)
	G.B. Shaw	Caesar and Cleopatra (1907)		19/9/1932	Old Vic (21)
	Tyrone Guthrie	Follow Me (1932)		11/11/1932	Westminster (11)
	G.B. Shaw	Getting Married (1908)		25/11/1932	Little (27)
	Dion Boucicault	The Streets of London; or, Poverty is No Crime (1857)		20/12/1932	Ambassadors (158)
1933 (399)	Oliver Goldsmith	She Stoops to Conquer (1773)		2/1/1933	Old Vic (21)
	Paul Vincent Carroll	Things That Are Caesar's (1932)	The Irish Players	11/1/1933	Arts (6)
	G.B. Shaw	The Admirable Bashville; or, Constancy Rewarded (1903)		13/2/1933	Old Vic (19)
	Lord Dunsany	The Lost Silk Hat (1921)		24/2/1933	Little (13)
	St. John G. Ervine	The Lady of Belmont (1924)		26/3/1933	Cambridge (1)
	Richard Brinsley Sheridan	The School for Scandal (1777)		27/3/1933	Old Vic (21)
	Richard Brinsley Sheridan	The Rivals (1775)		1/5/1933	Embassy
	Lennox Robinson	Is Life Worth Living? (1933) [Drama at Inish]		22/8/1933	Ambassador (102)
	G.B. Shaw	On the Rocks (1933)	Première	25/11/1933	Winter Garden (73)
	James B. Fagan	Treasure Island (1922) – from R.L. Stevenson		26/12/1933	New (23)

1934 (391)	Richard Brinsley Sheridan	*The Rivals* (1775)		18/1/1934	Ambassadors (37)
	Oscar Wilde	*The Importance of Being Earnest* (1895)		5/2/1934	Old Vic (28)
	Sean O'Casey	*Within the Gates* (1934)		7/2/1934	Royalty (40)
	George Shiels	*Paul Twyning* (1922)	The Irish Players	14/2/1934	Little (17)
	Lennox Robinson	*The Big House: Four Scenes in its Life* (1926)		21/2/1934	Playhouse (13)
	Sean O'Casey	*Juno and the Paycock* (1924)	The Irish Players, produced by Arthur Sinclair	1/3/1934	Little (20)
	Lennox Robinson	*All's Over, Then?* (1932)		11/5/1934	Comedy (2)
	G.B. Shaw	*Village Wooing* (1934)		19/6/1934	Little (33)
	Sean O'Casey	*Juno and the Paycock* (1924)	Produced by Fred O'Donovan	25/6/1934	Embassy
	G.B. Shaw	{*Androcles and the Lion* (1913)}		17/7/1934	Open Air (8)
	G.B. Shaw	{*The Six of Calais* (1934)}	Première	17/7/1934	Open Air (8)
	G.B. Shaw	*Androcles and the Lion* (1913)		20/9/1934	Winter Garden (28)
	Denis Johnston	*The Moon in the Yellow River* (1931)	Produced by Denis Johnston	24/9/1934	Westminster (16)
	Denis Johnston	*The Moon in the Yellow River* (1931)	Produced by Fred O'Donovan	23/11/1934	Haymarket (128)
	G.B. Shaw	*Saint Joan* (1923)		26/11/1934	Old Vic (35)
	Lennox Robinson	*The Whiteheaded Boy* (1916)		24/12/1934	Embassy
	James B. Fagan	*Treasure Island* (1922) – from R.L. Stevenson		26/12/1934	New (22)
1935 (455)	Lord Dunsany	*Mr. Sliggen's Hour* (1935)		13/1/1935	Kingsway (1)
	J.M. Synge	*In The Shadow of the Glen* (1903)	The Irish Players	27/1/1935	Kingsway (1)
	Lady Gregory	*The Rising of the Moon* (1907)		10/2/1935	Kingsway (1)
	G.B. Shaw	*Major Barbara* (1905)		4/3/1935	Old Vic (21)
	St. John Ervine	{*Ole George Comes to Tea* (1927)}		7/4/1935	Little (3)

Year	Author	Play	Company	Date	Venue
	St. John Ervine	{Progress (1922)}		7/4/1935	Little (3)
	Lady Gregory	{The Travelling Man (1910)}		7/4/1935	Little (3)
	Lady Gregory	{The Workhouse Ward (1908)}		7/4/1935	Little (3)
	Lord Longford	Yahoo (1933) – from Swift	Dublin Gate Theatre Company	3/6/1935	Westminster (8)
	Denis Johnston	The Old Lady Says 'No!' (1929)	Dublin Gate Theatre Company	10/6/1935	Westminster (8)
	Oliver Goldsmith	She Stoops to Conquer (1773)		1/7/1935	Westminster (8)
	G.B. Shaw	Arms and the Man (1894)		15/7/1935	Embassy
	G.B. Shaw	Man and Superman (1905)		12/8/1935	Cambridge (24)
	G.B. Shaw	Pygmalion (1913)		3/9/1935	Cambridge (25)
	G.B. Shaw	The Apple Cart (1929)		25/9/1935	Cambridge (21)
	W.B. Yeats	{The Hour Glass (1903)}		27/10/1935	Little (4)
	W.B. Yeats	{The Player Queen (1919)}		27/10/1935	Little (4)
	W.B. Yeats	{The Pot o' Broth (1902)}		27/10/1935	Little (4)
	St John Ervine	Anthony and Anna (1926)		8/11/1935	Whitehall (788)
	Richard Brinsley Sheridan	The School for Scandal (1777)		20/12/1935	Old Vic (22)
1936 (401)	Lord Longford	Armlet of Jade (1936)		13/4/1936	Westminster (16)
	Elsie T. Schauffler	Parnell (1936)		23/4/1936	Gate
	Denis Johnston	A Bride for the Unicorn (1933)		3/7/1936	Westminster (19)
	Denis Johnston	Storm Song (1934)		6/7/1936	Embassy
	Kate O'Brien	The Ante-Room (1936)		14/8/1936	Queen's (10)
	Elsie T. Schauffler	Parnell (1936)		4/11/1936	New (108)
	James B. Fagan	Treasure Island (1922) – from R.L. Stevenson		26/12/1936	Aldwych (18)
1937 (444)	G.B. Shaw	Candida (1897)		10/2/1937	Globe (101)
	G.B. Shaw	Heartbreak House (1920)		9/3/1937	Westminster (31)
	Lord Dunsany	Lord Adrian (1937)		16/4/1937	Gate
	J.M. Synge	The Tinker's Wedding (1909)		3/7/1937	Players'

	Sean O'Casey	Juno and the Paycock (1924)	The Irish Players, produced by A. Sinclair, transferred to Haymarket 9/8/37; Saville 6/9/37	/7/1937	Haymarket (90)
	Lord Longford	Carmilla (1932) – from J.S. Le Fanu		9/9/1937	Westminster (12)
	Denis Johnston	The Moon in the Yellow River (1931)		20/9/1937	Westminster (15)
	G.B. Shaw	Pygmalion (1913)		21/9/1937	Old Vic (23)
	Mary Manning	Youth Is the Season . . . ? (1931)		5/10/1937	Westminster (15)
	W.B. Yeats	At The Hawk's Well (1916)		12/10/1937	Arts (1)
	Lady Longford	Anything but the Truth (1937)		18/10/1937	Westminster (16)
	Oliver Goldsmith	She Stoops to Conquer (1773)		26/10/1937	Victoria Palace (1)
	Lord Longford	Yahoo (1933) – from Swift		2/11/1937	Westminster (15)
	G.B. Shaw	Cymbeline Refinished (1937)		16/11/1937	Embassy
	St. John G. Ervine	Robert's Wife (1937)		23/11/1937	Globe (489)
	Richard Brinsley Sheridan	The School for Scandal (1777)		25/11/1937	Queen's (65)
	J.M. Synge	Riders to the Sea (1937)	Opera – Ralph Vaughan Williams	30/11/1937	Royal College of Music
	Louis MacNeice	Out of the Picture (1937)		5/12/1937	Westminster (2)
	James B. Fagan	Treasure Island (1922) – from R.L. Stevenson		27/12/1937	Savoy (35)
1938 (385)	A.G. Thornton	Moonshine (19**)	The Irish Players	30/3/1938	Ambassadors (13)
	G.B. Shaw	You Never Can Tell (1899)		3/5/1938	Westminster (47)
	St. John G. Ervine	People of Our Class (1938)		11/5/1938	New (77)
	Richard Brinsley Sheridan	The Rivals (1775)		31/5/1938	Holborn Empire
	Ernst Toller / Denis Johnston	Blind Man's Buff (1936)		25/9/1938	Arts
	G.B. Shaw	The Man of Destiny (1897)		7/10/1938	Mercury

		G.B. Shaw	Man and Superman (1905)		21/11/1938	Old Vic (15)
		G.B. Shaw	Geneva (1938)		22/11/1938	Saville (237)
		Teresa Deevy	Katie Roche (1936)	The Irish Players	25/11/1938	Torch
		Richard Brinsley Sheridan	The Rivals (1775)		6/12/1938	Old Vic (14)
		James B. Fagan	Treasure Island (1922) – from R.L. Stevenson		26/12/1938	Savoy (18)
1939 (297)		G.B. Shaw	{Village Wooing (1934)}		10/1/1939	Torch
		G.B. Shaw	{Annajanska, the Bolshevik Empress (1917)}		10/1/1939	Torch
		G.B. Shaw	{The Dark Lady of the Sonnets (1910)}		10/1/1939	Torch
		Oliver Goldsmith	She Stoops to Conquer (1773)		24/1/1939	Old Vic (28)
		J.M. Synge	The Playboy of the Western World (1907)		27/1/1939	Mercury
		Oscar Wilde	The Importance of Being Earnest (1895)		31/1/1939	Globe (8)
		Lord Dunsany	{The Bureau de Change (1939)}		12/2/1939	Playhouse (3)
		G.B. Shaw	{The Shewing Up of Blanco Posnet (1909)}		12/2/1939	Playhouse (3)
		G.B. Shaw	The Doctor's Dilemma (1906)		17/2/1939	Westminster (35)
		G.B. Shaw	Saint Joan (1923)		20/2/1939	Winter Garden (2)
		St. John G. Ervine	Robert's Wife (1937)		6/3/1939	Savoy (87)
		G.B. Shaw	Candida (1897)		24/3/1939	Westminster (1)
		G.B. Shaw	The Doctor's Dilemma (1906)		28/3/1939	Whitehall (95)
		G.B. Shaw	Candida (1897)		24/4/1939	Westminster (16)
		Teresa Deevey	{The King of Spain's Daughter (1935)}		5/5/1939	Torch
		J.M. Synge	{The Tinker's Wedding (1909)}		5/5/1939	Torch
		G.B. Shaw	Jitta's Atonement (1939) – from S. Trebitsch		22/5/1939	Embassy
		G.B. Shaw	Pygmalion (1913)		29/5/1939	Embassy
		G.B. Shaw	Pygmalion (1913)		13/6/1939	Haymarket (21)
		G.B. Shaw	Misalliance (1910)		20/6/1939	Torch

	Author	Play	Notes	Date	Theatre
	Sean O'Casey	The Plough and the Stars (1926)		3/7/1939	Embassy
	Oscar Wilde	The Importance of Being Earnest (1895)		16/8/1939	Globe (92)
	J.M. Synge	The Playboy of the Western World (1907)		30/9/1939	Mercury
	Sean O'Casey	{A Pound on Demand (1939)}		16/10/1939	'Q'
	Sean O'Casey	{The End of the Beginning (1937)}		16/10/1939	'Q'
	Sean O'Casey	{A Pound on Demand (1939)}		23/10/1939	Embassy
	Sean O'Casey	{The End of the Beginning (1937)}		23/10/1939	Embassy
	J.M. Synge	The Playboy of the Western World (1907)		24/10/1939	Duchess (37)
1940 (177)	G.B. Shaw	Major Barbara (1905)		20/12/1939	Westminster (39)
	Denis Johnston	The Golden Cuckoo (1939)		2/1/1940	Duchess (15)
	G.B. Shaw	Misalliance (1910)		22/1/1940	Embassy (c.8)
	Lennox Robinson	Killycreggs in Twilight (1937)		23/1/1940	Torch (c.14)
	St. John Ervine	Robert's Wife (1938)		4/3/1940	Embassy (c.7)
	Sean O'Casey	The Star Turns Red (1940)	Première	12/3/1940	Unity (85)
	G.B. Shaw	In Good King Charles's Golden Days (1939)		9/5/1940	New (29)
1941 (167)	G.B. Shaw	The Devil's Disciple (1897)	-	24/7/1940	Piccadilly (54)
	-		-		-
1942 (191)	G.B. Shaw	The Doctor's Dilemma (1906)		4/3/1942	Haymarket (474)
	Oscar Wilde	The Importance of Being Earnest (1895)		14/10/1942	Phoenix (77)
	G.B. Shaw	{The Man of Destiny (1897)}		1/12/1942	Arts (8)
	G.B. Shaw	{Village Wooing (1934)}		1/12/1942	Arts (8)
1943 (188)	Oliver Goldsmith	She Stoops to Conquer (1773)		12/1/1943	Arts (8)
	Dion Boucicault	The Streets of London (1942)	Version of The Poor of New York (1857)	28/1/1943	Cambridge (20)
	G.B. Shaw	Androcles and the Lion (1913)		2/2/1943	Arts (40)

	Oliver Goldsmith	*She Stoops to Conquer* (1773)	2/2/1943	Mercury (*c.*21)
	J.M. Synge	*The Well of the Saints* (1905)	17/3/1943	Arts (34)
	G.B. Shaw	*Heartbreak House* (1920)	18/3/1943	Cambridge (236)
	G.B. Shaw	*Don Juan in Hell* (1907)	24/3/1943	Arts (27)
	Paul Vincent Carroll	*The Old Foolishness* (1940)	7/5/1943	Arts (36)
	Paul Vincent Carroll	*Shadow and Substance* (1934)	25/5/1943	Duke of York's (31)
	Maud Flannery / T. Brown	*Case 27, V.C.* (194*)	2/6/1943	Comedy (30)
	George Farquhar	*The Constant Couple* (1699)	27/7/1943	Arts (21)
	Richard Brinsley Sheridan	*The Rivals* (1775)	29/7/1943	Arts (18)
	G.B. Shaw	*Misalliance* (1910)	10/8/1943	Arts (20)
	Oscar Wilde	*An Ideal Husband* (1895)	16/11/1943	Westminster (263)
	George Farquhar	*The Recruiting Officer* (1706)	23/11/1943	Arts (19)
1944 (219)	G.B. Shaw	*The Philanderer* (1905)	6/4/1944	Arts (29)
	Kate O'Brien / J. Perry	*The Last of Summer* (1940)	7/6/1944	Phoenix (29)
	G.B. Shaw	*Arms and the Man* (1894)	5/9/1944	New (67)
	G.B. Shaw	*Fanny's First Play* (1911)	14/9/1944	Arts (38)
	St John Ervine	*Jane Clegg* (1913)	26/9/1944	Lyric, Hammersmith (23)
	G.B. Shaw	*Candida* (1897)	31/10/1944	Gateway (*c.*7)
	G.B. Shaw	*Too True to be Good* (1932)	31/10/1944	Lyric, Hammersmith (30)
	G.B. Shaw	*Candida* (1897)	14/11/1944	Lyric, Hammersmith (27)
	G.B. Shaw	{*The Dark Lady of the Sonnets* (1910)}	28/11/1944	Lyric, Hammersmith (13)

	G.B. Shaw	{(*Village Wooing* (1934)}		28/11/1944	Lyric, Hammersmith (13)
	G.B. Shaw	*Pygmalion* (1914)		12/12/1944	Lyric, Hammersmith (29)
	Richard Brinsley Sheridan	*The Critic* (1779)		26/12/1944	Arts (35)
1945 (168)	Sean O'Casey	*Juno and the Paycock* (1924)	Windsor Theatre Guild	**/1/1945	Unity
	G.B. Shaw	*The Simpleton of the Unexpected Isles* (1935)		7/3/1945	Arts (39)
	Oscar Wilde	*Lady Windermere's Fan* (1892)		21/8/1945	Haymarket (602)
	G.B. Shaw	*Getting Married* (1908)		5/9/1945	Arts (42)
	James Joyce	*Exiles* (1918)		11/9/1945	Torch (*c*.21)
	Richard Brinsley Sheridan	*The School for Scandal* (1777)		19/9/1945	Arts (44)
	George Farquhar	*The Constant Couple* (1699)		25/9/1945	Arts (35)
	Richard Brinsley Sheridan	*The Rivals* (1775)		25/9/1945	Criterion (166)
	G.B. Shaw	*Mrs. Warren's Profession* (1902)		2/10/1945	Torch
	Richard Brinsley Sheridan	*The Critic; or, a Tragedy Rehearsed* (1779)		18/10/1945	New (76)
	Sean O'Casey	*Juno and the Paycock* (1924)		**/12/1945	Unity
	G.B. Shaw	*Arms and the Man* (1894)		18/12/1945	New (17)
1946 (292)	Sean O'Casey	*Red Roses for Me* (1943)		26/2/1946	Embassy (*c*.32)
	Paul Vincent Carroll	*The Wise Have Not Spoken* (1944)		19/3/1946	King's, Hammersmith
	Sean O'Casey	*Red Roses for Me* (1943)		9/4/1946	Lyric, Hammersmith (32)
	W.B. Yeats	*The Resurrection* (1927)		25/4/1946	Mercury (*c*.28)
	Sean O'Casey	*Red Roses for Me* (1943)		28/5/1946	New/Wyndham's (85)

		G.B. Shaw	Don Juan in Hell (1907)		3/7/1946	Arts (27)
		Sean O'Casey	The Star Turns Red (1940)		24/7/1946	Unity (c.44)
		G.B. Shaw	The Apple Cart (1929)		7/8/1946	Arts (26)
		G.B. Shaw	{Back to Methuselah: Part I (1922)}		27/8/1946	Lindsey (c.21)
		G.B. Shaw	{Village Wooing (1934)}		27/8/1946	Lindsey (c.21)
		Richard Brinsley Sheridan	St.Patrick's Day; or, The Scheming Lieutenant (1775)		3/9/1946	Arts (30)
		J.B. Fagan	Treasure Island (1922) – from R.L. Stevenson		23/12/46	Whitehall (37)
1947 (339)		G.B. Shaw	Mrs. Warren's Profession (1902)		13/1/1947	Theatre Royal, Stratford E. (14)
		J.M. Synge	The Tinker's Wedding (1909)		30/1/1947	Unity (c.21)
		Paul Vincent Carroll	The Wise Have Not Spoken (1946)		4/2/1947	Arts (6)
		Walter Macken	Galway Handicap (1946)		4/2/1947	Lyric, Hammersmith (26)
		Micheál MacLiammóir	Ill Met by Moonlight (1946)		5/2/1947	Vaudeville (25)
		G.B. Shaw	Fanny's First Play (1911)		11/2/1947	Gateway (c.28)
		G.B. Shaw	Back to Methuselah: Part I (1922)		18/2/1947	Arts (to 27/4/47)
		G.B. Shaw	Back to Methuselah: Part II (1922)		19/2/1947	Arts (to 27/4/47)
		G.B. Shaw	Back to Methuselah: Part III (1922)		19/2/1947	Arts (to 27/4/47)
		G.B. Shaw	Back to Methuselah: Part IV (1922)		25/2/1947	Arts (to 27/4/47)
		Paul Vincent Carroll	The White Steed (1939)		3/3/1947	Embassy (c.21)
		G.B. Shaw	Back to Methuselah: Part V (1922)		4/3/1947	Arts (to 27/4/47)
		Paul Vincent Carroll	The White Steed (1939)		24/3/1947	Whitehall (24)
		G.B. Shaw	Candida (1897)		27/3/1947	Piccadilly (39)
		G.B. Shaw	The Apple Cart (1929)		16/4/1947	Gateway (c.14)
		Sean O'Casey	Oak Leaves and Lavender (1946)		13/5/1947	Lyric, Hammersmith (22)

	Richard Brinsley Sheridan	*The Rivals* (1775)		9/6/1947	Theatre Royal, Stratford E. (16)
	G.B. Shaw	*Pygmalion* (1913)		18/6/1947	Lyric, Hammersmith (29)
	Donagh MacDonagh	{*Happy as Larry* (1946)}		18/9/1947	Mercury
	Sean O'Casey	{*A Pound on Demand* (1939)}		18/9/1947	Mercury
	G.B. Shaw	*You Never Can Tell* (1899)		3/10/1947	Wyndham's (312)
	St John Ervine	*Private Enterprise* (1947)		25/11/1947	St James's (61)
	Denis Johnston	*The Moon in the Yellow River* (1931)		26/11/1947	Arts (23)
	G.B. Shaw	*John Bull's Other Island* (1904)	Dublin Gate Theatre Company	2/12/1947	Embassy (7)
	G.B. Shaw	*St. Joan* (1923)		3/12/1947	New (82)
	Denis Johnston	*The Old Lady Says No* (1929)	Dublin Gate Theatre Company	9/12/1947	Embassy (7)
	Micheál MacLiammóir	*Where Stars Walk* (1940)	Dublin Gate Theatre Company	16/12/1947	Embassy (7)
	Donagh MacDonagh	*Happy as Larry* (1947)		16/12/1947	Criterion (53)
1948 (335)	Elizabeth Bowen / J. Perry	*Castle Anna* (1948)		24/2/1948	Lyric, Hammersmith (30)
	J.M. Synge	*The Playboy of the Western World* (1907)		11/3/1948	Mercury
	G.B. Shaw	*Major Barbara* (1905)		30/3/1948	Arts (24)
	Richard Brinsley Sheridan	*The Rivals* (1775)		29/6/1948	St James's (15)
	Sean O'Casey	*Juno and the Paycock* (1924)		5/7/1948	Embassy (c.7)
	G.B. Shaw	*Too True to Be Good* (1932)		13/7/1948	Arts (16)
	Oscar Wilde	*The Importance of Being Earnest* (1895)		29/9/1948	Gateway (c.21)
	G.B. Shaw	*Captain Brassbound's Conversion* (1900)		13/10/1948	Lyric, Hammersmith (44)

1949 (327)	Richard Brinsley Sheridan	*The School for Scandal* (1777)		20/1/1949	New (74)
	G.B. Shaw	*Widowers' Houses* (1892)		2/2/1949	Arts (23)
	Oliver Goldsmith	*She Stoops to Conquer* (1773)		19/4/1949	Arts (32)
	George Farquhar	*The Beaux' Stratagem* (1707)		5/5/1949	Phoenix (532)
	G.B. Shaw	*Man and Superman* (1905)		17/5/1949	Embassy (*c*.14)
	G.B. Shaw	*Candida* (1897)		11/7/1949	Theatre Royal, Stratford E. (7)
	G.B. Shaw	*Village Wooing* (1934)		2/8/1949	Lyric, Hammersmith (23)
	Michael J. Molloy	*The King of Friday's Men* (1948)	London première	30/8/1949	Lyric, Hammersmith (38)
	Donagh MacDonagh	*Fading Mansion* (1946)		31/8/1949	Duchess (37)
	Oliver Goldsmith	*She Stoops to Conquer* (1773)		18/10/1949	New (57)
1950 (325)	G.B. Shaw	*Mrs Warren's Profession* (1902)		25/1/1950	Arts (39)
	G.B. Shaw	*Heartbreak House* (1920)		5/7/1950	Arts (31)
	Louis D'Alton	*They Got What They Wanted* (1949)		18/7/1950	Embassy
	J.M. Synge	{*Riders to the Sea* (1904)}		20/7/1950	Watergate (*c*.18)
	J.M. Synge	{*In the Shadow of the Glen* (1903)}		20/7/1950	Watergate (*c*.18)
	J.M. Synge	{*The Tinker's Wedding* (1909)}		20/7/1950	Watergate (*c*.18)
	Louis D'Alton	*They Got What They Wanted* (1949)		16/8/1950	Phoenix (29)
	Oliver Goldsmith	*The Good-Natured Man* (1768)		29/8/1950	Chepstow
	G.B. Shaw	*Far Fetched Fables* (1950)		6/9/1950	Watergate (*c*.21)
	Tyrone Guthrie	*Top of the Ladder* (1950)		11/10/1950	St. James's (91)
	G.B. Shaw	*The Man of Destiny* (1897)		28/11/1950	Chepstow
	James B. Fagan	*Treasure Island* (1922) – from R.L. Stevenson		26/12/1950	St. James's (20)
1951 (319)	G.B. Shaw	*Pygmalion* (1913)		23/1/1951	Embassy (*c*.14)

Oscar Wilde	*The Importance of Being Earnest* (1895)		26/1/1951	Gateway (c.4)
G.B. Shaw	*Candida* (1897)		12/2/1951	Boltons (c.21)
G.B. Shaw	*Man and Superman* (1905)		14/2/1951	New (255)
George Shiels	*The Passing Day* (1936)	Northern Ireland Festival Company	20/3/1951	Lyric, Hammersmith (22)
G.B. Shaw	{*The Dark Lady of the Sonnets* (1910)}		3/4/1951	St. Martin's (30)
G.B. Shaw	{*The Man of Destiny* (1897)}		3/4/1951	St. Martin's (30)
G.B. Shaw	{*Village Wooing* (1934)}		3/4/1951	St. Martin's (30)
G.B. Shaw	*Captain Brassbound's Conversion* (1900)		17/4/1951	Old Vic (27)
John D. Stewart	*Danger, Men Working* (1951)	Northern Ireland Festival Company	21/4/1951	Lyric, Hammersmith (16)
Charles Shadwell	*The Sham Prince* (1718)	Northern Ireland Festival Company	23/4/1951	Lyric, Hammersmith (8)
G.B. Shaw	{*The Admirable Bashville* (1903)}		26/4/1951	Arts (30)
G.B. Shaw	{*Great Catherine* (1913)}		26/4/1951	Arts (30)
G.B. Shaw	{*How He Lied to Her Husband* (1904)}		26/4/1951	Arts (30)
G.B. Shaw	{*Passion, Poison and Petrifaction* (1905)}		26/4/1951	Arts (30)
G.B. Shaw	*Caesar and Cleopatra* (1906)		10/5/1951	St James's (77)
G.B. Shaw	{*The Fascinating Foundling* (1928)}		16/5/1951	Arts (31)
G.B. Shaw	{*The Shewing-Up of Blanco Posnet* (1909)}		16/5/1951	Arts (31)
G.B. Shaw	{*Annajanska, the Bolshevik Empress* (1917)}		20/6/1951	Arts (7)
G.B. Shaw	{*Augustus Does His Bit* (1917)}		20/6/1951	Arts (7)
G.B. Shaw	{*The Glimpse of Reality* (1927)}		20/6/1951	Arts (7)
G.B. Shaw	{*Overruled* (1912)}		20/6/1951	Arts (7)
G.B. Shaw	{*Village Wooing* (1934)}		20/6/1951	Arts (7)
G.B. Shaw	*Arms and the Man* (1894)		26/6/1951	Embassy (c.12)
G.B. Shaw	{*The Dark Lady of the Sonnets* (1910)}		27/6/1951	Arts (23)
G.B. Shaw	{*The Man of Destiny* (1897)}		27/6/1951	Arts (23)

	Author	Play		Date	Venue
	G.B. Shaw	{*The Music-Cure* (1914)}		27/6/1951	Arts (23)
	G.B. Shaw	{*O'Flaherty, V.C.* (1920)}		27/6/1951	Arts (23)
	G.B. Shaw	{*The Six of Calais* (1934)}		27/6/1951	Arts (23)
	George Shiels	*The Passing Day* (1936)		3/7/1951	Ambassadors (70)
	James B. Fagan	"*And So to Bed*" (1926) – from Pepys		17/10/1951	New (323)
	G.B. Shaw	*Candida* (1897)		30/10/1951	Torch
1952 (306)	George Farquhar	*The Constant Couple* (1699)		14/3/1952	Winter Garden (42)
	Oscar Wilde	*Salomé* (1896)		20/5/1952	Torch (c.21)
	T.C. Murray	*Autumn Fire* (1924)		2/6/1952	Irving (c.23)
	G.B. Shaw	*The Millionairess* (1936)		27/6/1952	New (98)
	Arthur Murphy	*The Way to Keep Him* (1760)		9/7/1952	Arts (23)
	G.B. Shaw	*Village Wooing* (1934)		26/7/1952	Court (1)
	G.B. Shaw	*Don Juan in Hell* (1907)		8/9/1952	Arts (17)
	Dion Boucicault	*The Streets of London* (1864)		1/12/1952	Embassy (c.17)
1953 (347)	Paul Vincent Carroll	*The Devil Came from Dublin* (1951)	Revised version of *The Chuckeyhead Story* (1950)	21/1/1953	Embassy (c.14)
	Oscar Wilde	*A Woman of No Importance* (1893)		12/2/1953	Savoy (179)
	Sean O'Casey	*Juno and the Paycock* (1924)		16/3/1953	Theatre Royal, Stratford E. (14)
	G.B. Shaw	*Arms and the Man* (1894)		27/4/1953	Theatre Royal, Stratford E. (14)
	G.B. Shaw	*The Apple Cart* (1929)		7/5/1953	Haymarket (100)
	Sean O'Casey	{*The End of the Beginning* (1937)}	Première	22/5/1953	Unity
	Sean O'Casey	{*Time to Go* (1952)}	Première	22/5/1953	Unity
	Sean O'Casey	{*Hall of Healing* (1952)}	Première	22/5/1953	Unity
	J.M. Synge	*Riders to the Sea* (1937)	Opera – Ralph Vaughan Williams	11/6/1953	Sadler's Wells (3)
	G.B. Shaw	*Arms and the Man* (1894)		25/6/1953	Arts (30)

	Author	Play	Notes	Date	Venue
	G.B. Shaw			20/7/1953	Lyric, Hammersmith (8)
	Michael J. Murphy	*Le Heros et le Soldat* (1894) – Translated by A. & H. Hamon			
		Dust Under Our Feet (1953)	Ulster Group Theatre	11/8/1953	Arts (16)
	Sean O'Casey	*Juno and the Paycock* (1924)		10/9/1953	Irving
	Gerard McLarnon	*The MacRoary Whirl* (1953)	Original title *Wrestler's Honeymoon*	1/10/1953	Duchess (4)
	Denis Johnston / E. Toller	*Blind Man's Buff* (1936)		14/10/1953	St. Martin's (53)
	Lennox Robinson	*Drama at Inish* (1933)		21/10/1953	Arts (23)
	J.M. Synge	*Riders to the Sea* (1937)	Opera – Ralph Vaughan Williams	22/10/1953	Sadler's Wells (3)
	George Shiels	*The Ragged Path* (1940)		13/11/1953	Chepstow
	G.B. Shaw	*Pygmalion* (1914)		19/11/1953	St. James's (155)
1954 (323)	G.B. Shaw	*The Devil's Disciple* (1897)		16/3/1954	Theatre Royal, Stratford E. (13)
	Sean O'Casey	*Juno and the Paycock* (1924)		30/3/1954	Lindsey (c.28)
	Hugh Hunt	{*In the Train* (1937)} – from a story by Frank O'Connor		27/4/1954	Lindsey (c.30)
	J.M. Synge	{*The Well of the Saints* (1905)}		27/4/1954	Lindsey (c.30)
	Sean O'Casey	*Red Roses for Me* (1943)		4/5/1954	Theatre Royal, Stratford E. (19)
	Sean O'Casey	*The Plough and the Stars* (1926)		27/5/1954	Lindsey (c.60)
	Oscar Wilde	*Salomé* (1896)		20/7/1954	St. Martin's (22)
	Richard Brinsley Sheridan	*The Duenna* (1775)		28/7/1954	Westminster (134)
	G.B. Shaw	*Saint Joan* (1923)		29/9/1954	Arts (39)
1955 (262)	G.B. Shaw	*Saint Joan* (1923)		8/2/1955	St. Martin's (125)
	G.B. Shaw	{*Androcles and the Lion* (1913)}		29/3/1955	Theatre Royal, Stratford E. (20)

	Author	Play	Note	Date	Theatre (performances)
	G.B. Shaw	{O'Flaherty, V.C. (1917)}		29/3/1955	Theatre Royal, Stratford E. (20)
1956 (298)	Samuel Beckett	Waiting for Godot (1955)	London première	3/8/1955	Arts (263)
	G.B. Shaw	Misalliance (1910)		8/2/1956	Lyric, Hammersmith (53)
	Richard Brinsley Sheridan	The Rivals (1775)		23/2/1956	Saville (179)
	M.J. Fitzgerald	Midsummer Irish (19**)		25/2/1956	Candlelight
	J.M. Synge	Riders to the Sea (1937)	Opera – Ralph Vaughan Williams	29/2/1956	Sadler's Wells (4)
	G.B. Shaw	Widowers' Houses (1892)	Merseyside Unity	19/5/1956	Unity (c.12)
	Brendan Behan	The Quare Fellow (1954)		24/5/1956	Theatre Royal, Stratford E. (29)
	G.B. Shaw	Major Barbara (1905)		16/7/1956	Old Vic (16)
	Brendan Behan	The Quare Fellow (1954)		24/7/1956	Comedy (79)
	G.B. Shaw	Mrs. Warren's Profession (1902)		24/7/1956	Court (3)
	G.B. Shaw	Caesar and Cleopatra (1907)		30/7/1956	Old Vic (16)
	G.B. Shaw	The Doctor's Dilemma (1906)		4/10/1956	Saville (68)
	Michael Molloy	{The Paddy Pedlar (1952)}		8/10/1956	Lindsey
	Sean O'Casey	{The Shadow of a Gunman (1923)}		8/10/1956	Lindsey
	G.B. Shaw	The Devil's Disciple (1897)		8/11/1956	Winter Garden (36)
	G.B. Shaw	Captain Brassbound's Conversion (1900)		27/11/1956	Theatre Royal, Stratford E. (18)
1957 (307)	Teresa Deevey	{Light Falling (1948)}	The Irish Players	14/1/1957	Lyric, Hammersmith (40)
	Sean O'Casey	{The Shadow of a Gunman (1923)}	The Irish Players	14/1/1957	Lyric, Hammersmith (40)
	J.M. Synge	The Playboy of the Western World (1907)		16/1/1957	Theatre Royal, Stratford E. (23)
	Samuel Beckett	{Acte sans Parole I (1957)}		2/4/1957	Royal Court (6)
	Samuel Beckett	{Fin de Partie (1957)}		2/4/1957	Royal Court (6)

1958 (337)	Carolyn Swift / G.D. Hodnett	Dublin Pike Follies (1957)	Revue	25/11/1957	Lyric, Hammersmith (23)
	Gerard McLarnon	Tenebrae (195*)	Repertory Players	19/1/1958	Lyric (1)
	G.B. Shaw	The Man of Destiny (1897)		15/4/1958	Theatre Royal, Stratford E. (13)
	G.B. Shaw / A.J. Lerner / F. Loewe	My Fair Lady (1956)		30/4/1958	Drury Lane (2281)
	G.B. Shaw	Heartbreak House (1920)		6/6/1958	Unity (c.30)
	G.B. Shaw	Major Barbara (1905)		28/8/1958	Court (36)
	Nuala & Mairin O'Farrell	The Heart's a Wonder (1958) – from The Playboy of the Western World	Musical	18/9/1958	Westminster (44)
	Brendan Behan	The Hostage (1958)	London première	14/10/1958	Theatre Royal, Stratford E. (62)
	Samuel Beckett	{Endgame (1957)}		28/10/1958	Royal Court (38)
	Samuel Beckett	{Krapp's Last Tape (1958)}		28/10/1958	Royal Court (38)
1959 (291)	J.M. Synge	Riders to the Sea (1937)	Opera – Ralph Vaughan Williams	20/1/1959	Sadler's Wells (4)
	Brendan Behan	The Hostage (1958)	Transferred Wyndham's 11/6/59	14/5/1959	Theatre Royal, Stratford E. (452)
	Marjorie Barkentin	Ulysses in Nighttown (1958) – from James Joyce		21/5/1959	Arts (54)
	James Plunkett	The Risen People (1958)		22/5/1959	Unity
	Sean O'Casey	Cock-a-Doodle Dandy (1949)		17/9/1959	Royal Court (36)
	Oscar Wilde	The Importance of Being Earnest (1895)		13/10/1959	Old Vic (65)
1960 (166)	Samuel Beckett	Act without Words II (1959)		25/1/1960	ICA
	Allan McClelland	Bloomsday (1960) – from James Joyce		**/**/1960	Unity
	G.B. Shaw	Saint Joan (1923)		9/2/1960	Old Vic
	Sean O'Casey	Purple Dust (1943)		18/3/1960	Tower, Canonbury

	Author	Play	Note	Date	Venue
	Dominic Behan	Posterity Be Damned! (1960)		28/3/1960	Metropolitan Music Hall, W2
	G.B. Shaw	Pygmalion (1913)		29/3/1960	Pembroke, Croydon
	Patrick Kirwan	A Lodging for a Bride (1960)		18/4/1960	Westminster (16)
	Sam Thompson	Over the Bridge (1960)		4/5/1960	Prince's
	James Clancy	Ned Kelly (196*)		23/5/1960	Theatre Royal, Stratford E.
	G.B. Shaw	Candida (1897)		13/6/1960	Piccadilly (160)
	J.M. Synge	The Playboy of the Western World (1907)	Dublin Festival Company	12/10/1960	Piccadilly (110)
	John B. Keane	Sive (1959)		24/10/1960	Lyric, Hammersmith (16)
	G.B. Shaw	Androcles and the Lion (1913)		28/10/1960	Unity
	Micheál MacLiammóir / O. Wilde	The Importance of Being Oscar (1960)		31/10/1960	Apollo (16)
	Oliver Goldsmith	She Stoops to Conquer (1773)		8/11/1960	Old Vic
	Sean O'Casey	The Drums of Father Ned (1960)		8/11/1960	Queen's, Hornchurch
	Oliver Goldsmith	The Good-Natured Man (1768)		18/11/1960	Tower, Canonbury
1961 (167)	Micheál MacLiammóir / O. Wilde	The Importance of Being Oscar (1960)		23/1/1961	Royal Court (32)
	Brendan Behan	The Hostage (1958)		13/2/1961	Lyric, Hammersmith (48)
	Fergus Linehan	Glory Be! (1961)	Musical	3/4/1961	Theatre Royal, Stratford E. (35)
	Samuel Beckett	Waiting for Godot (1955)		15/5/1961	Theatre Royal, Stratford E. (35)
	Sean O'Casey	The Bishop's Bonfire (1955)		26/7/1961	Mermaid (53)
	G.B. Shaw	Caesar and Cleopatra (1907)		31/8/1961	Duchess (22)

	Author	Play	Note	Date	Theatre
	Thomas Murphy	*A Whistle in the Dark* (1961)	Transferred Apollo 17/10/1961	11/9/1961	Theatre Royal, Stratford E. (91)
	George Farquhar	*The Recruiting Officer* (1706)		22/9/1961	Unity
	G.B. Shaw	{*Androcles and the Lion* (1913)}		3/10/1961	Mermaid (54)
	G.B. Shaw	{*The Shewing Up of Blanco Posnet* (1909)}		3/10/1961	Mermaid (54)
	G.B. Shaw	*Heartbreak House* (1920)		1/11/1961	Wyndham's (117)
	Richard Brinsley Sheridan	*The Rivals* (1775)		14/11/1961	Pembroke, Croydon
	Patrick Galvin	*And Him Stretched* (1961)		**/**/1961	Unity
1962 (187)	G.B. Shaw	*Arms and the Man* (1894)		20/3/1962	Mermaid (33)
	James McKenna	*The Scatterin'* (1960)	Dublin Theatre Festival	2/4/1962	Theatre Royal, Stratford E. (35)
	Richard Brinsley Sheridan	*The School for Scandal* (1777)		5/4/1962	Haymarket (258)
	Robert Crean	*A Time to Laugh* (1962)		24/4/1962	Piccadilly (22)
	David Rudkin	*Afore Night Come* (1960)	Royal Shakespeare Company (RSC)	7/6/1962	Arts
	Mary Manning	*The Voice of Shem* (1961) – from *Finnegan's Wake*	Dublin Theatre Festival		Theatre Royal, Stratford E. (13)
	Sean O'Casey	*Purple Dust* (1943)		15/8/1962	Mermaid (31)
	Sean O'Casey	*Red Roses for Me* (1942)		4/9/1962	Mermaid (33)
	Sean O'Casey	*The Plough and the Stars* (1926)		25/9/1962	Mermaid (33)
	Donagh McDonagh	*Step-in-the-Hollow* (1962)		13/10/1962	Questors, Ealing
	Samuel Beckett	*Happy Days* (1961)		1/11/1962	Royal Court
	Edna O'Brien	*Cheap Bunch of Nice Flowers* (1962)		20/11/1962	New Arts
	Samuel Beckett	*End of Day* (1962)	Anthology	16/12/1962	New Arts
1963 (187)	G.B. Shaw	*Misalliance* (1910)		8/1/1963	Royal Court (54)

	Hugh Leonard	*Stephen D.* (1962)		12/2/1963	St. Martin's (120)
	G.B. Shaw	*The Doctor's Dilemma* (1906)		23/4/1963	Haymarket (84)
	Richard Brinsley Sheridan	*The Rivals* (1775)		23/4/1963	Lyric, Hammersmith (22)
	Micheál MacLiammóir / O. Wilde	*The Importance of Being Oscar* (1960)		29/4/1963	Aldwych (36)
	Micheál MacLiammóir	*I Must Be Talking to My Friends* (1963)	Première	2/5/1963	Aldwych (36)
	George Farquhar	*The Beaux' Stratagem* (1707)		6/5/1963	Ashcroft, Croydon
	J.M. Synge	{*The Tinker's Wedding* (1909)}	{New Pike Theatre,	29/7/1963	Theatre Royal, Stratford E. (14)
	J.M. Synge	{*In the Shadow of the Glen* (1903)}	Festival of Irish	29/7/1963	Theatre Royal, Stratford E. (14)
	Brendan Behan	{*The Big House* (1963)} - British Première	Comedy}	29/7/1963	Theatre Royal, Stratford E. (14)
	M.J. Molloy	*The Wood of the Whispering* (1953)	New Pike Theatre	12/8/1963	Theatre Royal, Stratford E. (14)
	Hugh Leonard	*Madigan's Lock* (1958)	New Pike Theatre	26/8/1963	Theatre Royal, Stratford E. (14)
	Dominic Behan	*Behan Bein' Behan*		23/9/1963	Prince Charles
	G.B. Shaw	*Saint Joan* (1923)	National Theatre (NT)	30/10/1963	Old Vic
	Samuel Beckett	*Happy Days* (1961)		9/12/1963	Theatre Royal, Stratford E. (12)
	George Farquhar	*The Recruiting Officer* (1706)	National Theatre	10/12/1963	Old Vic
1964 (215)	Hugh Leonard	*The Poker Session* (1963)		11/2/1964	Globe (40)
	Samuel Beckett	*Play* (1963)	National Theatre	7/4/1964	Royal Court
	Sean O'Casey	*Juno and the Paycock* (1924)	Abbey Theatre	20/4/1964	Aldwych (6)
	Sean O'Casey	*The Plough and the Stars* (1926)	Abbey Theatre	27/4/1964	Aldwych (6)

	O. Wilde / T. Sturge Moore	*A Florentine Tragedy* (1908)		19/5/1964	Little Theatre Club, WC2
	David Rudkin	*Afore Night Come* (1960)	RSC	25/6/1964	Aldwych
	Samuel Beckett	*Act Without Words II* (1959)	RSC	2/7/1964	Aldwych
	Samuel Beckett	*Endgame* (1957)	RSC	9/7/1964	Aldwych
	George Farquhar	*The Recruiting Officer* (1706)	National	7/10/1964	Old Vic
	Samuel Beckett	*Waiting for Godot* (1955)		30/12/1964	Royal Court (70)
	Micheál MacLiammóir / O. Wilde	*The Importance of Being Oscar* (1960)	One-man show	31/12/1964	Queen's (68)
1965 (181)	Micheál MacLiammóir	*I Must Be Talking to My Friends* (1963)	One-man show	31/12/1964	Queen's (68)
	G.B. Shaw	*Widowers' Houses* (1892)		12/3/1965	Theatre Royal, Stratford E. (24)
	Samuel Beckett	*Oh les Beaux-Jours* (1961)	Jean-Louis Barrault Théâtre de France	3/4/1965	Aldwych (1)
	G.B. Shaw	*Mrs. Warren's Profession* (1902)		22/4/1965	Hampstead Theatre Club (18)
	Sean O'Casey	*The Drums of Father Ned* (1960)	London première	21/5/1965	Canonbury Tower, Islington
	G.B. Shaw	*Too True to be Good* (1932)		22/9/1965	Strand (138)
	G.B. Shaw	*Fanny's First Play* (1911)		29/9/1965	Mermaid (67)
	G.B. Shaw	*Man and Superman* (1905)		23/11/1965	New Arts (232)
	Oscar Wilde	*An Ideal Husband* (1895)		16/12/1965	Strand (360)
1966 (183)	G.B. Shaw	*You Never Can Tell* (1899)		12/1/1966	Haymarket (284)
	G.B. Shaw	*The Philanderer* (1905)		27/1/1966	Mermaid (34)
	Sean O'Casey	*Juno and the Paycock* (1924)	NT, directed by Laurence Olivier	26/4/1966	Old Vic
	J.M. Synge	*The Playboy of the Western World* (1907)	East 15 Acting School	**/**/1966	Unity

	G.B. Shaw	The Doctor's Dilemma (1906)		2/6/1966	Comedy (36)
	Paul Shyre / Sean O'Casey	Pictures in the Hallway (1966)	Autobiography	30/8/1966	Mermaid (19)
	G.B. Shaw	{The Man of Destiny (1897)}		14/9/1966	Mermaid (49)
	G.B. Shaw	{O'Flaherty, V.C. (1917)}		14/9/1966	Mermaid (49)
	Micheál MacLiammóir / O. Wilde	The Importance of Being Oscar (1960)	One-man show	19/9/1966	Haymarket (14)
	Micheál MacLiammóir	I Must Be Talking to My Friends (1963)	One-man show	26/9/1966	Haymarket (1)
	Michael Voysey / G.B. Shaw	An Evening with G.B.S. (1966)	One-man show	28/9/1966	Criterion (38)
	Richard Brinsley Sheridan	The Rivals (1775)		6/10/1966	Haymarket (108)
	Oscar Wilde	Lady Windermere's Fan (1892)		13/10/1966	Phoenix (181)
1967 (204)	G.B. Shaw	{Augustus Does His Bit (1917)}		31/1/1967	Mermaid (49)
	G.B. Shaw	{Press Cuttings (1909)}		31/1/1967	Mermaid (49)
	G.B. Shaw	{Passion, Poison and Petrifaction (1905)}		31/1/1967	Mermaid (49)
	Sean O'Casey	{The Shadow of a Gunman (1923)}		5/4/1967	Mermaid (67)
	Sean O'Casey	{A Pound on Demand (1939)}		5/4/1967	Mermaid (67)
	G.B. Shaw	Getting Married (1908)		19/4/1967	Strand (149)
	George Farquhar	The Constant Couple (1699)		29/6/1967	New (19)
	Brian Friel	Philadelphia, Here I Come! (1964)		20/9/1967	Lyric (53)
	G.B. Shaw	Heartbreak House (1920)		9/11/1967	Lyric (116)
	Oscar Wilde	A Woman of No Importance (1893)		28/11/1967	Vaudeville (54)
1968 (170)	G.B. Shaw / B. Ashmore	{The Adventures of the Black Girl in Her Search for God (1968)}		7/2/1968	Mermaid (37)
	G.B. Shaw / B. Ashmore	{Aerial Football (1968)}		7/2/1968	Mermaid (37)
	Oscar Wilde	The Importance of Being Earnest (1895)		8/2/1968	Haymarket (282)

Year	Author	Play	Notes	Date	Venue
	G.B. Shaw	Passion, Poison and Petrifaction (1905)		22/2/1968	Arts (21)
	Samuel Beckett	Come and Go (1966)		28/2/1968	Royal Festival Hall
	Dion Boucicault	The Shaughran (1874)	Abbey Theatre	20/5/1968	Aldwych (11)
	Wilson John Haire	The Clockin' Hen (1968)		**/**/1968	Hampstead
	Wilson John Haire	Divil Era (1968)		**/**/1968	Hampstead
1969 (197)	Hugh Leonard	The Au Pair Man (1968)		23/4/1969	Duchess
	Oliver Goldsmith	She Stoops to Conquer (1773)		7/5/1969	Garrick
	G.B. Shaw	Back to Methuselah, Part I (1922)	National Theatre	31/7/1969	Old Vic
	G.B. Shaw	Back to Methuselah, Part I (1922)	National Theatre	1/8/1969	Old Vic
	Wilson John Haire	The Diamond, Bone and Hammer and Along the Shoughs of Ulster (1968)		8/8/1969	Unity
	Brian Friel	Lovers (Winners and Losers) (1968)	London première	25/8/1969	Fortune
	Sean O'Casey	The Silver Tassie (1928)	RSC	10/9/1969	Aldwych
	Samuel Beckett	Oh! Les Beaux Jours (1961)	Directed by Roger Blin	29/9/1969	Royal Court
	Thomas Murphy	Famine (1968)		9/11/1969	Royal Court
1970 (180)	G.B. Shaw	{How He Lied to Her Husband (1904)}		26/1/1970	Fortune
	G.B. Shaw	{Village Wooing (1934)}		26/1/1970	Fortune
	G.B. Shaw	{Press Cuttings (1909)}		26/1/1970	Fortune
	G.B. Shaw	The Apple Cart (1929)		5/3/1970	Mermaid (36)
	Samuel Beckett	Waiting for Godot (1955)		18/3/1970	Jeanetta Cochrane
	Samuel Beckett	{Play (1963)}		1/4/1970	Royal Court Theatre Upstairs
	Samuel Beckett	{Come and Go (1966)}		1/4/1970	Royal Court Theatre Upstairs
	Samuel Beckett	{Cascando (1963)}		1/4/1970	Royal Court Theatre Upstairs
	George Farquhar	The Beaux' Stratagem (1707)	National Theatre	8/4/1970	Old Vic
	G.B. Shaw	Widowers' Houses (1892)		14/4/1970	Royal Court
	Samuel Beckett	Krapp's Last Tape (1958)		29/4/1970	Aldwych

	Author	Title	Notes	Date	Venue
	G.B. Shaw	Back to Methuselah (1922)	National Theatre	7/6/1970	Cambridge
	Dion Boucicault	London Assurance (1841)	RSC	23/6/1970	Aldwych
	James Joyce, et al.	Here Are Ladies (1970)	Siobhan McKenna	28/7/1970	Criterion
	J.M. Synge	{The Well of the Saints (1905)}	Abbey Theatre	3/8/1970	Old Vic (6)
	George Fitzmaurice	{The Dandy Dolls (1913)}	Abbey Theatre	3/8/1970	Old Vic (6)
	G.B. Shaw	Saint Joan (1923)		3/9/1970	Mermaid
	G.B. Shaw	Major Barbara (1905)	RSC	19/10/1970	Aldwych
	Samuel Beckett	Waiting for Godot (1955)		4/11/1970	Young Vic
	James Joyce	Exiles (1918)	Directed by Harold Pinter	12/11/1970	Mermaid
	G.B. Shaw	Mrs Warren's Profession (1902)	National Theatre	30/12/1970	Old Vic
1971 (172)	Samuel Beckett	Endgame (1957)		2/2/1971	Young Vic
	G.B. Shaw	Captain Brassbound's Conversion (1900)		18/2/1971	Cambridge
	G.B. Shaw	Max-Adrian as G.B.S. (1971)		29/3/1971	Haymarket
	Samuel Beckett	{Krapp's Last Tape (1958)}	Directed by Samuel Beckett	29/4/1971	Aldwych
	Samuel Beckett	{Endgame (1957)}	Directed by Samuel Beckett	29/4/1971	Aldwych
	G.B. Shaw	John Bull's Other Island (1904)		13/5/1971	Mermaid
	Rory O'Briain Bell	Black Girl (1971)		**/**/1971	Unity
	Rory O'Briain Bell	Rebellion from Erin to Eureka (1971)		**/**/1971	Unity
	Samuel Beckett	Happy Days (1961)		1/6/1971	Young Vic
	Hugh Leonard	The Patrick Pearse Motel (1971)		17/6/1971	Queen's
	G.B. Shaw	The Devil's Disciple (1897)	Theatre inauguration	5/7/1971	Shaw (39)
	James Joyce	Exiles (1918)	Directed by Harold Pinter	7/10/1971	Aldwych
	Micheál MacLiammóir	Talking About Yeats (1971)	One-man show	13/10/1971	Duke of York's
	G.B. Shaw	Geneva (1938/45)		4/11/1971	Mermaid

	Author	Play		Date	Theatre
	Oliver Goldsmith	The Good-Natured Man (1768)	National Theatre	9/12/1971	Old Vic
1972 (174)	Wilson John Haire	Within Two Shadows (1971)		**/**/1971	Royal Court
	Oliver Goldsmith	She Stoops to Conquer (1773)		3/2/1972	Young Vic
	Dion Boucicault	London Assurance (1841)		5/4/1972	New
	Wilson John Haire	Within Two Shadows (1972)		12/4/1972	Theatre Upstairs (28)
	Richard Brinsley Sheridan	The Rivals (1775)		1/5/1972	Sadler's Wells
	Richard Brinsley Sheridan	The School for Scandal (1777)	National Theatre	11/5/1972	Old Vic
	Brendan Behan	The Hostage (1958)		30/5/1972	Theatre Royal, Stratford East
	Sean O'Casey	The Shadow of a Gunman (1923)		4/7/1972	Young Vic
	Brendan Behan	Richard's Cork Leg (1972)		19/9/1972	Royal Court
	Tom MacIntyre	Eye-Winker, Tom Tinker (1972)		12/10/1972	Theatre Upstairs
	Edna O'Brien	A Pagan Place (1972)		2/11/1972	Royal Court
1973 (150)	Samuel Beckett	{Not I (1972)}		16/1/1973	Royal Court
	Samuel Beckett	{Krapp's Last Tape (1958)}		16/1/1973	Royal Court
	G.B. Shaw	Man of Destiny (1897)		18/1/1973	Open Space
	Brian Friel	The Freedom of the City (1973)		27/2/1973	Royal Court
	G.B. Shaw	Misalliance (1910)		18/4/1973	Mermaid
	Sean O'Casey	Juno and the Paycock (1924)		2/7/1973	Mermaid
	Samuel Beckett	Endgame (1957)		12/7/1973	Shaw
	David Rudkin	Cries from Casement as his Bones are Brought to Dublin (1973)	RSC	4/10/1973	The Place
1974 (165)	David Rudkin	Ashes (1974)		9/1/1974	Open Space
	George Farquhar	The Recruiting Officer (1706)	Belt and Braces	**/**/1974	Unity
	Oscar Wilde	The Importance of Being Earnest (1895)		8/3/1974	Shaw
	G.B. Shaw	Pygmalion (1913)		15/5/1974	Albery

				//1974	Unity
1975 (151)	Samuel Beckett	*Not I* (1972)		29/1/1975	Royal Court
	G.B. Shaw	*Heartbreak House* (1920)	National Theatre	25/2/1975	Old Vic
	Samuel Beckett	*Happy Days* (1961)	National Theatre	13/3/1975	Old Vic
	Oscar Wilde	*The Importance of Being Earnest* (1895)	Directed by Jonathan Miller	20/3/1975	Greenwich
	G.B. Shaw	*The Doctor's Dilemma* (1906)		21/4/1975	Mermaid
	David Rudkin	*Ashes* (1974)		11/6/1975	Young Vic
	G.B. Shaw	*On the Rocks* (1933)		21/8/1975	Mermaid
	G.B. Shaw	*Too True to Be Good* (1932)	RSC	23/10/1975	Aldwych
	J.M. Synge	*The Playboy of the Western World* (1907)	National Theatre	29/10/1975	Old Vic
	Wilson John Haire	*Echoes from a Concrete Canyon* (1975)		**/**/1975	Royal Court
1976 (av. 296)	G.B. Shaw	*Too True to Be Good* (1932)	RSC transfer	1/1/1976	Globe
	Samuel Beckett	*La Dernière Bande* (1958)	Directed by Samuel Beckett	8/3/1976	Greenwood
	Samuel Beckett	*Happy Days* (1961)	First performance at new National Theatre	12/3/1976	Lyttelton
	Richard Brinsley Sheridan	*The Duenna* (1775)	Musical	16/3/1976	Collegiate
	G.B. Shaw	*Widowers' Houses* (1892)		30/3/1976	Wimbledon
	Samuel Beckett	*Waiting for Godot* (1955)	Schiller Theatre, Berlin, dir. Beckett	21/4/1976	Royal Court
	Samuel Beckett	*Endgame* (1961)	Directed Donald McWhinnie	6/5/1976	Royal Court
	Samuel Beckett	{*Play* (1963)}	Directed by Donald McWhinnie	20/5/1976	Royal Court

	Author	Play	Notes	Date	Venue
	Samuel Beckett	{That Time (1976)}	Directed by Donald McWhinnie	20/5/1976	Royal Court
	Samuel Beckett	{Footfalls (1976)}	Directed by Donald McWhinnie	20/5/1976	Royal Court
	Patrick Galvin	We Do It For Love (1975)	Lyric Players Theatre, Belfast	1/6/1976	Young Vic
	G.B. Shaw	Pygmalion (1913)		7/7/1976	Ashcroft, Croydon
	G.B. Shaw	The Devil's Disciple (1897)		13/7/1976	Aldwych
	Stewart Parker	Spokesong or The Common Wheel (1975)	Musical	14/9/1976	King's Head
	J.M. Synge	The Playboy of the Western World (1907)	National Theatre	7/10/1976	Olivier
	Stewart Parker	The Actress and the Bishop (1976)		8/12/1976	King's Head
	John O'Keefe	Wild Oats (1791)	RSC	14/12/1976	Aldwych
1977 (av. 296)	Sean O'Casey	The Silver Tassie (1928)		9/2/1977	Theatre Royal, Stratford E.
	Stewart Parker	Spokesong or The Common Wheel (1975)	Transfer	16/2/1977	Vaudeville
	Oscar Wilde	Salomé (1896)		21/2/1977	Round House
	G.B. Shaw	Saint Joan (1923)	Prospect	4/5/1977	Old Vic
	G.B. Shaw	Candida (1897)		23/6/1977	Albery
	Hugh Leonard	Da (1973)		20/7/1977	King's Head
	G.B. Shaw	Man and Superman (1905)	RSC	16/8/1977	Savoy
	Samuel Beckett	Happy Days (1961)	National Theatre	19/9/1997	Lyttelton
	Sean O'Casey	The Plough and the Stars (1926)	National Theatre	20/9/1977	Olivier
	G.B. Shaw	The Apple Cart (1929)		7/11/1977	Phoenix
	Thomas Kilroy	Talbot's Box (1977)	Abbey Theatre	22/11/1977	Royal Court (25)
	Oscar Wilde	The Importance of Being Earnest (1895)		15/12/1977	Round House
	Oscar Wilde	The Importance of Being Earnest (1895)		21/12/1977	Young Vic

1978 (av. 296)	Stewart Parker	*Kingdom Come* (1977)		17/1/1978	King's Head
	Ron Hutchinson	*Says I, Says He* (1978)		18/1/1978	Theatre Upstairs
	Oscar Wilde	*An Ideal Husband* (1895)		2/2/1978	Greenwich
	G.B. Shaw	*Saint Joan* (1923)	Prospect	9/2/1978	Old Vic
	G.B. Shaw	*Arms and the Man* (1894)	Horniman Season	17/4/1978	Greenwich
	Ron Hutchinson	*Eejits* (1978)		18/5/1978	Bush
	Wilson John Haire	{*Lost Worlds – Newsflash* (1978)}	National Theatre	25/5/1978	Cottesloe
	Wilson John Haire	{*Lost Worlds – Wedding Breakfast* (1978)}	National Theatre	25/5/1978	Cottesloe
	Wilson John Haire	{*Lost Worlds – Roost* (1978)}	National Theatre	25/5/1978	Cottesloe
	Lady Gregory	{*The Rising of the Moon* (1907)}	Horniman Season Golden Cradle	14/6/1978	Greenwich
	W.B. Yeats	{*The Cat and the Moon* (1924)}	Horniman Season Golden Cradle	14/6/1978	Greenwich
	W.B. Yeats	{*Purgatory* (1938)}	Horniman Season Golden Cradle	14/6/1978	Greenwich
	W.B. Yeats	{*The Pot of Broth* (1902)}	Horniman Season Golden Cradle	14/6/1978	Greenwich
	J.M. Synge	{*Riders to the Sea* (1904)}	Horniman Season Golden Cradle	14/6/1978	Greenwich
	Bill Morrison	*Flying Blind* (1977)		20/6/1978	Royal Court
	G.B. Shaw	{*The Man of Destiny* (1897)}		17/7/1978	Open Air, Regent's Park
	G.B. Shaw	{*The Dark Lady of the Sonnets* (1910)}		17/7/1978	Open Air, Regent's Park
	G.B. Shaw	*The Philanderer* (1905)	National Theatre	7/9/1978	Lyttelton
	Richard Brinsley Sheridan	*The Rivals* (1775)	Prospect	10/9/1978	Old Vic
	Peter Sheridan	*Emigrants* (1978)	Pirate Jenny	21/9/1978	Theatre Upstairs
	Dave Allen	*An Evening with Dave Allen* (1978)	Revue	4/10/1978	Vaudeville

	Samuel Beckett	{*Krapp's Last Tape* (1958)}	San Quentin Drama Workshop	18/10/1978	Open Space
	Samuel Beckett	{*Endgame* (1957)}	San Quentin Drama Workshop	18/10/1978	Open Space
1979 (av. 296)	Ron Hutchinson	*Anchorman* (1978)		9/1/1979	Theatre Upstairs
	Hugh Leonard	*Da* (1973)		11/1/1979	Greenwich
	Bryan MacMahon	*The Honey Spike* (1978)	Green Fields and Far Away	30/1/1979	Irish Club, Eaton Square
	Kevin O'Connor	*James Joyce and Co.* (1978)		12/3/1979	King's Head
	Samuel Beckett	*Happy Days* (1961)	Directed by Samuel Beckett	7/6/1979	Royal Court
	John O'Keefe	*Wild Oats* (1791)	RSC	7/7/1979	Aldwych
	G.B. Shaw	*The Philanderer* (1905)	National Theatre	11/7/1979	Lyttelton
	David Rudkin	*Hippolytus* (1979) – from Euripides		18/7/1979	Warehouse
	Oscar Wilde	*The Importance of Being Earnest* (1895)	Premiere of 4-act full-length version	29/7/1979	Adeline Genee
	G.B. Shaw	{*O'Flaherty, V.C.* (1917)}		13/8/1979	Open Air, Regent's Park
	G.B. Shaw	{*Overruled* (1912)}		13/8/1979	Open Air, Regent's Park
	G.B. Shaw	*You Never Can Tell* (1899)		18/10/1979	Lyric, Hammersmith
	G.B. Shaw / A.J. Lerner / F. Loewe	*My Fair Lady* (1956)		25/10/1979	Adelphi
	Glyn Jones	*The 88* (1979)		8/11/1979	Old Vic
	Oliver Goldsmith	*She Stoops to Conquer* (1773)		13/12/1979	Greenwich
1980 (av. 296)	Hugh Leonard	*A Life* (1979)	Abbey Theatre – "A Sense of Ireland"	4/2/1980	Old Vic

Author	Work	Date	Venue
James Plunkett	*The Risen People* (1958, revised version 1977)	7/2/1980	Project Arts Centre – "A Sense of Ireland"	ICA
Michael McGrath	*The Key Tag* (1980)	7/2/1980	World première – "A Sense of Ireland"	Theatre Upstairs
Ian McPherson	*Jack Doyle, the Man Who Boxed Like John McCormack* (1980)	11/2/1980	World première – Green Fields and Far Away	Lyric Studio, Hammersmith
Stewart Parker	*Catchpenny Twist* (1977)	21/2/1980	Musical	King's Head
Flann O'Brien / Ken Campbell	*The Third Policeman* (1980)	26/2/1980	Science Fiction Theatre of Liverpool – "A Sense of Ireland"	ICA
Peter Sheridan	*The Liberty Suit* (1977)	28/2/1980	Project Arts Centre – "A Sense of Ireland"	Royal Court
J.M. Synge	*The Playboy of the Western World* (1979)	4/3/1980	Irish Ballet + The Chieftains – "A Sense of Ireland"	Sadler's Wells
Dion Boucicault	*The Streets of London* (1864)	18/3/1980		Theatre Royal, Stratford E.
Michael McGrath	*Third Flight* (1980)	16/4/1980		Bush
G.B. Shaw	*Pygmalion* (1913)	7/5/1980		Shaw
G.B. Shaw	*John Bull's Other Island* (1904)	29/5/1980		Greenwich
Samuel Beckett	{*Krapp's Last Tape* (1958)}	29/7/1980	San Quentin Drama Workshop	Young Vic (12)

	Samuel Beckett	{*Endgame* (1957)}	San Quentin Drama Workshop	29/7/1980	Young Vic (12)
	G.B. Shaw	*Androcles and the Lion* (1913)		5/8/1980	Open Air, Regent's Park
	Samuel Beckett	*Company* (1980)	Stage reading of novel	1/9/1980	Cottesloe
	Sean O'Casey	*Juno and the Paycock* (1924)	RSC	7/10/1980	Aldwych
	Oscar Wilde	*The Importance of Being Earnest* (1895)	Haymarket, Leicester – 4-act full-length version	14/10/1980	Old Vic
	Howard Brenton	*The Romans in Britain* (1980)	National Theatre	16/10/1980	Olivier
	Dion Boucicault	*The Streets of London* (1864)		21/10/1980	Her Majesty's
	Geraldine Aron	*A Galway Girl* (1980)		23/10/1980	Lyric Studio, Hammersmith
	Seamus Finnegan	*Act of Union* (1980)		10/11/1980	Soho Poly
	Ron Hutchinson	*The Irish Play* (1980)		18/11/1980	Warehouse
	Richard Brinsley Sheridan	*The Rivals* (1775)		18/12/1980	Greenwich
1981 (311)	G.B. Shaw	*Man and Superman* (1905)	National Theatre	22/1/1981	Olivier
	G.B. Shaw	*Pygmalion* (1913)		28/1/1981	Young Vic
	Edna O'Brien	*Virginia* (1981)		29/1/1981	Theatre Royal, Haymarket (78)
	Samuel Beckett	*Waiting for Godot* (1955)	South African company	18/2/1981	Old Vic (30)
	Brian Friel	*Faith Healer* (1979)	London première	2/3/1981	Royal Court (19)
	Brian Friel	*Translations* (1980)		12/5/1981	Hampstead Theatre Club (52)
	G.B. Shaw	*The Doctor's Dilemma* (1906)		4/6/1981	Greenwich (37)
	Samuel Beckett	*Waiting for Godot* (1955)		9/6/1981	Round House (18)
	Samuel Beckett	*Texts* {*Texts for Nothing* + *How It Is*} (1981)	Based on novels	17/6/1981	Riverside Studios

	Author	Title	Notes	Date	Venue
	James Pettifer	The Other Side (1981)		29/6/1981	Irish Club, Eaton Square (12)
	G.B. Shaw	Androcles and the Lion (1913)		7/7/1981	Open Air, Regents Park (50)
	Sean O'Casey	The Shadow of a Gunman (1923)	RSC	24/7/1981	Warehouse (35)
	Brian Friel	Translations (1980)	National Theatre	6/8/1981	Lyttelton
	G.B. Shaw	Pygmalion (1913)		18/8/1981	Young Vic (11)
	G.B. Shaw	Village Wooing (1934)		8/10/1981	New End, Hampstead (16)
	G.B. Shaw	Arms and the Man (1894)		15/10/1981	Lyric (199)
	Richard Brinsley Sheridan	The School for Scandal (1777)		17/12/1981	Greenwich (36)
1982 (333)	Seamus Finnegan	James Joyce and the Israelites (1982)		10/3/1982	Lyric Studio (17)
	G.B. Shaw	Captain Brassbound's Conversion (1899)		10/6/1982	Theatre Royal, Haymarket (51)
	Samuel Beckett	Waiting for Godot (1955)		15/7/1982	Young Vic (13)
	G.B. Shaw	{Dark Lady of the Sonnets (1910)}		10/6/1982	Open Air, Regents Park (25)
	G.B. Shaw	{The Admirable Bashville (1901)}	Cashel Byron's Confession	10/6/1982	Open Air, Regents Park (25)
	George Farquhar	The Twin Rivals (1702)	RSC	26/7/1982	The Pit, Barbican
	Oliver Goldsmith	She Stoops to Conquer (1773)		10/8/1982	Lyric, Hammersmith (38)
	Oscar Wilde	The Importance of Being Earnest (1895)	National Theatre	16/9/1982	Lyttelton
	G.B. Shaw	Major Barbara (1905)	National Theatre	27/10/1982	Lyttelton
	Peter Sheridan	Diary of a Hunger Strike (1982)	Hull Truck	11/11/1982	Round House (23)
	Robin Glendinning	Stuffing It (1982) aka Jennifer's Vacation		15/11/1982	Tricycle (19)
	G.B. Shaw	Man and Superman (1905)		18/11/1982	Theatre Royal, Haymarket (90)
	Samuel Beckett	Rockaby (1981)	National Theatre	9/12/1982	Cottesloe

Year	Author	Title		Date	Venue
1983 (358)	Richard Brinsley Sheridan	The School for Scandal (1777)		6/1/1983	Theatre Royal, Haymarket (60)
	G.B. Shaw	Heartbreak House (1920)		10/3/1983	Theatre Royal, Haymarket (90)
	Daniel Mornin	Kate (1983)		11/3/1983	Bush (28)
	Richard Brinsley Sheridan	The Rivals (1775)	National Theatre	12/4/1983	Olivier
	Daniel Mornin	Short of Mutiny (1983)		26/4/1983	Theatre Royal, Stratford East (25)
	Brian Friel	The Communication Cord (1982)	Field Day Theatre	6/5/1983	Hampstead
	G.B. Shaw / B. Green / D. King	Bashville (1983)	Musical	2/8/1983	Open Air, Regent's Park (22)
	Richard Brinsley Sheridan	The School for Scandal (1777)		15/12/1983	Duke of York's
	Ron Hutchinson	The Dillen (1983) – from Angela Hewins			
1984 (355)	Mick Egan / Peter Sheridan	The Kips, The Digs, The Village (1983)		5/1/1984	Theatre Upstairs (6)
	Peter Sheridan	Pledges and Promises (1983)		6/1/1984	Theatre Upstairs (7)
	Mick Egan	A Hape a' Junk (1983)		7/1/1984	Theatre Upstairs (8)
	Stewart Parker	Nightshade (1980)		17/1/1984	King's Head (39)
	G.B. Shaw	Saint Joan (1923)	National Theatre	16/2/1984	Olivier
	Mustapha Matura	Playboy of the West Indies (1984) – from Synge		21/2/1984	Tricycle (17)
	Seamus Finnegan	North (1984)		22/2/1984	Cockpit (17)
	Shane Connaughton	Lily (1984)	The Irish Company	2/4/1984	Old Red Lion (19)
	G.B. Shaw	Pygmalion (1913)		15/5/1984	Shaftesbury (22)
	J.H. Dean	The Importance (1984) – from Wilde	Musical	31/5/1984	Ambassadors (17)
	Seamus Finnegan	Mary's Men (1984)		12/6/1984	Drill Hall (18)
	G.B. Shaw	Back to Methuselah: Parts I-V (1922)		18/6/1984	Shaw (12)

Year	Author	Play	Company	Date	Venue
	G.B. Shaw / B. Green / D. King	*Bashville* (1983)	Musical	31/7/1984	Open Air, Regent's Park (25)
	Samuel Beckett	{*Ohio Impromptu* (1981)}		28/8/1984	Warehouse (18)
	Samuel Beckett	{*Catastrophe* (1982)}		28/8/1984	Warehouse (18)
	Samuel Beckett	{*What Where* (1983)}		28/8/1984	Warehouse (18)
	J.M. Synge	*The Playboy of the Western World* (1907)		30/8/1984	Riverside Studios (37)
	Ron Hutchinson	*Rat in the Skull* (1984)		4/9/1984	Royal Court (32)
	Aidan Carl Matthews	*The Diamond Body* (1984)	Operating Theatre, Dublin	2/10/1984	Bush (25)
	Oliver Goldsmith	*She Stoops to Conquer* (1773)	National Theatre	8/10/1984	Lyttelton
	Christina Reid	*Tea in a China Cup* (1983)	Sphinx	12/10/1984	Riverside Studios (20)
	Marie Jones / Martin Lynch, et al.	*Drill Hall* (1984)	Charabanc, Belfast	6/11/1984	Drill Hall, Chenies St. (6)
	Marie Jones / Martin Lynch, et al.	*Oul Delf and False Teeth* (1984)	Charabanc, Belfast	13/11/1984	Drill Hall, Chenies St. (6)
	Samuel Beckett	*Happy Days* (1961)	Shared Experience	20/11/1984	Donmar Warehouse (18)
1985 (407)	Peter McDonald	*Light* (1985)	Wooden O	4/2/1985	Soho Poly (12)
	Peter Cox	*The Garden of England* (1985)	7:84 Theatre Company (England)	18/2/1985	Shaw (12)
	J.M. Synge	*The Playboy of the Western World* (1907)	Druid Theatre Company, Galway	26/2/1985	Donmar Warehouse (24)
	Bill Morrison	*Scrap!* (1982)		1/3/1985	Half Moon (30)
	Seamus Finnegan	*Gombeen* (1985)	Pascal Theatre Company	9/4/1985	Theatre Downstairs, EC1 (18)
	Ron Hutchinson	*Rat in the Skull* (1984)		1/7/1985	Royal Court (20)
	Ron Hutchinson	*The Dillen* (1983) – from Angela Hewins	RSC	15/7/1985	The Other Place

	Sean O'Casey	*The Shadow of a Gunman* (1923)	Claddagh Theatre Company	1/8/1985	Falcon, NW1 (10)
	Marie Jones, et al.	*Now You're Talkin* (1985)	Charabanc, Belfast	4/9/1985	Drill Hall, Chenies St. (24)
	Richard Brinsley Sheridan	*The Critic* (1779)	National Theatre	12/9/1985	Olivier
	Daniel Mornin	*The Murderers* (1985)	National Theatre	23/9/1985	Cottesloe (7)
	Kerry Lee Crabbe	*Flann O'Brien's Hard Life* (1985)		30/9/1985	Tricycle (27)
	G.B. Shaw	*Mrs. Warren's Profession* (1894)	National Theatre	10/10/1985	Lyttelton
	Peter Cox	*The Garden of England* (1985)	National Theatre	14/11/1985	Cottesloe (9)
	Anne Devlin	*Ourselves Alone* (1985)		21/11/1985	Royal Court, Theatre Upstairs (30)
1986 (400)	Anne Devlin	*Ourselves Alone* (1985)		14/1/1986	Royal Court, Theatre Upstairs (17)
	Kerry Lee Crabbe	*Flann O'Brien's Hard Life* (1985)		20/1/1986	Tricycle (19)
	Samuel Beckett	{*Enough* (1986)}	Short story read by Billie Whitelaw	30/1/1986	Riverside Studios (10)
	Samuel Beckett	{*Footfalls* (1976)}		30/1/1986	Riverside Studios (10)
	Samuel Beckett	{*Rockaby* (1980)}		30/1/1986	Riverside Studios (10)
	Christina Reid	*Joyriders* (1986)		18/2/1986	Tricycle (28)
	Tom Murphy	*Bailegangaire* (1985)	Druid Theatre Company	19/2/1986	Donmar Warehouse (24)
	G.B. Shaw	*The Apple Cart* (1929)		20/2/1986	Theatre Royal, Haymarket (85)
	Bernard Farrell	*I Do Not Like Thee Doctor Fell* (1979)	Claddagh Theatre Company	26/2/1986	Old Red Lion (21)
	David Rudkin	*The Saxon Shore* (1986)		27/2/1986	Almeida (23)
	Shane Connaughton	*I Do Like To Be* (1986)	The Irish Company	12/3/1986	Soho Poly (9)
	Marie Jones	*Gold in the Streets* (1986)	Charabanc, Belfast	18/3/1986	Watermans, Brentford (4)

Author	Play	Notes	Date	Venue
George Farquhar	*The Beaux' Stratagem* (1707)		8/4/1986	Lyric, Hammersmith (39)
Thomas Kilroy	*Double Cross* (1986)	Field Day Theatre Company	10/5/1986	Royal Court (21)
Samuel Beckett	{*Krapp's Last Tape* (1958)}	Max Wall	10/6/1986	Riverside Studios (26)
Samuel Beckett	{*Endgame* (1957)}		10/6/1986	Riverside Studios (26)
Shane Connaughton	*I Do Like To Be* (1986)	Revised version	7/7/1986	Tricycle (19)
Samuel Beckett / Barry McGovern	*I'll Go On* (1985) – adaptation of three novels	Dublin Gate Theatre	23/7/1986	Riverside Studios (18)
Frank McGuinness	*Observe the Sons of Ulster Marching towards the Somme* (1985)		24/7/1986	Hampstead (37)
G.B. Shaw	*Arms and the Man* (1894)		5/8/1986	Open Air, Regent's Park
Tom Paulin	*The Riot Act* (1985) – from Sophocles		20/8/1986	Tabard (10)
Anne Devlin	*Ourselves Alone* (1985)		27/8/1986	Royal Court (25)
Marcy Kahan	*Intimate Memoirs of an Irish Taxidermist* (1986)	One-man show with Ben Keaton	22/9/1986	Donmar Warehouse (6)
G.B. Shaw	*Misalliance* (1910)	RSC	8/10/1986	Barbican
Brendan Behan	*The Hostage* (1958)		13/10/1986	Tricycle (53)
Seamus Finnegan	*The Spanish Play* (1986)	Pascal Theatre Company	15/10/1986	The Place (10)
Dave Allen	*Dave Allen Live* (1986)	One-man show	30/10/1986	Albery (104)
Seamus Finnegan	*The German Connection* (1986)	Pascal Theatre Company	5/11/1986	Young Vic Studio (22)
G.B. Shaw	*Too True to Be Good* (1932)		5/11/1986	Riverside Studios (25)
Marie Jones	*The Girls in the Big Picture* (1986)	Charabanc, Belfast	12/11/1986	Drill Hall (10)
David Rudkin	*Ashes* (1973)		20/11/1986	Bush (43)
Tom MacIntyre	*The Great Hunger* (1986) – from P. Kavanagh	Abbey Theatre	25/11/1986	Almeida (18)
Marie Jones	*Gold in the Streets* (1986)	Charabanc, Belfast	25/11/1986	Drill Hall (11)

	G.B. Shaw	*Candida* (1897)		8/12/1986	Kings Head (25)
1987 (492)	Marcy Kahan	*Intimate Memoirs of an Irish Taxidermist* (1986)	One-man show with Ben Keaton	24/1/1987	Battersea Arts Centre (2)
	Seamus Finnegan	*Ghetto* (1987)	Pascal Theatre Company	11/3/1987	Riverside Studios (25)
	Peter Sheridan	*Shades of the Jelly Woman* (1986)		23/3/1987	Watermans, Brentford (6)
	Daniel Magee	{*Mainland* (1987)}		2/4/1987	Watermans, Brentford (16)
	Michael McKnight	{*Ronnie's Doing Well* (1987)}		2/4/1987	Watermans, Brentford (16)
	Daniel Mornin	*Built on Sand* (1987)		13/5/1987	Theatre Upstairs (30)
	Robin Glendinning	*Mumbo Jumbo* (1986)		15/5/1987	Lyric, Hammersmith (35)
	James Joyce / Pamela Leventon	*Molly Bloom* (1987)		7/7/1987	Offstage Downstairs (6)
	Brian Friel	*Fathers and Sons* (1987) – from Turgenev	National Theatre	9/7/1987	Lyttelton
	Niall Ward	*Maguire Speaking* (1987)		5/8/1987	Etcetera (19)
	Brian Friel	*The Freedom of the City* (1973)	National Youth Theatre	24/8/1987	Shaw (19)
	J.M. Synge	{*When the Moon Has Set* (1900-03)}	First prof. performance – Four Corners Theatre	9/9/1987	Gate (18)
	J.M. Synge	{*The Shadow of the Glen* (1904)}	Four Corners Theatre	9/9/1987	Gate (18)
	J.M. Synge	{*Riders to the Sea* (1905)}	Four Corners Theatre	9/9/1987	Gate (18)
	Marie Jones	*Somewhere Over the Balcony* (1987)	Charabanc, Belfast	10/9/1987	Drill Hall (17)
	Oscar Wilde	*The Importance of Being Earnest* (1895)		11/9/1987	Royalty (36)
	Tom Murphy	*Conversations on a Homecoming* (1985)		16/10/1987	Donmar Warehouse (21)

	Oscar Wilde / Lou Stein	*The Importance of Being Earnest* (1895/1987)		2/11/1987	Whitehall (94)
	Matthew Brady	*Death of a Dragonfly* (1987)		4/11/1987	Tabard (20)
	Samuel Beckett	*Waiting for Godot* (1955)	National Theatre	25/11/1987	Lyttelton
	G.B. Shaw	*You Never Can Tell* (1899)	Theatr Clwyd, Mold	18/12/1987	Theatre Royal, Haymarket (150)
	Christina Reid	*Did You Hear the One about the Irishman?* (1982)		**/**/1987	King's Head
	Hugh Leonard	*The Mask of Moriarty* (1986)		**/**/1987	Haymarket
1988 (480)	G.B. Shaw	*Candida* (1897)	King's Head Theatre Club	12/1/1988	Arts (24)
	Samuel Beckett / Katherine Worth	*Company* (1987)	Adapted from novel	20/1/1988	Donmar Warehouse (17)
	Cecil Jenkins	*Our Own Red Blood* (1988)		3/2/1988	Man in the Moon (24)
	Billy Roche	*A Handful of Stars* (1988)		15/2/1988	Bush (26)
	Aidan C. Mathews	*Exit Entrance* (1988)	Abbey Theatre	29/3/1988	Donmar Warehouse (25)
	Ben Keaton	*Gone with the Wind 2* (1988)		12/4/1988	ICA (18)
	Dion Boucicault	*The Shaughran* (1874)	National Theatre	11/5/1988	Olivier
	Nell McCafferty	*The Worm in the Heart* (1988)	Theatre of Open Secrets	11/5/1988	Drill Hall (18)
	Frank McGuinness	*Factory Girls* (1982)	Druid Theatre Company	12/5/1988	Riverside Studio 2 (10)
	Brian Friel	*Aristocrats* (1979)	English première	2/6/1988	Hampstead (37)
	Seamus Finnegan	*The Murphy Girls* (1988)	Pascal Theatre Company	2/6/1988	Drill Hall (17)
	George Farquhar	*The Recruiting Officer* (1706)		26/7/1988	Royal Court (106)
	Hugh Carr	*Encounter in the Wilderness* (1978)		5/8/1988	Tabard (35)
	Arthur Murphy	*The Way to Keep Him* (1760)		9/9/1988	Orange Tree, Richmond (30)
	Frank McGuinness	*Baglady* (1988)	Bristol Old Vic	14/9/1988	Riverside Studio 2 (10)
	G.B. Shaw	*Candida* (1897)		21/9/1988	Boulevard (24)
	G.B. Shaw	*The Millionairess* (1935)		10/10/1988	Greenwich (39)

	Richard Brinsley Sheridan	The Rivals (1775)		18/10/1988	New End (18)
	Nick Perry	{The Vinegar Fly (1988)}	Dry Boke	28/10/1988	Soho Poly (21)
	Nick Perry	{Smallholdings (1986)}	Dry Boke	28/10/1988	Soho Poly (21)
	Brian Friel	Making History (1988)	Field Day Theatre Company	5/12/1988	Cottesloe
1989 (551)	G.B. Shaw	{Village Wooing (1934)}	London Theatre Laboratory	5/1/1989	Theatre Museum (25)
	G.B. Shaw	{Overruled (1912)}	London Theatre Laboratory	5/1/1989	Theatre Museum (25)
	Stewart Parker	Pentecost (1987)	Tricycle Theatre Company	9/1/1989	Lyric Studio (19)
	Sean O'Casey	Juno and the Paycock (1924)	National Theatre	22/2/1989	Lyttelton
	Samuel Beckett	Waiting for Godot (1955)		23/2/1989	Young Vic Studio (30)
	Oscar Wilde	An Ideal Husband (1895)		24/4/1989	Westminster (210)
	Edward Callan	I am of Ireland (1988)	Tribute to W.B. Yeats	23/4/1989	Riverside (7)
	Peter Sheridan	Shades of the Jelly Woman (1986)		24/4/1989	Riverside (1)
	Sean Lawlor	The Watchman (1988)		26/4/1989	Riverside (3)
	Donal O'Kelly	Bat the Father, Rabbit the Son (1988)		27/4/1989	Riverside (3)
	Oscar Wilde	The Importance of Being Earnest (1895)	Talawa Theatre Company	16/5/1989	Bloomsbury (12)
	Oscar Wilde	The Importance of Being Earnest (1895)	Voices Theatre Company	23/5/1989	Latchmere (25)
	Tom Murphy	A Whistle in the Dark (1961)	Abbey Theatre	7/7/1989	Royal Court
	Frank McGuinness	Carthaginians (1988)		13/7/1989	Hampstead (30)
	Brendan Kennelly	Medea (1988) – from Euripides		18/7/1989	Purcell Room (10)
	Dion Boucicault	The Shaughran (1874)	National Theatre	10/8/1989	Olivier
	George Farquhar	The Recruiting Officer (1706)		10/8/1989	Royal Court (50)
	Richard Brinsley Sheridan	The Rivals (1775)		15/8/1989	Holland Park (10)

	Maggie Cronin	A Most Notorious Woman (1989)	One-woman show	6/9/1989	Battersea Arts Centre (12)
	G.B. Shaw	Mrs. Warren's Profession (1902)		8/9/1989	Orange Tree, Richmond (30)
	Frank McGuinness	Mary and Lizzie (1989)	RSC	27/9/1989	The Pit (35)
	Oscar Wilde	Salomé (1896)	National Theatre	7/11/1989	Lyttelton
	Billy Roche	Poor Beast in the Rain (1989)		13/11/1989	Bush (40)
	George Farquhar	The Beaux' Stratagem (1707)	National Theatre	14/11/1989	Lyttelton
	G.B. Shaw	Heartbreak House (1920)		21/11/1989	Riverside Studios (12)
	Declan Donellan	Lady Betty (1989)	Cheek by Jowl	30/11/1989	Almeida (24)
	Seamus Finnegan	1916 (1989)	Pascal Theatre Company	11/12/1989	ICA (2)
	Dion Boucicault	London Assurance (1841)	Chichester Festival Theatre	13/12/1989	Theatre Royal, Haymarket (92)
1990 (574)	Brian Behan	Boots for the Footless (1990)		8/1/1990	Tricycle (47)
	Samuel Beckett	{Krapp's Last Tape (1958)}		11/1/1990	Riverside (16)
	Samuel Beckett	{Catastrophe (1982)}		11/1/1990	Riverside (16)
	Oscar Wilde	Salomé (1896)		22/1/1990	Phoenix (33)
	Brendan Somers	{Wake (1990)}		30/1/1990	Latchmere (13)
	Brendan Somers	{Knife (1990)}		30/1/1990	Latchmere (13)
	Seamus Finnegan	Mary Maginn (1990)	National Theatre	28/2/1990	Drill Hall (18)
	Christina Reid	My Name, Shall I Tell You My Name (1987)	Yew Theatre Company, Ballina, County Mayo	8/3/1990	Young Vic Studio (17)
	Ray Brennan	Sidewind (1985)	Portrait Theatre Co., Siol Phadraig Fest. of Irish Arts	8/3/1990	Battersea Arts Centre (11)
	Terry Eagleton	Saint Oscar (1989)	Field Day Theatre Company	9/3/1990	Hampstead (28)

Flann O'Brien / Paul Lee	The Poor Mouth (1989)	Dry Bread Theatre, Siol Phadraig Fest. of Irish Arts	14/3/1990	Battersea Arts Centre (5)
Richard Brinsley Sheridan	The School for Scandal (1777)	National Theatre	24/4/1990	Olivier
Marie Jones	The Hamster Wheel (1990)	Charabanc Theatre Company	2/5/1990	Riverside Studio 2 (18)
Frank McGuinness	Three Sisters (1990) – from Chekhov	Gate Theatre, Dublin	24/7/1990	Royal Court (67)
Richard Brinsley Sheridan	The School for Scandal (1777)		24/7/1990	Holland Park Open Air (5)
Arthur Murphy	The Way to Keep Him (1760)		4/9/1990	Duke's Head (27)
Dermot Bolger	The Lament for Arthur Cleary (1989)	Arthur Cleary Productions, A Sense of Ireland Festival	2/10/1990	Riverside Studio 1 (6)
Roma Tomelty	The Wind and the Sleeping Harp (1990)	Newry Arts Centre, A Sense of Ireland Festival	3/10/1990	Riverside Studio 2 (2)
Edward Callan	I am of Ireland (1988)	Tribute to W.B. Yeats, A Sense of Ireland Festival	7/10/1990	Riverside Studio 2 (1)
Frank McGuinness	The Factory Girls (1982)		8/10/1990	Tricycle (33)
Colin Teevan	The Big Sea (1990)	Galloglass Theatre Co., A Sense of Ireland Festival	9/10/1990	Riverside Studio 2 (1)
Eamon Morrissey	The Brother (1974) – from Flann O'Brien	One-man show, A Sense of Ireland Festival	12/10/1990	Riverside Studio 1 (2)

	Author	Work	Company	Date	Venue
	Brian Friel	Dancing at Lughnasa (1990)	Abbey Theatre	15/10/1990	Lyttleton (75)
	Paul O'Hanrahan	The Wake (1990) – from James Joyce	Balloonatics Theatre Company	18/10/1990	Bush (11)
	G.B. Shaw	Arms and the Man (1894)	Voices Theatre Company	13/11/1990	Duke's Head (27)
	G.B. Shaw	Arms and the Man (1894)	Orpheus Theatre Company	13/11/1990	Greenwich Studio (20)
1991 (727)	Samuel Beckett	Endgame (1957)	Three Legged Company	9/1/1991	Etcetera (19)
	Hugh Carr	Heloise and Abelard (1991) previously titled Encounter in the Wilderness (1978)		10/1/1991	Lyric Studio (17)
	Jeremy Monson	A Night in Belfast (1991)		29/1/1991	Hen and Chickens (18)
	G.B. Shaw	The Millionairess (1936)		7/2/1991	Battersea Arts Centre (25)
	Dave Allen	An Evening with Dave Allen (1991)	One-man show	18/2/1991	Strand (46)
	Arthur Murphy	All in the Wrong (1761)		25/2/1991	Orange Tree (34)
	James Doherty	The Rising of the Moon (1991)		27/2/1991	Old Red Lion (25)
	Maciek Reszczynski	Cromwell (1991) – from Brendan Kennelly	Theatre Unlimited, Kilkenny, Siol Phadraig Fest. of Irish Arts	1/3/1991	Bush (16)
	Johnny Hanrahan	The Battle of Aughrim (1991)	London Irish Theatre, Siol Phadraig Fest. of Irish Arts	13/3/1991	Battersea Arts Centre (12)
	Brian Friel	Dancing at Lughnasa (1990)	Abbey Theatre	25/3/1991	Phoenix (275 +)
	Seamus Heaney	The Cure at Troy (1990)	Field Day Theatre Company	4/4/1991	Tricycle (24)
	Marie Jones	{Weddin's, Wee'ins and Wakes (1989)}	Charabanc Theatre Company	10/4/1991	Drill Hall (18)

Author	Play	Company	Date	Venue
Marie Jones	{*The Blind Fiddler of Glenadaugh* (1990)}	Charabanc Theatre Company	10/4/1991	Drill Hall (18)
Julia O'Faolain / Colin Watkeys	*Melancholy Baby* (1991)	Myrtle	18/4/1991	Finborough (18)
G.B. Shaw	*The Man of Destiny* (1897)	Merriman Theatre Company	25/4/1991	Latchmere (18)
Eamon Morrissey	*The Brother* (1974) – from Flann O'Brien	One-man show	1/5/1991	Tricycle (18)
Sean O'Casey	*The Plough and the Stars* (1926)		7/5/1991	Young Vic (46)
Geraldine Aron	*Same Old Moon* (1991)		13/5/1991	Globe (39)
Antoine O Flatharta	*Grace in America* (1991)		13/6/1991	Old Red Lion (17)
Richard Brinsley Sheridan	*The Scheming Lieutenant* (1775) (*St Patrick's Day*)	Moth Theatre Company	13/8/1991	Man in the Moon (18)
Eamon Morrissey	*The Brother* (1974) – from Flann O'Brien	One-man show	28/8/1991	Tricycle (23)
Una Ellis-Fermor	*Hedda Gabler* (19910 – trans. from Ibsen	Abbey Theatre	3/9/1991	Playhouse (32)
Richard Brinsley Sheridan	*The Rivals* (1775)	National Youth Theatre	5/9/1991	Greenwich (10)
Rona Munro	*Bold Girls* (1990)		9/9/1991	Hampstead (27)
Daniel Mornin	*At Our Table* (1991)	National Theatre	19/9/1991	Cottesloe
Samuel Beckett	*Waiting for Godot* (1955)		30/9/1991	Queen's (75)
Oscar Wilde	*Salomé* (1896)		1/10/1991	Theatre Museum (12)
Richard Brinsley Sheridan	*The Rivals* (1775)		1/10/1991	Rheingold's Theatre Club (32)
Oscar Wilde	*A Woman of No Importance* (1893)	RSC	2/10/1991	Barbican (28)
Billy Roche	*Belfry* (1991)		18/11/1991	Bush (26)
G.B. Shaw	*The Philanderer* (1905)		19/11/1991	Hampstead (55)
Oscar Wilde	*Lady Windermere's Fan* (1892)		7/12/1991	Lilian Bayliss (15)
G.B. Shaw	*The Millionairess* (1936)		10/12/1991	Rose (30)

	Sean Hughes	*Sean Hughes Live* (1991)	One-man show	27/12/1991	Purcell Room (7)
1992 (637)	Tom Murphy	*The Gigli Concert* (1983)	English premiere	7/1/1992	Almeida (46)
	Brian Friel	*Faith Healer* (1979)	Abbey Theatre	24/1/1992	Royal Court (23
	G.B. Shaw	*Caesar and Cleopatra* (1898)		4/2/1992	Greenwich (45)
	Maureen O'Brien	*The Cutting* (1992)		10/2/1992	Bush (32)
	Ron Hutchinson	*Pygmies in the Ruins* (1992)		24/2/1992	Royal Court (32)
	George Farquhar	*The Recruiting Officer* (1706)	National Theatre	12/3/1992	Olivier
	Karl MacDermott	*An Afternoon with Klaus Barbie's Pen-Pal* (1991)	One-man show	17/3/1992	Battersea Arts Centre Studio (13)
	Brendan Behan	*Richard's Cork Leg* (1972)	Not the Abbey Theatre	18/3/1992	Pentameters (5)
	G.B. Shaw	*Heartbreak House* (1920)		19/3/1992	Theatre Royal, Haymarket (90)
	Declan Hughes	*Digging for Fire* (1991)	Rough Magic Theatre Company, Dublin	20/3/1992	Bush (21)
	Michael Skelly	*Rat Play* (1992)		24/3/1992	Old Red Lion (24)
	Thomas Shadwell	*The Virtuoso* (1676)	RSC	2/4/1992	The Pit
	Eamon Morrissey	*Just the One* (1992)	One-man show	8/4/1992	Tricycle (38)
	G.B. Shaw	*Pygmalion* (1938)	National Theatre	9/4/1992	Olivier
	Sebastian Barry	*White Woman Street* (1992)		23/4/1992	Bush (32)
	George Farquhar	*Love and a Bottle* (1698)	Rough Magic Theatre Company, Dublin	3/6/1992	Tricycle (25)
	Brian Friel	*Philadelphia, Here I Come!* (1964)	Transferred to Wyndham's 28/7/1992	4/6/1992	King's Head (45+)
	Thomas Shadwell	*The Libertine* (1740)		26/6/1992	Pentameters (24)
	Michael Harding	*Una Pooka* (1989)		6/7/1992	Tricycle (32)

Frank McGuinness	*Someone Who'll Watch over Me* (1992)	Premiere. Transferred to Vaudeville 9/9/1992	10/7/1992	Hampstead (43)
Oscar Wilde	*A Woman of No Importance* (1893)	RSC	13/7/1992	Theatre Royal, Haymarket (114)
Billy Roche	*Amphibians* (1992)	RSC	3/9/1992	The Pit
G.B. Shaw / D. King / B. Green	*Valentine's Day* (1991)	Musical from *You Never Can Tell*	17/9/1992	Globe (24)
Michael Harding	*Misogynist* (1992)	Monologue	2/10/1992	Bush (9)
Sean O'Casey	{*The End of the Beginning* (1937)}	Three Shadows from a Hill – O'Casey Theater Co.	12/10/1992	Lilian Baylis (6)
Sean O'Casey	{*A Pound on Demand* (1939)}	Three Shadows from a Hill – O'Casey Theater Co.	12/10/1992	Lilian Baylis (6)
Sean O'Casey	{*Bedtime Story* (1952)}	Three Shadows from a Hill – O'Casey Theater Co.	12/10/1992	Lilian Baylis (6)
David Ian Neville	*Exile* (1992)		13/10/1992	Bush (12)
G.B. Shaw	*Village Wooing* (1933)		13/10/1992	Village (18)
Noel MacAoidh	*The Changing Reason* (1992)	"New Voices"	15/10/1992	Royal Court (22)
Ger Fitzgibbon	*The Rock Station* (1992)		28/10/1992	Cockpit (24)
Oscar Wilde	*An Ideal Husband* (1895)	Directed by Peter Hall	11/11/1992	Globe (218)
Oliver Goldsmith	*She Stoops to Conquer* (1773)		17/11/1992	New End (34)
Billy Roche	*A Handful of Stars* (1988)	*Wexford Trilogy*	6/11/1992	Bush (45)
Billy Roche	*Poor Beast in the Rain* (1989)	*Wexford Trilogy*	13/11/1992	Bush (39)

	Billy Roche	*Belfry* (1991)	*Wexford Trilogy*	19/11/1992	Bush (34)
	Flann O'Brien / J. Haynes / A. Barr	*The Third Policeman* (1992)	Ridiculusmus Theatre Company	9/12/1992	Aras na nGael, NW6 (38)
1993 (721)	Gavin Kostick	*The Ash Fire* (1993)		27/1/1993	Tricycle (24)
	Claire Booker	*Irish Roulette* (1993)		4/2/1993	Man in the Moon (24)
	Samuel Beckett	*Krapp's Last Tape* (1958)		24/2/1993	Etcetera (19)
	Pat McCabe	*Frank Pig Says Hello* (1993) – from *The Butcher Boy*	Co-Motion Theatre Company, Dublin	10/3/1993	Theatre Upstairs
	Declan Hughes	*New Morning* (1993)	Rough Magic Theatre Company, Dublin	2/4/1993	Bush (23)
	Bill Morrison	*The Marriage* (1993)	*A Love Song for Ulster*	27/3/1993	Tricycle (28)
	Bill Morrison	*The Son* (1993)	*A Love Song for Ulster*	3/4/1993	Tricycle (28)
	Bill Morrison	*The Daughter* (1993)	*A Love Song for Ulster*	10/4/1993	Tricycle (28)
	Frank McGuinness	*Carthaginians* (1988)		14/4/1993	Greenwich Studio (19)
	Marina Carr	*Low in the Dark* (1989)		6/5/1993	Theatro Technis (16)
	Sean O'Casey	*Juno and the Paycock* (1924)	Gate Theatre, Dublin. Transferred to Wyndham's 13/7/93 (32)	19/5/1993	Albery (30)
	Christina Reid	*The Belle of Belfast City* (1989)		7/6/1993	Orange Tree Room (26)
	Brian Friel	*Translations* (1981)		9/6/1993	Donmar Warehouse (45)
	Oscar Wilde / R.S. Philips	*The Picture of Dorian Gray* (1993)		30/6/1993	Baron's Court (15)
	Vincent Woods	*At the Black Pig's Dyke* (1992)	Druid Theatre Company, Galway (LIFT)	7/7/1993	Tricycle (24)
	G.B. Shaw	*Widowers' Houses* (1892)		16/7/1993	Chelsea Theatre Centre (21)
	Oliver Goldsmith	*She Stoops to Conquer* (1773)	Directed by Peter Hall	25/10/1993	Queen's (130)

	Author	Title	Company	Date	Venue
	Sean Hughes / Owen O'Neill	*Patrick's Day* (1991)		27/10/1993	Battersea Arts Centre (17)
	Helen Edmundsen	*The Clearing* (1993)		22/11/1993	Bush (32)
	Oliver Goldsmith	*The Good-Natur'd Man* (1768)		7/12/1993	Orange Tree (52)
	Mustapha Matura	*Playboy of the West Indies* (1984) – from Synge		14/12/1984	Tricycle (46)
	Peter Cox / Robert Era	*The Bodhran Makers* (1993) – from John B. Keane's novel		6/12/1993	Galtymore Ballroom, NW2 (10)
	Flann O'Brien / J. Haynes / A. Barr	*The Third Policeman* (1992)	Ridiculusmus Theatre Company	29/12/1993	Battersea Arts Centre 2 (18)
1994 (665)	Billy Roche	*The Cavalcaders* (1993)	Abbey Theatre	7/1/1994	Royal Court (30)
	Samuel Beckett	*Waiting for Godot* (1955)		11/2/1994	Lyric Studio (22)
	Samuel Beckett	*Endgame* (1957)		17/2/1994	Battersea Arts Centre 2 (24)
	Samuel Beckett	*Waiting for Godot* (1955)		1/3/1994	Pentameters (27)
	Samuel Beckett	{*Rough for Theatre 1* (1976)}		1/3/1994	White Bear (20)
	Samuel Beckett	{*Rough for Theatre 2* (1976)}		1/3/1994	White Bear (20)
	Oscar Wilde / R.S. Philips	*The Picture of Dorian Gray* (1993)		1/3/1994	Baron's Court (33)
	Daniel Magee	*Paddywack* (1994)		2/3/1994	Cockpit (30)
	James Joyce	*Ulysses Blooms* (1994) – from Chapter 13 "Nausicaa"	Cracked Mirror Theatre Company	2/3/1994	Hens and Chickens (18)
	Frank McGuinness	*Peer Gynt* (1988) – from Ibsen	RSC	3/3/1994	Barbican (10)
	Samuel Beckett	*Footfalls* (1976)		14/3/1994	Garrick (6)
	Oscar Wilde	*Salomé* (1896)		18/3/1994	Camden Studio (22)
	Jon Kenny / Pat Shortt	*One Hell of a Do* (1993)	Southern Comedy Theatre Company	22/3/1994	Tricycle
	Oscar Wilde	*Lady Windermere's Fan* (1892)	Rough Magic Theatre Company, Dublin	14/4/1994	Tricycle (24)
	Samuel Beckett	*Happy Days* (1961)		3/6/1994	French Institute (17)

Author	Title	Company	Date	Venue
Oscar Wilde / R.S. Philips	Lord Arthur Savile's Crime (1994)		10/6/1994	Baron's Court (29)
Oscar Wilde / A. O'Callaghan / A.K. Daniel	The Innocence of Dorian Gray (1994)		16/6/1994	Hen and Chickens (16)
Oliver Goldsmith	She Stoops to Conquer (1771)		28/6/1994	Pentameters (20)
Samuel Beckett	Endgame (1957)		4/7/1994	Arts (28)
G.B. Shaw	Saint Joan (1923)	Theatr Clwyd, Mold	21/7/1994	Strand (71)
Oscar Wilde	Lady Windermere's Fan (1892)	Birmingham Repertory Theatre	25/7/1994	Albery (170)
J.M. Synge	The Playboy of the Western World (1907)		5/9/1994	Almeida (40)
J.M. Synge	The Playboy of the Western World (1907)	Traffic of the Stage	6/9/1994	Pentameters (26)
G.B. Shaw	The Devil's Disciple (1897)	Royal National Theatre	8/9/1994	Olivier
Oscar Wilde / N. Bartlett	The Picture of Dorian Gray (1994)		12/9/1994	Lyric, Hammersmith (33)
Brendan Behan	The Hostage (1958)	RSC	14/9/1994	Barbican
Samuel Beckett	Not I (1972)	Bitesize Theatre Company	29/9/1994	DOC (16)
Richard Brinsley Sheridan	The Rivals (1775)	Akimbo	27/10/1994	Southwark Playhouse (22)
Thomas McLaughlin	Iron May Sparkle (1994)	Charabanc Theatre Company	3/11/1994	Drill Hall (25)
Brian Friel	Molly Sweeney (1994)	Gate Theatre, Dublin	3/11/1994	Almeida (50)
Oscar Wilde	An Ideal Husband (1895)	Pilgrim Theatre	8/11/1994	Pentameters (26)
Frank McGuinness	Innocence (1986)		1/12/1994	Cage, SW9 (22)
Richard Brinsley Sheridan	The Rivals (1775)	Chichester Festival Theatre	13/12/1994	Albery (30)

1995 (651)	Flann O'Brien / Audrey Welsh	At-Swim-Two-Birds (1995)	Ridiculusmus Theatre Company	3/1/1995	Battersea Arts Centre 2 (18)
	Richard Brinsley Sheridan	The Rivals (1775)		9/2/1995	Southwark Playhouse (22)
	Geraldine Aron	{The Stanley Parkers (1995)}	Attic Theatre Company	23/2/1995	Wimbledon Studio (16)
	Geraldine Aron	{The Donahue Sisters (1995)}	Attic Theatre Company	23/2/1995	Wimbledon Studio (16)
	Kate O'Riordan	The Jaws of Darkness (1995)		23/2/1995	Orange Tree Room (22)
	Marie Jones	A Night in November (An Afternoon in June) (1994)	DubbelJoint, One-man show	28/2/1995	Tricycle (33)
	Anne Devlin	After Easter (1994)	RSC	3/4/1995	The Pit
	Sebastian Barry	The Steward of Christendom (1995)	Out of Joint	3/4/1995	Theatre Upstairs (20)
	Frank McGuinness	Uncle Vanya (1995) – from Chekhov	Field Day Theatre Company	10/4/1995	Tricycle (20)
	Alex Ferguson	Casement (1995)	Moving Theatre	25/4/1995	Riverside 2 (11)
	Sean O'Casey	The Silver Tassie (1928)	Directed by Lynne Parker	10/5/1995	Almeida (44)
	Cathy Belton, et al.	True Lines (1995)	Bickerstaffe, Dublin	12/5/1995	Bush (21)
	G.B. Shaw	Don Juan In Hell (1905)	Final Act of Man and Superman	19/5/1995	Riverside 2 (2)
	Marie Jones	Ethel Workman Is Innocent (1995)		8/6/1995	Chelsea Centre (24)
	Gina Moxley	Danti-Dan (1995)	Rough Magic Theatre Company	13/6/1995	Hampstead (18)
	Oscar Wilde	The Importance of Being Earnest (1895)	Directed by Terry Hands, Birmingham Repertory Theatre	3/7/1995	Old Vic (135)
	Joseph O'Connor	Red Roses and Petrol (1995)	Pigsback Theatre Company, Dublin	11/7/1995	Tricycle (25)
	Sebastian Barry	The Steward of Christendom (1995)	Out of Joint	5/9/1995	Royal Court (46)

	John O'Keefe	*Wild Oats* (1791)	Royal National Theatre	7/9/1995	Lyttelton
	Bill Whelan	*Riverdance* (1995)	Dance Show	3/10/1995	Labatt's Apollo (103)
	Ron Hutchinson	*Rat in the Skull* (1984)	Royal Court Classics	11/10/1995	Duke of York's (37)
	Joseph Crilly	*Shuttle* (1994)		16/11/1995	Red Room (16)
	G.B. Shaw	*The Simpleton of the Unexpected Isles* (1935)		4/12/1995	Orange Tree (53)
	Fergus Linehan	*The Streets of Dublin* (1995) – from Boucicault	Musical	18/12/1995	Brixton Shaw (32)
1996 (690)	Maeve Murphy	*The Miracle People* (1996)		5/1/1996	Etcetera (24)
	Oscar Wilde	*An Ideal Husband* (1895)	Directed by Peter Hall	17/1/1996	Theatre Royal, Haymarket (92)
	Samuel Beckett	{*Act Without Words I* (1957)}	London Mime Festival	18/1/1996	Battersea Arts Centre (2)
	Samuel Beckett	{*Act Without Words I* (1959)}	London Mime Festival	18/1/1996	Battersea Arts Centre (2)
	Samuel Beckett	{*Breath* (1969)}	In Motion Theatre Company	2/2/1996	Etcetera (24)
	Samuel Beckett	{*Rockaby* (1980)}	In Motion Theatre Company	2/2/1996	Etcetera (24)
	Samuel Beckett	{*Footfalls* (1976)}	In Motion Theatre Company	2/2/1996	Etcetera (24)
	Samuel Beckett	{*Not I* (1972)}	In Motion Theatre Company	2/2/1996	Etcetera (24)
	Samuel Beckett	{*Come and Go* (1966)}	In Motion Theatre Company	2/2/1996	Etcetera (24)
	Martin McDonagh	*The Beauty Queen of Leenane* (1996)	Druid Theatre Company, Galway	5/3/1996	Theatre Upstairs (19)
	Frank McGuinness	*Observe the Sons of Ulster Marching towards the Somme* (1985)	Abbey Theatre	6/3/1996	Barbican (11)

Paul Mercier	Buddleia (1995)		12/3/1996	Donmar Warehouse (5)
Bryan James Ryder	The Soldier's Song (1996)	Passion Machine, Four Corners Season	18/3/1996	Theatre Royal, Stratford E.
Dermot Bolger	Baby Jean (1996)	Lucid Productions, Irish Festival	19/3/1996	Battersea Arts Centre (15)
Dermot Bolger	In High Germany (1990)	Lucid Productions, Irish Festival	22/3/1996	Battersea Arts Centre (10)
Christina Reid	Clowns (1996)		22/3/1996	Orange Tree Room (21)
Jimmy Murphy	Brothers of the Brush (1993)	Directed by Lynne Parker	25/3/1996	Arts (72)
Eamon Morrissey	{Byrne (1996)}	One-man show	25/3/1996	Tricycle (32)
Eamon Morrissey	{The Brother (1974)} – from Flann O'Brien	One-man show	25/3/1996	Tricycle (32)
Samuel Beckett	Endgame (1957)		17/4/1996	Donmar Warehouse (38)
Ger Fitzgibbon	The Rock Station (1992)	Liffey Street Theatre Company	9/5/1996	Finborough (17)
Marina Carr	Portia Coughlan (1996)	Abbey Theatre	14/5/1996	Royal Court (17)
G.B. Shaw	Mrs. Warren's Profession (1902)		14/5/1996	Wimbledon Studio (12)
Brendan O'Carroll	The Course (1995)		28/5/1996	Bloomsbury (4)
Shivaun O'Casey / Niall Buggy	Song at Sunset (1996) – from O'Casey	O'Casey Theater Company	11/6/1996	Hampstead (12)
Conor McPherson	This Lime Tree Bower (1995)		5/7/1996	Bush (36)
Michael Flatley	Lord of the Dance (1996)	Dance Show	23/7/1996	Coliseum (25)
Stewart Parker	Pentecost (1987)	Rough Magic Theatre Company	5/9/1996	Donmar Warehouse (24)
G.B. Shaw	Mrs. Warren's Profession (1902)		21/10/1996	Lyric, Hammersmith (33)
Gerard Stembridge	The Gay Detective (1996)		29/10/1996	Tricycle (32)
Samuel Beckett	Happy Days (1961)		30/10/1996	Almeida (10)

	Author	Title	Company/Notes	Date	Venue
	Nicholas Kelly	*The Future is Betamax* (1996)	Royal Court Young Writers' Festival	30/10/1996	Royal Court Upstairs (17)
	Paul Sellar	*The Bedsit* (1996)		7/11/1996	Tabard (17)
	Martin McDonagh	*The Beauty Queen of Leenane* (1996)	Druid Theatre Company, Galway	2/12/1996	Royal Court Downstairs (47)
1997 (725)	Martin McDonagh	*The Cripple of Inishmaan* (1997)	Royal National Theatre	7/1/1997	Cottesloe
	Michael Flatley	*Lord of the Dance* (1996)	Dance Show	7/1/1997	Wembley Arena (12)
	Paul Mercier	*Kitchensink* (1997)	Passion Machine, Dublin	3/2/1997	Tricycle (27)
	Samuel Beckett	*First Love* (1997)	Theatre Dark, adaptation	20/2/1997	Etcetera (18)
	Conor McPherson	*St. Nicholas* (1997)	Monologue	21/2/1997	Bush (37)
	Marie Jones	*Women on the Verge of HRT* (1996)	DubbelJoint	3/3/1997	Vaudeville (60)
	Jon Kenny / Pat Shortt	*"I Doubt It," Says Pauline* (1996)	Southern Comedy Theatre Company	6/3/1997	Tricycle (24)
	Lin Coghlan	*Waking* (1997)	Soho Theatre Company	10/3/1997	21 Dean Street (20)
	Micheál MacLiammóir / O. Wilde	*The Importance of Being Oscar* (1960)	One-man show, Simon Callow	18/3/1997	Savoy (52)
	Oscar Wilde	*Lady Windermere's Fan* (1892)	Royal Exchange Theatre Company	1/4/1997	Theatre Royal, Haymarket (61)
	Daragh Carville	*Language Roulette* (1996)	Tinderbox Theatre Company, Belfast	4/4/1997	Bush (21)
	Declan Hughes	*Halloween Night* (1997)	Rough Magic Theatre Company, Four Corners Season	9/4/1997	Donmar Warehouse (11)
	G.B. Shaw	{*The Man of Destiny* (1897)}		17/4/1997	Wimbledon Studio (24)

Author	Play	Note	Date	Venue
G.B. Shaw	{Annajanska, the Bolshevik Empress (1917)}		17/4/1997	Wimbledon Studio (24)
Tom Murphy	Bailegangaire (1985)		23/4/1997	Royal Court Upstairs (25)
Marina Carr	The Mai (1994)		28/4/1997	Tricycle (10)
Donal O'Kelley	Asylum! Asylum! (1994)		11/5/1997	Tricycle
Hugh Leonard	Da (1973)	Hibernia Theatre	13/5/1997	White Bear (26)
W.B. Yeats	{On Baile's Strand (1904)}		15/5/1997	Pentameters (25)
W.B. Yeats	{The Dreaming of the Bones (1919)}		15/5/1997	Pentameters (25)
W.B. Yeats	{The Cat and the Moon (1924)}		15/5/1997	Pentameters (25)
W.B. Yeats	{The Words Upon the Window Pane (1934)}		15/5/1997	Pentameters (25)
W.B. Yeats	{Purgatory (1938)}		15/5/1997	Pentameters (25)
Sebastian Barry	Prayers of Sherkin (1990)	Peter Hall Company	19/5/1997	Old Vic
Samuel Beckett	Waiting for Godot (1955)	Directed by Peter Hall	27/6/1997	Old Vic
Conor McPherson	The Weir (1997)		8/7/1997	Royal Court Upstairs (19)
Brian Friel	Lovers (1968)	Kassiopia	22/7/1997	Riverside 3 (13)
Martin McDonagh	The Beauty Queen of Leenane (1996)	Leenane Trilogy	26/7/1997	Royal Court Downstairs (50)
Martin McDonagh	A Skull in Connemara (1997)	Leenane Trilogy	26/7/1997	Royal Court Downstairs (50)
Martin McDonagh	The Lonesome West (1997)	Leenane Trilogy	26/7/1997	Royal Court Downstairs (50)
G.B. Shaw	Pygmalion (1913)		28/7/1997	Albery (68)
Oscar Wilde	An Ideal Husband (1895)	Directed by Peter Hall	6/8/1997	Theatre Royal, Haymarket (65)
G.B. Shaw	Heartbreak House (1920)	Directed by David Hare	3/9/1997	Almeida (38)

	Enda Walsh	*Disco Pigs* (1996)	Corcadorca Theatre Company	5/9/1997	Bush (23)
	Hilary Fanning	*Mackerel Sky* (1997)		3/10/1997	Bush (35)
	Frank McGuinness	*Electra* (1997) – from Sophocles		23/10/1997	Donmar Warehouse (42)
	Bill Whelan	*Riverdance* (1995)	Chichester Festival Theatre Dance Show	10/11/1997	Labatt's Apollo (60)
	Frank McGuinness	*Mutabilitie* (1997)	Royal National Theatre	20/11/1997	Cottesloe
	Samuel Beckett	*Oh Les Beaux Jours* (1961)	Directed by Peter Brook	27/11/1997	Riverside (10)
	Arthur Murphy	*All in the Wrong* (1761)		1/12/1997	Orange Tree (51)
	Jim O'Hanlon	*Ready or Not* (1997)	Monologue	3/12/1997	Man in the Moon (8)
	John B. Keane	*Sive* (1959)	Directed by Ben Barnes	4/12/1997	Tricycle (44)
	Michael Skelly	*Redemption* (1997)		**/**/1997	Old Red Lion
1998 (774)	Oscar Wilde	*The Kaos Importance of Being Earnest* (1998)	Kaos Theatre, Cirencester	9/1/1998	Oval House (14)
	Ron Hutchinson	*Flight* (1998) – from Mikhail Bulgakov	Royal National Theatre	12/2/1998	Olivier
	Samuel Beckett	*Happy Days* (1961)	Leap of Faith	13/2/1998	Battersea Arts Centre Main (16)
	Conor McPherson	*The Weir* (1997)		23/2/1998	Royal Court Downstairs (34)
	Gary Mitchell	*In a Little World of Our Own* (1997)	Foundry, Four Corners Season	4/3/1998	Donmar Warehouse (4)
	Samuel Beckett	*Krapp's Last Tape* (1958)	RSC	10/3/1998	The Pit (24)
	Samuel Beckett	*Waiting for Godot* (1955)	Directed by Peter Hall	10/3/1998	Piccadilly (45)
	Brian Friel	*Give Me Your Answer, Do!* (1997)		30/3/1998	Hampstead (40)

	Carlo Gebler	*The Dance of Death* (1998) – from Strindberg		31/3/1998	Tricycle (27)
	Greg Banks	*Tír Na N-Og* (1998) – from Jim Sheridan's film *Into the West*	Traveling Light Theatre Company, Bristol	1/4/1998	Unicorn (25)
	G.B. Shaw	*Candida* (1897)		2/4/1998	New End (25)
	W.B. Yeats	{*At the Hawk's Well* (1916)}	Cuchulain Cycle; Theatre Machine, Dublin	2/4/1998	Riverside (10)
	W.B. Yeats	{*The Green Helmet* – extract (1910)}	Cuchulain Cycle; Theatre Machine, Dublin	2/4/1998	Riverside (10)
	W.B. Yeats	{*On Baile's Strand* (1904)}	Cuchulain Cycle; Theatre Machine, Dublin	2/4/1998	Riverside (10)
	W.B. Yeats	{*The Only Jealousy of Emer* (1919)}	Cuchulain Cycle; Theatre Machine, Dublin	2/4/1998	Riverside (10)
	W.B. Yeats	{*The Death of Cuchulain* (1939)}	Cuchulain Cycle; Theatre Machine, Dublin	2/4/1998	Riverside (10)
	Declan Croghan	*Choirboys* (1998)	Theatre Machine, Dublin	9/4/1998	Finborough (23)
	Sebastian Barry	*Our Lady of Sligo* (1998)	Royal National Theatre	16/4/1998	Cottesloe
	Eamon McDonnell	*Singing About Laundry Basket Killers in Northern Ireland* (1998)	The Best of Briefs	22/4/1998	Lyric Studio (24)
	G.B. Shaw	*Major Barbara* (1905)	Directed by Peter Hall	14/5/1998	Piccadilly
	G.B. Shaw	*The Doctor's Dilemma* (1906)		3/6/1998	Almeida (25)
	Conor McPherson	*Rum and Vodka* (1992)		9/6/1998	Canal Café (18)

Author	Play	Company/Note	Date	Venue
Enda Walsh	*Disco Pigs* (1996)	Corcadorca Theatre Company	11/6/1998	Arts (45)
G.B. Shaw	*Back to Methuselah* – Part I (1922)		8/7/1998	Union, SE2 (24)
Lennox Robinson	*The Whiteheaded Boy* (1916)	Liber Theatre	14/7/1998	Greenwich (5)
Aodhan Madden	*Sea Urchins* (1998)	Barabbas … the Company	11/8/1998	Grace (19)
Conall Morrison	*Tarry Flynn* (1996) – from Patrick Kavanagh	Abbey Theatre	20/8/1998	Lyttelton
Declan Croghan	*Choirboys* (1998)	Theatre Machine, Dublin	1/9/1998	Old Red Lion (19)
Brian Friel	*Dancing at Lughnasa* (1990)	National Youth Theatre	3/9/1998	Arts (16)
Mark Ravenhill	*Handbag, or the Importance of Being Someone* (1998) – from O. Wilde	Actors Touring Company	14/9/1998	Lyric Studio (27)
Declan Croghan	*The Redeemer* (1998)	"Cells"	22/9/1998	Finborough (18)
Oscar Wilde / B. Kinseg	*The Importance of Being Earnest* (1998)	Strangefruit Stageworks	24/9/1998	Etcetera (17)
Samuel Beckett	*Play* (1963)		29/9/1998	Riverside (17)
Kate O'Reilly	*Yard* (1998)		2/10/1998	Bush (30)
Conor McPherson	*The Weir* (1997)		12/10/1998	Royal Court Downstairs (108)
Brian Friel	*Volunteers* (1975)	British première	22/10/1998	Gate (19)
Richard Brinsley Sheridan	*The School for Scandal* (1777)	RSC	3/11/1998	Barbican (18)
Antoine O Flatharta	*Blood Guilty* (1989)		26/10/1998	Old Red Lion (6)
Oscar Wilde	*The Importance of Being Earnest* (1895)		9/11/1998	Richmond (6)
Frank McGuinness	*The Storm* (1998) – from A. Ostrovsky		17/11/1998	Almeida (33)
Samuel Beckett	*Molloy* (1998) – from Part 1 of novel	Gare St. Lazare	24/11/1998	Riverside (18)
Oscar Wilde	*Salomé* (1896)		25/11/1998	Riverside (18)
J.M. Synge	{*Riders to the Sea* (1904)}	"Shadows" – RSC	9/12/1998	The Pit

1999 (804)	J.M. Synge	{*The Shadow of the Glen* (1903)}	"Shadows" – RSC	9/12/1998	The Pit
	W.B. Yeats	{*Purgatory* (1938)}	"Shadows" – RSC	9/12/1998	The Pit
	Samuel Beckett	*Krapp's Last Tape* (1958)	RSC	5/1/1999	Arts (32)
	Samuel Beckett	*Breath* (1969)	RSC; London première	5/1/1999	Arts (32)
	Christine Molloy / Joe Lawlor	*Play-boy* (1999) – after J.M. Synge	Desperate Optimists	27/1/1999	Young Vic Studio (11)
	Eamon Morrissey	*And the Brother Too . . .* (1999) – from Flann O'Brien	One-man show	9/2/1999	Tricycle (19)
	Mark O'Rowe	*Howie the Rookie* (1999)		12/2/1999	Bush (32)
	The Nualas	*The Nualas* (1999)		19/2/1999	Drill Hall (23)
	Declan Croghan	*Paddy Irishman, Paddy Englishman and Paddy . . . ?* (1999)		1/3/1999	Tricycle (20)
	Dion Boucicault	*The Shaughran* (1874)		11/3/1999	Upstairs/Gatehouse (20)
	Gary Mitchell	*Trust* (1999)		15/3/1999	Royal Court Upstairs Circle (19)
	Dion Boucicault	*The Colleen Bawn* (1860)	Abbey Theatre	18/3/1999	Lyttelton (10)
	Daragh Carville	*Dumped* (1999)	National Youth Theatre	13/4/1999	Battersea Arts Centre (13)
	J.M. Synge	*Deirdre of the Sorrows* (1910)		30/4/1999	Riverside (17)
	Brian Friel	*A Month in the Country* (1992) – from Turgenev	RSC	4/5/1999	The Pit (5)
	Colin Teevan	*Svejk* (1999) – from J. Hasek		10/5/1999	Gate (25)
	Donal O'Kelley	*Catalpa* (1996)	Solo	11/5/1999	Tricycle (25)
	Brian Friel	*Lovers* (1968)		27/5/1999	New End (17)
	Joseph O'Connor	*True Believers* (1999)	Fishamble	5/7/1999	Tricycle (13)
	Brendan O'Carroll	*Mrs. Brown's Last Wedding* (1999)		13/7/1999	Lyric, Hammersmith (12)
	Oscar Wilde	*The Importance of Being Earnest* (1895)		4/8/1999	Theatre Royal, Haymarket (100)

	Declan Croghan	The Shop (1999)	Juno Theatre Company	10/8/1999	Etcetera (19)
	Marie Jones	Stones in His Pockets (1996)	Lyric Theatre, Belfast	1/9/1999	Tricycle (18)
	Samuel Beckett	Waiting for Godot (1955)	BITE 99, Gate Theatre, Dublin	1/9/1999	Barbican (12)
	Samuel Beckett	{Come and Go (1965)}	BITE 99, Gate Theatre, Dublin	2/9/1999	The Pit (1)
	Samuel Beckett	{Act Without Words II (1956)}	BITE 99, Gate Theatre, Dublin	2/9/1999	The Pit (1)
	Samuel Beckett	{Play (1963)}	BITE 99, Gate Theatre, Dublin	2/9/1999	The Pit (1)
	Samuel Beckett	Krapp's Last Tape (1958)	BITE 99, Gate Theatre, Dublin	2/9/1999	The Pit (15)
	Samuel Beckett	{Not I (1972)}	BITE 99, Gate Theatre, Dublin	7/9/1999	The Pit (2)
	Samuel Beckett	{What Where (1983)}	BITE 99, Gate Theatre, Dublin	7/9/1999	The Pit (2)
	Samuel Beckett	{Act Without Words I (1957)}	BITE 99, Gate Theatre, Dublin	7/9/1999	The Pit (2)
	Samuel Beckett	Happy Days (1961)	BITE 99, Gate Theatre, Dublin	9/9/1999	Barbican (3)
	Samuel Beckett	{Footfalls (1975)}	BITE 99, Gate Theatre, Dublin	10/9/1999	The Pit (2)
	Samuel Beckett	{Rough for Theatre I (1976)}	BITE 99, Gate Theatre, Dublin	10/9/1999	The Pit (2)
	Samuel Beckett	{Rockaby (1980)}	BITE 99, Gate Theatre, Dublin	10/9/1999	The Pit (2)
	Samuel Beckett	{Ohio Impromptu (1981)}	BITE 99, Gate Theatre, Dublin	14/9/1999	The Pit (2)

Author	Work	Date	Venue
Samuel Beckett	{*Rough for Theatre II* (1976)}	14/9/1999	BITE 99, Gate Theatre, Dublin	The Pit (2)
Samuel Beckett	{*Catastrophe* (1982)}	14/9/1999	BITE 99, Gate Theatre, Dublin	The Pit (2)
Samuel Beckett	*Endgame* (1957)	16/9/1999	BITE 99, Gate Theatre, Dublin	Barbican (3)
Samuel Beckett	{*Breath* (1969)}	17/9/1999	BITE 99, Gate Theatre, Dublin	The Pit (2)
Samuel Beckett	{*That Time* (1976)}	17/9/1999	BITE 99, Gate Theatre, Dublin	The Pit (2)
Samuel Beckett	{*A Piece of Monologue* (1980)}	17/9/1999	BITE 99, Gate Theatre, Dublin	The Pit (2)
The Nualas	*The Big Shiny Dress Tour* (1999)	14/9/1999		Drill Hall (18)
Sean O'Casey	*Juno and the Paycock* (1924)	20/9/1999		Donmar Warehouse (46)
W.B. Yeats	*Purgatory* (1938)	5/10/1999	"Together Alone"	Etcetera (19)
Oscar Wilde	*The Kaos Importance of Being Earnest* (1998)	26/10/1999	Kaos Theatre, Cirencester	Bloomsbury (2)
Hugh Leonard	*Da* (1973)	9/11/1999	Hibernia Theatre	Riverside 3 (26)
Colin Teevan	*Marathon* (1999) – translated from from Edoardo Erba	19/11/1999		Gate (22)
Edna O'Brien	*Our Father* (1999)	24/11/1999		Almeida (27)
Frank McGuinness	*Hedda Gabler* (1999) – from H. Ibsen	30/11/1999		Richmond (5)
Seamus Egan	*Dancing on Dangerous Ground* (1999)	6/12/1999	Dance show	Theatre Royal, Drury Lane (60)
David King	*Spirit of the Dance* (1999)	15/12/1999	Dance show	Grand Hall, Wembley (30)
Oliver Goldsmith / C. Hart / H. Goodall	*The Kissing-Dance, or She Stoops to Conquer* (1999)	28/12/1999	Musical	Linbury Studio, Royal Opera House (9)

200 (708)	G.B. Shaw	Widowers' Houses (1892)	NT Mobile Tour	11/1/2000	Cottesloe
	Samuel Beckett	Krapp's Last Tape (1958)	Gate Theatre, Dublin	27/1/2000	New Ambassadors (43)
	Tom O'Brien	Money From America (2000)	Two Colour Theatre Company	27/1/2000	Tabard (17)
	Mark-Anthony Turnage	The Silver Tassie (2000) – from Sean O'Casey	Opera	16/2/2000	London Coliseum
	Conor McPherson	Dublin Carol (2000)	Previewed at Old Vic 15/1/2000	22/2/2000	Royal Court (26)
	Patricia Burke Brogan	Eclipsed (2000)	Irish Women's Theatre Workshop	16/3/2000	Riverside (15)
	Marie Jones	Stones in his Pockets (1996)	Lyric, Belfast	4/4/2000	Tricycle (46)
	Seamus Finnegan	Life after Life (2000)		6/4/2000	Old Red Lion (17)
	Gary Mitchell	The Force of Change (2000)		10/4/2000	Theatre Upstairs (20)
	Howard Brenton	The Romans in Britain (1980)		10/4/2000	Man in the Moon (27)
	Ron Hutchinson	Burning Issues (2000)		25/4/2000	Hampstead (39)
	Sean O'Casey	The Shadow of a Gunman (1923)	Phoenix Theatre Company	16/5/2000	White Bear (19)
	Frank McGuinness	Dolly West's Kitchen (1999)	Abbey Theatre	17/5/2000	Old Vic (72)
	Marie Jones	Stones in his Pockets (1996)	Lyric, Belfast	24/5/2000	New Ambassadors (86)
	Oscar Wilde / Merlin Holland	De Profundis (2000)	"Matters of Life and Death"	1/7/2000	Battersea Arts Centre (1)
	Samuel Beckett	En Attendant Godot (1953)	Theatre Vidy, Lausanne / Scott Walker's Meltdown	30/6/2000	Queen Elizabeth Hall (1)
	Strathcona	The Salt Garden (2000)	Strathcona	3/7/2000	National Maritime Museum (5)
	Marina Carr	On Raftery's Hill (2000)	Druid, Theatre, Galway	3/7/2000	Royal Court (27)
	Ken Harmon	{Wideboy Gospel (2000)}	Bedrock, Dublin	5/7/2000	Greenwich (4)

David Woods / Jon Hough	{Say Nothing (2000)}	Ridiculusmus	5/7/2000	Greenwich (4)
Alex Johnson	{Salty Dog 2: Black Dog (2000)}	"The Car Show" – Corn Exchange, Dublin	5/7/2000	Cutty Sark Gardens (3)
Terry O'Hagan	{5 (2000)}	"The Car Show" – Corn Exchange, Dublin	5/7/2000	Cutty Sark Gardens (3)
Arthur Riordan	{Love Me? (2000)}	"The Car Show" – Corn Exchange, Dublin	5/7/2000	Cutty Sark Gardens (3)
Annie Ryan / Michael West	{Untitled (2000)}	"The Car Show" – Corn Exchange, Dublin	5/7/2000	Cutty Sark Gardens (3)
Roderick O'Grady	A Foolish Fancy (2000)		13/7/2000	Etcetera (18)
Samuel Beckett	I'll Go On (2000) – from novels	Gate, Dublin	13/7/2000	The Pit (17)
Marie Jones	Stones in his Pockets (1996)	Lyric, Belfast	21/8/2000	Duke of York's, transferred to New Ambassadors 21/7/2003 (1364)
Oscar Wilde / R.S. Phillips	The Picture of Dorian Gray (2000)		31/8/2000	Westminster (24)
G.B. Shaw	Pygmalion (1913)		31/8/2000	Greenwich Playhouse (18)
Lin Coghlan	Clean Break (2000)	Clean Break	7/9/2000	Battersea Arts Centre (18)
G.B. Shaw	Arms and the Man (1894)		8/9/2000	Orange Tree (37)
Thomas Kilroy	The Secret Fall of Constance Wilde (1997)	Abbey Theatre	28/9/2000	Barbican (10)
David Woods / Jon Hough	Say Nothing (2000)	Ridiculusmus	17/10/2000	Battersea Arts Centre (2)
Tom O'Brien	Bottom Dog (2000)		24/10/2000	Tabard (18)

	Tom O'Brien	Money From America (2000)		26/10/2000	Pentameters (18)
	Mark O'Rowe	Howie the Rookie (1999)	Two monologues	27/10/2000	Bush (15)
	Oscar Wilde / Merlin Holland	De Profundis (2000)		7/11/2000	Cottesloe
	The Nualas	The Nualas (2000)		7/11/2000	Lyric, Hammersmith (12)
	Gary Mitchell	The Force of Change (2000)		8/11/2000	Royal Court (17)
	James Joyce / Mario Borciani / Anna Zaparoli	Molly Bloom – A Musical Dream (2000)		9/11/2000	Jermyn Street (24)
	Billy Roche	{A Handful of Stars (1988)}	Oxford Stage Company	9/12/2000	Tricycle (56)
	Billy Roche	{Poor Beast in the Rain (1989)}	Oxford Stage Company	9/12/2000	Tricycle (56)
	Billy Roche	{Belfry (1991)}	Oxford Stage Company	9/12/2000	Tricycle (56)
	Oscar Wilde	The Canterville Ghost (2000)	Traffic of the Stage	13/12/2000	Pentameters (30)
	Richard Brinsley Sheridan	The Rivals (1775)		18/12/2000	Barbican
2001 (674)	Oscar Wilde	The Importance of Being Earnest (1895)		23/1/2001	Savoy (80)
	Kenneth McLeish / Frederic Raphael	Medea (2000) – from Euripides	Abbey Theatre	30/1/2001	Queens (74)
	G.B. Shaw	Back to Methuselah (1922)	RSC	20/2/2001	The Pit
	J.M. Synge	The Playboy of the Western World (1907)	Royal National Theatre	20/2/2001	Cottesloe
	Conor McPherson	Port Authority (2001)		22/2/2001	New Ambassadors (38)
	Colin Teevan	The Walls (2001)	Royal National Theatre	14/3/2001	Cottesloe
	G.B. Shaw / A.J. Lerner / F. Loewe	My Fair Lady (1956)	Royal National Theatre	15/3/2001	Lyttelton

	Author	Title	Company	Date	Venue
	Jimmy Murphy	*The Kings of the Kilburn High Road* (2001)	Red Kettle Theatre Company	19/3/2001	Tricycle (26)
	Conor McPherson	{*Rum and Vodka* (2001)}	Solo play	1/5/2001	Soho (10)
	Conor McPherson	{*The Good Thief* (2001)}	Solo play	1/5/2001	Soho (10)
	Seamus Finnegan	*Diaspora Jigs* (2001)		2/5/2001	Old Red Lion (18)
	Ron Hutchinson	*The Beau* (2001)		24/5/2001	Theatre Royal, Haymarket (30)
	Brian Campbell / Laurence McKeown	*The Laughter of Our Children* (2001)	Dubbeljoint	19/6/2001	Hackney Empire Bullion Room (6)
	G.B. Shaw / A.J. Lerner / F. Loewe	*My Fair Lady* (1956)	Royal National Theatre	21/7/2001	Theatre Royal, Drury Lane (630)
	Daragh Carville	*The Holyland* (2001)	National Youth Theatre	30/8/2001	Lyric Studio (17)
	Brian Friel	*The Enemy Within* (1962)		4/9/2001	White Bear (20)
	G.B. Shaw	*Saint Joan* (1923)	Isleworth Actors	4/9/2001	Isleworth Public Hall (18)
	Richard Brinsley Sheridan	*The Rivals* (1775)	Logos	11/9/2001	Wimbledon Studio (20)
	Gary Mitchell	*As the Beast Sleeps* (1998)	Lyric Theatre, Belfast	19/9/2001	Tricycle (25)
	David Rudkin	*Afore Night Come* (1960)		29/9/2001	Young Vic (15)
	Brian Friel	*Faith Healer* (1979)		28/11/2001	Almeida at Kings Cross (50)
	Colin Teevan	*Monkey* (2001) – from Wu Ch'eng En		5/12/2001	Young Vic (44)
	Oscar Wilde	*The Importance of Being Earnest* (1895)	Galleon Theatre Company	13/12/2001	Greenwich Playhouse (30)
2002 (694)	Martin McDonagh	*The Lieutenant of Inishmore* (2000)	RSC	2/1/2002	The Pit
	Billy Roche	*The Cavalcaders* (1993)		7/1/2002	Tricycle (33)

Author	Play	Company	Date	Venue
Enda Walsh	Bedbound (2001)		15/1/2002	Royal Court Upstairs (18)
Marina Carr	Portia Coughlan (1995)	Strawberry Theatre	15/1/2002	Man in the Moon (18)
Samuel Beckett	Endgame (1957)	Liquid Theatre	7/2/2002	Battersea Arts Centre (18)
Oscar Wilde	Lady Windermere's Fan (1892)		21/2/2002	Theatre Royal Haymarket (108)
Sebastian Barry	Hinterland (2002)	Out of Joint / Abbey Theatre	4/3/2002	Cottesloe
Kate O'Reilly	Peeling (2002)	Graeae	4/4/2002	Soho (10)
Frank McGuinness	Observe the Sons of Ulster, Marching Towards the Somme (1985)		9/4/2002	Pleasance (20)
Helen Edmundson	The Clearing (1993)	Shared Experience	24/4/2002	Tricycle (31)
Seamus Finnegan	Murder in Bridgport (2002)		25/4/2002	Old Red Lion (17)
Bernard Farrell	Happy Birthday Dear Alice (2002)		26/4/2002	Orange Tree (23)
Bill Whelan	Riverdance (1995)	Dance Show	16/5/2002	London Apollo (37)
Colin Teevan	Bacchai (2002) – translated from Euripides	Royal National Theatre	17/5/2002	Olivier
Martin McDonagh	The Lieutenant of Inishmore (2000)	RSC	26/6/2002	Garrick (130)
Marie Jones	A Night in November (An Afternoon in June) (1994)		11/7/2002	Tricycle (17)
Sean O'Brien	The Birds (2002) – from Aristophanes	Royal National Theatre / Mamaloucos Circus	26/7/2002	Lyttelton
Ade Morris	I Dreamed I Dwelt in Marble Halls (2002) – from story by Bryan Gallagher		30/7/2002	Tricycle (19)
Marie Jones	A Night in November (An Afternoon in June) (1994)		6/8/2002	Etcetera (20)
Patrick McCabe	Frank Pig Says Hello (1992)		22/8/2002	Finborough (24)
Ron Hutchinson	Lags (2001)		5/9/2002	Latchmere (24)

	Owen McCafferty	Closing Time (2002)	Royal National Theatre	9/9/2002	Lyttelton Loft (13)
	Brian Friel	Dancing at Lughnasa (1990)	Watermill, Newbury	17/9/2002	Greenwich (5)
	Brian Friel	Afterplay (2002) – sequel to plays by Chekhov		19/9/2002	Gielgud (74)
	Samuel Beckett	Lessness (2002) – from poems	Gare St Lazare Players	25/9/2002	Cottesloe
	G.B. Shaw	Mrs. Warren's Profession (1902)		10/10/2002	Strand (100)
	Eugene O'Brien	Eden (2001)	Directed by Conor McPherson; Abbey Theatre	30/10/2002	Arts (45)
	Frank McGuinness	Someone Who'll Watch Over Me (1992)		4/11/2002	Southwark Playhouse (6)
	Oliver Goldsmith	She Stoops to Conquer (1773)	Out of Joint	17/12/2002	Cottesloe
	Rosalind Scanlon, et al.	Molly Malone – the Musical (2002)	Irish Women's Theatre Company	19/12/2002	Riverside (16)
2003 (710)	Marie Jones	A Night in November (An Afternoon in June) (1994)		11/2/2003	Tricycle (26)
	Geraldine Aron	My Brilliant Divorce (2003)	Directed by Garry Hynes	24/2/2003	Apollo (83)
	Greg Allen, Ben Schneider, Danny Thompson	The Complete Works of Samuel Beckett (2003)		6/3/2003	Riverside (37)
	Ron Hutchinson	Lags (2001)		27/3/2003	Battersea Arts Centre (17)
	Owen McCafferty	Scenes from the Big Picture (2003)	Royal National Theatre	10/4/2003	Cottesloe
	Dennis Kelly	Debris (2003)		17/4/2003	Latchmere (17)
	Owen McCafferty	Mojo Mickybo (1998)	Kabosh	1/5/2003	Lyric Studio (17)
	Samuel Beckett	{Rough for Theatre I (1976)}		27/5/2003	Rose & Crown (18)
	Samuel Beckett	{Rough for Theatre II (1976)}		27/5/2003	Rose & Crown (18)
	Conor Mitchell	Have a Nice Life (2002)	Musical	29/5/2003	Pleasance (24)

	Author	Title	Company	Date	Venue
	Conor Grimes & Alan McKee with Martin Lynch	*The History of the Troubles (acordin' to my Da)* (2003)		3/6/2003	Tricycle (26)
	Colin Teevan	*Cuckoos* (2000) – translated from Guiseppe Manfridi		24/6/2003	The Pit (19)
	G.B. Shaw	*Press Cuttings* (1909)	"The Women's War"	14/8/2003	Finborough (24)
	Martin McDonagh	*The Beauty Queen of Leenane* (1996)	Not the National Theatre	3/9/2003	Bloomsbury (4)
	G.B. Shaw	*John Bull's Other Island* (1904)		15/9/2003	Tricycle (40)
	Oscar Wilde	*A Woman of No Importance* (1893)		16/9/2003	Theatre Royal Haymarket (137)
	Tom Paulin	*The Riot Act* (2003) – from Sophocles' *Antigone*		17/9/2003	Gate (25)
	Samuel Beckett	*Waiting for Godot* (1955)	The Godot Collective	6/11/2003	Finborough (24)
	Gary Mitchell	*Loyal Women* (2003)		11/11/2003	Royal Court (33)
	Samuel Beckett	*Happy Days* (1961)		18/11/2003	Arts (74)
	Stella Feehily	*Duck* (2003)	Out of Joint	27/11/2003	Royal Court Upstairs (44)
	Oscar Wilde / Annie Wood	*The Selfish Giant* (2003)		2/12/2003	Polka (82)
2004 (653)	Samuel Beckett	*Waiting for Godot* (1955)	The Godot Collective	3/3/2004	Pleasance (12)
	Samuel Beckett	*Endgame* (1957)		10/3/2004	Albery (52)
	Richard Brinsley Sheridan	*The Rivals* (1775)	Compass Theatre Company	16/3/2004	Greenwich (5)
	David Rudkin	*Red Sun* (2004)	ajtc	17/3/2004	Warehouse, Croydon (18)
	Samuel Beckett	*First Love* (2004) – from short story		30/3/2004	Lion & Unicorn (12)
	Dennis Kelly	*Debris* (2003)		30/3/2004	Battersea Arts Centre (26)

Author	Play	Company	Date	Venue (performances)
Brendan Behan	The Quare Fellow (1954)	Oxford Stage Company / Liverpool Everyman	16/4/2004	Tricycle (23)
Sebastian Barry	Whistling Psyche (2004)		12/5/2004	Almeida (30)
Brian Friel	Winners (1968)		27/5/2004	Young Vic (7)
Samuel Beckett	{Ohio Impromptu (1981)}	The Godot Collective	31/5/2004	Southwark Playhouse (20)
Samuel Beckett	{Rough for Theatre I (1976)}	The Godot Collective	31/5/2004	Southwark Playhouse (20)
Samuel Beckett	{Rough for Theatre II (1976)}	The Godot Collective	31/5/2004	Southwark Playhouse (20)
Geraldine Hughes	Belfast Blues (2004)	That's Us Productions	4/6/2004	Soho (30)
Robert Welch	Protestants (2004)	Ransom Productions	8/6/2004	Soho (26)
Conor McPherson	Shining City (2004)		9/6/2004	Royal Court (60)
Sean Buckley	Matches for Monkeys (2002)		24/6/2004	Chelsea (24)
Lin Coghlan	Mercy (2004)		13/7/2004	Soho (26)
G.B. Shaw	Androcles and the Lion (1913)	The Steam Industry	5/8/2004	The Scoop (31)
John B. Keane	Sive (1959)	Irish Repertory Theatre	12/8/2004	Riverside (18)
David Rudkin	The Master and Margarita (2004) – from Mikhail Bulgakov	National Youth Theatre	23/8/2004	Lyric Hammersmith (20)
Conall Morrison	Hard to Believe (2004)	Storytellers	3/9/2004	Riverside (24)
Frank McGuinness	Hecuba (2004) – from Euripides		14/9/2004	Donmar Warehouse (30)
Kaite O'Reilly	Henhouse (2004)		23/9/2004	Arcola (17)
Sean O'Casey	The Shadow of a Gunman (1923)		4/10/2004	Tricycle (33)
Frank McGuinness	Gates of Gold (2004)	Charm Offensive / Concordance	25/11/2004	Finborough (24)
Marina Carr	By the Bog of Cats (1998)		1/12/2004	Wyndham's

	Mustapha Matura	Playboy of the West Indies (1984) – from Synge	Nottingham Playhouse	6/12/2004	Tricycle (47)
2005 (623)	Tom O'Brien	Johnjo (2005)	Irish Theatre Company	11/1/2005	Courtyard (20)
	Ron Hutchinson	Head/Case (2005)	RSC / Belgrade, Coventry	13/1/2005	Soho (17)
	Conor Mitchell	Have a Nice Life (2002)	Musical	14/1/2005	Union (16)
	Sean O'Casey	The Plough and the Stars (1926)	Abbey Theatre Centenary	19/1/2005	Barbican (11)
	Enda Walsh	The Small Things (2005)	Paines Plough	3/2/2005	Chocolate Factory (25)
	Conor McPherson	This Lime Tree Bower (1995)	Young Vic	9/2/2005	Theatre 503 (12)
	Gerald Murphy	Take Me Away (2004)	Rough Magic	10/2/2005	Bush (30)
	Owen McCafferty	Days of Wine and Roses (2005) – from J.P. Miller		22/2/2005	Donmar Warehouse (40)
	Danny Morrison	The Wrong Man (2005)	New Strung Theatre Company	15/3/2005	Pleasance (20)
	Oscar Wilde / Simon Vinnicombe	Wilde Tales (2005)		18/3/2005	Southwark Playhouse (16)
	Sean O'Casey	Cock-a-Doodle Dandy (1959)	Red Mick Theatre Company	22/3/2005	Barons Court (27)
	Oscar Wilde	The Importance of Being Earnest (1895)	British Theatre Playhouse, Singapore	30/3/2005	Greenwich (11)
	Tom Murphy	The Gigli Concert (1983)	Charm Offensive	31/3/2005	Finborough (24)
	Frank McGuinness	Hecuba (2004) – from Euripides	RSC	7/7/2005	Albery (31)
	Richard Norton-Taylor / Eamonn McCann (eds.)	Bloody Sunday: Scenes from the Saville Enquiry (2005)	Verbatim drama	11/4/2005	Tricycle (20)
	Frank McGuinness	Someone Who'll Watch Over Me (1993)	Background Theatre Company	19/4/2005	New Ambassadors (61)
	Lin Coghlan	Kingfisher Blue (2005)		20/5/2005	Bush (30)

	Brian Friel	The Home Place (2005)	Dublin Gate Theatre	25/5/2005	Comedy (93)
	Brendan Behan	The Quare Fellow (1954)		25/5/2005	Tricycle (37)
	Dion Boucicault	The Shaughran, or the Vagabond (1874)	Oxford Stage Company	25/5/2005	Albery (53)
	Oscar Wilde	The Importance of Being Earnest (1895)	Abbey Theatre	8/6/2005	Pit (31)
	Enda Walsh	Chatroom (2005)	Ridiculusmus	9/6/2005	Cottesloe (1)
	Brian Friel	Aristocrats (1979)	Boomerang Theatre Company, Cork	6/7/2005	Lyttelton
	Samuel Beckett	{Play (1963)}	Royal National Theatre	12/7/2005	Battersea Arts Centre (20)
	Samuel Beckett	{Not I (1972)}		19/7/2005	Battersea Arts Centre (20)
	Christopher Hanvey	Justice (2005)	Tiger Theatre Productions	19/7/2005	Old Red Lion (17)
	Michael Toumey	Dancing with the Angels (2005)	Be Lucky Productions	4/8/2005	Union (17)
	Conor McDermottroe	Swansong (2005)	Benrae Productions	1/9/2005	Finborough (17)
	Seamus Heaney	The Cure at Troy (1990) – from Sophocles	Floodtide Productions	8/9/2005	Cockpit (17)
	Owen McCafferty	Shoot the Crow (1997)		11/10/2005	Trafalgar Studios (60)
	G.B. Shaw	You Never Can Tell (1896)	Peter Hall Company	7/11/2005	Garrick (124)
	Tom Murphy	Alice Trilogy (2005)		16/11/2005	Royal Court (25)
	Brian Friel	Translations (1981)	Royal National Theatre	16/11/2005	Cottesloe (16)
	Brian Friel	The Freedom of the City (1973)		1/12/2005	Finborough (23)
	Oscar Wilde / John Kane	The Canterville Ghost (2005)		5/12/2005	Southwark Playhouse (19)
2006 (673)	Stella Feehily	O Go My Man (2006)		17/1/2006	Royal Court (26)

Author	Play	Company	Date	Venue
Elizabeth Kuti	The Sugar Wife (2005)	Rough Magic	19/1/2006	Soho (24)
Frank McGuinness	The Factory Girls (1982)		20/1/2006	Arcola (30)
Colin Teevan	Missing Persons: Four Tragedies and Roy Keane (2006)		2/2/2006	Trafalgar Studio 2 (24)
Frank McGuinness	Speaking Like Magpies (2006)	RSC	15/2/2006	Trafalgar Studio 1 (11)
Ron Hutchinson	Rat in the Skull (1984)	Royal Court 50 reading	27/2/2006	Royal Court (1)
Jim Nolan	Blackwater Angel (2001)		3/3/2006	Finborough (23)
Martin McDonagh	The Beauty Queen of Leenane (1996)	Royal Court 50 reading	15/3/2006	Royal Court (1)
Enda Walsh	Chatroom (2005)	Royal National Theatre	15/3/2006	Cottesloe
Sean O'Casey	{Bedtime Story (1950)}	Young Vic Direct Action	17/3/2006	Union (14)
Sean O'Casey	{The End of the Beginning (1932)}	Young Vic Direct Action	17/3/2006	Union (14)
Samuel Beckett	{Rockaby (1980)}	Gate, Dublin	22/3/2006	Pit (7)
Samuel Beckett	{Ohio Impromptu (1981)}	Gate, Dublin	22/3/2006	Pit (7)
Conor McPherson	Shining City (2004)	Royal Court 50 reading	24/3/2006	Royal Court (1)
Samuel Beckett	{Come and Go (1965)}	Beckett Centenary Festival	31/3/2006	Pit (10)
Samuel Beckett	{Footfalls (1975)}	Beckett Centenary Festival	31/3/2006	Pit (10)
Tom Murphy	A Whistle in the Dark (1961)	Royal Exchange, Manchester	3/4/2006	Tricycle (33)
Samuel Beckett	Waiting for Godot (1955)	Beckett Centenary Festival	5/4/2006	Barbican (10)
Mark Doherty	Trad (2005)	Galway Arts Festival	6/4/2006	Bush (24)
Enda Walsh	Disco Pigs (1996)	Pure Theatre	8/4/2006	Pleasance (30)

Samuel Beckett	{*Play* (1963)}	Beckett Centenary Festival	13/4/2006	Pit (10)
Samuel Beckett	{*Catastrophe* (1982)}	Beckett Centenary Festival	13/4/2006	Pit (10)
Samuel Beckett	*Endgame* (1958)	Beckett Centenary Festival	20/4/2006	Barbican (4)
Frank McGuinness	*Phaedra* (2006) – from Racine		21/4/2006	Donmar Warehouse (42)
Samuel Beckett	*Krapp's Last Tape* (1958)	Beckett Centenary Festival	26/4/2006	Pit (10)
Jacqueline McCarrick	*The Mushroom Pickers* (2006)		4/5/2006	Southwark Playhouse (17)
Owen McCafferty	*Cold Comfort* (2006)	Prime Cat Productions	18/5/2006	Theatre 503 (22)
John B. Keane	*The Field* (1965)		31/5/2006	Tricycle (32)
Oscar Wilde	*Lady Windermere's Fan* (1892)		31/5/2006	Landor (18)
Des Keogh	*The Love-Hungry Farmer* (2006) – from John B. Keane		12/6/2006	Jermyn Street (19)
Marina Carr	*Woman and Scarecrow* (2006)		21/6/2006	Royal Court Upstairs (24)
Colin Teevan / Hideki Noda	*The Bee* (2006) – from Yasutaka Tsutui		27/6/2006	Soho (18)
Samuel Beckett	*Eh Joe* (1965)	Adapted by Atom Egoyan	30/6/2006	Duke of York's (16)
Brian Friel	*Performances* (2003)		4/7/2006	Wilton's Music Hall (12)
Gregory Burke	*Liar* (2006)	Galway Youth Theatre	18/7/2006	Olivier (1)
James Joyce	*Exiles* (1915)	Royal National Theatre	2/8/2006	Cottesloe
Rosalind Scanlon	*Dance Hall Days* (2006)	Irish Repertory Theatre	12/8/2006	Riverside (16)
Frank McGuinness	*Yerma* (2006) – from Federico Garcia Lorca		25/8/2006	Arcola (28)

Abbie Spallen	Pumpgirl (2006)		13/9/2006	Bush (32)
Conor McPherson	The Seafarer (2006)	Royal National Theatre	28/9/2006	Cottesloe
Samuel Beckett	Waiting for Godot (1955)	Directed by Peter Hall	9/10/2006	New Ambassadors (39)
Samuel Beckett	Krapp's Last Tape (1958)	With Harold Pinter	14/10/2006	Royal Court Upstairs (8)
G.B. Shaw	Major Barbara (1905)		20/10/2006	Orange Tree (35)
Eoin Colfer	Artemis Fowl – Fairies, Fiends and Flatulence (2006)	Solo show	22/10/2006	Trafalgar Studio 1 (8)
Marie Jones	Stones in His Pockets (1996)		7/11/2006	Duchess (26)
G.B. Shaw	{Augustus Does His Bit (1917)}	Triple Bill A	13/11/2006	Orange Tree (13)
G.B. Shaw	{O'Flaherty VC (1917)}		13/11/2006	Orange Tree (13)
G.B. Shaw	{Press Cuttings (1909)}		13/11/2006	Orange Tree (13)
G.B. Shaw	{How He Lied to Her Husband (1904)}	Triple Bill B	13/11/2006	Orange Tree (13)
G.B. Shaw	{Overruled (1912)}		13/11/2006	Orange Tree (13)
G.B. Shaw	{Village Wooing (1934)}		13/11/2006	Orange Tree (13)
Frank McGuinness	Gates of Gold (2002)	Charm Offensive / Doublethink	23/11/2006	Trafalgar Studio 2 (24)
Stella Feehily, et al.	Catch (2006)		5/12/2006	Royal Court Upstairs (18)

List of Contributors

Richard Allen Cave is Professor of Drama and Theatre Arts in the Department of Drama and Theatre at Royal Holloway, University of London.

Enrica Cerquoni teaches in the School of Drama, English, and Film at University College, Dublin.

Peter Harris is Professor of English Literature at the State University of São Paulo (UNESP) in the city of São José do Rio Preto in Brazil.

Peter Kuch holds the Eamon Cleary Chair of Irish Studies at the University of Otago, New Zealand.

Cathy Leeney is Subject Leader in Drama in the School of Drama, English, and Film at University College, Dublin.

Ben Levitas is Senior Lecturer in the Department of Theatre at Goldsmiths College, University of London.

Michael McAteer is a Lecturer in the School of English, Queen's University Belfast.

Wallace McDowell is completing his doctoral thesis on 'Performance and Performativity within Ulster Loyalist Working-class Communities since the Good Friday Agreement' at the University of Warwick.

Tim Miles lectures in the Department of Drama at the University of the West of England.

Jerry Nolan is an independent scholar with affiliations to the British Association of Irish Studies and the International Association for the Study of Irish Literatures.

Graham Saunders lectures in the Department of Film, Theatre and Television at the University of Reading.

Elizabeth Schafer is Professor of Drama and Theatre Studies in the Department of Drama and Theatre at Royal Holloway, University of London.

Jonathan Statham is completing his doctoral thesis on 'Yeats's Anti-Theatre' in the Department of Drama and Theatre at Royal Holloway, University of London.

Carmen Szabó lectures in the School of Drama, English and Film at University College, Dublin.

Index

A

Abbey Theatre, 4, 15, 19, 23, 26-30, 33, 37, 41, 49-50, 53- 55, 57, 64, 66, 69, 84, 98-99, 139, 155, 157, 179, 180-181, 184-86
Act of Union (1801), 36
Adelphi Theatre (London), 7, 133
Allgood, Sara, 55
An Claidheamh Soluis, 39
Anderson, Linda, 108, 111
Archer, William, 16, 21, 31, 57, 65
Ashton, Frederick, 151
Asmus, Walter, 90
Asquith, Herbert, 22, 29-33
Athenaeum, The, 130
Auden, W.H., 5, 69, 74, 77
Avenue Theatre (London), 4, 35, 47

B

Baker, Thomas, 133
Balanchine, George, 149
Balfe, Michael William, 8, 129-30, 134, 140
  The Bohemian Girl, 129, 130
Balfour, Arthur, 22, 32-33
Ballets Russes, Les (The Russian Ballet), 148
Ballymacarratt Arts and Cultural Society, 118
Barbican Centre (London), 80, 93
Barker, H. Granville, 21-23, 29, 33
Barr, Ian, 118, 126
Barrie, J.M., 29, 33
  The Twelve Pound Look, 29, 33
Barry, Sebastian, 79, 83, 88-89
Barthes, Roland, 189, 191
Baylis, Lilian, 150-51
Beardsley, Aubrey, 47
Beckett Country, 82, 94, 95
Beckett on Film, 5, 79, 80-81, 84, 86-93, 96
Beckett, Samuel, 5, 41, 68, 77, 79-96, 161, 182
  Act Without Words II, 92
  All That Fall, 84-85, 95
  Come and Go, 91-92
  Company, 54, 67, 69, 75, 83, 129, 138, 149, 158, 177, 179-81
  Eh Joe, 84, 93
  Embers, 93
  Endgame, 81, 89, 90, 92

Footfalls, 92
Happy Days, 81, 87, 89, 92
Malone Dies, 83
Molloy, 83
More Pricks Than Kicks, 82
Not I, 83, 89, 91, 95
Ohio Impromptu, 91
Play, 65, 84, 93, 99, 110, 172-75
That Time, 83-84
Waiting for Godot, 80-84, 87, 89-90, 92-94
What Where, 92
Beerbohm, Max, 21
Behan, Brendan, 70, 83
Belfast Harp Festival, 132
Beltaine, 39
Benedict, Julius, 8, 99, 110, 129, 130, 133, 136, 140-42
The Lily of Killarney, 8, *129-30, 133, 137-39, 141*
Bignell, Jonathan, 81, 94
Billington, Michael, 99, 101-103, 105, 110, 111, 124
Bishop, Tom, 79
Black and Tans, The, 5, 54, 60
Bleeker, Maaike, 188, 190
Blue Angel Productions, 87
Blunt, Wilfred Scawen, 28
Bookman Review, The, 41, 49
Boucicault, Dion, 3, 8, 16-17, 31, 130, 133, 135-36, 138-39, 141-42
Arrah-na-Pogue, 133, *139*, 141
Robert Emmet, *131*, 133
The Colleen Bawn, *133*, 136, *139*
The Shaughraun, *133*, *139*
Bourke, P.J., 139, 141, 178
Boveri, Margaret, 170, 182

Treason in the Twentieth Century, 170, 182
Bowen, Elizabeth, 63
The Last September, 63
Bowles, Graham, 152, 156
Bradby, David, 83, 94
Bratton, Jacky, 10, 144-45, 154
Brennan, Paul, 170, 182
Brewer, John D., 115, 125
Brown, Terence, 36, 48, 79, 140-41
Bryson, Norman, 184
Bull, Ole, 4, 7, 15-17, 20-21, 23, 26, 28-33, 39
Bunn, Alfred, 129-30
Bunting, Edward, 132, 138, 141
A General Collection of the Ancient Music, 132
Burton, Frederic William, 124, 132, 141
Byrne, Ophelia, 99, 110, 145-46, 154
Byron, Lord George Gordon Noel, 131

C

Calder, John, 84, 95
Cambridge Festival Theatre, 150
Campbell, Julie, 22, 86, 95
Campbell-Bannerman, Sir Henry, 22
Canadian Journal of Irish Studies, The, 103, 111
Carlyle, Thomas, 61
Carr, Marina, 88
Catholic Emancipation Bill, 2
Cave, Richard, 1, 10, 95, 109, 156
Cavendish, Dominic, 107, 111
Cecchetti, Enrico, 148
Centre Georges Pompidou (Paris), 79

Cerquoni, Enrica, 9, 11, 183
Chamberlain, Sir Neville, 10, 28, 70
Chancellor, Betty, 161
Chandos, John, 69, 71, 76
Chanticleer Theatre Company, 69
Chekhov, Anton, 180
  Uncle Vanya, 180
Chorley, H.F., 130
Clandillion, Seamus, 87
Colgan, Michael, 79-81, 84, 86, 88-89, 92-93, 95
Collins, Michael, 60, 106
Colum, Padraic, 19, 38
  Broken Soil, 19
  The Saxon Shillin', 38
Conneely, Paddy, 132, 141
Connolly, James, 28, 32
Connolly, Roy, 117, 126
Conquering England: Ireland in Victorian England, 2, 10
Corkery, Daniel, 136, 141
Cornell, Jennifer, 103, 106, 108, 111-12
Corrs, The, 88
Coveney, Michael, 99, 110, 186, 190
Covent Garden (Theatre Royal, Covent Garden, London), 2, 76, 130, 143, 153, 155
Coward, Noel, 158-60
  The Vortex, 158-59
Coxhead, Elizabeth, 46, 50
Crane Bag, The, 68, 75
Cronin, John, 134, 141
Crowley, Nicholas, 10
Cullen, Fintan, 2, 10-11
Cumann na nGaedhal, 39
Cusack, Cyril, 83

D

Dackombe, Amanda, 86, 95
Daily Chronicle, The, *41, 49*
Daily Express (Dublin), *23, 32, 64*
Daily Mail (London), *99, 107, 110, 155*
Daily News, The (London), *56, 60, 65*
Daily Telegraph, The (London), 21, 29, 31-33, 107, 111, 120, 126
Dancing Times, The, 145, 155
Davis, Thomas, 31-32, 95, 132, 137, 141
de Jongh, Nicholas, 99, 110, 161-66
de l'Isle-Adam, Villiers, 38, 49
  Axël, *38, 49*
de Valois, Dame Ninette, 8, 143, 144-56
  Come Dance With Me, *143, 148, 153-56*
Deane, Seamus, 67, 75, 141, 171, 180, 182
Der Ring des Nibelungen, *130*
Derrida, Jacques, 172, 182
Diaghilev, Sergei, 148-50, 154
Dillingham, Charles, 58
Docherty, Sean, 104
Dolin, Anton, 151
Donmar Warehouse (London), 99, 118, 123, 125
Donoghue, Denis, 67-68, 75
Dowling, Joe, 187, 189-190
Drogheda, Earl of (C.G.P. Moore), 152, 156
Drury Lane Theatre (Theatre Royal, Drury Lane), 129
Dublin Drama League, The, 55, 64

Dublin International Theatre
    Festival, 82
Dubost, Thierry, 170, 182
Duffy, Charles Gavin, 55, 57, 59-60,
    62, 138
Dun Emer Press, 71, 76

E

Edgar, David, 33, 106
Edward VII, King, 22
Edwards, Hilton, 158, 165-66
Egoyan, Atom, 89
'Eglinton, John' (W.K. Magee), 71-
    72, 76-77
    Some Essays and Passages, 71, 76
    Two Essays on the Remnant, 71
Eloquent Dempsey, The (William
    Boyle), 57
Emergency, The, 69
Emmet, Robert, 131, 133, 136
Era, The, 55, 65
Ervine, St. John, 54
Espinosa, Edouard, 148, 156
Euripides, 21
    The Hippolytus, 21
Eurovision Song Contest, 91
Evening Standard (London), 56, 65,
    99-100, 110

F

Fabian Society, The, 25
Fagan, James Bernard, 55, 56, 65
Faithful, Marianne, 88
Farley, Charles, 2, 10
    *Harlequin Pat; or, The Giant's
        Causeway, 2*
Farquhar, George, 1
Farr, Florence, 41, 49

Fay, Frank, 29, 37-40, 42, 48-49
Fay, William G., 29, 37-40, 42, 48-
    49
Fenwick, Harry, 81, 94
Ferguson, Samuel, 133, 141
Festival d'Automne (Paris), 86
Field Day Theatre Company, 9, 67-
    69, 75, 141, 170-71, 175-77, 179-82
Finnigan, Kate, 144-45, 154
Fisher Unwin, T., 47
Fitzgerald, Nan, 55
Fitzgerald, Scott, 63
    The Great Gatsby, 63
Flannery, James, 37-38, 40, 49
Fokine, Michel, 149
Fonteyn, Margot, 143-44, 155
Foster, Roy F., 2, 10, 11, 44, 49-50,
    64, 141-42, 166, 190
Foucault, Michel, 169, 182
Frazer, Sir James, 45, 50
    The Golden Bough, 45, 50
Frazier, Adrian, 37, 40, 49
Friel, Brian, 9, 16, 31, 67-68, 108,
    112, 161, 175, 180-85, 190
    *Dancing at Lughnasa, 9, 181,
        183-85, 187*
    Philadelphia, Here I Come!, 161
    The Home Place, 108, 112
    Translations, 16, 175, 181
Frost, Everett C., 91, 96
Fuchs, Elinor, 183, 190
Fugard, Athol, 177
    Boesman and Lena, 177

G

Gaelic League, The, 17
Gaiety Theatre (Manchester), 55, 65,
    146

Galsworthy, John, 22
Gambon, Michael, 90, 93
Gardner, Lynn, 100, 110, 123, 126
Gate Theatre (Dublin), The, 79, 93, 157, 160, 165, 187
Gay, John, 157, 160
   The Beggars' Opera, 160
George V, King, 29, 32
Gibbons, Fiachra, 103, 111
Gibbons, Luke, 87, 96, 142
Gilpin, Heidi, 184, 190
Glendinning, Robin, 117
Globe, The, 23, 32
Good Friday Agreement, The, 99
Gowen, Peter, 188
Grand Opera House (Belfast), 107
Grant, Elizabeth, 50, 147
Gray, Terence, 150, 155
Gregory, Lady Augusta, 1, 5, 29, 33, 35, 37, 39, 45-46, 48- 50, 54, 69, 138
Grene, Nicolas, 16, 32-33, 64, 119, 126
Griffin, Gerald, 134-36, 139, 141
   The Collegians, 134, 136, 141
Griffith, Arthur, 24, 50
Grimes, Conor, 107, 111, 138
Guardian, The (London), *57, 65, 99-101, 103-104, 107, 109-112, 120, 126*
Gwynn, Stephen, 47

H

Haire, John Wilson, 100
   Within Two Shadows, 100
Hall, Anna Maria, 10
   The Groves of Blarney, 10
Hall, Sir Peter, 87, 90, 93

Hanley, Ellen, 135
Harrington, John, 90, 94, 96
Harris, Peter, 10, 124
Hauptmann, Gerhart, 22
Havel, Vaclav, 106
Haymarket Theatre (London), 7
Heaney, Seamus, 67-68, 137, 141
Hederman, Mark Patrick, 67, 75
Hellman, Lillian, 159
   The Children's Hour, 159
Helpmann, Robert, 144, 151
Hemmings, Sarah, 107, 111
Henry Miller's Theatre (New York), 58
Hilton, Matthew, 63, 66, 158, 165-66
   Smoking in British Popular Culture, 63, 66
Holdsworth, Nadine, 103, 104, 111
Holloway, Joseph, 43, 50
Holloway, Stanley, 139
Home Rule Bill, The Third, 15, 29
Horniman, Annie E.F., 19, 26, 49, 55
Howard, Alan, 87
Howard, Pamela, 11, 190
   What is Scenography?, 11, 190
Hudson, Edward, 131, 141
Hughes, Eamon, 98, 100, 110
Hurt, John, 89, 96
Hutchinson, Ron, 75, 119, 124-26

I

Ibsen, Henrik, 22, 39, 44, 81
   A Doll's House, 33, 44
Independent Theatre Company, The, 16, 21
Independent, The, 16, 21, 23-24, 32, 64, 96, 99, 102, 107, 111, 182

Inghinidhe na hÉireann, 42
In The Name of the Father
IRB (Irish Republican Brotherhood), 54
Irish 'Ring', The, 7
Irish Independent, The, 23, 32, 64
Irish Literary Society (London), The, 17, 19
Irish Literary Theatre, The, 17, 138, 140
Irish National Theatre Society, The, 19, 37
Irish Players, The, 4, 53-58, 64
Irish Theatrical Diaspora Project, 2, 15
Irish Times, The, 23, 32, 64, 85, 97, 99, 110

J

Jackson, Kevin, 76, 179, 182
Johns, Ian, 107, 111
Jones, Marie, 108, 112, 114, 119, 126
   A Night in November, 108, 112, 119-20, 122, 126
Jones, Robert, 187-89
Jordan, Neil, 89
Joyce, James, 45, 50, 67-68, 75-77, 82, 131, 137, 171-75
   Dubliners, 15, 83, 131
   Ulysses, 45, 50, 68, 76, 82, 138, 142

K

Kean, Edmund, 134
Kearney, Richard, 67-68, 74-75, 77
Kelem Films, 139
Kendall, Felicity, 87
Kent, Nicholas, 84, 108, 146

Kilroy, Tom, 9, 169-80, 182
   Double Cross, 9, 169-71, 175, 179-80, 182
   The Madam MacAdam Travelling Theatre, 9
Kingsley, Ben, 87
Knowlson, James, 82, 86, 94, 95
Koenig, Rhoda, 107, 111
Kuch, Peter, 4, 53, 64

L

Laura Keene's Theatre (New York), 133
Lawrence, W.J., 38, 49
Leech, John, 133
Leeney, Cathy, 8, 157
Leerssen, Joep, 16, 31
Legat, Nicolas, 148
Leigh, J.H., 21, 190
Leventhal, A.J., 83, 94
Levitas, Ben, 1, 4, 15, 39, 42, 49-50, 142
Lila Field Academy, 148
Lincoln Centre (New York), 80
Linehan, Rosaleen, 87, 89
Llewellyn-Jones, Margaret, 121, 126
Loane, Tim, 119, 126
Logan, Brian, 97, 110, 120, 126
Longford Company, The, 158
Lopokova, Lydia, 151
Love, Stewart, 49, 117, 131
Lover, Samuel, 3, 7, 32
   Handy Andy, 23, 32
   Rory O'More, 7
   The White Horse of the Peppers, 7
Lynch, Martin, 107, 111
Lynch, Martin (with Conor Grimes and Alan McKee)

The History of the Troubles (Accordin' to my Da), 107, 111
Lyric Theatre (Belfast), 97, 99, 106, 116-17, 125-26
Lyric Theatre (London), 21, 95

M

Macarthy, Eugene, 3
Macaulay, Alastair, 61, 123, 126
MacCarthy, Desmond, 21, 31
MacGowran, Jack, 84
MacGreevy, Thomas, 85
MacLiammóir, Micheál, 8, 158, 160, 163-66
Maclise, Daniel, 7, 10, 131-32
  The Origin of the Harp, 10, 132
Macnamara, Brinsley, 157
MacSwiney, Terence, 28, 32
Maeterlinck, Maurice, 22
Magee, Patrick, 71, 84
Malina, Jaroslav, 183, 185, 190
Maloney, Alan, 80-81, 89, 96
Manchester City News, The, 55-56, 65
Manchester Guardian, The, 57, 65
Manchester Weekly Times, The, 55, 65
Mangan, James Clarence, 138
Manning, Mary, 8, 157-63, 165-66
Markievicz, Constance, 43, 50
Markova, Alicia, 144, 151, 153
Martin, Edward, 69, 71, 73, 88, 107, 111, 182
Marx, Karl, 30, 37, 44, 46, 48, 50-51
  The Communist Manifesto, 37, 46, 48
Masefield, John, 22
Mason, Patrick, 185-87, 189

Massine, Léonide, 149
Mays, J.C.C., 84, 95
McAteer, Michael, 4, 35
McCarthy, Gerry, 90, 96
McCormack, John, 76, 131
McDonagh, Martin, 88
McDonald, Henry, 109, 112
McDonald, Ronan, 84, 95
McDowell, Wallace, 6, 32, 113
McFetridge, Paula, 97, 99, 108, 110-11, 126
McGovern, Barry, 79, 83, 89
McGuinness, Frank, 94, 114, 119, 180, 182
McKay, Susan, 109
McKee, Alan, 107, 111
McMullan, Anna, 91, 96
McPherson, Conor, 89-90, 96
  The Weir, 89
Mercier, Vivian, 82, 84-85, 94-95
Merritt, Henry, 45, 50
Michael Collins, 60, 106
Miles, Tim, 6, 97, 190
Mitchell, Billy, 103-104, 111
Mitchell, Gary, 6, 97-125
  As the Beast Sleeps, 97, 100, 101-110
  In a Little World of Our Own, 98-99, 105, 108-110
  Independent Voice, 99, 102
  Loyal Women, 97, 100-101
  Marching On, 101, 110, 118
  Red, White and Blue: A Protestant Tale, 102, 110
  Splinters, 100
  Stranded, 109, 112
  Tearing the Loom, 117

The Force of Change, 97-98, 100, 103-104
Trust, 54, 100, 104, 121, 156
Modern Drama, 103, 111
Moore, George, 16, 17, 42
  The Strike at Arlingford, 16
Moore, Henry, 137
Moore, Julianne, 89
Moore, Thomas, 131-32, 137-38, 141-42
  Irish Melodies, 7, 10, 141
  Lalla Rookh: An Oriental Romance, 137
Moran, D.P., 38, 49
Morash, Christopher, 16, 31, 64, 116, 125
Morgan, Eileen, 88, 94, 96
Morgan, Sydney, 55
Morrison, Bill, 119
Morrison, Conal, 105
  Hard to Believe, 105, 111
Morrison, Danny, 106
  The Wrong Man, 106
Motley, 165, 166
Murphy, Daniel J., 46, 50
Murphy, Johnny, 89
Murray, Christopher, 64, 83, 85, 94-95, 142, 166
Murray, Gilbert, 21
Murray, Rupert, 187

N

Nation, The, 49, 71, 94, 132, 138, 142, 166
National Literary Society, The (Dublin), 17
National Portrait Gallery, The (London), 2, 10, 112

New Century Theatre, The, 21
Newell, George, 118
Nietzsche, Friedrich, 70-71
Nijinska, Bronislava, 149
Nolan, Jerry, 7, 129
Nolan, Jim, 176, 180

O

O'Casey, Sean
  The Drums of Father Ned, 82
  The Shadow of a Gunman, 106
O'Malley, Pearse, 117
Olcott, Sidney, 139
Old Vic, The (London), 150

P

Paget, Dorothy, 41, 47
Paisley, Ian, 76, 106, 108, 114-15
Pall Mall Gazette, The, 57, 60, 65-66
Parker, Stewart, 114, 116-17, 119, 121, 125-26
  Pentecost, 119, 121
Parkinson, Alan F., 105, 119, 126
  Ulster Loyalism and the British Media, 105, 126
Parnell, Charles Stewart, 16, 149
Pavis, Patrice, 188, 191
Payne-Townshend, Charlotte, 25
Pearse, Padraic, 39, 117, 138
Peasant and Irish Ireland, 23, 32
Pethica, James, 46, 50
Petrie, George, 132, 141
Pilkington, Lionel, 42, 49
Pirandello, Luigi, 73, 180
  Six Characters in Search of an Author, 180
Pleasance Theatre (London), 107
Porter, Norman, 28, 50, 115, 125

Power, Tyrone, 1-3, 7, 10
Power, William, 132
Provisional IRA, The, 67
Puccini, Giacomo, 140
Punch, 133, 141
Pussin, Nicolas, 188, 190

Q

Queen, The, 19, 32, 62, 123, 133, 138

R

Radio Telefis Eireann (RTE), 87
Rea, Stephen, 93, 179-80, 182
Reid, Christina, 106, 119
Reid, Graham, 116, 117, 119
Rhys, Ernest, 40
Rising, The Easter, 15, 30, 75, 117
Riverdance, 6, 87, 91
Robinson, Lennox, 54-60, 62, 64-66
   A Young Man from the South, 63, 66
   The Lost Leader, 55
   The Whiteheaded Boy, 4, 60
Robinson, Mary, 154, 187
Roche, Anthony, 83, 86, 88, 90, 94-96, 123-24, 170, 182
Roof, Judith, 82-84, 94-95
Rough Magic Theatre Company, 123
Royal Ballet School, The, 152, 155-56
Royal Ballet, The, 8, 143-44, 152, 154-56
Royal Court Theatre, The (London), 4, 15, 21-25, 29-30, 91, 100, 118-19, 124-25, 170-71, 177, 179
Royal National Theatre (London), 19, 21, 30, 37, 39, 49, 84, 99, 118, 184, 187
Royalty Theatre (London), 19

Rudkin, David, 177
   The Saxon Shore, 177
Russell, Richard R., 103, 111
Russell, Sean, 70
Ryan, Frederick, 28, 32
Ryan, W.P., 23, 28, 32

S

Sadler's Wells Ballet, 144, 154-55
Sadler's Wells Theatre, 150
Samhain, 39
Samuel, Raphael, 3, 7, 22, 32, 79, 83, 91-92, 94-96, 133, 141, 161
Saunders, Graham, 5, 79, 141
Savoy Theatre (London), 23
Scanlan, John, 135
Schafer, Elizabeth, 8, 143
Shakespeare, William, 61, 80, 81, 150, 156, 177
   2 Henry IV, 61
   The Tempest, 61
Shaw, George Bernard, 4, 7, 15-35, 40, 48-49, 67, 81, 83, 139
   Arms and the Man, 17, 35, 40, 48-49
   John Bull's Other Island, 4, 7, 15, 17, 31-33
   Man and Superman, 20
   The Quintessence of Ibsenism, 17
Sheridan, Jim, 176
   In the Name of the Father, 106
Sheridan, Richard Brindsley, 81, 176
Shiels, George, 157
Sinclair, Arthur, 54-55
Singleton, Brian, 79, 86, 90-91, 93, 95-96
Sinn Féin, 32, 38, 106

Sleeping Beauty, 146
Socialist Review, The, 104, 111
Society for the Preservation and Publication of the Melodies of Ireland, 132
Solomon, Alisa, 161, 166
Spencer, Charles, 120, 126
Stage Society (London), The, 21
Stage, The, 10, 21, 31, 55, 56, 58, 60, 65, 93, 94, 96, 139, 155, 166, 190
Stannus, Edris (see under de Valois), 8, 143, 145-46, 148, 153-54
Stansfield, Lisa, 88
Statham, Jonathan, 5, 67
Stevenson, Sir John, 132
Stokes, Whitely, 133, 141
Strindberg, August, 45, 50
   The Ghost Sonata, *45, 50*
Suess, Barbara, 37, 48
Sullivan, Stephen, 135
Sun, The, 105, 111
Sunday Times, The, *96, 107*
Sydney Morning Herald, The, 60-61, 66
Synge, John Millington, 15, 19, 23, 60, 83, 95, 132, 139, 141
   In the Shadow of the Glen, *19*
   Riders to the Sea, *19*

T

Taylor, Neil, 81, 93
Theatre Royal, The (Dublin), 23, 24, 43
Thewlis, David, 90
Time Out, 97, 110
Times, The (London), 21, 23, 31-33, 50, 55, 57-58, 60-61, 64-66, 85, 94, 96-97, 99, 107, 110-11, 126, 145, 155, 165-66, 190
Todhunter, John, 35, 40, 48
   A Comedy of Sighs, *35, 48*
Torchiana, Donald, 43, 50
Tricycle Theatre, The, 109, 119
Trimble, David, 92, 108
Trinity College, Dublin, 79, 96, 131, 133
Twickenham Studios, 139
Tyrone Productions, 87

U

U2, 88
Ulster Defence Association (UDA), 97-98, 102, 109
United Irishman, The, 37, 38, 39, 40, 71

V

Vaněk, Joe, 185-86
Verdi, Giuseppe, 140
Victoria, Queen, 133

W

Wagner, Richard, 39, 130, 140
Wallace, William Vincent, 6, 8, 113, 129-30, 134, 140
   Maritana, *129-30*
Walshe, Eibhear, 163, 166
Waugh, Evelyn, 63
   Brideshead Revisited, *63*
Webb, Beatrice, 22
Webb, Sidney, 22
Welch, Robert, 48, 108
   Protestants, *108*
Weldon's, 62

Wells, H.G., 25, 144, 150-52, 154-56
Wesker, Arnold, 108
Westminster Theatre (London), 158, 160, 164
Wilde, Oscar, 7, 16-17, 31, 35, 41, 81, 132, 141, 161, 163, 182
Wilde, Sir William, 132
Willmore, Alfred (see under MacLiammóir), 8, 163
Wilson, A.P., 54, 100, 190
Wilton, Penelope, 93
Worth, Katharine, 81, 85, 93-95
Wright, Elizabeth, 161, 166
Wyndham Land Act, 26

Y

Yeats, Jack B., 83
Yeats, W.B., 1, 5, 7, 10, 16-17, 19-20, 22, 31, 35-50, 54, 60, 64, 67-77, 83, 85, 91, 93- 94, 137-38, 140, 142-43, 147, 150, 152-56, 166
A Pot of Broth, 19
A Vision, 73- 74
Autobiographies, 10, 31, 49
Cathleen ní Houlihan, 49- 50
Four Plays for Dancers, 152
Responsibilities, 15
The King's Threshold, 19
The Land of Heart's Desire, 4, 17, 35-50
The Unicorn From the Stars, 5
Young Ireland, 132, 133, 166

Carysfort Press was formed in the summer of 1998. It receives annual funding from the Arts Council.

The directors believe that drama is playing an ever-increasing role in today's society and that enjoyment of the theatre, both professional and amateur, currently plays a central part in Irish culture.

The Press aims to produce high quality publications which, though written and/or edited by academics, will be made accessible to a general readership. The organisation would also like to provide a forum for critical thinking in the Arts in Ireland, again keeping the needs and interests of the general public in view.

The company publishes contemporary Irish writing for and about the theatre.

Editorial and publishing inquiries to:
CARYSFORT PRESS Ltd
58 Woodfield, Scholarstown Road,
Rathfarnham, Dublin 16,
Republic of Ireland

T (353 1) 493 7383   F (353 1) 406 9815
e: info@carysfortpress.com
www.carysfortpress.com

NEW TITLES

ECHOES DOWN THE CORRIDOR: IRISH THEATRE – PAST, PRESENT, AND FUTURE
EDITED BY PATRICK LONERGAN AND RIANA O'DWYER

This collection of fourteen new essays explores Irish theatre from exciting new perspectives. How has Irish theatre been received internationally - and, as the country becomes more multicultural, how will international theatre influence the development of drama in Ireland? These and many other important questions.

ISBN   978-1-904505-25-9
€20

GOETHE AND ANNA AMALIA: A FORBIDDEN LOVE?
BY ETTORE GHIBELLINO, TRANS. DAN FARRELLY

In this study Ghibellino sets out to show that the platonic relationship between Goethe and Charlotte von Stein – lady-in-waiting to Anna Amalia, the Dowager Duchess of Weimar – was used as part of a cover-up for Goethe's intense and prolonged love relationship with the Duchess Anna Amalia herself. The book attempts to uncover a hitherto closely-kept state secret. Readers convinced by the evidence supporting Ghibellino's hypothesis will see in it one of the very great love stories in European history – to rank with that of Dante and Beatrice, and Petrarch and Laura.

ISBN   978-1-904505-24-2
EAN   9781904505242
€25

NEW TITLES

EDNA O'BRIEN
'NEW CRITICAL PERSPECTIVES'
EDITED BY KATHRYN LAING
SINÉAD MOONEY AND MAUREEN O'CONNOR

The essays collected here illustrate some of the range, complexity, and interest of Edna O'Brien as a fiction writer and dramatist... They will contribute to a broader appreciation of her work and to an evolution of new critical approaches, as well as igniting more interest in the many unexplored areas of her considerable oeuvre.

ISBN 1-904505-20-1
€20

THE THEATRE OF MARTIN MCDONAGH
'A WORLD OF SAVAGE STORIES'
EDITED BY LILIAN CHAMBERS AND
EAMONN JORDAN

The book is a vital response to the many challenges set by McDonagh for those involved in the production and reception of his work. Critics and commentators from around the world offer a diverse range of often provocative approaches. What is not surprising is the focus and commitment of the engagement, given the controversial and stimulating nature of the work.

ISBN 1-904505-19-8
€30

IRELAND ON STAGE:
BECKETT AND AFTER
EDITORS: HIROKO MIKAMI, MINAKO
OKAMURO, NAOKO YAGI

A collection of ten essays on contemporary Irish theatre. The focus is primarily on Irish playwrights and their works, both in text and on the stage, in the latter half of the twentieth century. The essays range from Samuel Beckett to Brian Friel, Frank McGuinness, Marina Carr, and Conor McPherson. There is frequent reference back to Wilde, Yeats, Synge, Shaw, O'Casey, and Joyce.

ISBN 978-1-904505-23-5
€20

BRIAN FRIEL'S DRAMATIC ARTISTRY
'THE WORK HAS VALUE'
EDITED BY DONALD E. MORSE, CSILLA
BERTHA, AND MÁRIA KURDI

Brian Friel's Dramatic Artistry presents a refreshingly broad range of voices: new work from some of the leading English-speaking authorities on Friel, and fascinating essays from scholars in Germany, Italy, Portugal, and Hungary. This book will deepen our knowledge and enjoyment of Friel's work.

ISBN 1-904505-17-1
€25

OUT OF HISTORY
'ESSAYS ON THE WRITINGS OF SEBASTIAN BARRY'
EDITED WITH AN INTRODUCTION BY CHRISTINA HUNT MAHONY

The essays address Barry's engagement with the contemporary cultural debate in Ireland and also with issues that inform postcolonial criticial theory. The range and selection of contributors has ensured a high level of critical expression and an insightful assessment of Barry and his works.

ISBN 1-904505-18-X
€20

IRISH THEATRE ON TOUR
EDITED BY NICHOLAS GRENE AND CHRIS MORASH

'Touring has been at the strategic heart of Druid's artistic policy since the early eighties. Everyone has the right to see professional theatre in their own communities. Irish theatre on tour is a crucial part of Irish theatre as a whole'. *Garry Hynes*

ISBN 1-904505-13-9
€20

GEORGE FITZMAURICE: 'WILD IN HIS OWN WAY'
BIOGRAPHY OF AN ABBEY PLAYWRIGHT
BY FIONA BRENNAN
WITH A FOREWORD BY FINTAN O'TOOLE

Fiona Brennan's...introduction to his considerable output allows us a much greater appreciation and understanding of Fitzmaurice, the one remaining under-celebrated genius of twentieth-century Irish drama.
Conall Morrison

ISBN 1-904505-16-3
€20

THE POWER OF LAUGHTER
EDITED BY ERIC WEITZ

The collection draws on a wide range of perspectives and voices including critics, playwrights, directors and performers. The result is a series of fascinating and provocative debates about the myriad functions of comedy in contemporary Irish theatre. *Anna McMullan*

As Stan Laurel said, it takes only an onion to cry. Peel it and weep. Comedy is harder. These essays listen to the power of laughter. They hear the tough heart of Irish theatre – hard and wicked and funny. *Frank McGuinness*

ISBN 1-904505-05-8
€20

NEW TITLES

EAST OF EDEN
NEW ROMANIAN PLAYS
EDITED BY ANDREI MARINESCU

Four of the most promising Romanian playwrights, young and very young, are in this collection, each one with a specific way of seeing the Romanian reality, each one with a style of communicating an articulated artistic vision of the society we are living in.
Ion Caramitru, General Director Romanian National Theatre Bucharest

ISBN 1-904505-15-5
€10

SYNGE: A CELEBRATION
EDITED BY COLM TÓIBÍN

A collection of essays by some of Ireland's most creative writers on the work of John Millington Synge, featuring Sebastian Barry, Marina Carr, Anthony Cronin, Roddy Doyle, Anne Enright, Hugo Hamilton, Joseph O'Connor, Mary O'Malley, Fintan O'Toole, Colm Toibin, Vincent Woods.

ISBN 1-904505-14-7
€15 Paperback

POEMS 2000–2005
BY HUGH MAXTON

Poems 2000-2005 is a transitional collection written while the author – also known to be W. J. Mc Cormack, literary historian – was in the process of moving back from London to settle in rural Ireland.

ISBN 1-904505-12-0
€10

HAMLET
THE SHAKESPEAREAN DIRECTOR
BY MIKE WILCOCK

"This study of the Shakespearean director as viewed through various interpretations of HAMLET is a welcome addition to our understanding of how essential it is for a director to have a clear vision of a great play. It is an important study from which all of us who love Shakespeare and who understand the importance of continuing contemporary exploration may gain new insights."

From the Foreword, by Joe Dowling, Artistic Director, The Guthrie Theater, Minneapolis, MN

ISBN 1-904505-00-7
€20

NEW TITLES

GEORG BÜCHNER: WOYZECK
A NEW TRANSLATION BY DAN FARRELLY

The most up-to-date German scholarship of Thomas Michael Mayer and Burghard Dedner has finally made it possible to establish an authentic sequence of scenes. The widespread view that this play is a prime example of loose, open theatre is no longer sustainable. Directors and teachers are challenged to "read it again".

ISBN 1-904505-02-3
€10

MUSICS OF BELONGING: THE POETRY OF MICHEAL O'SIADHAIL
EDITED BY MARC CABALL AND DAVID F. FORD

An overall account is given of O'Siadhail's life, his work and the reception of his poetry so far. There are close readings of some poems, analyses of his artistry in matching diverse content with both classical and innovative forms, and studies of recurrent themes such as love, death, language, music, and the shifts of modern life.

Paperback €25
ISBN 978-1-904505-22-8

Casebound €50
ISBN: 978-1-904505-21-1

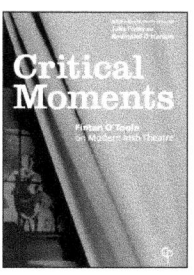

CRITICAL MOMENTS
FINTAN O'TOOLE ON MODERN IRISH THEATRE
EDITED BY JULIA FURAY & REDMOND O'HANLON

This new book on the work of Fintan O'Toole, the internationally acclaimed theatre critic and cultural commentator, offers percussive analyses and assessments of the major plays and playwrights in the canon of modern Irish theatre. Fearless and provocative in his judgements, O'Toole is essential reading for anyone interested in criticism or in the current state of Irish theatre.

ISBN 1-904505-03-1
€20

THE THEATRE OF MARINA CARR
"BEFORE RULES WAS MADE" - EDITED BY ANNA MCMULLAN & CATHY LEENEY

As the first published collection of articles on the theatre of Marina Carr, this volume explores the world of Carr's theatrical imagination, the place of her plays in contemporary theatre in Ireland and abroad and the significance of her highly individual voice.

ISBN 0-9534-2577-0
€20

NEW TITLES

THEATRE TALK
VOICES OF IRISH THEATRE PRACTITIONERS
EDITED BY LILIAN CHAMBERS & GER FITZGIBBON

"This book is the right approach - asking practitioners what they feel."
Sebastian Barry, Playwright

"...an invaluable and informative collection of interviews with those who make and shape the landscape of Irish Theatre."
Ben Barnes, Artistic Director of the Abbey Theatre

ISBN 0-9534-2576-2
€20

SACRED PLAY
SOUL JOURNEYS IN CONTEMPORARY IRISH THEATRE BY ANNE F. O'REILLY

'Theatre as a space or container for sacred play allows audiences to glimpse mystery and to experience transformation. This book charts how Irish playwrights negotiate the labyrinth of the Irish soul and shows how their plays contribute to a poetics of Irish culture that enables a new imagining. Playwrights discussed are: McGuinness, Murphy, Friel, Le Marquand Hartigan, Burke Brogan, Harding, Meehan, Carr, Parker, Devlin, and Barry.'

ISBN 1-904505-07-4
€25

THEATRE OF SOUND
RADIO AND THE DRAMATIC IMAGINATION BY DERMOT RATTIGAN

An innovative study of the challenges that radio drama poses to the creative imagination of the writer, the production team, and the listener.

"A remarkably fine study of radio drama – everywhere informed by the writer's professional experience of such drama in the making...A new theoretical and analytical approach – informative, illuminating and at all times readable." *Richard Allen Cave*

ISBN 0-9534-2575-4
€20

PLAYBOYS OF THE WESTERN WORLD
PRODUCTION HISTORIES
EDITED BY ADRIAN FRAZIER

'Playboys of the Western World is a model of contemporary performance studies.'

'The book is remarkably well-focused: half is a series of production histories of Playboy performances through the twentieth century in the UK, Northern Ireland, the USA, and Ireland. The remainder focuses on one contemporary performance, that of Druid Theatre, as directed by Garry Hynes. The various contemporary social issues that are addressed in relation to Synge's play and this performance of it give the volume an additional interest: it shows how the arts matter.' *Kevin Barry*

ISBN 1-904505-06-6
€20

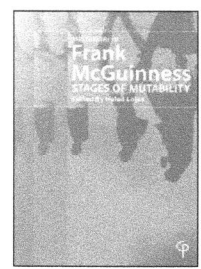

THE THEATRE OF FRANK MCGUINNESS
STAGES OF MUTABILITY
EDITED BY HELEN LOJEK

The first edited collection of essays about internationally renowned Irish playwright Frank McGuinness focuses on both performance and text. Interpreters come to diverse conclusions, creating a vigorous dialogue that enriches understanding and reflects a strong consensus about the value of McGuinness's complex work.

ISBN 1-904505-01-5
€20

THE DRUNKARD
TOM MURPHY

'The Drunkard is a wonderfully eloquent play. Murphy's ear is finely attuned to the glories and absurdities of melodramatic exclamation, and even while he is wringing out its ludicrous overstatement, he is also making it sing.'
The Irish Times

ISBN 1-904505-09-0
€10

TALKING ABOUT TOM MURPHY
EDITED BY NICHOLAS GRENE

Talking About Tom Murphy is shaped around the six plays in the landmark Abbey Theatre Murphy Season of 2001, assembling some of the best-known commentators on his work: Fintan O'Toole, Chris Morash, Lionel Pilkington, Alexandra Poulain, Shaun Richards, Nicholas Grene and Declan Kiberd.

ISBN 0-9534-2579-7
€15

THREE CONGREGATIONAL MASSES
BY SEÓIRSE BODLEY,
EDITED BY LORRAINE BYRNE

'From the simpler congregational settings in the Mass of Peace and the Mass of Joy to the richer textures of the Mass of Glory, they are immediately attractive and accessible, and with a distinctively Irish melodic quality.' *Barra Boydell*

ISBN 1-904505-11-2
€15

THE IRISH HARP BOOK
BY SHEILA LARCHET CUTHBERT

This is a facsimile of the edition originally published by Mercier Press in 1993. There is a new preface by Sheila Larchet Cuthbert, and the biographical material has been updated. It is a collection of studies and exercises for the use of teachers and pupils of the Irish harp.

ISBN 1-904505-08-2
€35

GOETHE AND SCHUBERT
ACROSS THE DIVIDE
EDITED BY LORRAINE BYRNE & DAN FARRELLY

Proceedings of the International Conference, 'Goethe and Schubert in Perspective and Performance', Trinity College Dublin, 2003. This volume includes essays by leading scholars – Barkhoff, Boyle, Byrne, Canisius, Dürr, Fischer, Hill, Kramer, Lamport, Lund, Meikle, Newbould, Norman McKay, White, Whitton, Wright, Youens – on Goethe's musicality and his relationship to Schubert; Schubert's contribution to sacred music and the Lied and his setting of Goethe's Singspiel, Claudine. A companion volume of this Singspiel (with piano reduction and English translation) is also available.

ISBN 1-904505-04-X
Goethe and Schubert: Across the Divide. €25

ISBN 0-9544290-0-1
Goethe and Schubert: 'Claudine von Villa Bella'. €14

GOETHE: MUSICAL POET, MUSICAL CATALYST
EDITED BY LORRAINE BYRNE

'Goethe was interested in, and acutely aware of, the place of music in human experience generally - and of its particular role in modern culture. Moreover, his own literary work - especially the poetry and Faust - inspired some of the major composers of the European tradition to produce some of their finest works.' *Martin Swales*

ISBN 1-904505-10-4
€30

THEATRE STUFF (REPRINT)

CRITICAL ESSAYS ON
CONTEMPORARY IRISH THEATRE
EDITED BY EAMONN JORDAN

Best selling essays on the successes and debates of contemporary Irish theatre at home and abroad.

Contributors include: Thomas Kilroy, Declan Hughes, Anna McMullan, Declan Kiberd, Deirdre Mulrooney, Fintan O'Toole, Christopher Murray, Caoimhe McAvinchey and Terry Eagleton.

ISBN 0-9534-2571-1
€20

URFAUST

A NEW VERSION OF GOETHE'S
EARLY "FAUST" IN BRECHTIAN MODE
BY DAN FARRELLY

This version is based on Brecht's irreverent and daring re-interpretation of the German classic.

"Urfaust is a kind of well-spring for German theatre… The love-story is the most daring and the most profound in German dramatic literature." *Brecht*

ISBN 0-9534257-0-3
€10

IN SEARCH OF THE SOUTH AFRICAN IPHIGENIE

BY ERIKA VON WIETERSHEIM
AND DAN FARRELLY

Discussions of Goethe's "Iphigenie auf Tauris" (Under the Curse) as relevant to women's issues in modern South Africa: women in family and public life; the force of women's spirituality; experience of personal relationships; attitudes to parents and ancestors; involvement with religion.

ISBN 0-9534-2578-9
€10

THE STARVING AND OCTOBER SONG

TWO CONTEMPORARY IRISH PLAYS
BY ANDREW HINDS

The Starving, set during and after the siege of Derry in 1689, is a moving and engrossing drama of the emotional journey of two men.

October Song, a superbly written family drama set in real time in pre-ceasefire Derry.

ISBN 0-9534-2574-6
€10

BACK LIST

SEEN AND HEARD (REPRINT)
SIX NEW PLAYS BY IRISH WOMEN
EDITED WITH AN INTRODUCTION
BY CATHY LEENEY

A rich and funny, moving and theatrically exciting collection of plays by Mary Elizabeth Burke-Kennedy, Síofra Campbell, Emma Donoghue, Anne Le Marquand Hartigan, Michelle Read and Dolores Walshe.

ISBN 0-9534-2573-8
€20

UNDER THE CURSE
GOETHE'S "IPHIGENIE AUF TAURIS",
IN A NEW VERSION BY DAN FARRELLY

The Greek myth of Iphigenie grappling with the curse on the house of Atreus is brought vividly to life. This version is currently being used in Johannesburg to explore problems of ancestry, religion, and Black African women's spirituality.

ISBN 0-9534-2572-X
€10

HOW TO ORDER
TRADE ORDERS DIRECTLY TO

CMD
Columba Mercier Distribution,
55A Spruce Avenue,
Stillorgan Industrial Park,
Blackrock,
Co. Dublin

T: (353 1) 294 2560
F: (353 1) 294 2564
E: cmd@columba.ie

*FOR SALES IN NORTH AMERICA
AND CANADA*

Dufour Editions Inc.,
124 Byers Road,
PO Box 7,
Chester Springs, PA 19425,
USA

T: 1-610-458-5005
F: 1-610-458-7103

www.ingramcontent.com/pod-product-compliance
Ingram Content Group UK Ltd.
Pitfield, Milton Keynes, MK11 3LW, UK
UKHW021838210426
5322IPUK00021B/347